Living
Between the Lines

Lucy McCormick Calkins

Teachers College, Columbia University

with

Shelley Harwayne

Teachers College Writing Project

HEINEMANN
Portsmouth, NH

IRWIN PUBLISHING
Toronto, Canada

HEINEMANN EDUCATIONAL BOOKS, INC.
361 Hanover Street   Portsmouth, NH 03801-3959
Offices and agents throughout the world

Published simultaneously in Canada by
IRWIN PUBLISHING
1800 Steeles Avenue West   Concord, Ontario, Canada L4K 2P3

Acknowledgments for borrowed material begin on page xiii.

Library of Congress Cataloging-in-Publication Data

Calkins, Lucy McCormick.
     Living between the lines / Lucy McCormick Calkins with Shelley
Harwayne.
         p.   cm.
     Includes bibliographical references.
     ISBN 0-435-08538-7
     1. Language arts.   2. English language—Composition and exercises—
Study and teaching.   I. Harwayne, Shelley.   II. Title.
     LB1576.C3123   1990
     372.6—dc20   90-43146
                                                               CIP

Canadian Cataloguing in Publication Data

Calkins, Lucy McCormick
     Living between the lines

Includes bibliographical references.
ISBN 0-7725-1816-5

1. Reading (Elementary).   2. English language—
Composition and exercises—Study and teaching
(Elementary).   3. Creative writing (Elementary
education).   I. Harwayne, Shelley.   II. Title.

LB1576.C35 1990   372.6′044   C90-095056-0

Designed by Jenny Greenleaf.
Cover and interior photos © 1990 by Peter Cunningham.
Calligraphy by Allison Zaeder.
Printed in the United States of America.
91 92 93 94 95 9 8 7 6 5 4 3 2

For Hindy List
advisor, colleague, friend

Contents

In Appreciation ix

Acknowledgments xiii

1 Big Dreams and Tall Ambitions in the Teaching of Writing 1

2 A Place for Writing and Reading 11

3 Shared Stories Turn Classrooms into Communities 27

4 The Notebook: A Tool for Writing and Living 35

5 Rereading and Reflecting: Adding Growth Rings of Meaning to Our Writing 55

6 From Notebooks to Projects 71

7 Revision of Teaching 99

8 When Writers Clear the Sills of Their World 105

9 Silent Spaces and Study Groups in the Reading and Writing Workshop 117

10 New Frontiers 127

Contents

11 Picture Books and the Magic of "Once upon a Time" 137

12 Memoir: Reading and Writing the Story of Our Lives 165

13 And the Walls Come Tumbling Down: Bringing Our
    Lives to Nonfiction Research 187

14 Learning to Confer in Ways That Last a Lifetime 225

15 Records of Growth 243

16 Hopes and Horizons: Understanding Our Children's
    Images of Good Writing 261

17 Density in Writing: When Texts Take Writers and
    Readers on Significant Journeys 269

18 On Loving Words 283

19 Nurturing Writing, Nurturing Teaching 301

Works Cited 307

In Appreciation

At a recent Writing Project gathering, my colleague Bonnie Uslianer said, "I found a beginning for your acknowledgments, Lucy." She opened Anne Morrow Lindbergh's *A Gift from the Sea* (1965) and started to read:

> I began these pages for myself in order to think out my own living . . . but as I went on writing and simultaneously talking with others . . . these chapters, fed by conversations, arguments and revelations from men and women of all groups, became more than my individual story, until I decided in the end to give them back to the people who had shared and stimulated many of these thoughts. Here, then, with my warm feelings of gratitude and companionship for those working along the same lines, I return my gift. (9–11)

The passage was perfect, and the moment emblematic of the ways this book has grown, gathering in a great many voices and ideas. *Living Between the Lines* is indeed more than one person's story; it is more, even, than two people's story. It has grown out of eight years of leisurely Thursdays devoted to reading, writing, talking, and musing within the community of educators in the Teachers College Writing Project. It has also grown out of many years of working side by side with teachers in their classrooms and of meeting with them and Project staff members in the study groups that have formed the scaffold of our classroom work.

Living Between the Lines has grown, above all, from a decade of thinking and teaching and living alongside Shelley Harwayne, Co-Director of the Teachers College Writing Project. Shelley is, without doubt, the most brilliant, most natural, and most joyous teacher any one of us in the Project has ever known. She learns as effortlessly as others breathe. Because we have worked so closely, our ideas are all of a piece, hers the warp and mine the woof in the fabric of our joint thinking. Shelley has been a contributing author in the truest sense of the word. She has joined me in the lifework of this book, working with teachers and children in order to push back the frontiers of our knowledge on the teaching of reading and writing. This book reflects this mutuality of learning; readers will be aware of Shelley's presence in many of the classrooms, and they'll hear her ideas on most subjects. But even when she is not cited or quoted, Shelley has been a behind-the-scenes presence, helping me design chapters, rethink drafts, and revise ideas. I only hope I can be equally helpful to her as she works on her book, *Lasting Impressions.*

Although writing this book has been an unusually collegial process, there have still been long and lonely stretches of deskwork. I've needed company, and, in addition to Shelley, I've reached out to several very special people. I am more grateful than I can ever say to Joanne Hindley, Laurie Pessah, Lydia Bellino, Hindy List, and Randy Bomer. Joanne Hindley is one of those best friends we have when we are very young and never stop longing to have once we are grown up. For many of us in the Project, her friendship has helped blur the boundaries between work and play, allowing us to bring all that we are to our teaching. Laurie Pessah and Lydia Bellino have joined Shelley and me in bringing ideas to life in classrooms and then in learning from those class-rooms, those ideas. Hindy List has been an invaluable guide, advisor, and friend throughout all my years of association with the New York City schools. Randy Bomer is an astute and generous reader; in even a brief conversation, he has been able to reorient my thinking, remind me of what I know, and revive my belief in the work we do together.

I have also benefited tremendously from working with Dorothy Barn-house and Vicki Vinton. I especially value their ability to rethink and rearticulate the deepest and simplest truths about writing. It was Dorothy, especially, who helped us unlearn old ideas about the writing process, and Vicki has joined her in giving us important seeds of thought about memoir, language, and writing to learn.

There are a great many others to thank. Ellin Keene of Denver, Colorado, read through the entire manuscript, and the comments she wrote on every page astonished me. How could someone know so clearly what the manuscript needed? Georgia Heard's reading of *Living Between the Lines* led to important revisions, not only in the manuscript but also in my life.

I'm grateful to Judy Davis of P.S. 183, to all the teachers of P.S. 148, to teachers at P.S. 87, P.S. 7, P.S. 41, and to a great many others who have welcomed Shelley and me into their classrooms and joined us as we have learned from their teaching and their children. It is no coincidence that in each of the schools I have listed, there is an extraordinary educator at the helm, and I am grateful also to these individuals.

Susan Pliner has ably administered the Project while I have been preoccu-pied and offered her wise response to early drafts of the book. Cathy Hale has been the mind behind the scenes, helping with word processing, references, revisions, permissions, and countless other details, and she's done all this with wisdom, confidence, and dedication.

When the manuscript was transferred from Cathy's hands to those of Philippa Stratton, Linda Howe, Bob Thomas, and Donna Bouvier at Heinemann, it continued to receive careful, wise attention. In the end, when Donna and I talked about which photographs to open which chapters and where to place the figures, it felt as though she knew and cared about *Living* as much as I do. What a gift it has been to have that kind of investment from someone so talented.

I am also indebted to Rebecca Sheridan, to Mary Winsky, Mimi Aronson, Bonnie Uslianer, JoAnn Curtis, Ralph Fletcher, and to all my Writing Project colleagues. In helping me care for my children, Marian Sundloff has allowed me the peace of mind I needed in order to write.

Finally, I'm grateful to my family. My parents, Evan and Virginia Calkins, have given me an image of what childhood can be, and I return to this knowledge again and again as I teach and write. My sons, Miles and Evan, were born during the lifeline of this book, and they have filled my life with unbelievable joy and helped me know that the living that surrounds what we do at the desk nourishes our writing. And to John, my husband and my best friend, who has always been there, luring me away from the desk when he can, supporting me when he can't . . . I'm done. Now there will again be time for hikes and tennis and reading, side by side.

Acknowledgments

This book has grown, layer by layer, out of all of my life. Friends, colleagues, and children have been part of its growth, but in the end, in order to write, a person needs to create a space separate from one's world and in that space not only Shelley Harwayne but also other authors have provided me with company and inspiration. I am grateful to Annie Dillard for her thundering prose. I am grateful to Katherine Paterson for saying all the things I want to say. I am grateful to Donald Murray, who has made the writing life accessible and yet endlessly challenging, and who long ago discovered many of the ideas I have discovered in living towards this book.

There are other authors, too, who have kept me company. I've learned endlessly from Donald Graves. I have quoted and cherished much of what Cynthia Rylant, Mem Fox, and Jean Little have written and have read their books, hoping their language would rub off on me. As I write, I stand on the shoulders of Ken and Yetta Goodman, Jerry Harste, Peter Elbow, Frank Smith, and many others. I have been astonished and inspired by the writing of many children, but especially Chris Ralph. And I have relied tremendously on *Language Arts* and *The Horn Book*.

I am grateful to all the writers for permission to reprint borrowed material, and to the following for permission to reprint previously published material:

"The Writer" from *The Mind-Reader: New Poems*, copyright © 1971 by Richard Wilbur, reprinted by permission of Harcourt Brace Jovanovich, Inc., and Faber and Faber Ltd.

Extract from "Sea-Fever" by John Masefield. Reprinted by permission of The Society of Authors as the literary representative of John Masefield.

From *Tales of a Gambling Grandma*, by Dayal Kaur Khalsa. Copyright © 1986 by Dayal Kaur Khalsa. Reprinted by permission of Clarkson N. Potter, Inc.

From Byrd Baylor, *I'm in Charge of Celebrations*. Reprinted by permission of Charles Scribner's Sons, an imprint of Macmillan Publishing Company, from *I'm in Charge of Celebrations* by Byrd Baylor. Copyright © 1986 Byrd Baylor.

Text excerpts from *Hey World Here I Am!* by Jean Little, illustrated by Sue Truesdell. Text copyright © 1986 by Jean Little. Illustrations copyright © 1989 by Susan G. Truesdell. Reprinted by permission of Harper & Row, Publishers, Inc. and Kids Can Press Ltd.

Dan Jaffe, "The Forecast," *Prairie Schooner* 38 : 1 (Spring 1964), p. 48. Reprinted by permission of the author.

From *Diana, Maybe* by Crescent Dragonwagon. Text copyright © 1987 by Crescent Dragonwagon. Reprinted with permission of Macmillan Publishing Company and Curtis Brown, Ltd.

"The Sound of Freedom" by Barbara Marin-Rivas. Reprinted by permission.

"Bring the Cattle Home" by the Rishile Poets. From *Uphu Van Der Merwe*. In *My Drum: South African Poetry for Young People* (Parklands, South Africa: The Hippogriff Press, 1988). Reprinted by permission of the publisher.

Excerpt from *Fierce Attachments: A Memoir* by Vivian Gornick. Copyright © 1987 by Vivian Gornick. Reprinted by permission of Farrar, Straus and Giroux, Inc. and Virago Press.

From Sandra Cisneros, *The House on Mango Street* (Houston, TX: Arte Publico Press, 1986), p. 12. Reprinted by permission of the publisher.

From *Homesick, My Own Story* by Jean Fritz, copyright © 1982 by Jean Fritz. Reprinted by permission of G. P. Putnam's Sons and Gina Maccoby Literary Agency.

Eve Merriam, "A Lazy Thought," from *JAMBOREE Rhymes for All Times* by Eve Merriam. Copyright © 1962, 1964, 1966, 1973 by Eve Merriam. All rights reserved. Reprinted by permission of Marian Reiner for the author.

From "Poetry and Word Processing: One or the Other, But Not Both" by Louis Simpson, *The New York Times Book Review*, January 3, 1988. Copyright © 1988 by The New York Times Company. Reprinted by permission.

Excerpts from *The Writing Life* by Annie Dillard. Copyright © 1989 by Annie Dillard. Reprinted by permission of Harper & Row, Publishers, Inc., and Blanche C. Gregory, Inc.

Every effort has been made to ensure that copyright holders and all other writers—including teachers and children—have given their permission to reprint borrowed material. (The use of full names for these writers signifies our having been able to contact them.) We regret any oversights that may have occurred and would be happy to rectify them in future printings of this book.

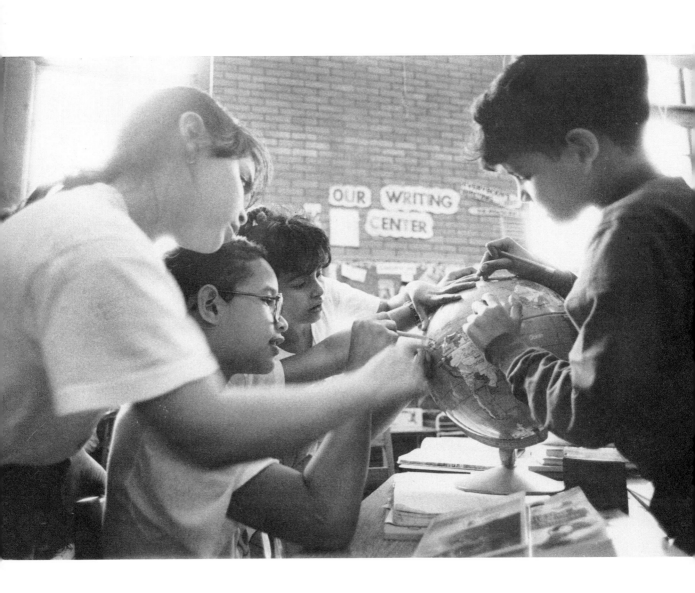

1

Big Dreams and Tall Ambitions in the Teaching of Writing

$\mathbf{A}$s a child, I draped plaid blankets between the sofa and chair, and when the sunlight streamed in, my shadowy forts became castles with stained glass windowpanes. I lashed birch logs together to make walls for forest forts and turned tree stumps into tables and chairs. My forts were a lot of work, but childhood was a time of industriousness, of projects. It was a time of secret chemistry experiments in the attic, of carefully fashioned yarn dolls, of elaborate dams along the Eighteen Mile Creek.

When I moved into my present house several years ago and saw that there was a swamp across the street, I couldn't wait to see the children poling their homemade rafts through the tall reeds, searching for muskrats and jellied strings of frog eggs to incubate in the bathtub and for their own magical Terabithia. But the neighborhood children aren't there.

I wonder if they are sitting glassy-eyed in front of the VCR, the television, the Nintendo game. I wonder if they are being driven from soccer to computer camp, from gymnastics to aerobics, or if they are drifting around the shopping mall. James Howe, author of *Bunnicula*, recently said, "My greatest worry for children today is that they are losing their capacity to play, to create a city out of blocks, to find a world in a backyard, to dream an adventure on a rainy afternoon. My greatest fear for children today is they are losing the capacity to play" (1987).

When I think of the long afternoons I spent building forts, I cannot help but wonder whether I was playing or working. Perhaps our fear should be not that children are losing the capacity to play so much as that they are losing the recognition that there can be a thin line between work and play.

It has not been lost altogether. If we asked our students for the highlight of their school careers, most would choose a time when they dedicated themselves to an endeavor of great importance. I am thinking of Paula Bower's second graders, who worked during lunch and before and after school to turn the empty lot beside their school into a flower garden. I am thinking of Liz Dolan's seventh graders, who led weekly book talks with the residents of a South Bronx nursing home, joining the senior citizens in writing dialogue journals in response to Katherine Paterson's *Bridge to Terabithia.* I am thinking of the youngsters from P.S. 321, who have launched a ·Save-the-Tree campaign to prevent the oaks outside their school from being cut down. I am thinking of children who write the school newspaper, act in the school play, organize the playground building committee. In endeavors such as these, no one asks, "How long does it have to be?" No one asks, "Will it be graded?" or "Are you going to collect it?" No one whines, "My arm hurts." On projects such as these, youngsters will work before school, after school, during lunch. Our youngsters want to work hard on endeavors they deem significant.

John Chambers, a principal in Katonah-Lewisboro, New York, recently rediscovered this. Chambers decided he wanted to take a small group of high school students on a five-day sail. The crew members would have to raise the money for expenses themselves and participate in an extracurricular study of the literature and science of the sea. If any high school students were interested, Chambers suggested, they might gather one evening in the art gallery in town. When Mary Winsky arrived with her sixteen-year-old daughter Pam, the street was already lined with cars. The gallery was so crowded with teenagers and their parents that Mary and her daughter could barely see the slides Chambers was showing of a previous sail. With each slide, Chambers described the dedication and work involved. "If these kids look tired, it's because they sailed through the night." "Notice the pile of papers on the right-hand corner; that's where we were plotting our course." Sometimes Chambers would pause to ask, "Are you still interested?"

Each time the crowd would respond with a resounding "Yes." Pam Winsky turned to her mother and said, "Oh, Mom, I wish I could get down on my knees and beg for the chance to be part of that sail." My goal is for students to have that kind of passion toward reading and writing.

My goal in a reading-writing workshop is to launch ships. My goal is to help youngsters set off on endeavors significant enough that they will want to write and learn with heart and soul. Launching ships. My metaphors have certainly changed over time. Not long ago, I said our job in the writing workshop was to be like the circus men who run about keeping plates spinning on the ends of sticks. But in many writing workshops, the plates are spinning. The writing folders are filling. The teacher keeps it going: "Why not read it to a friend?" "You could add a line." "Would you tell me more?" "Why not fix it up?" "I'd copy it over." Rehearse, draft, revise, edit. The plates are spinning. Rehearse, draft, revise, edit. Second verse same as the first, a little bit longer and a little bit worse . . .

The plates are spinning, but are they going anywhere? As we move about the writing classroom, we need to help children spin through the stages of writing, but we also need to send them off on important endeavors. Listen to the intensity, the ambition, in Richard Wilbur's young writer:

The Writer

In her room at the prow of the house
Where light breaks, and the windows are tossed with linden,
My daughter is writing a story.

I pause in the stairwell, hearing
From her shut door a commotion of typewriter-keys
Like a chain hauled over a gunwale.

Young as she is, the stuff
Of her life is a great cargo, and some of it heavy:
I wish her a lucky passage.

But now it is she who pauses,
As if to reject my thought and its easy figure.
A stillness greatens, in which

The whole house seems to be thinking,
And then she is at it again with a bunched clamor
Of strokes, and again is silent.

I remember the dazed starling
Which was trapped in that very room, two years ago;
How we stole in, lifted a sash

And retreated, not to affright it;
And how for a helpless hour, through the crack of the door,
We watched the sleek, wild, dark

And iridescent creature
Batter against the brilliance, drop like a glove
To the hard floor, or the desk-top,

And wait then, humped and bloody,
For the wits to try it again; and how our spirits
Rose when, suddenly sure,

It lifted off from a chair-back,
Beating a smooth course for the right window
And clearing the sill of the world.

It is always a matter, my darling,
Of life or death, as I had forgotten. I wish
What I wished you before, but harder.

Our darlings need, through their writing, to clear the sill of the world. They need to do work that is gigantic in scope and consequence.

When Shelley Harwayne, codirector of the Teachers College Writing Project, drew a chair alongside Ipolito Diaz's desk, the boy sighed deeply. "I don't have anything to write about," he said. "Nothing happens in my life. All I do is watch TV, feed the pigeons, watch TV, feed the pigeons."

"Is one of those topics especially important?" Shelley asked.

"Well," Ipolito answered, "I suppose feeding the pigeons is more important because if I don't feed them they'll starve." When Shelley suggested that Ipolito write on that topic, he looked dubious. "It'll be awful short," he answered, and to illustrate his point, Ipolito recited the story. "I—feed—pigeons."

Undaunted, Shelley pulled a small assignment pad from her satchel. "You know what you could do?" she said. "You could be like a reporter and take a notebook with you. Next time you're on the roof feeding the pigeons, write down everything you notice, all the details."

Several weeks later, Ipolito stood before his classmates and read the draft shown in Figure 1–1 aloud to them:

> Boo, Coo a soft whisper
> Calls me to the yard
> Grey, silver birds
> Greeting me
> Crowding me, watching me, pecking at my feet.
> Piles of yellow, minute, hard corn
> Stampedes of homers, flights, tiplits, maggies,
> Rollers, turbans, owls swooping and charging.
> Pecking, pushing, struggling
> Done!
> The same scramble for a drink
> Full and lazy
> Time to sleep
> Goodnight pigeons.

Charlene didn't lift her head up from her desk when Ipolito read his poem aloud. Shelley queried the teacher. "What's the matter with the beautiful girl in the back?" The teacher explained that because Charlene had been abused by her parents, she was now staying with an aunt across the city. "She travels an hour each way on the subway," she said, "so she often falls asleep in class." Then she added, "Let's try to talk with her." At first when they approached the desk, Charlene did not lift up her head. "What are you writing about?" Shelley asked. Charlene shrugged, looked as if she was about to say something, then retreated again into a shrug. Shelley nodded and gently said, "You've got something to write about, don't you?"

Charlene shook her head in protest. "All I have is, is, just, is, just, about this bag lady . . . " she said, her voice trailing off. Because Shelley waited, Charlene began haltingly to tell the story. A week earlier, it turned out, Charlene had been on the brink of running away. She cried as she walked down the street.

"What's the matter, girl?"

Figure 1–1   Ipolito's Draft

Looking around, Charlene had realized the voice belonged to a homeless woman sitting on the curb. Charlene said, "I don't know what happened, but all of a sudden I was telling this lady the whole story and she was putting her arm around me and telling me not to run away. Now, I look for her every morning. I've told her all about me. Maybe if I hear all about *her*, I could write it."

Shelley and Charlene's teacher exchanged glances. "If you published that story in a newspaper," Shelley said, "I bet no one who reads the paper would ever think of homeless people in the same way." When they moved on to the next student, Charlene did not put her head back onto her desk.

Juliet was next. "How can I help?" Shelley asked.

"I am thinking about how you said that literature often comes from family stories," Juliet answered, "but I can't think of any family stories."

Shelley nodded. Sometimes she couldn't think of stories either. Tentatively, thinking as she spoke, she said, "Sometimes, Juliet, family stories are attached to objects, to things we have that are very important to us. Can you imagine walking through your house touching all the special things, the objects that tell stories?" Pausing, she added, "Does this help you think of family stories, family memories?"

Juliet was quiet. "The most precious, the oldest thing in our apartment is a little sack of garlic," she said. "When you have a bad dream, you put it under your pillow."

"Where do you keep it?"

"It's centuries old," Juliet answered, "and it doesn't have its smell so we keep it surrounded by fresh garlic in a little cupboard my father built. We each wear a tiny key around our necks and if you have a bad dream you open the cupboard and get the garlic out."

"Juliet, you're going to have to think very hard about what to do with that lovely story. Do you want to turn it into a picture book? I can just see you creeping through the house in the night with the key to that cupboard. Or do you want to collect other stories and write a book called *Tales from Yugoslavia?* Or you could work with other children and write *Tales and Traditions from Many Lands. . . .* "

Tanameeca Dingle brought a finished piece of writing to her conference. When Shelley read it, she looked with great excitement at Tanameeca. "Your writing reminds me of a book I just love," she said. "Do you know Cynthia Rylant's *When I Was Young in the Mountains*?" Looking together at Tanameeca's text, they noticed the ways it was similar to Cynthia Rylant's book. Tanameeca had written:

When I Was Down South
by Tanameeca Dingle

When I was down south I met a lot of people.
When I was down south I played with a lot of friends.
When I was down south it was very hot.
When I was down south it was like home.
When I was down south I hoped that more friends came with me.
When I was down south there was a lot of animals like dogs, cats, pigs, puppies and bats.

Tanameeca begins her lines "When I was down south," and Cynthia Rylant begins hers "When I was young in the mountains." For each writer, too, the repeating phrase introduces a verbal snapshot of a scene.

"Tanameeca, maybe you could take Cynthia Rylant on as your writing teacher," Shelley said. "You could study what she has done and, because you two write in similar ways, you'd probably learn a lot from her. You could think about what advice she might give you on your draft."

As she moved about the room, Shelley launched Ipolito, Charlene, Juliet, and Tanameeca onto endeavors of scope and significance. She did more than encourage one student to add some details and another to clarify the setting. Instead she also invited students to document pigeon behavior, to embark on the study of an author, to collect an anthology of traditions from many lands, to interview a homeless person.

We've come a long way in the teaching of writing. Not long ago the writing process, for us, meant listing several topics and selecting one, producing a page full of possible leads and then another page of freewriting, then writing, revising, and editing a draft. Not long ago the writing process was deskwork. For Ipolito, Charlene, Juliet, and Tanameeca, writing extends far beyond the desk. Writing happens when pigeons scramble for food on the roof of your apartment building, and it happens on the street curb and in the library. Writing is lifework, not deskwork.

Those of us who staff the Teachers College Writing Project, like teachers of writing throughout the world, are fascinated by stories of authors. We each have bulging files of author anecdotes. We each pore through back issues of the *Horn Book* and squeeze into crowded sessions at national conferences to hear authors speak. We love knowing that Byrd Baylor's writing begins when she shoulders her knapsack and heads into the desert to watch hawk nests and collect turquoise beads and remnants of Indian pottery. We're fascinated to learn that Dr. Seuss's first book resulted from trying to put words to the rhythm of the ship's engine during a long, rainy cruise across the Atlantic. We love knowing that Robert McCloskey kept four squawking mallards in his Greenwich Village apartment while he worked on *Make Way for Ducklings* and that E. B. White's original drafts of *Charlotte's Web,* which he wrote while sitting on a bale of hay in his barn, is full of sketches of pigs, barns, and a spider at work.

For those of us who teach writing, these aren't just cute author anecdotes. They are revolutionary.

We collect and cherish author anecdotes because they remind us that writers live their lives differently because they write. They remind us that if we regard writing only as a sequence of deskwork—rough drafts and conferences, cumulative folders and editing checklists—we are inadvertently squeezing the life out of the writing process. They remind us that writing is meant to unfold, stretch into, and disturb every aspect of a writer's world. They remind us that, as Toni Morrison says, "If writing is thinking and discovery and selection and order and meaning, it is also awe and reverence and mystery and magic" (1987b, 111).

When it sometimes seems that writing workshops have become perfunctory, that our students are cranking out lifeless ditties, that writing is more like spinning plates than launching ships, we shouldn't be disheartened. The task we've taken on is gigantic.

The challenge we've taken on in establishing reading-writing workshops is not only to help children write well, but also to help them live well. That's huge. That's bigger than a school's yearly goal. It's bigger than a district's five-year plan.

And so we—Shelley Harwayne and I—offer this book as one more contribution to the continuing dialogue about the teaching and learning of writing and reading. *Living Between the Lines* stands on the shoulders of ideas that have now become part of the established currency on the teaching of writing. Those ideas, as described especially by Donald Graves's *Writing: Teachers and Children at Work,* Nancie Atwell's *In the Middle,* and my *The Art of Teaching Writing,* long ago brought heart and soul, rigor and direction to our teaching. In this book, we challenge, revise, and extend those earlier ideas. We imagine new possibilities and explore new frontiers. We have been able to do so only because we've had shoulders to stand upon. We have been willing to do this only because we know these ideas will also live in classrooms where they, too, will be questioned, revised, and extended. This is as it should be.

The challenge of helping children write well—and live well—is bigger than any of us and bigger than any of our theories. It's a challenge that's big enough to live for.

2

A Place for Writing and Reading

At a recent conference of the National Council of Teachers of English, a teacher asked the author Avi, "What do you suggest doing if kids won't write?"

"Well, first you have to love them," Avi responded. "If you can convince your children that you love them, then there's nothing you can't teach them" (1987). One of the challenges we as writing teachers face is that we must begin teaching writing before we've grown to love each child. Once we can look at loud, blustery Joel and know the vulnerability and earnestness just beneath the surface, it's not hard to teach him. Once we have found that quiet Diana has so much to say if only we listen, once we've become proud of Marcella's feistiness and her social consciousness, it's not hard to teach them. But in September, when Joel seems loud, Diana withdrawn, and Marcella a stranger, it's hard to help them write well. Our first objective, then, is to fall in love with our children, and to do so quickly.

Establishing a School for Children in Our Classrooms

Years ago, founders of the Bank Street College of Education realized that if they wanted to help preservice teachers study and appreciate children, they needed classrooms in which children were doing all the wondrous things children do: planning, painting, talking, critiquing, building, choosing, organizing, collecting, dreaming, constructing. . . . Because they could find few such classrooms, Bank Street established its own School for Children. In a sense, each teacher who wants to observe and understand children—to fall in love with children—must do the same.

The way to establish a School for Children in each classroom is not to rush about filling the room with a variety of paper, bulletin boards, conference areas, editing checklists, and an author's chair—these will all come in time—

but instead, to fill the classroom with children's lives. Imagine the message we would convey if we began the year by asking everyone to bring photograph albums from home and spend an hour in twos and threes sharing the moments and people in our lives. Imagine the message we would convey if, during the first few weeks of school, we had potluck lunches together on Fridays, talking in clusters about our families, favorite nooks and crannies, and our collections. Imagine what it would mean to children if we instituted classroom museums for displaying stamps, insects, marbles, books, fossils, and artwork. Three children with shell collections could collaborate with a child who sails in the summer and one whose father is in the Navy, and together they could create a museum of oceanography. The museum needn't be fancy; it's a grand enough thing for children to label and display their abalone and mussel shells and bring in photographs and awards and memories from their fathers' stints in the Navy or their own sailing adventures. It's a grand enough thing for children to search the library for reference books and journal articles to accompany their displays and to brainstorm stories, lessons, and plans they might share in a seminar with interested classmates.

If we want to establish Schools for Children in our classrooms, if we want our children to be living fully as themselves in our classrooms, then instead of stapling scalloped edges and cardboard horns of plenty onto our bulletin boards, we might let youngsters use bulletin boards as a place for announcements, jokes, news about ticket sales, displays of artwork, writing, quotes and posters, maps and photographs. Instead of beginning the year with a neatly arranged library, we might suggest that each person bring in a beloved book to contribute to the library. Later, students can help unbox other library books, deciding how to categorize them and designing sign-out procedures. Instead of beginning the year by asking children to take turns reading aloud from a textbook, we might ask them to read their favorite poems and books aloud, and especially to read in their native languages.

Imagine the message we would convey if children began the year by surveying each other about topics of real concern and then making bar graphs depicting which children read the front page of the newspaper, which native languages are represented in the classroom, who believes in boycotting tuna fish companies, and how many in the class are only children. Mimi Aronson, a teacher of teachers with the Writing Project, recently suggested that different children might use their hobbies to illustrate letters on the alphabet chart, with Ipolito, for example, drawing pigeons for the *Pp* letter and Juliet drawing Yugoslavia for the *Yy*. Mimi also suggests that during the first week of school, children (and their teacher, of course) might bring in and discuss artifacts that are emblematic of themselves. They might put colored pins onto a world map in order to locate and mark their ethnic origins and talk about their roots. They might turn their desks into work spaces for themselves, bringing in photographs, artwork, quotations to live by, special paper, or small mascots.

Not so very long ago, we urged teachers to bring children's lives into classrooms, because then writers wouldn't be able to hide behind excuses like

"I have nothing to write about" and "Nothing happens in my life." Now we realize that the reason to invite children's lives into the classroom has less to do with finding topics for writing than with the fact that we cannot learn unless we're alive to our existence. Above her writing desk, Annie Dillard has a photograph that might be hung above every classroom door. The photograph is of a little Amazonian boy whose face is sticking out of river rapids. White water is pounding all around his head and his dark eyes are looking up. "That little boy is completely alive," Dillard says. "He's letting the mystery of existence beat on him. He's having his childhood, and I think he knows it. And I think he will come out of the water strong, and ready to do some good" (1987, 58).

The intensity and engagement with life in Annie Dillard's photograph is exactly what is missing in too many classrooms. When one watches children at play—building a dam across the creek, running wires between light bulbs and battery nodes, organizing a neighborhood pet show—it is incomprehensible that a classroom filled with more than twenty children could actually be characterized as having a flat, unemotional tone and a sense of passivity. But in his study of American classrooms, John Goodlad (1984) found that emotional neutrality and student passivity are the norm in American education. Children sit passively at their desks and listen with glassy eyes. They expect someone to tell them what to do. They go through the motions of filling out dittos, answering reading questions, doing math exercises, copying off a chalkboard—and when the school day is over, they burst through the schoolhouse door and into their lives.

It's no accident that the photograph over Annie Dillard's writing desk is not about writing but about being alive to one's existence. Literacy is inseparable from living. If we invite youngsters to address topics of great significance during the writing workshop and then find that instead of writing with heart and soul, their writing is lifeless and rote, we do not necessarily need to change anything we're doing in the writing workshop. Sometimes it's more important to look at the life that surrounds writing, at the messages children hear during and outside the school day. How can we expect students to write with vigor and voice if they are silenced throughout the rest of the day? How can we expect students to write from the particulars of their lives if they feel as Susanne does about school (Figure 2–1):

My teddy bear, I love my teddy bear.
I sleep with my teddy bear.
I eat with my teddy bear.
I play with my teddy bear.
I go shopping with my teddy bear.
Except! I don't bring my teddy bear to school.

How can we expect children to write well when we don't know their stories? David Booth (1989) points out, "Our children story about *us* all the

Figure 2–1   Susanne's "Teddy Bear" Piece

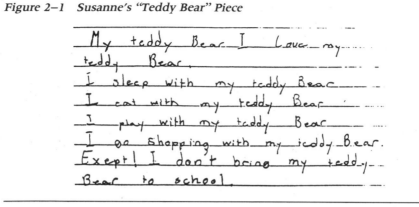

My teddy Bear I Love my
teddy Bear.
I sleep with my teddy Bear
I eat with my teddy Bear
I play with my teddy Bear
I go shopping with my teddy Bear.
Exept! I don't bring my teddy
Bear to school.

time. They story about our new shirt (Was it for our birthday?) and about our suntans (Where did she go over vacation?)." But some teachers don't "story" with their kids. Shouldn't shared stories be at the heart of writing workshops?

If cutting down the rain forests in Brazil threatens plant life in Connecticut, then surely writing workshops are affected by the straight, silent rows of desks, short-answer questions, stratified groupings, grammar drills, and science dittos that surround too many writing workshops. The ecology of the school is at least as interconnected as the ecology of the planet.

We don't need to have carpets, salt-water aquariums, elaborate learning centers, and frequent field trips to lead effective reading and writing workshops. But if we're going to teach reading and writing well, our classrooms must be filled with our students' voices and their lives. We don't need to be Superteachers to teach children to write, but we do need to love and respect our children and to help them love and respect each other—and themselves.

Coming to Know Our Children's Stories

We needn't establish Schools for Children on our own. When children fill their classrooms with collections and areas of expertise, native languages and favorite books, they are joining us in supplying the prerequisite materials for writing, reading, and growing up. Parents, too, can be invaluable partners in the effort to establish classrooms that brim over with our children's voices and lives. Mary Ellen Giacobbe, a former first-grade teacher from Atkinson Academy in New Hampshire, used to begin the school year by inviting her children's parents to a wine and cheese bookmaking party, which provided the classroom with 400 blank books and gave parents the chance to be insiders in the reading-writing workshop. Other teachers have asked parents to help build files of available experts, so that parents and local people can become mentors for children. As wonderful as it is to ask for parents' help with bookbinding and expertise files, it's even more crucial to ask for parents' help in knowing and teaching their children. Teachers in New York City, London, England, Stratham, New Hampshire, and many other places have recently begun the year by writing letters like this one by three Hewlett-Woodmere teachers:

Dear Parents,

I'm writing to ask you to help me become a partner with you in your child's education. I will only have your child for a short time in this trip through life—just one fleeting school year—and I want to make a contribution that lasts a lifetime.

I know my teaching must begin with making your child feel at home in my classroom, and with helping all the children come together into a learning community made up of particular, unique individuals, each with his or her own learning style and interests and history and hopes. Would you help me teach well by taking a quiet moment to write me about your child? What is your youngster like? What are the things you, as a parent, know that would be important for me to know? What are the child's interests? I want to know how your child thinks and plays and how you see your child as a learner and a person.

Respectfully yours,
Carol Pollock
Rose Weinstein
Joan Boccio

Anyone who has ever been a parent, who has ever zipped up a son's or daughter's jacket and watched as that child heads off with lunch box in hand, ready (or not) for the first day of school, knows how much it would mean for a teacher to write, "Will you help me make your child feel at home in our classroom?" When parents write back, their letters are full of information about their children, but they also convey an overwhelming sense of the infinite preciousness of each child.

Barbara Novack's letter about her son Joshua began like this:

As I begin to think and write about my one and only child, my first thought is to thank you for wanting to receive my insights on him. I've just watched Joshua and his two cousins setting up a lemonade stand on a warm Saturday afternoon. I love the excitement, gleam, and joy he's experiencing as he sets out to do business and makes a sale. . . . I have to tell you that the joy and love I receive every morning when I see my son's face gives me the understanding of what life is about. . . .

Once Joshua's teacher has received a letter like this one, it won't be hard to teach Joshua to write. The letter makes Joshua very real and precious . . . yet there are countless people in school systems who are never brought to life in this way. In his inaugural address as Commissioner of Education for New York State, Tom Sobol talked (without intending to do so) about the importance of knowing people's stories. He said,

> Each of the thousands of young men who will spend their youth in prison, each of the 1725 young women (age 10 to 14) who last year in New York State became pregnant, is an individual with a heart that hurts every bit as much as 18-month-old Jessica who fell in a well shaft last week, her tiny foot wedged against her head. Drillers worked feverishly to save her, and the nation watched and listened. We need to care as much and direct as much attention to the thousands of young men in prison, to the 1725 young girls who became pregnant last year, as the nation did to baby Jessica. (1987)

The nation cared about baby Jessica just as we cared about the three whales trapped in a diminishing pocket of Alaskan water, because when we know the particulars of a human being's (or a whale's) story we are called out of ourselves to care.

When Hewlett-Woodmere teachers asked parents to write letters about their sons and daughters, those teachers were inviting parents to help them fall in love. Letter after letter spoke in a voice similar to Mrs. Novak's, straight from the hearts of mothers and fathers who were touched to have been given the chance to look a teacher in the eye and say, "Please, listen well to my little one. You'll hear he has so much to say," and "Give her time to warm up to you. She can be cautious and distant at first, but that will pass," and "Forgive her loudness. It's exuberance and zest." Some of the letters cried out for help, telling of children who are caught in court cases, in family illnesses, in split families, and telling of youngsters who have grown up in the shadow of a dazzlingly successful older sibling or of a handicapped brother. Many of the letters also helped teachers begin to understand each child's history as a reader and writer. Sarah loves to make detailed, maplike drawings with roads, tunnels, and bridges, and she uses Legos, blocks, and road sets to create similar empires. Reading and talking about reading are Amanda's favorite activities, short of brushing her hair or discussing stickers. She also loves to buy clothes, polish her nails, and do her hair. When she has time and her nails are dry, she enjoys writing stories and poems. Scott's mother drilled him every day all summer long on initial consonants and sounds, and he doesn't like to read.

In journalism there is a rule of thumb that says, "The more you know, the more you can learn." If we know about the intricate worlds Sarah creates in drawing and play, then we wonder whether she builds worlds through her written narratives as well. If we know the sustained attention she gives to Legos and balsa models, then we're especially surprised when her writing shows hurry and impatience. Once we begin building up mental portraits of each child as a learner and a person, then it's almost impossible to avoid constantly learning and needing to learn more. If we find that Sarah loves to write long science fiction stories in which she builds and inhabits imaginary worlds, then we're filled with questions when we notice her writing a short poetic piece. "Sarah," we say, "can we talk today about your writing?"

Teachers who receive letters from children's parents and who invite children to bring their lives into the classroom will probably want to interview children about their histories as readers and writers.

"What kind of books do you read at home?" Shelley Harwayne asked after six-year-old Simone had settled herself comfortably onto a milk crate. Simone didn't pause for an instant before answering. "Hard ones," she said, and taking a Roald Dahl book from the shelves, she showed Shelley the kinds of hard books she reads outside her first-grade classroom. Then Simone said,

> I have piles. One pile is travel books, if you want to take a trip to South America. One pile is books I haven't read in a long, long time. Then there's a pile of early reading books like Dr. Seuss, and there's books like *Charlie and the Chocolate Factory* in a harder pile. I read to my mother and my babysitter, and if I don't know a word, I try to sound it out or they just tell me the word. No guessing allowed. Like Mum said, "Don't guess." I'm six, so I read the books myself. I'm too old for bedtime stories or sucking my thumb.

Interviews such as this one are full of places in which we're tempted to switch from interviewing to instruction. We want to tell Simone that six isn't too old for bedtime stories, and that guessing is the best possible way to deal with unfamiliar words. But it's often important to postpone instruction, to remember that interviews are meant as opportunities for understanding rather than reforming youngsters. If we postpone the temptation to correct Simone's perspective and try instead to understand it, an integrated portrait will begin to emerge. It's interesting to notice, for example, what Simone said later.

> My favorite area in the classroom is the worksheet area and the reading games because I feel grown up doing them. You write words—it's fun—you spell.

> I'm in the blue reading group, which is the middle group. Red is for the hard group. Blue is the second hardest. Yellow is the third hardest. I want to be in the red group, but the teacher doesn't pick me to change. I don't know why.

Interviewing students takes time, and time is a scarce resource in the schools. But it's hard to imagine any activity more worthy of the time it takes than these interviews. When we understand our children as readers and writers, our teaching does not feel as if we are spinning our wheels in the air. Our wheel connects with the child's wheel, and teaching and learning can become one and the same motion.

We can also learn about children's lifelines as readers and writers, particularly in the upper grades, by asking them to write about them. When John Chambers, the principal who took high school students on a five-day sail, and Mary Winsky, the writing staff developer in the Katonah-Lewisboro district, cotaught a secondary school writing workshop, they often joined students in free writing about their histories and hopes as readers and writers. "Let's begin the workshop today with a few minutes to gather and share our thoughts on this," Mary or John would say, and then they and their students would think together about issues such as:

- As a reader, I . . .
- As a writer, I . . .
- In this workshop, I hope that we . . .
- If you're going to respond well to my writing (or reading), you need to know . . .
- My greatest fear as a writer (reader) is . . .
- One thing you may still not know about me as a writer (reader) is . . .
- My ambition as a writer (reader) is to . . .

Others have asked students to select a single scene from their lifelines that best conveys who they are as writers or as readers. Some teachers invite students to make time lines depicting their reading/writing histories and to turn back on these in order to reflect on their stages of growth and turning points. When Project staff member Randy Bomer taught eighth grade, he suggested that students begin their reading response logs with autobiographies of themselves as readers. These are excerpts from some of their entries:

One of my fondest memories of reading is that our whole family would gather on Monday nights and read *Uncle Arthur's Bedtime Stories.* All of us kids would get comfortable on the couch while Mom and Dad got situated and ready to read. We'd all choose which story to read . . .

NATHAN

"A comb, a hush and a bowl full of mush." This is from *Goodnight Moon,* one of the first books I remember. When I was little I'd recite along as my Mom or Dad read it to me. Now all I remember is that one phrase, and the pictures of rabbits getting ready for bed and the room growing darker like it was night . . .

MEGAN

My life history as a writer is a long and painstaking one because I have dyslexia. When I was younger, I went to so many doctors and specialists to see what the problem was. I had enough EKG tests done on me and enough tutors to last two or three lifetimes.

In class when I have to read I always read a paragraph or two ahead so that when I read aloud, I won't mess up. It used to piss me off so bad when I would be reading and I would say the wrong word but know what it really was. I'd know what it was but it stuck in my throat.

I shouldn't say this like it doesn't happen anymore because it does. People say the right word and I know what it is, and I say, "Shut up." It is hard and always will be.

JEROD

I remember when I was very little that I couldn't wait for Saturday nights because my brother would come home from boarding school and bring me chocolate he'd saved from his lunches and a Mickey Mouse book. I learned to read early, and I'd read stories over and over because I wanted to make my mom proud and happy. If I could read and write without mistakes, my mother would allow me to sleep for an hour with my dad in the big bed, and I just loved to stay close to my dad and to hear all the beautiful stories he told me.

As I grew older, I loved to go in the back of the house where the roses are and sit on a very short tree and read my book. My favorite books were given me for my birthday, written just for me, and I was the main character, with my Mom, Dad, brother and sister.

ROBERT

Sharing Intimacy, Adventure, and Books

We can also get to know students by working and playing together. Several students in Isoke Nia's class were walking past a used furniture store when they spotted a wooden chair with luxurious green velvet cushions. A few days later the whole class was at that store, deciding together that yes, this was to be their author's chair. Then came the brainstorming and the work of raising $36, and eventually, the fun of carrying the chair down the road, through the school, and into the classroom. In the room that day, the children sang African spirituals as they polished the chair.

At Harvard University, many freshmen begin their year with a week of biking or mountain climbing. They come back to campus dirty, ragged, worn-out, and full of shared stories and memories. In public schools, adventures such as these tend to come in May and June, when it's too late for them to make a difference. How important it is to do in September what we normally do in June.

We learned this, especially, at 5:00 A.M. on a rainy morning. Storm clouds were gathering and the wind was picking up momentum when building principals from twenty of our New York City schools began arriving at South Street Seaport, Pier 13. Each of us eyed the grey skies as we walked down the plank onto the eighty-foot schooner that awaited us.

At 6:00 A.M. we set sail, two of us at *The Bowdoin*'s helm, another two reading the radar, others hauling up the sails, four on the mainsail's throat halyard, four on the mainsail's peak halyard, straining and pulling to lift the thousands of pounds of canvas. As we rounded the bend, the skies opened with rain, and from the hatch below came the slightly smelly plastic orange coats with hoods. We gathered for John Masefield's "Sea-Fever":

I must go down to the seas again, to the lonely sea and the sky,
And all I ask is a tall ship and a star to steer her by,
And the wheel's kick and the wind's song and the white sail's shaking,
And a grey mist on the sea's face and a grey dawn breaking.

We read, two taking one part and the rest chiming in. So began our day.

That morning, eighteen of us squashed into the cabin, sitting on narrow, creaking cots, listening as Norm Sherman read *Thomas' Snowsuit* by Robert Munsch. Later, many of the rest of us crowded into a lifeboat, sharing stories of our first days as teachers and administrators. Principals Ed Funk and Millicent Gormandy were on their hands and knees on the ship's deck, hammering at the claws of lobsters. Other principals in slickers and life vests sat cross-legged on the slushy wet floor talking about the struggles and loneliness they face back home in their buildings.

We learned something that day about organizing effective writing workshops. We learned that the spirit and intimacy of the workshop are much more important than the structures: the mini-lessons, workshops, and share meetings we put together like so many Legos. And that spirit, that intimacy, comes from sharing bits of life. Normally, Writing Project staff and building principals tend to sit with the principal's big desk between us, talking of schedules and arrangements, of who's to do what and when. On the schooner, we hauled in ropes and cracked lobster shells together, and talked about books and the sea, about people we love and dreams we have lost. Normally, we teachers also tend to maintain a polite distance from our students. We sit with the teacher's big desk and the teacher's big curriculum between us. We talk of schedules and assignments, of who's to do what and when. How good it would be to bring classrooms of children to Pier 13, just as the storm clouds were gathering, to wear orange raincoats and read "I must go down to the seas again," to share lobsters and talk about books and the sea and childhood memories and dreams we've lost, about hopes and plans and ways of learning.

Of course I'm not really saying that writing teachers need to march into administrators' offices and tell them that in addition to writing portfolios, staplers, scotch tape, and author's chairs, we now need a schooner and stormy skies. But I do believe that the classroom that has reading and writing at its heart needs the spirit of that schooner. Those of us who have written within a community of writers and read within a community of readers know that these communities have a different feel. They have a sense of intimacy and of adventure. The most important thing to do in September, then, is not to establish routines and rituals but to nurture the intangible spirit that can matter more than anything. Surely one way of doing this is to share incredible pieces of literature with our children.

In their classrooms, Writing Project teachers have invited children to climb inside books and travel together—to Narnia, to the backwoods of the Ozarks, to Caddie Woodlawn's one-room schoolhouse, to the Arctic seas, to the Emerald City of Oz, to Puddleby. Together, teachers and children have mourned the death of a friend, salvaged whatever they could from a shipwreck, reared lion cubs, kayaked among icebergs, seen families gassed in death chambers, and made friends with spiders and crickets and fawns. And we have learned that reading together is powerful stuff. "Reading," Franz Kafka says, "is an ice axe to break the sea frozen inside us." Reading can also be an ice axe to break the sea frozen within our classrooms.

I think, for example, of a teacher in Queens whose classroom has, for years, been one of those in which everything seems to be done perfectly well but there's just no chemistry. This particular teacher had a lovely author's chair, two sets of writing folders for each child, a daily writing workshop . . . but it often seemed that her students were merely going through the motions. Then one day, Ralph Fletcher, a staff person from the Project, arrived to find that everything was different. The room was charged with energy and intention. Kids were pouring their hearts out onto paper, writing about the death of a grandparent, about not fitting in with their classmates, about a brother coming home drunk, about growing up as an only child. "What happened?" Ralph asked.

The teacher nodded knowingly. "Can you believe it?" she said. "If I don't stop them, they'll write and write and write all day."

"What did you do?" Ralph asked, still big-eyed in amazement.

"We read together," the teacher said. "That's all. We read sad, sad stories like *Roll of Thunder, Hear My Cry* and *A Taste of Blackberries.*" Then she said, "I think I'd been pretending that stories have happy endings, and reading those sad books, it tapped into the pain in the children's lives and in mine. I started talking to the children about how my parents are moving and it's killing me. I told them about all my years of plastic surgery on my face and how I always thought I was ugly . . . and they started telling their stories, too, and writing them."

One child said, "When my mother hurts inside, she cries. I want to cry too, but I don't because I know she'll just feel worse."

A tiny little boy wrote about seeing his father go into diabetic shock and fall on the floor, hitting his head on the dishwasher. Then another child began writing about her father being released from jail, and how she hugs him and he hugs her and, she says, they have the greatest love of all. In that teacher's classroom, it only took two incredible novels to make moments, in Anne Tyler's words, "bristle with meaning." Literature can do that. "Great literature, if we read it well," Donald Hall has said, "opens us up to the world and makes us more sensitive to it, as if we acquired eyes that could see through things and ears that could hear smaller sounds."

In a reading-writing workshop, something has to give you an extra consciousness. Something has to make moments bristle with meaning. A friend of Anne Tyler's once said, "In order to be a writer, you have to have suffered childhood arthritis, buried a son, or gone to a foreign country and lived in utter loneliness." Anne Tyler responds that although she has never done any of these things, she does believe that in order to write, something has to separate you from the nondescript cottonwool of everyday life (1980, 13).

Books can make that difference. They can make classrooms bristle with meaning. More and more, teachers throughout the world are trusting that shared books can create a world for writing. Priorities are changing. Good teachers are less concerned about whether we make elaborate helping hand charts or begin the year with homemade board games and more concerned than ever about beginning the year with wonderful literature, carefully selected by both teachers and children.

Rather than reading aloud what Margaret Atwood calls "thumbsucking" books, the kind that publishing companies replace each year with others just like them, teachers are selecting books that can act as lifelines. The notion of books as lifelines comes from Hazel Rochman's article about Maya Angelou, who was traumatized as a child and, as a result, stopped talking. She was punished and beaten, but nothing helped. Then a woman named Mrs. Flowers began lending her books and reading aloud to her from Dickens. In sharing her books, Angelou says, Mrs. Flowers was holding out "a 'lifeline,' freeing her from the grim confines of her private sorrow. The best books can do that" (1988a, 39). More and more, our teachers are looking for books that offer children a lifeline.

Lydia Bellino, a teacher of teachers who recently came to the New York City schools after years of staff development work on Long Island, begins her work with children by simply reading aloud from the most powerful books she can find. She says, "For the first three days of school, almost all I did was read. When I closed *A Taste of Blackberries,* the room was hushed because words weren't needed. . . . The tears brimming in our eyes said it all. . . . I knew we were ready to write."

This year, Lydia read Doris B. Smith's *A Taste of Blackberries* differently than she had in previous years. "Instead of doling the book out in evenly measured bits, a chapter a day, we let the story grab hold of us and take over everything. Once we got into the book, we read it constantly, morning, noon, and night. We couldn't put it down. Even when we were not reading we were talking and thinking about the book."

One of the reasons Lydia Bellino's students thought about the book is that they talked about it. Each day after reading aloud, children clustered together informally, right on the floor where they'd been sitting for the story, and talked and talked and talked. Sometimes Lydia guided the talk by saying, "Before we begin talking in our pairs, can each of us think for a moment about this: If you could only say one thing in response to this book, what would it be?" Another time just prior to reading aloud, Lydia said, "Today let's talk, among other things, about whether there is a significant scene that stands out for us." Often Lydia suggested that as the children listened to the story, they each let their own stories come to mind. "Let's tell each other about the parts of our lives the book calls to mind," Lydia said.

Listening to *A Taste of Blackberries* one child muttered, half under his breath, "That reminds me of when my cousin got sick." Another said, "That reminds me of when I kept laughing at this old lady and then all of a sudden she was dead and I felt so bad." And Lydia did not say, "Could we get back to the story?" because, of course, our children's stories are as important as those of literature. To teach writing well, we need to know those stories.

Why Reading and Writing Matter

When children bring their lives into the classroom and we come to know those lives well, we cannot help but want to enrich them. Teachers of writing and reading throughout the world have come to care passionately about workshop teaching, in part because reading and writing are ways in which human beings find significance and direction, beauty and intimacy, in their lives.

These are hard times for children. The rate of child suicide has risen 300 percent in the last decade. Thirty thousand young people in West Virginia alone are alcoholics. In New York City every day, sixty thousand young people roam the streets, preferring the streets and what they offer to class-rooms and what they offer. One in twenty infants in New York City is born with AIDS.

These are hard times for our children, even the so-called lucky ones. A recent survey showed that when today's young people were asked, "Who are your heroes?" they did not name statesmen, writers, teachers, politicians, physicians, musicians . . . but actors and athletes. These are hard times for children. When we teachers were children, we made doll clothes from scraps of fabric, turned shoeboxes into cradles, and wove our fantasies and fears into stories for our dolls and teddy bears; now dolls come with ready-made names and story lines and weapons. Back then, we rolled and stretched and shaped play dough into families of snakes and dishes with grapes and pancakes; now youngsters merely turn the lever of a machine and out pop perfectly formed stars and hearts. Back then, the neighborhood children gathered at dusk, just as the frogs and crickets were beginning to sing, for Kick the Can and Ring-a-levio; now youngsters don't have to get on their bikes and round up the neighborhood kids or even get off the sofa: the electronic games supply teammates and opponents, and all today's youngsters have to do is push the buttons.

In a speech about the world's problems, Katherine Paterson, the beloved author of *A Bridge to Terabithia,* paused and asked, "What am I doing while the world is falling apart?" Then she answered,

I am sitting in my little study in front of my typewriter. . . . Sometimes
I see this as an evasion of responsibility . . . but still I believe that . . .
to give the children of the world the words they need is to give them
life and growth and refreshment. (1981, 6)

The reason that many of us care so much about the teaching of reading and
writing is that we, too, have found that when we give the children of the world
the words they need, we are giving them life and growth and refreshment.

3

Shared Stories
Turn Classrooms into
Communities

Our students need what readers and writers the world over need. They need places to go and things to do. They need supplies: paper, pens, pencils of all sorts and sizes, typewriters, and word processors, if possible; stamps, envelopes, phone books, catalogues, and files of addresses; paper clips, staplers, scissors, carbon paper, tape, and white out; file folders, file drawers, and ways to index their work; dictionaries, encyclopedias, atlases, and thesauruses. They need lots and lots of time to write and doodle and dream and play. They need ways to get advice, to gain distance, to settle down and write, to take a break. But more than all this, they need to feel at home. They need to feel safe and respected and free to be themselves.

Launching the Writing Workshop
"Let's push all the desks against the walls," Shelley Harwayne said as she and fourth-grade teacher Anne Gianatiempo began "preparing the soil" for writing in Room 417 of P.S. 148. Readers of this book will become familiar with Anne, with Laurie Pessah, the staff developer who nurtures and guides teachers in this building, and with Public School 148. There are eighteen different dialects spoken here. The front foyer is always filled with clusters of new immigrant children waiting for their class assignments, and every turn of the hallway reveals another circle of beautiful, wide-eyed children drawn closely around a ten-year-old "teacher." These youngsters, like their mentors inside the classroom, teach with easels, newsprint stories, tape recorders, clipboards, and literature. This is a school for literacy. Reading and writing hang from the ceiling and fill the halls. Inside the door to the library there is a white wicker baby basket filled with new books, labeled "New Arrivals." Each year the fifth graders of the school hold a "Bed and Books" sleepover at the school. Bulletin boards are full of announcements of network meetings, study sessions,

reading and writing groups for teachers. Even in a school such as P.S. 148, children need to be called together into a community, and they need to re-discover over and over again that yes, indeed, they have observations to make, stories to tell, lessons to teach.

"Instead of squeezing into our traditional meeting area, let's form a big circle, one that includes all the observing teachers and principals," Shelley said. As the children began to gather, she added, "You needn't bring pencils or paper." After the circle was formed, Shelley said, "We're going to be in this circle for a long while, so let's get very comfortable." When the rustling and shifting stopped and the room filled with an expectant stillness, Shelley began, first sweeping the circle of faces with her eyes as if to gather people together, and then quietly said, "Today, and often, we're going to share stories, memories, moments. In every family there are stories we tell over and over. These are stories that hold us together as a family; stories of coming to America, of how one child got his name, of the day we found a turtle on the highway, or named our dog, or got stuck in a rainstorm."

With no further explanation, and no mention about topic choice or the writing workshop, Shelley launched into a story. "Last night my mother told me the familiar story about how, when she was a child in a small village in Poland, she made her own toys. She spoke of drying the small bones of a chicken's neck to use as jacks, and gathering hairs from cows to mold into a ball, and carving checkers out of bits of broken brick. It's a story I've heard many times before," Shelley added, "but somehow I never get tired of hearing it."

One story leads to another. Jonas told about how, on his sister's wedding day, she opened the door to leave for the church and a puppy with muddy paws ran in, scampering right up the long train of her white bride's dress. Norman told of asking his grandmother, "Where do people get babies?" and his grandmother answering that babies come on a boat from a land full of babies. Ariel told about how her mom had been rescued by an American helicopter pilot in Vietnam a few weeks before she gave birth, and that she was born in America. Alex told about his father bringing his mother home to meet his parents, who served rabbit stew for the occasion. Alex's mother detested this stew, and so she slipped it under the table to her fiancé, little by little, lest she insult her in-laws-to-be.

Every family has stories that are called forth again and again, stories that start with the chorus, "Remember the time when. . . . " Bill Martin and John Archambault's picture book *Knots on a Counting Rope* begins with a young Indian boy saying to his grandfather,

> Tell me the story again, Grandfather.
> Tell me who I am.
>> I have told you many times, Boy.
>> You know the story by heart.
> But it sounds better
> when you tell it, Grandfather . . .

> Once there was a boy-child . . .
> No, Grandfather.
> Start at the beginning.
> Start where the storm
> was crying my name . . .
> Start, "It was a dark night . . . "

In the same way, the children who sat around the circle that day told stories they'd heard again and again. As one person after another shared a story, something cumulative happened in the room. There was a welling up, a growing sense of "What lives we lead!"

After a bit Shelley intervened to say, "Sometimes the seeds for our stories are not contained in family tales, but in private treasures. I'm thinking of the drawer or the shoebox full of stuff that your mother calls junk. In a way she's right, but somehow you can't bring yourself to throw it away, and you're not sure why." Bringing out an old wrinkled black-and-white photo of a man reading to a child, Shelley said, "This photograph was in the attic of our house when we moved in. Even though I don't know the people, for some reason I keep looking at their picture."

Although Shelley did not mention it that day, she could have told the circle of children that James Howe, author of *Bunnicula*, keeps a treasure box under his bed containing cowboy boots from a boyhood trip to a dude ranch and the official membership certificate from when he joined the Mickey Mouse Club. Shelley could have told the circle of children that, in *One Writer's Beginnings*, Eudora Welty talks about finding treasures in her mother's bottom drawer: a braid of chestnut-colored hair, a tiny cardboard box containing buffalo nickels, which Welty later learned had lain on the eyelids of a baby brother she had never known. Shelley could have read from Dayal Kaur Khalsa's picture book, *Tales of a Gambling Grandma*, in which a little girl looked forward to the days when her grandma would slowly slide open her special drawer. The girl recalls the drawer, saying:

> I liked that drawer.
> First there was the smell of sweet perfume and musty old pennies. Then there was a tiny dark blue bottle of Evening in Paris cologne, shaped like a seashell; a square snapshot of my grandma holding me as a baby; big, thick, wriggly legged black hairpins; and stuck in corners so I had to use the hairpins to get them out, dull brown dusty pennies.
> But most fascinating of all were my grandma's false teeth. (1986, 10)

Shelley could have brought these stories into the fireside sharing in Anne Gianatiempo's classroom, but that morning the children needed very little priming before sharing their own shoeboxes full of unexpected treasures.

"I have this thing," one boy said, backing up to add, "Don't laugh," then, "I have this thing, this little grey bunny. It's all worn out and raggedy, but I think he's like my protector, and I won't let my mom throw him out."

Marcella's story tumbled out quickly. "When I went to leave Colombia, I couldn't bring this patchwork doll with me and so I made a bed for it way back in the closet underneath Grandpa's fishing stuff, and when I went back last summer, she was still there, and my Grandma had found her and made new clothes for her."

As the others talked, a tall, thin boy with a punk hairstyle, who had initially been leaning back away from the circle, drew in and began to talk too. "Your stories are reminding me of something. There's this picture of my grandpa, framed. He died the day I was born. Whenever I'm waiting for my grandma to get dressed, I just stare at the picture. I never met the man, but I can't keep from staring at his picture."

No one spoke between stories; instead, the community of children seemed to understand instinctively the Quaker-meeting-like uses of silence. When Shelley joined in, she tended to do so in ways that called forth yet another kind of story. She said, for example, "I'm wondering if any of us have scenes or images that we can't shake out of our minds."

Judy Davis, who was one of several teachers visiting P.S. 148 that day, spoke first. She told how, as a thirteen-year-old girl, she was charged with the responsibility of giving her grandmother her insulin shot. "Grandpa had always given her the shots, but he was rushed to the hospital suddenly, and even though I was a child myself, everyone looked to me to do it," Judy said. "I'll never forget what it was like to lift up my grandma's skirt and see her bone-thin leg, all bruised and dark from my grandpa's shaking grip on the syringe, and to know it was my turn to puncture that thin, fragile skin."

Billy broke the silence to say, "Where I live there's a big pothole, and after it rains, this old man comes out and sits there all day with his fishing pole." Marcella talked of how, on the top floor of a gutted, abandoned building, she had seen flowerpots with bright red geraniums.

There were other images. Of an old woman who spends hours in the park, crouched down among pigeons, and then leaves with a burlap bag that wobbles and coos. Of staring blankly at a hospital only to see a window, high up in the building, flung open, a face appear, and a telephone go flying through the air. Of an old man in a wheelchair, wheeling to school in the morning with a golden-haired little girl on his lap.

Stories and images cascaded over each other that morning. There was, in that room, a tumbling richness of stories, one resonating against another, some dichotomous, some overlapping, but always gathering abundantly, and there was laughter too, and people listening to each other with tears brimming. There were exclamations of "That happened to me, too," and "You must have some family." There was among us a growing sense of "Here we stand, in the presence of life itself," of "What a privilege it is to be part of this community," of "What voices, what stories, what lives."

Writers need this sense of fullness, of readiness to write, of responsiveness. It can come from storytelling, it can come from shared responses to literature, it can come from bringing boxes and files of writing we've done in our lives and reading excerpts aloud appreciatively with each other. It can come from camping together and sharing thoughts and stories around the campfire. However it comes, it's terribly important. In Anne's classroom, it was the most natural thing in the world for Anne to build on the energy of that moment by suggesting that each person begin honoring his or her memories, images, moments, and ideas by recording them in a writer's notebook.

Moving Beyond Our Resistance to Notebooks and New Ideas

Over the past five years, few things have altered and invigorated life in our writing classrooms more than those notebooks: our own, and those that our students keep. Now, looking back at the process of discovering, then resisting, then tentatively exploring the use of small looseleaf notebooks, spirals, and marble-covered composition books, and of eventually letting them influence all that we do in the writing workshop, we are flabbergasted that they could so drastically challenge the norms of our writing workshop. But they have. In the next three chapters, I show how notebooks have helped us discover the importance both of rehearsal and of writing that is meant simply to generate ideas. I explore the ways notebooks have replaced our daily writing folders and daily rough drafts, and the ways they have helped us and our youngsters build the momentum necessary for larger writing projects. I talk about ways notebooks have given us a new sense of revision. In our workshops, revision usually begins with seeing themes and entries that have the potential to become more, then growing and writing our way into those ideas and collecting parallel entries about them, and finally, standing on the shoulders of all we have written and read in order to write several pieces, usually with particular purposes and audiences in mind for each one.

Both Anne Gianatiempo and Judy Davis, along with other Writing Project teachers, had at first been reluctant to incorporate writers' notebooks into their workshops. "I finally feel comfortable teaching the writing process," Judy said, her voice tense with anxiety, "and now everything's changing." Confused, she asked, "So daily writing folders are out and notebooks are in?" For Anne, too, it was as if all the hard-earned changes she had made in her teaching were being called into question. Was writing process going the route of every other new program? Was it, too, going to be a revolving door with writing process "out" and notebooks "in"?

Although Anne and Judy didn't know it, when we first brought notebooks into writing classrooms, we hated them. We first learned about them from Dorothy Barnhouse, a writer in the Project. She was at home with notebooks, and could draw on her own experiences with them as she shared them with us and with children. But when we tried incorporating notebooks into our teaching, it was awful, it was maddening. How could a little thing like notebooks so shake our confidence? We felt as if we had to learn all over again how to teach a writing workshop. We tripped over our words and didn't know where to put our bodies. Nothing was second nature anymore. The notebooks pulled our routines out from under us and made us self-conscious and confused. Like Anne and Judy, our ambivalence came partly because we had had some success with preexisting ideas about writing. Success, even partial success, can be dangerous. It sucks you in. You end up not wanting to deviate from what you've been doing.

We longed to go back to our old method of launching the workshop by saying to children, "Today we're all going to be authors. What does an author do?" We could anticipate their response: "Authors write books!" We knew our retort: "Yes, and today *we're* going to begin writing books. The first thing an author does is to decide what to write about. Let's see, I might write about. . . . "

We longed to abandon the idea of notebooks and return to the comfort of our old ways, but we didn't. We didn't because, in truth, we'd had questions all along about what we'd been doing. We knew the emphasis writers put on germinating ideas, on rehearsal, on waiting. Donald Murray talks about writers needing to have the courage to wait for their topics. "Waiting means time," he says, "time for staring out of windows, time for thinking, time for dreaming, time for doodling, time for rehearsing, planning, drafting, restarting . . . for moving closer, backing off, coming at it from a different angle, circling again, trying a new approach" (1989, 22–23).

We knew Kafka had one word over his writing desk: "Wait." We knew that for Kafka, Murray, and so many others, writing has everything to do with waiting and gathering and seeing pieces combine and gather momentum . . . and we knew that for many of the young writers in our classrooms, there had not been much delay, or planning, or opportunity for gathering momentum between beginning a piece and drafting it, or between producing one piece of writing and another.

Then, too, neither Shelley nor I nor any of the other writers on the Project staff begin writing by choosing a topic and producing a draft. Instead, each of us begins writing by generating coexisting entries and notes and ideas. Once we have an occasion, a form, a focus, an audience, a voice—a position in relationship to our material—we push off into rough drafts.

Finally, we persisted with notebooks because once the idea of notebook writing was on our front burner, we could no longer avoid seeing that almost all the authors we'd read—Annie Dillard, Gail Godwin, Joyce Carol Oates, Virginia Woolf, Gretel Ehrlich, Katherine Mansfield, Mary Gordon, Don Graves, Maurice Sendak, Ursula K. LeGuin, Donald Murray, Norman Mailer, and many others—have a journal, diary, daybook, notebook, or file out of which beginnings of writing projects emerge.

And so even when notebooks were a total failure in our writing workshops, we persisted. We persisted ultimately because we'd been feeling for a while that in too many instances good teachers, especially in grades two and up, were struggling with writing workshops. In too many instances, kids were churning out dutifully revised little pieces. We persisted because for a while we'd had an unsettled sense that something was needed to enrich the chain of life in some of our writing classrooms. We persisted because the very thing that made notebooks difficult also made them important. Notebooks, from the start, stood a chance of being more than a new tool, more than a place for writing. They stood a chance of altering the existing ecology of our writing workshops, of affecting the cycle of life in the classrooms. That was scary, because change is scary. But it was also enormously hopeful.

4

The Notebook: A Tool for Writing and Living

In her memoir, *Little by Little,* Jean Little remembers the moment she began to live like a writer. She was home, sick in bed, and her mother brought her a fleet of orange slices on a white plate. Jean says, "I lined the bright little boats up, one behind the other, on the windowsill beside me. The world outside was dark, and the wood of the windowsill was a mahogany brown. The orange segments glowed against the sombre background. I loved the look of them. I could hardly bear to spoil it by eating one." As Jean took the farthest-away orange slice and began to chew the pulp, she realized with a pang that in a day she'd forget how beautiful the line of glowing orange boats looked. "It's part of my life," she thought, "and I am forgetting it." She straightened her shoulders, stared at the brave little fleet and said, "I will remember, as long as I live, how these orange boats look right now." Reflecting back on this moment in her memoir, Jean says, "What mattered was that for the first time I saw my world and my life as something that belonged to me, and began to put small scraps of time away in a place where I could take them out and look at them whenever I needed to remember" (1987, 92–93).

When people ask those of us who staff the Teachers College Writing Project about our goals, we sometimes answer that our first goal is for young people to cherish the sight of orange slices lined up on a windowsill. We cannot give youngsters rich lives. We cannot give them long family suppers full of shared stories, rainbow-colored markers and sheaves of drawing paper, photograph albums full of memories, and beautiful picture books lined up beside their beds. We can't give children rich lives, but we can give them the lens to appreciate the richness that is already there in their lives. Notebooks validate a child's existence. Notebooks say, "Your thoughts, your noticings, your fleet of orange slices matter."

Byrd Baylor's wonderful picture book, *I'm in Charge of Celebrations*, has helped all of us understand that the process of keeping a notebook is an act of listening and celebration. The book opens with a girl from the Southwest desert country saying, "Sometimes people ask me, 'Aren't you lonely out there with just desert around you?'" It is a question that can be asked of all of us and all our children. "Aren't you lonely out there with just your classroom and your apartment?" "Aren't you lonely out there with whatever your life holds?" When Byrd Baylor's heroine is asked, "Aren't you lonely out there with just desert around you?" she responds, in astonishment,

> I guess they mean
> the beargrass
> and the yuccas
> and the cactus
> and the rocks.
>
> I guess they mean
> the deep ravines
> and the hawk nests
> in the cliffs
> and the coyote trails
> that wind
> across the hills.
>
> *"Lonely?"*
>
> I can't help
> laughing
> when they ask me
> that.
>
> I always look at them . . .
> surprised.
> And I say,
> "How could I be lonely?
> I'm the one
> in charge of
> celebrations."

As the girl proceeds to explain, it is her notebook that helps her see and appreciate her life and her landscape. In her notebook, she captures moments and scenes she plans to remember for the rest of her life. "You can tell what's worth a celebration," she says, "because your heart will POUND . . . and you'll catch your breath like you were breathing some new kind of air."

Helping Youngsters Anticipate the Role of Notebooks

The way to launch notebooks, then, is for us teachers to buy ourselves a book—or find a file, a box, a bag—and begin living our lives with the consciousness that "My life belongs to me, it matters. I need to put scraps of time and thought away in order to take them out later, to live with and linger with them." Once we have begun to incorporate notebooks into our lives, we can invite youngsters to do the same.

Many of us in the Teachers College Writing Project—teachers, children, and Project staff alike—carry our notebooks with us all the time. We read with notebooks beside us. We listen to the news and teach and travel and eat with our notebooks in hand. Like the young girl Kate in Jean Little's book, *Hey World, Here I Am!,* we have found it important to choose our own notebook. Kate writes:

> When Mother told my sister Marilyn that I loved to write, she sent me a journal for my birthday. . . . It had a shiny pink cover with MY DIARY written on it in scrolled, gold letters. . . . Every page had two skimpy sections, with a date at the top of each. There was space enough for maybe three sentences if your handwriting was small. My handwriting scrawls. Besides, my life is too big to fit into those squinched-up pages. I gave it to my friend Lindsay Ross. She adores it. She has a smaller life . . .
>
> Then Dad gave me a journal. It is elegant . . . I love it. Maybe, someday, my life will be elegant enough to match it. I hope so. I'm saving it carefully just in case. (1986, 73)

The notebook Kate bought for herself has lots of room, and there are no dates at the top of each page. Some days she fills seven pages; other days she writes only "Another day lived through!" "Getting a journal," she says, "is like buying shoes. You have to find the one that fits. And you are the only person who can tell if it pinches" (1986, 74).

Teachers and children will want to choose their own notebooks. Mine is a looseleaf notebook. Shelley's is a bound book with blank pages. Anne Gianatiempo's is a composition book covered with a quilted fabric. Judy Davis turned an empty spiral into her notebook. Each person must carefully choose the form his or her notebook will take.

When I returned to Anne's classroom after the storytelling circle, almost every child had a notebook to hold overhead and wave in the air, and the diversity of notebooks was well worth celebrating. Marcella had brought a blank book that her mother had given her. Other students had brought marble-covered notebooks, steno pads, small spirals. Over time, some children would cover their notebooks with richly colored African fabrics, others with laminated paper. Some would make special sacks for carrying their notebooks and others would staple together their own tiny portable notepads, which they would periodically disassemble and paste into their notebooks. "It's the bond between the writer and his or her notebook that matters most," Project member Vicki Vinton says.

Nothing magical happens simply because youngsters bring notebooks to school. Notebooks can be just another place for writing, or they can represent a new way of thinking about the writing process. The most obvious way in which notebooks have altered my views of writing is that they have served as a concrete, physical invitation to write without requiring me to view my scrawlings as rough drafts of anything in particular. Notebooks have embodied the idea that we put bits of our lives and our thinking into print not only to produce compositions but also because we do not want to walk around unwritten (Gass 1979). Notebooks have been, for me and for the students with whom I work, an invitation to generate entries, notes, lists, drafts, observations, ramblings on millions of topics and on no particular topic at all. In bringing the idea of notebooks into classrooms, the challenge is more than finding a way for young writers to go through the motions of keeping such a notebook. The challenge is, instead, for them to be so clear about the value of writing that they, too, do not want to walk around unwritten. We want youngsters to value writing. We hope they will begin to carry pencils and pads of paper with them, that they will keep pens beside the phone and in the car and near their books. This is important, first because such writing changes our living, and then because it also changes the composing we eventually do.

Even if youngsters are just at the stage of beginning to collect bits of their lives, it's enormously helpful for them to have a farsighted vision of the role these entries might eventually play in creating finished pieces of writing. When Judy Davis introduced notebooks to her youngsters, therefore, she did so by sharing with them examples of children's writing from Anne Gianatiempo's P.S. 148 classroom. Judy read aloud from the opening pages of Luz Gordillo's notebook, in which Luz roamed about among many topics. Luz chronicled a relationship with her friend, recalled the day her cousin died, commented on the ending of a book, talked about mysterious footprints she found outside her front door, and described herself looking at the empty apartment in which her best friend had once lived.

Judy used an overhead projector to show her students how the appearance and tone of Luz's entries changed over the course of those days. On September 17 Luz wrote the piece shown in Figure 4–1:

> Today was my first time me and Andrea had a fight. We are fighting because Andrea doesn't want to be Jamie's friend but I do.

Figure 4–1 Luz's Writing, September 17

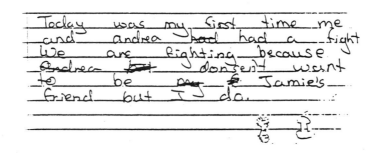

About a week later, Luz wrote the entry shown in Figure 4–2:

> My Grandmother may not be the kind who makes cakes and cookies for me. She may not be the one kind of grandmother who sits and tells me stories or the one who knits clothes for me. She's got great long hair and she's pretty old. My grandmother doesn't live next to me or doesn't kiss me all the time. My grandma says she loves me the way her grandmother loved her. Only by the heart.

Luz is a skilled writer, and it is not surprising that this entry, like many others, reads like a very nice first draft. The year before, in third grade, Luz would certainly have stayed with her grandmother piece, fixing it up and filing it into her Final Writing Folder. This year, however, Anne had encouraged Luz to wait over the course of many entries for a topic to emerge that had the potential to become not just a nice piece of writing but a writing project with scope and significance.

As Judy explained to her students, in order to find the seed for a longer writing project, Luz read and reread her notebook. One of the things she looked for was bits of language—a phrase, a paragraph, a page—that felt alive. Sometimes Luz took those bits and expanded them into entries that branched off from earlier entries. Luz also reread her notebook looking for selections that surprised her, that troubled her, that deserved more attention.

Figure 4–2 Luz's Writing, a Week Later

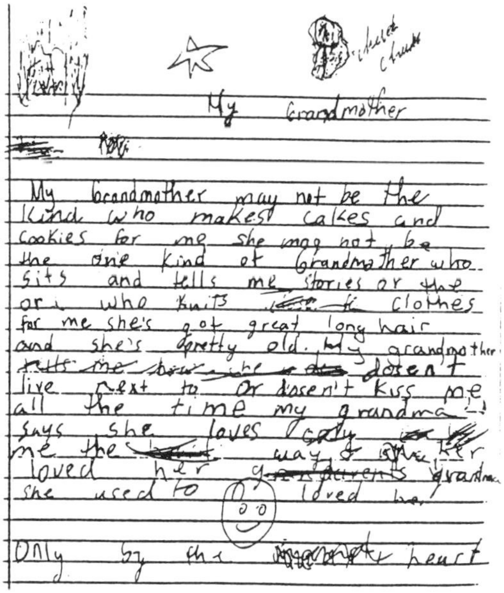
My Grandmother
My grandmother may not be the
kind who makest cakes and
cookies for me she may not be
the one kind of grandmother who
sits and tells me stories or the
one who knits clothes
for me she's got great long hair
and she's pretty old. My grandmother
doesn't
live next to Or doesn't kiss me
all the time my grandma
says she loves
me the way
loved her
she used to loved her
Only by the heart

Above all, she looked for entries or sentences or themes that mattered to her. Anne Gianatiempo had been surprised when Luz circled back to this very early entry about her father in a tree:

> Once upon a time there was a little boy. He used to climb a tree and think it was an airplane that would bring him all the way to New York City. This boy was my very own father. He used to love to get up on a tree and pretend he was on his way to the United States.

This had not been one of Luz's best entries, but if this entry lifted itself off the page saying, "Write me," Luz was right to return to it. After writing more about her father leaving Colombia, Luz shifted into the long, rambling entry shown in Figure 4–3, which recaptured the life she loved in Colombia. Judy read a passage of this aloud to her children. She read:

> When I'm back from school at 3:00 the sun is up and it's up high. It gives light so everyone could dance outside. At night around my neighborhood there's hundreds of stars. They all are night lights wait-

Figure 4–3 *Luz's Writing About Columbia*

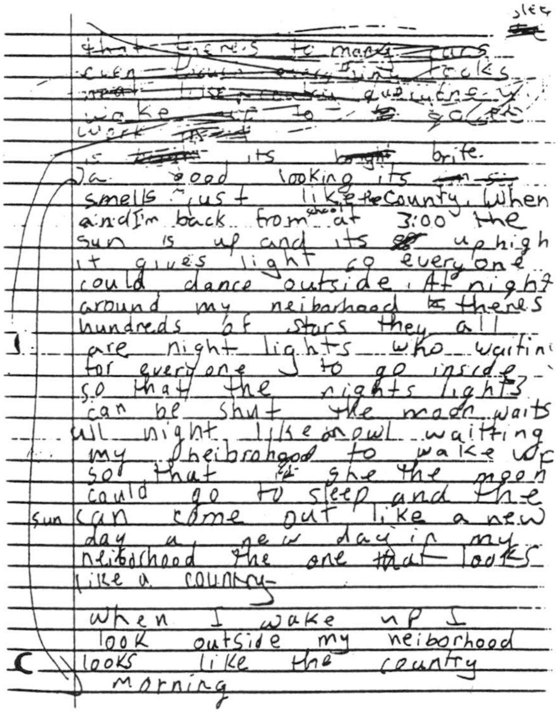

ing for everyone to go inside so that the night lights can be shut off. The moon waits all night like an owl waiting for my neighborhood to wake up. . . . I look outside. My neighborhood looks like the country morning.

By this time, Judy told her class, a center of gravity had emerged in Luz's notebook. Luz had decided on her topic but still wasn't ready to start on a rough draft. She needed more time to live with her topic, to fill herself with it. Luz now made sure most of her entries addressed the theme of leaving Colombia for the United States. She wrote a long, focused entry about being afraid that when she arrived in the United States, unable to speak the language, children would look at her as if she were some kind of animal. She wrote a detailed account of packing her suitcases. She interviewed her sister about coming to America.

Because somewhere along the way Luz had decided she was writing rough drafts rather than entries, she moved from her notebook onto composition paper. Luz tried three different versions of a lead sentence and altered her draft somewhat based on a peer conference. Now her writing process was very much like it had been the year before, and it was very much like the process I describe in *The Art of Teaching Writing*. One of Luz's drafts began like this:

As the plane took off, I looked out the window. I could see all the little houses, everything. I was sad and unhappy. Everything I left behind was now a long memory, my whole life was only a memory. My house, my school, my friends were disappearing in clouds as we went up and up. I could only see the clouds now. I felt a tear fall on my face. It was a magical tear. This was going to be my last cry. I remember the look on my grandma's face. She was as red as an apple about to explode and throw out all her tears onto the new shiny airplane. She would wash it and clean up with her memories. My grandpa took her hand and held her close. I didn't want to throw away all those happy times and sad times. I looked again at my grandparents' faces. They were about to throw out our memories in a whole bunch of tears. . . .

Luz decided this long, rich draft could become a source of several pieces of writing, including a poem, a letter to her Colombian grandmother, and a picture book. This is the text of her picture book:

We were on our way to the airport. We were on our way to leave Colombia forever. Everything seemed so ugly, so unfair. My whole life, my whole world, would soon be just a memory.

In the airplane, I looked at my mother. She just sat there. My sister was quiet as a turtle. My grandpa had stopped crying but I knew he still felt terrible. The houses of Colombia below me looked like toys, and I wanted them. I felt like an infant crying out for my mother to buy me toys.

I can still envision my grandpa's face. He was quiet. All he could do was hold my grandma's hand. His tears fell quietly down his cheeks. Grandma only stared; no words, no tears.

Finally we arrived. In a little room, a man told me to sign a paper and I'd be legally from the United States. "But I want to be legally from Colombia," I said to my mother.

We finally got out of the little room, and we got our pack. I saw two men. One was my Uncle Ruben. The other was short and skinny. He reached to pick me up. It was my father. I gave him a kiss. I had lost my country but won my father.

Judy showed her class other examples of children using notebooks, and these examples included work by younger children as well as by less skilled writers. She told them about Arthur, who noticed upon rereading his notebook that he had several entries in which he depicted his life in a hotel for the homeless. Anne Gianatiempo had helped Arthur realize that those entries could become a letter asking someone—perhaps Governor Cuomo—to do something about the crack addicts in the stairwell and the starving babies wailing from behind closed doors. Once Arthur decided to tackle this project, he spent a few days collecting more memories and descriptions of the hotel, and then, before he moved to rough draft paper, he searched through magazines and newspapers for letters to the editor that could serve as models for him.

Judy also told her students about a cluster of youngsters who noticed they each had entries about animals. They decided to make an anthology of animal stories modeled after Cynthia Rylant's *Every Living Thing*. To do this, they made posters that read, "Writers at P.S. 148 are invited to submit manuscripts." On these posters, they listed details about the board of reviewers and the process of selection for the anthology. Then, while they waited for incoming manuscripts, they each lived with and extended their animal entries, turning them into stories.

Notebooks Help Us Lead Wide-Awake Lives

For all of this to happen in our classrooms, teachers must not only keep notebooks, but we must also let those notebooks nudge us toward living with the sense that "my life and my ideas are important enough to me. I am going to record and savor them." The important thing is that we let those notebooks help us lead more wide-awake lives.

In speaking about the essential contribution writing can make to a person's life, Katherine Paterson described watching the cicada bug shed its skin. She and her son David watched as a tiny slit in the bug's back was gradually pulled down, as though the bug had a waist-length zipper, and they saw a hint of color through the slit. Then there were more colors—green, yellow, aqua, cream, and flecks of gold like jewelry on its head. Then the wings emerged, first crumpled ribbons, then stretched out. As they watched, the cicada bug swung like an acrobat onto a new twig and eventually flew off, "oblivious to the wake of wonder it had left behind." Paterson says, "As I let that wonder wash over me I realized that this was the gift I really wanted to give my children, for what good are straight teeth and trumpet lessons to a person who cannot see the grandeur that the world is charged with?" (1981, 20).

It's not only children who overlook the grandeur the world is charged with. Most of us live with blinders on. It's particularly hard to see the grandeur of the world when we are in schools, where the watchword has often been "Clear your desks off so we can begin." The title of Albert Cullum's book, *The Geranium on the Window Sill Just Died, But Teacher You Went Right On,* not only speaks of what schools do to children, it also speaks of what schools do to teachers. Our schools and our age are well characterized in Dan Jaffe's poem, "The Forecast":

> Perhaps our age has driven us indoors.
> We sprawl in the semi-darkness . . .
> But we have snapped our locks, pulled down our shades,
> Taken all precautions. We shall not be disturbed.
> If the earth shakes, it will be on a screen;
> And if the prairie wind spills down our streets
> And covers us with leaves, the weatherman will tell us.

When students and teachers have snapped the locks and pulled down the shades, it's not enough in writing workshops to give us topic choice, time for writing, and mini-lessons on focus and telling details. Notebooks can become a habit of life, one that helps us recognize that our lives are filled with material for writing. "Look at the world," notebooks seem to say. "Look at the world in all its grandeur and all its horror. Let it matter."

For this to happen, it is crucial that notebooks leave the four walls of the classroom, and it is also crucial that they be out on children's desks throughout the school day. When writers carry notebooks everywhere, the notebooks nudge us to pay attention to the little moments that normally only flicker into our consciousness. Roy writes, "When my baby brother doesn't go to sleep, I tell him about tomorrow. When he still doesn't, I tell him about his party." Annabelle writes, "I was just thinking about how much I miss my cats. This might sound weird, but my two cats loved all the same music and movies that I did." Annabelle's entry about her cats is accompanied by several small sketches. She, like many other children, includes flow charts, portraits, and diagrams in her notebook. Sandra writes, "When I saw these old ladies in my building and how they stop talking when I get there, I always wonder what they were talking about," and later, "I'm always wondering how people are going to look when they grow up. I don't know why, but I wonder this about a lot of people." Angelo writes, "I remember my father and my mother would have fist fights. I was too small to break things but I used to watch with my fists clenched." Ten-year-old Chris Ralph writes, "My tooth is loose. It's probably the last tooth I have to lose." Later that same day, he writes the entries in Figure 4–4.

"I compost my life," Murray says in describing "the great garage sale of junk" from which his notebook—and eventually, his writing—is made, "piling up phrases which do not yet make sense, lines overheard in a restaurant, scenes caught in the corner of my eyes, pages not yet understood, questions not yet shaped, thoughts half begun, problems unsolved, answers without questions" (1989, 242). Children, the great collectors of life, learn to use notebooks in similar ways.

Figure 4–4   Chris's Three Entries

> why do pepole die? Do they die
> to live again? Maybe peple die to be punished
> or rewarded. I would like to know, but
> I want to have fun while I live.
>
> What makes people cry?
>
> I look out the window and see
> tiny drops of water being blown by the
> wind. They run from current to current,
> like a billion little ants in a war over
> bred. Attacking, retreating, attacking, retreating, attacking
> and they hit the ground dead until it rains
> again.
>
> I was reading The Swiss
> Family Robinson and kept noticing
> that the author kept saying
> saying "replied I" or "said I".
> I was surprised when this happened.
> It is an interesting way to say
> something. I think it makes
> a simple saying look complicated and mature.
>
> I find it amazing when an
> author knows some tricks, or uses
> great language, but doing both is
> fantastic. It really shows
> the talent of the author.

In her notebook, seven-year-old Sunit relived a single moment at the grocery store. She'd fetched carrots for her mother and had thrown them into the shopping cart when she said to herself, "I love my mom," and hugged the familiar legs of the lady beside her. Looking up, her arms still around the skirt, Sunit saw her mother across the aisle. "Then whose legs am I hugging?" she thought. After skipping a few lines in her notebook, Sunit went on to jot down the words to "Mary Mary, Quite Contrary." Then she taped in a magazine advertisement for a breed of dwarf horses and listed what she'd done over the weekend. Then she took part of that list, "Saturday morning, playing in the park," and in hurried print, she wrote:

> An empty park
> Lots of benches
> Lots of checker boards.
> No leaves on trees
> A cold day
> A sunny day
> Very sunny.
> A quiet day
> It's easy to find people in the yard.

Without pausing for a transition, Sunit shifted to a related memory.

Mini-Lessons, Conferences, and Share Sessions That Encourage Wide-Awakeness

The diversity in Chris's and Sunit's notebooks—which demonstrates a crucial willingness to take in life through many different lenses—did not happen automatically or accidentally. If left to their own devices, Sunit and Chris might have filled their notebooks with memories, each beginning, "I remember when . . . " and each filling a single page. Alternatively, depending on their sense of what was expected of them, they might have filled their notebooks with a cryptic list of possible topics, or with emotional ventings, or with summaries of the preceding day's events. Instead, they have done all of these and more. Their notebooks are collages, "garage sales of junk," treasure chests.

When notebooks are very new in a classroom, the workshops sometimes begin with everyone gathering for a mini-lesson in which writers learn some ways in which others have used notebooks in their lives. In these mini-lessons, we may tell the class about how Jane Yolen pulled off the highway in a snowstorm to scrawl down a phrase she'd heard on the car radio. The announcer, trying to sell a fence, described it as "horse-high, hog-tight, and bull-strong." Yolen thought the words were too good to lose. Months later, they led to the first paragraph of *The Inway Investigators*:

> What makes a good fence? Grandad used to say being "horse-high, hog-tight, and bull-strong." And Uncle Henry, my guardian, winks

and says, "Good neighbors make good fences." Only when I ask him what he means by that, he just laughs and says I'll understand in a while. (1973, 15)

Once teachers and children in the Project learn that Jane Yolen copies down phrases she has overheard and glories in the way people talk, this strategy becomes contagious. Tiffany Wooten, for example, explored the way her mother's talk changes when they return to her mother's childhood home in North Carolina:

But when we go to North Carolina my mother's talk is different. She tells me about the times she was tough like a boy. She tells me how she scared her sister and how she had the biggest responsibility because she was the oldest. "Tiff, doesn't it feel good to smell the country air and listen to the birds, walk on grass in wintertime and get things so cheap?" she says, and then we laugh. Thinking about my mother, so lucky to be born in North Carolina, I can't forget North Carolina talk.

Sharon Taberski, a teacher of teachers in Brooklyn, found it revealing when a colleague described teaching first grade as being like pulling teeth.

She found it revealing when a little girl said, after working and reworking a poem, "I've got the words, but I'm trying to get the music into them." Weeks later, the little girl's words were the opening to a speech Sharon Taberski made to 150 Project principals. "My colleagues and I often feel that we, too, 'have the words' but are trying 'to get the music into them,' " Sharon said.

It's important that Sharon let her students and her colleagues know not only that she recorded overheard language in her notebook, but also that these phrases ignited a whole process of thinking and writing. What Sharon has done is an essential part of composition. She saw a little girl sitting with wads of discarded drafts, struggling to make her words sing. Sharon jotted down some notes about the way the girl described her struggles. She recorded the girl's sentence for no particular reason except that it resonated for her, and then Sharon continued to go about her life with the notebook at her side. Later, as she watched a teacher struggle to feel at home with new ideas on teaching, Sharon was suddenly reminded of what the little girl said: "I've got the words, but I'm trying to get the music into them." It ignited a spark in Sharon's mind, and she began to write her way into a brand new idea.

It is as we explore possibilities with our own notebooks that we generate possibilities for our children's notebooks—and vice versa. Everything we and our colleagues do and everything our students do provides seeds for mini-lessons, conferences, share sessions. There is, therefore, lots of shop talk about notebooks among the circle of notebook keepers in our Project. How many pages a day? Lined or unlined paper? Are the entries dated, numbered, neither? How many of the entries are abbreviated jottings? Clippings, quotes, lists, freewritings, drafts?

In a mini-lesson or in a writing conference, we may tell the class about how we or another author described a scene, excerpted lines from a story, interviewed an authority, explored a puzzling thought, listed questions, returned to an earlier entry, or outlined possible stories. The writers in Sunit's class, for example, may learn about the nursery rhyme she included in her notebook. They may learn about pasting clippings and copying quotations into their notebooks. They may learn about savoring the image of a fleet of orange segments. They may learn that some writers keep notebooks close at hand as they read, knowing that if a book is right for them, they may end up wanting to write something that pushes off from the text. We scout for these mini-lessons by learning what published authors do, by seeing what we and our colleagues do, and most of all, by celebrating what the young writers in our classrooms do.

In a mini-lesson or a conference, for example, we might let youngsters know that other writers in the classroom use notebooks as research instruments. We may tell children, for example, about how Ipolito brought his notebook onto the roof to record what his pigeons do as he feeds them. We may tell children about how Erin, a pixielike seven-year-old, overheard her teacher describing someone as having salt-and-pepper hair and scribbled the phrase in her notebook. When Erin inserted the phrase into a third-person fictional story she wrote months later, she learned that research doesn't have to involve stacks of carefully coded index cards and footnotes and worry over bibliographies, and that it isn't confined to the genre of research reports. Research is what learners do as we live our lives.

In mini-lessons and conferences we will also want to tell youngsters about how we and others use notebooks as a place for responding to reading. When Judy Davis read Jean Fritz's memoir, *Homesick,* aloud to her class, many children wrote entries in response. *Homesick* tells the story of growing up in China and of Jean Fritz's desperate loneliness for the magical country of America. When Jean finally reaches America, she finds herself out of place here, too, and so, ultimately, this is a book about everyone's search to belong.

As Hau Ha Lam listened to her teacher reading *Homesick,* she wrote wrenchingly in her notebook:

My heart has split in two; one belongs to China and the other belongs to the people who filled my life with joy.

The great memories of China always fill my heart with joy. The big blue river of China makes beautiful waves and oh, how I remember the sun and how it made me want to shout with glee. On hot summer days the sea seemed to call me. How can I sum up the way I feel about a place? If you looked at the sea, all you would see are people on the river in their boats. . . .

When I walk into my house [in New York City], I feel like some-body locked me in. The walls are closing in on me. There are more dishes to be washed and a little brother to be looked after. Soon I can't see the sunlight. . . . Why not stay happy and playful. . . . Now I know how growing up feels.

Natalia does not share Fritz's and Hau Ha Lam's Chinese heritage, but she does share their sense of being displaced. In her notebook she wrote:

Leaving Poland was hard. Leaving those beautiful castles, leaving my grandparents, leaving the milkman who comes every morning and the walks to the bakery and my cousins and their rabbits was hard. Anytime I have to leave I cry big, sad tears. When I look out the window of the airplane my insides turn to mush.

Now that I'm not in Poland, I talk to my parents about Poland a lot. Anytime I see a boxer, I think about my grandfather's dog. I talk about my cousins, etc., etc. When I am walking down a street and I feel a wind that is like a "Polish wind," my mind switches and sud-denly I'm in Lodz.

Often, teachers and children will write notebook entries in response to the books we read on our own. In Karen Rosner's Bronx classroom, for example, Ramell Craven wrote a brief entry in response to Katherine Paterson's *Park's Quest:*

I'm reading this book because my father was in Vietnam but he didn't die. But if he would of died, I would be like Park.

Later, Ramell went back to this entry and expanded it on a separate sheet of paper he then slid into his notebook. This time he wrote the piece in Fig-ure 4–5:

When my father was in Vietnam I wasn't around. He sent letters home to my mother and brothers and sisters. I know they were scared.

In 1978 I was born. My father was already home. One morning my father James found his medal in his junk closet.

I never imagined growing up without a father. He could of died in that war. I never thought of it that way. I'm sure my mother did. The subject never comes up at home. But I think of it every night.

In the Army you have to get shot to get a Purple Heart. Being shot at is good enough. I wonder what I would do if I was in the Army?

Lt. Craven, it has a nice ring to it. Jogging 20 miles, 50 push-ups, and cheap food.

Just watching war movies I know what my father went through. I'm glad he's home and everyone's happy.

Figure 4–5   Ramell's Piece

When my father was in
Vietnam I wasn't around.
He sent letters home to
my mother and brothers
and sisters. I know they
were scared.
In 1978 I was born.
My father was already home.
One morning my father James
found his medal in his junk
closet.
I never imagined growing
up without a father. He could
of died in that war. I never
thought of it that way. I'm
sure my mother did. The subjec-
never comes up at home. But
I think of it every night.
In the Army you have to
get shot to get a Purple Heart
Being shot at is good enough.
I wonder what I would do if
I was in the Army?
Lt. Craven, it has a nice
ring to it. Jogging 20 miles,
50 push ups, and cheap food.
Just watching war movies
I know what my father went
through. I'm glad he's home
and everyone's happy.

Ramell and his classmates at P.S. 7 do not keep their reading logs separate from their notebooks. Instead, in their notebooks they move from recording cherished phrases from a book to commenting on their sister, from questioning why an author wrote a story to recalling a hurt dog they saw in the alley. Entries that explore why they've lost interest in a book are set alongside entries that explore memories and feelings. This juxtaposition is a powerful brew—and a logical one. Writer Vicki Vinton, who supports this way of physically merging reading and writing, says, "After all, the me who notices something at the Metropolitan Museum isn't any different from the me who notices something in a book or from the me who writes a story or teaches a class."

There are other Project classrooms, however, in which children do keep their reading logs separate from their notebooks. This is most apt to happen if the reading log serves institutional as well as personal purposes. If children are including lists of books they have read and predictions of how stories might end in their reading logs, if they are exploring questions that will be discussed in response groups, then it may seem best to keep reading logs separate from notebooks. In these classrooms, however, teachers will want to encourage children to copy and question and bounce ideas from the reading logs into their notebooks. Teachers will also want to urge youngsters to have their notebooks open when they read aloud to the class.

In conferences with a child, then, as well as in mini-lessons, we may want to encourage the child to use the notebook as a place for responding to his or her reading. "What has Anne Frank's *The Diary of a Young Girl* made you feel about your own life?" we might ask in a writing conference. But the most important reading a writer can do is the reading of his or her own words. In another conference, we might say, "Last night I reread my notebook and just started noticing the ways I write and the ways I don't. I noticed, for example, that I never just list things, that most of my entries are long, that I write more about what I'm thinking than what I'm seeing. You may want to look over your notebook and take an inventory of what you do in it." The teacher may invite two children to study their notebooks together, talking about what each has and has not included. The teacher may ask a child whether the entries written at home seem different from entries written in the writing workshop. Also, as we move among the desks or talk with students at the back of the room, we may want to pick up on threads introduced in our mini-lessons.

For the first week or two in the year, when the mini-lessons tend to be about ways of noticing the world and when most children are still collecting and generating writing, it probably will not be appropriate for writers in share sessions to read their rough drafts aloud and receive questions and suggestions from the audience, as they did in the share sessions I described in *The Art of Teaching Writing*. Instead, teachers might use share sessions as opportunities for students to reread, celebrate, and learn from their notebooks. When the class gathers in a circle at the close of the workshop, the teacher may suggest that everyone search through their notebook pages together for illustrations of the kind of entry that was highlighted that morning. "Did anyone use their notebook as a place for recording an interview?" the teacher might ask, or "Has anyone included questions and things they wonder about in their notebook?" "Does anyone have an entry that begins by discussing one topic and then meanders to other, surprising and new topics?"

The risk is that when teachers invite children to record observations, for example, this can be regarded as a mandate, and notebook entries can begin to reflect the child's dutiful effort to please the teacher rather than that child's actual thoughts and impressions. There's no easy way to avoid this, because if we simply suggest that youngsters write whatever occurs to them, children tend to reproduce the kinds of writing they felt pleased a previous teacher or to record daily summaries because they equate notebooks with journals. Notebooks are not journals, nor are they a collection of the same rough drafts children would normally keep in their folders. The reason to let youngsters know that they can copy sections of a book, raise questions, or create long fantasies in their notebooks is that this may prompt youngsters to see notebooks as something new and open-ended.

And so, as teachers we walk a thin line. We want to suggest possibilities for using notebooks, but we also want to give youngsters the space to invent their own. The best way to walk this line may be to bring a stack of our children's notebooks home often and look through them, hoping to learn not only about our children and their writing but also about ourselves and our teaching. We will inevitably notice patterns across many of the notebooks, and those patterns can give us windows onto our teaching. If many children begin entries with phrases such as "There are things in my house that I wouldn't throw away . . . " and "There are sayings in my family such as . . . ," we will realize that while we thought we were encouraging diversity and wide-awakeness in notebook entries, we have inadvertently been giving our students story starters and assigned topics. There's no great harm in the fact that we've done this; we have, after all, prompted only a jotted entry and not a major piece of writing. But the power of the notebook—or the lifebook, as some children call it—is greatly diminished if a well-intended teacher's hand is evident throughout.

The wonderful thing is that when not only teachers but students, too, are encouraged to experiment and play with lots of different kinds of entries and bring notebooks home to reflect on the kinds of entries they have written, we can learn a lot about ourselves and our interests as writers. The question "What does it mean that I write in this manner?" can be a light, easy question or one that acts as a plumb line to the most important issues of our lives.

The Wells We Draw from When We Introduce Notebooks

How do we create a climate in our classroom in which this will happen? I know of only one answer: we write. We keep our own notebook (or file box, folder, daybook, stack of papers) beside us as we live. When we and our colleagues keep notebooks of our own, we have wells to draw on when we teach. Then, if we see Rebecca tearing a giant wad of paper from her notebook during social studies because she forgot to bring paper to school, our dismay is deeply felt. "How could you? This is your notebook," we say, and it's not so much what we have said that reaches through to Rebecca but what we have felt.

When we keep our own notebooks, if John seems to scribble only one or two brief entries into his notebook each day, we remember doing the same thing. "When I first started keeping a notebook," we say to him, "I filled it with lists of ideas that I might write about, but I didn't think of the notebook as a place for actually writing the pieces out. Is that how you're thinking?" When John answers, "No, it's just boring to put down what I see and stuff," we remember that our notebook became more important to us once we'd seen how it can nourish the process of producing publishable writing, and so we begin to talk with John about the possibility of moving into a project.

If we keep notebooks ourselves and move from those notebooks into larger writing projects, then we can anticipate and respond to the predictable problems that will emerge. But more than this, if we keep notebooks, we will expect and welcome diversity. We will soon come to know, in a deep-seated way, that there are wide variations in how and why writers keep notebooks. Some people always write in sentences and paragraphs; others often include lists and sketches. Some people do most of their writing in jotted notes as they carry their notebook about with them, and others write mostly at their desks during a predictable period each day. Some people continue with their notebook even when they are drafting and revising a piece, and others let the notebook slip into the background when a writing project moves into the foreground. Some people prefer not to have a notebook at all but instead gather and muse on papers they keep in files or shoeboxes, and others do none of this generative and reflective writing. And that is as it should be. In the end, it will be the diversity in our classrooms rather than our mini-lessons and conferences that extends what we and our students do in our notebooks.

5

Rereading and Reflecting: Adding Growth Rings of Meaning to Our Writing

Isoke Nia's thirty-two children drew closely around her. Their teacher waited dramatically. Everything about Isoke is dramatic. Her long, sweeping dress, her giant beaded necklace, her low, vibrant voice, the green-cushioned author's chair in which she sat. Once the children around her had settled down, Isoke began to talk. "When I was pinning your work onto the bulletin board, I remembered open-school night when I was young," she said. "Everyone, it seemed, came in holding their parents' hands. My hands were empty. I wrote that memory into my notebook and, while writing, it dawned on me that in my foster family, we never held hands." Then Isoke said, "A few days later, I reread the notebook and started thinking. The only memories I have of my foster mother's hands were in church when she was clapping and on Sunday mornings when she made biscuits. Her hands were strong and loving then. I wrote about that too."

Rereading her notebook, Isoke listened for sections that made her heart feel differently. She looked for something to lift itself off the page, saying, "Do something with me." Because there was something alive about the overlapping images of hands, Isoke wrote about them in her notebook again, lingering on those childhood scenes. Then she took these brief scenes and, in a separate draft, worked them into a memoir. Her children listened, big-eyed, as she read an excerpt to them:

Knead

By Isoke Nia

I watched with my small oval Black face tilted as her cocoa-colored hands kneaded the dough. No wonder those biscuits tasted so good. They were loved. At that moment I felt jealous. Envious of the flour, the shortening, the baking powder, the salt, the milk that formed the white lump my foster mother so carefully caressed. I longed to be a white shapeless lump, instead of a tiny Black child. To be void of form and content instead of filled with ideas and feelings and notions and love. I wanted out of my Blackness, my smallness, myself. I wanted a HUG. No hug was given that Sunday or any Sunday to follow. And though all living things need love to grow, I grew regardless. At age 15, I surprised everyone who didn't know me (and that was everyone) by leaving. Biscuits just weren't enough anymore.

The four years that followed contained one day each. And on each of those four days I did something special for me. On day 1, I discovered my Africaness and I clothed myself with the pride of my ancestors and America became tolerable. On day 2, I met a man who was to be the father of my children and on day 3 and 4 I gave birth and was loved and loved and loved . . . and made biscuits on Sundays.

Isoke's process—turning back to reflect on her early jottings and then living with a few lines from her notebook until they gathered growth rings of meaning around them—is an absolutely fundamental part of the composing process. When she lingered with the image of her empty hands, asking, "Why does this image matter so much to me today?" and "Have I always felt my hands were empty?" she was engaged in a process of thought that underlies not only writing but learning. Writing is a powerful tool for thinking, because when we write, we fasten thoughts, observations, and feelings onto paper. We ask, "What have I said?" and we mean, "What am I trying to say?" "Why is this on my mind?" "What other ideas connect with this one?" "What surprises me about this?"

In *The Art of Teaching Writing*, I talk about this kind of questioning as an act of revision. Now I realize that I underestimated the importance of taking a half step backward from our lives. Reflecting on our thoughts, asking questions, letting our insights take root and grow . . . all of this underlies not only revision but thought itself.

In chapter 4, I cite Jean Little's attention to orange slices and Katherine Paterson's to a cicada bug. Writing begins with wide-awakeness to one's world, I conclude. But Jean Little and Katherine Paterson not only notice and cherish orange slices and a cicada bug; they also compose meaning from them. Whether these authors first jotted descriptions of those bits of life into their notebooks is not important; the concrete, physical notebook is not important. It's the process that is important. What matters is that their writing process involved returning to the images of orange slices and cicada bugs in order to make meanings from these "precious particles." In order to include the orange slices in her memoir, Jean probably asked, "What was happening around me that I was in bed that day and that these orange slices were brought to me on a white plate?" and then she probably either recalled or created the larger story of how she was home, sick in bed. She certainly asked, "Why do I still remember those orange slices?" and "How do those orange slices fit into the larger story of my journey towards being a writer?" Similarly, Katherine

Paterson's observations of a cicada bug shedding its skin became important to us as readers (and probably to her as the writer) because she not only celebrates each vivid detail of the process but also returns to this moment—to this anecdote, this image, this "precious particle"—in order to make meaning from it. The event becomes important when she shifts from the telephoto to the wide-angle lens and says, "As I let that wonder wash over me I realized that this was the gift I really wanted to give my children, for what good are straight teeth and trumpet lessons to a person who cannot see the grandeur that the world is charged with?" (1981, 20).

Vera John-Steiner ends her introduction to *Notebooks of the Mind* by saying, "To think, it seems to me, is to hold an idea long enough to unlock and shape its power" (1985, 9). In the hurry of our lives and in the rush of the inflated curriculum, we need rituals and tools that invite us to pause and make meaning from the bits of our lives. In order for this to happen in classrooms, teachers and children need to listen not only to each other but also to themselves.

Most of us are not very experienced at listening to ourselves. We listen to everyone else: to principals, supervisors, specialists, students, professors, publishers, researchers, parents, critics, editors, reviewers and friends . . . but when it comes to listening to ourselves, we don't have the time or the faith. Most of us nod in agreement when we hear Donald Murray saying, "I must somehow as a teacher, a husband, a son, a father, a colleague, a citizen, a professional, a busy-busy-busy man, so proud of the busyness, find time to listen so I will hear what I have to say."

Notebooks alone won't change habits of life. We cannot assume that a bound book—or a clipboard, portfolio, or sketch pad, for that matter—will give us or our youngsters habits of thought. Children, like adults, can all too easily keep notebooks without lingering over their observations, questions, and astonishments. But tools of the hand can become tools of the mind. What is at first done in concrete, active, and interactive ways can often be done later abstractly and alone. My colleagues and I in the Teachers College Writing Project, therefore, have tried to develop ways to highlight the process of lingering with one's notebook entries, with one's observations and ideas, in order to make this crucial aspect of writing more visible, more concrete, and more inviting for our students and ourselves. We have found, for example, that if children reread their notebooks and star their favorite entries, underline key words, draw arrows between related entries, write marginal notes alongside entries, and share all of this with each other and with their teacher, in time this process of reflecting, of standing on the shoulders of their thinking, becomes a natural part of their writing process.

Whole-Class Meetings Offer a Time and Place for Reflection

When children gather for whole-class share meetings at the beginning or end of a writing workshop (and when we meet with them individually in writing conferences), we can invite them to share their strategies for gathering notebook entries, but we can also invite them to join us in rereading and reflecting on their notebook entries. We can do this by suggesting that everyone take a few quiet moments to reread his or her notebook, searching for a particular thing.

For example, Susan Radley, a second-grade teacher at P.S. 87 in Manhattan, recently began a share meeting by asking whether any of the children had followed Byrd Baylor's example and included in their notebooks moments and scenes they plan to remember for the rest of their lives. For Byrd Baylor's desert girl in *I'm in Charge of Celebrations,* the selected moments were small ones: seeing a jack rabbit standing in the mist, watching a cloud take on the shape of a parrot, coming to know a horned toad. That day, children who had entries like these shared them in pairs and talked for a few minutes about whether this one important memory led them to still others.

Another day, Susan Radley said, "I notice that in my notebook I've become adventurous with language. Sometimes I play around with trying to say something really well, sometimes I use weird words. . . . Can all of us look for a moment for entries or lines in which we've done something unusual with language?"

Seven-year-old Vanessa Gravenstine said, "I put shortcuts in my entries." Then she read the entry in Figure 5–1, in which she had used -n- as an abbreviation for *and:*

> I remember when the snow comes down -n- I try to catch it with my mouth.

Her classmate, Max Siegal, announced that he'd done three things in one entry. He'd used a list, a Yiddish expression, and a surprise ending:

> Madame Tussaud's was great. I saw Elvis, Willie Wonka, the Royal Family tree, Mr. T, Beethoven, Dolly Parton, Abraham Lincoln, William Shakespeare, Hans Christian [Andersen], Charles Dickens, George Bush, John F. Kennedy, Lyndon B. Johnson, George Washington. In a cafe, my mom pointed to a real person—oy.

Many teachers have suggested that writers reread their notebooks, asking questions about their entries. "Let's question the gaps between our entries, too." "What made us move from one thought to another?" Hau Ha Lam noticed that she'd given an odd title to one of her entries. "What did the title mean?" she asked.

Figure 5–1 ***Vanessa's Abbreviation for "And"***

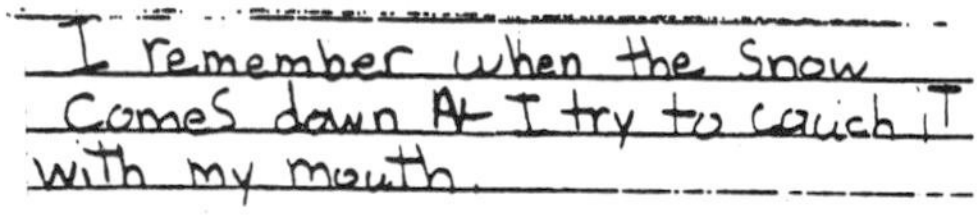
I remember when the Snow
ComeS down -n- I try to caich iT
with my mouth.

Time

When my mom is home she tells me about when she was young in China. She tells me that she had to work very hard doing the housework. "You have to work just like me," my mom says. Your life is about how well you do and work.

Ten-year-old Desiree Grand had lots of second thoughts and questions about the entry shown in Figure 5–2, in which she'd written in one column about the book she was reading, *After the Dancing Days,* and in another column about her responses to the book. Rereading the page, Desiree wrote in the margin, "Why? Why didn't I help people in the hospital?" Then she wrote another longer entry:

My sister is studying to be a doctor. I went to my sister's hospital job for a party. By mistake I wound up on the 2nd floor. The 2nd floor is where the sick people were. There were people crying in the hallway "I'm going to die." I wanted to help. But I didn't.

It was very confusing. I really didn't know what to do. I felt sorry for them. Also I felt scared because maybe someday I will be like that. That gets me scared. I never want to look like that. I wonder how those people feel when they look at themselves.

Figure 5–2   Desiree's Two-Column Entry

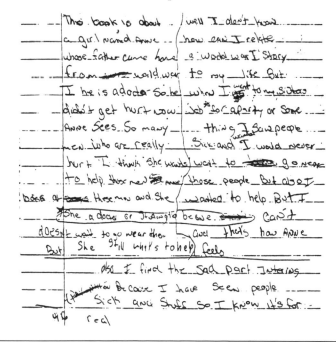

I wanted to go to them and sit down right next to them. I wanted to find out why did they look like that. But somehow I wanted to do that and I didn't want to do that. It was something I couldn't understand at all.

Another teacher told students that she sometimes rereads her notebook and tries to predict what her entries could eventually become. "My notes about my son might someday be part of a book I write for him, or an article on parenting," she said. She doesn't intend to work on the book or article now, but she jots a note beside the entry and lets the prospect of such a project simmer on the back burner. Children will have their own ideas about what their entries might become; if they don't, they might try reading an entry aloud and asking classmates to help them imagine the possibilities.

Eight-year-old Carol Ward asked, "What might I do with this entry?" to the circle of classmates in her writing workshop:

> One day my grandma gave my mom a sweatshirt.
>
> My mom had that sweatshirt for a few years. My mom liked that sweatshirt very much because it is very pretty. The sweatshirt is gray with painted flowers and a couple of rhinestones.
>
> When my mom didn't want the sweatshirt anymore, she gave it to my sister. My sister had the sweatshirt for a few years then she grew out of it. So she gave it to me. I was so happy because I finally got the sweatshirt.

The children suggested that Carol might write her grandmother a letter about what happened to the sweatshirt. Or she might write to the next recipient of the family sweatshirt, informing that person of the sweatshirt's legacy. Or she might turn the story of the sweatshirt into a picture book, post "Manuscripts Wanted" signs in the hallway and edit an anthology on family treasures, or research whether others in her class have surprising heirlooms.

Like her teacher, Carol jotted some of these possibilities in the margin next to her entry. She might indeed end up writing more entries as a result of this note and decide to begin working toward one of these projects.

On still other occasions, children might share entries in which they feel their voice as writers sounds exactly like them, or selections that seem particularly alive, or bits that come more from their imaginations than from their experiences. They might share entries that make them think of other things, entries that puzzle them, or entries that link up with still other entries.

Young authors can learn to jot notes in the margins of their entries. Sometimes they will use the white space underneath or across from an entry for related or second thoughts or for questions about what they've written. Sometimes they invent codes to show that one entry connects to (or contradicts) another, or to indicate a favorite line or a passage that deserves more attention. Such marks may seem small, but they can act as a fulcrum for big thoughts.

It is not a small matter that Vanessa has written "Think Big" alongside an entry she knows deserves more attention, and that Esther has used stars to set apart all the entries that relate to her childhood in Spain, and that Luz has inserted extra pages into her notebook and filled them with entries that grow out of earlier ones. When Randalio rereads his entries and decides they deserve a response in his reading log, and when Rory rereads hers and fills the margins with "This reminds me of . . . ," they are pursuing chains of thought in ways that are fundamental to writing.

These writers are learning about themselves, but they are also learning about the writing process. They are learning that just as there are countless reasons to read and to write, there are also countless reasons to reread. Children need to know that as writers, we run our hands over and over and over the bumpy fabric of our work. We touch and stroke and finger and smooth out our thinking . . . and we do this habitually, all the time, for no reason and for millions of reasons, over and over. And so, in share sessions—and in mini-lessons, conferences, and alone at the desk—we look back at the trail of our thinking in order to see what we have said, to hear tunes and rhythms in our language, to feel the power of an idea, to see how one insight links with another and another and another, to gather momentum for more writing, to notice, to be surprised, to marvel, to listen.

Opportunities for Deeper, Slower Reflection

This kind of rereading and listening needs to happen in little ways all the time as we write, but it is also important to provide ourselves with occasions for deeper kinds of reflectiveness. We learned this in a writing group for Project staff members, when we experimented with the idea of taking a few minutes to reread our notebooks to ourselves while thinking, "What can I learn from noticing the topics I have and have not addressed in my notebook?" We agreed to jot our thoughts down and then to share them.

When Ellen Goldberg read her thoughts to us, it challenged some of the ways we'd been teaching. Ellen had written,

> I began rereading my notebook and found entries I can't remember writing, including one important entry about my mother. I need to reread more tonight, and to reflect. I'm questioning the whole idea of speedy reflection, inserted into the school day. "Hurry up and reflect" —an oxymoron.

That night at home, Ellen wrote a much longer entry, and when she later shared it with us, we realized how necessary it is to create occasions for quiet reflection during the hurry of our teaching. Here is the entry Ellen eventually shared with us and with her students:

> I just finished rereading this notebook from the beginning. Some of what I wrote surprised me, some was embarrassingly awful, and some was really good writing. I didn't realize how many of the entries

came from what I'd been reading. Most of these were written during the summer, and those entries also had a flow and train of thought that's missing in the school year entries.

I knew I'd written a lot about school but I was surprised at just how much. And disappointed that most of the school entries were about the stress of the job, and that there were fewer entries about my actual work and its satisfactions, about how I enter Sari's classroom with a smile which grows wider by the minute, or about Evelyn's, Carol's, Cathy's classrooms . . .

There were lots of entries about my sons but they are sketchy. I haven't written at all about Jeff leaving for Israel next month. Is it avoidance? Is it that it will be such major writing that I need to make lots of time to deal with it? *Can* I deal with it? Am I refusing to? Am I being like my mother—ignore it and it will pass?

Although Ellen needed time at home in order to think in big, sweeping ways about her notebook, we find that before children can do this kind of thinking alone at home, they need first to develop a sense of what this kind of thinking is like. More and more, therefore, we are trying to re-create the mood and pace of the storytelling circle, only now when we gather together to share, we are sharing our thoughts about writing. "What's it been like for you to keep a notebook?" Dorothy Barnhouse recently asked a group of children. As it happened, the first child to respond said, "Frustrating." Had Dorothy responded defensively, the energy gathered in that room would have collapsed on the spot. Instead, Dorothy responded with real interest. "That's fascinating," she said. "Do you know why? What's the frustrating part?" Later that day, teachers and children addressed other questions. "How do you find your own voice in your notebook?" Dorothy asked. "As you keep a notebook, do you find that you gather entries with a sense of purpose? What is that purpose?"

Once children have had experience in talking at some length about issues such as these, they, like Ellen Goldberg, will benefit from occasional invitations to take a block of time to reflect on the journey recorded in their notebook. In some classrooms, the advance schedule gives each child one day a month during which the entire workshop time is devoted to rereading and reflecting on his or her writing. Children are invited to do this thinking with the knowledge that their teacher will bring their notebook home that night to read and will respond not only to the writing but also to the child's thoughts about it. On one such occasion Daniel Nasaw included this in his letter to his teacher:

Sometimes I think that I should stop my study of Nazis because sometimes I get so afraid that Nazis are going to come into my room and kill me that I look for places to hide. I already know that my Nazi reading and my Nazi entries have changed my life.

Philippa wrote,

When I was rereading my notebook, I wished I was still doing things I have down here. When I was little I used to take my mother's clean dishes, dump them into the sink, then pour soap onto them and scrub and talk about why I use this soap instead of another as if I was on a television commercial. When we went to the park I used to chase the flocks of pigeons and I'd drink my apple juice. Life was easier at my young age. Now I get free time only at night and Saturdays and Sundays and since a baby is in the house I do a lot of babysitting. I wish I could spend more time with myself like I used to.

The Payoff for Rethinking Is Not Revision, But Insight

At a recent staff development workshop after I had shared these ways to invite children to reread and reflect, one of the teachers spoke up to ask, "This sounds like a drumroll leading up to . . . what? How do you move from the rereading to the revision?" It's a good question. Once the writer has found and reflected upon beautiful language, puzzling lines, anecdotes that reveal something bigger . . . then what? Where does the drumroll lead?

It leads to insight. It leads to questions, to memories, to discovering feelings we didn't know were there. It leads us to uncover layers of meaning around the bits of life we collect. It does not necessarily lead to repairing or refining an entry for publication. This is crucial. When our students turn back in their traces to reread and reflect, we teachers must be very careful not to assume that this rereading and rethinking should necessarily function as an impetus for revision as we have known it. After youngsters read and share their entries, we must not hurry them into a constricting process of adding to or repairing those entries. But the rereading can lead toward re-visioning in the broadest sense of the word.

In order for this to happen, we need to encourage writers to work towards composing significant pieces of writing both by adding new layers of meaning to the particles in their notebooks and also by watching for entries, lines, ideas, and genres that evoke in them a sense of possibility. Within the first few weeks of the writing workshop, writers will want to decide on a direction for their writing. For example, perhaps a writer will choose to write more about an entry describing the bee sting he got at Bear Mountain park. The writer may then devote a few pages of his notebook to this topic. "Why does the bee sting stand out as more important than my other entries?" he wonders, and consequently describes his disappointment over having to come home early from the park and his longing for more time in the country. The writer then goes on to gather images about the hot city summers and the cool lushness of the park. The important thing to notice is that once a writer chooses to work with an entry or a pattern between entries, he or she begins by living with and collecting around the chosen entries, rather than repairing them. The revision process most of us know best—rethinking the lead, adding and clarifying information, tightening loose sections—is usually only appropriate after writers have lived with a topic for a while, written their way into it, and used all this living and writing to create a draft.

In many ways, the interpretation of revision we are calling for is not new. Years ago, Donald Murray said,

> The act of writing might be described as a conversation between two workmen muttering to each other at the workbench. The self speaks, the other self listens and responds. The self proposes, the other self considers. The self makes, the other self evaluates. The two selves collaborate: a problem is spotted, discussed, defined; solutions are proposed, rejected, suggested, attempted, tested, discarded, accepted. (1982, 165)

In countless classrooms over the last decade, teachers have done a yeoman's job of trying to convince young writers that rereading and revising are essential aspects of the writing process. As a result, in writing workshops throughout the world, children now write rough drafts in which they focus on content rather than spelling and punctuation. The fact that these children return to drafts to add missing ideas and to polish what they've said marks a gigantic step ahead from the days when youngsters regarded writing as a display of their best penmanship, spelling, and vocabulary. But it is probably fair to say that in a great many writing workshops, despite a good deal of effort on the part of teachers, the idea of living with a piece of writing and revising it extensively has not caught hold. Even in classrooms that contain all the accumulated components of the writing workshop—author's chairs, editing charts, author studies, and the like—children tend to write rough drafts, make minor improvements and editorial changes in them, and then move straight to final drafts.

It could be argued that what has happened is that children, in all their wisdom, have let us know that our enthusiasm for revision was unrealistic and unnecessary. When children are devoting some time each day to their writing, does it really matter whether they are redoing old work or simply moving on to new endeavors? Won't they be growing as writers either way? There is wisdom in this line of thought. Yet there are also limitations.

Because, in fact, Don Murray was wise to describe the act of writing as a conversation between two workers, one self speaking and the other self listening and responding. But what I have learned recently is that when the two selves collaborate, they are doing far more than spotting, discussing, and defining problems; they are doing more than proposing, suggesting, rejecting, and attempting solutions. When the two selves collaborate, one self proposes, the other self marvels at the proposal and takes it a step farther. One self makes, and the other self admires the creation and makes another like it. One self notices the cicada bug shedding its skin, and another self thinks about how often we overlook miracles such as this. Problems are found in the writing, yes, but also in the chains of thought. Solutions are proposed, celebrated, used, extended. Above all, one self lives and the other self is conscious of living. One self speaks and the other self listens. One self remembers an incident, and the other self remembers another like it. In the writer's interior dialogue between one self and the other self, we hear less evaluation and critiquing, and more articulation and rearticulation, more "That also makes me think . . . " and more "But how does that relate to . . . ?" The goal is not evaluating and improving writing; not yet, and in some instances, not ever. The goal, instead, is for writing and writers to grow.

When, in a notebook conference, Randy Bomer asked Dana to identify the entry that said the most about him, Dana silently pointed to this one:

> Mom and I got into a discussion about athletics. I asked her how strong Dad was when he wrestled. She told me his arms and shoulders were huge and he was very strong. We talked about how he used to be an infantry machine-gunner when he was drafted to go to Vietnam. He had to carry a 60 to 80 pound pack through the jungle in 100° heat. Most men only carried a seven-pound rifle.

Randy read the entry and then, looking over at Dana, he asked, "Why's this so important, Dana? Why is it on your mind today?"

"I have to know what kind of man my dad was so I can figure out what kind of man I'm going to be," Dana answered, and Randy understood. That day the two young men—twelve-year-old Dana and his courageous, sensitive teacher—talked about fathers, and about growing up as a man in today's society. Dana never changed the entry about his father's muscles. But throughout the year, Dana and Randy would often return to this topic in their writing. By June, Dana had published an interview with his father, several memoirs about his relationship with his father, and a nonfiction piece about Vietnam—and Randy Bomer had submitted the manuscript of a novel for adolescents to a major publisher.

When eight-year-old Warren reread his notebook looking for patterns, he saw right away that many of his entries were about being strong; one was about joining a wrestling class, another about a fight on the street, another about his muscles. When his teacher asked if there were any other related entries, Warren found further examples about being strong.

"What about this?" Warren's teacher asked, calling the boy's attention to an entry about how, as a newborn baby, he had spent his first month of life in an incubator, too fragile to be held.

"No," Warren said, "there is no connection. There's no connection between that puny little baby with that ol' bear that slept beside him . . . and the wrestling club, the fights on the street." The conversation shifted to other topics and so did Warren's writing. But the tenor of Warren's notebook changed after that. In a later entry he told about asking his mother whether she was disappointed that he was born so small and sick. Another time, he wrote about looking up to his big brother and about being afraid on the subway. Whether Warren realized it or not, an insight had germinated and was growing in his notebook. Perhaps he'd write about it some day, perhaps not. For now, he was living with it . . . and living is, after all, a crucial part of writing.

The process of living with and learning from our writing inevitably affects future writing. But this does not always happen in ways that are deliberate and conscious. Ten-year-old Chris Ralph, whose entries about raindrops, crying, and *The Swiss Family Robinson* were cited earlier, had also written many entries about his father's job interviewing and the view from the window at which he wrote. Then, on October 31, he jotted down a strange and wonderful entry that moved out from both these subjects:

> It was a bright sunny day, the shades were wide open. The sun shone with every last ounce of light it had left. As I watched the train run along the wire, I caught a glance of the building I live in. It stood tall like a giant guarding all his gold.
>
> Suddenly that giant seemed smaller, like he was six feet tall. The building looked like my dad standing over me, waking me up after he got back from Chicago at a job interview. He told me what happened. He was picked up in a limo. They bought him dinner. Then he went to a hotel with room service and a pool.
>
> He said he also applied for other jobs in San Francisco and New Jersey. I want to stay here in New York because I live in a nice house and there are lots of things to do.
>
> "Well, I will see what I can do, but I doubt I can do anything."

A day later, Chris jotted down some thoughts about discrimination:

> Other people go someplace and get humiliated for being themselves. Everyone is different. They should be treated equally. Like blacks. People should be who they are and expect other people to respect that.

The next day, Chris returned to the view outside his window, merging this with his reflections on racism:

> Roots of buildings wet like the top of a glazed donut, by-by goes the tram full of people, white and black together, equal like the world should be. Yellow penthouse sticking out of the top of a building like an overflowing pot of gold, heads in the class bobbing up and down like a pianist playing a floating solo, cars driving by throwing water from their tires like a cheese grater, and me sitting here writing it all down to be in memory forever, like clay tablets from Mesopotamia 1500 B.C.

Learning to Think on Paper

The process of thinking and then standing on the shoulders of our thoughts can even happen over the course of writing a single entry. I remember sitting in the window seat of our lakeside cabin in the woods of northern Michigan. The screen door closed, and the particular sound of that particular door called to mind the childhood summers I had spent in the same cabin, and the cardboard boxes stored on top of the logs near that screen door. In my notebook, I jotted down memories of the tiny worlds I used to build in those boxes and of the tiny toads that inhabited them. As I wrote, I recalled the valleys of sand, the pine-bough trees and pie-tin lakes. Then I began thinking and writing about the Michigan cabin itself as a world created by my parents for the nine children in my family. From there, I began exploring the idea that world-building is what my colleagues and I are doing now in education. One thing led to another.

William Stafford describes the process of finding new things to think this way:

> When I write, I get pen and paper, take a glance out of the window (often it is dark out there), and wait. It is like fishing. But I do not wait very long, for there is always a nibble—and this is where receptivity comes in. To get started I will accept anything that occurs to me. Something always occurs. . . . If I put something down, that thing will help the next thing come, and I'm off. If I let the process go on, things will occur to me that were not at all in my mind when I started. . . . For the person who follows with trust and forgiveness what occurs to him, the world remains always ready and deep, an inexhaustable environment. (1982, 17–18, 20)

Children, too, can learn to think on paper. But the strategies for thinking on paper are very different from the strategies for producing clear, logical, tightly focused compositions. It's important, therefore, that we teachers learn to defer some concerns until late in the composing process, when the goal shifts from thinking on paper to producing an organized composition. For example, in a finished piece of writing, every line and every example should usually address the main idea of the text. When I encourage students to focus I often quote an unknown writer who said, "Readers are like sheep. If there's an open gate to the right or the left they will surely go through it." The insinuation is that we need to block off the gates to prevent readers from being detoured as they read over our texts. But when writing notebook entries, when trying to generate thoughts and insights and meanings, those gates to the right and the left are crucial and life-giving. Our message to young writers and to ourselves must be, "Open the gates and go through."

When Joshua Bazán reread this entry about his little brother Nicholas, he found a line in it that didn't fit his topic at all and yet seemed important. The entry read:

Ever since my brother Nicholas was born, I loved him. That was, until he was 5 years old. Then it started to become a war, a war between me and him, a war for respect and for the most toys. Sometimes we don't fight, and sometimes it's head to head in Battleship. I destroy his ship, he destroys my ship. And that's where Mom comes in. She destroys everybody, including my dad.

That pest Nicholas tries to sneak my brand new toys to school. He says that I always bring his toys to school when that's not even true.

Because Joshua knows that one of the ways to learn from your writing is to pay attention to the surprising, troubling parts, he copied the line in which he said his mother "destroys everybody, including my dad," onto the top of a new page of his notebook and used it to start another entry.

Sometimes—often—the process of "going through the gates to the right or the left" happens not only when we return to our old writing but also when we are in the act of writing. Notice how Rafaela Villar explores and even uses the associations that attach themselves to her very sensory memories of her mother's homeland, the Dominican Republic. She writes:

I remember the first time I was going to visit the Dominican Republic. I was terrified because I thought it would be all dirty and grimy, and not comfortable. But I was wrong. When I got to the Dominican Republic, it was heaven. The birds were chirping so happily and the butterflies were clinging to the leaves while the wind blew. The flowers were pretty. I would pick one and smell it. It smelled like my mother, all dressed up to go out, when she'd put perfume behind her ears. Now I know the Dominican Republic can be as beautiful as the inside of a warm, gentle person.

As I read what Rafaela wrote and remember Joshua's courage, I'm reminded of Annie Dillard's advice to writers:

Examine all things intensely and relentlessly. Probe and search each object in a piece of art. Do not leave it, do not course over it, as if it were understood, but instead follow it down until you see it in the mystery of its own specificity and strength. (1989, 78)

Once, in an effort to encourage children to listen to and follow their writing, and to generate ideas as they write, Anne Gianatiempo began a share meeting by saying, "Let's all see if we have entries in which we begin by thinking about one thing and then wind our way to other thoughts." Esther Portela, a quiet girl with big brown eyes and long braids, read her entry only after Anne again insisted that they weren't sharing focused final pieces but instead rich, thoughtful, meandering ones. In fact, a subject and mood do emerge in Esther's entry, and the entry gathers momentum and focus in a powerful way.

> It's a rainy day and I am in the fourth floor of my school. I look out the window and I see the clouds gray and mean. They seem to come to you and eat you with their big black mouths. When the birds go through them and it all seems normal again I want to be asleep with my medicine that makes me sleep, and with the clouds. I really feel like sleeping. But I don't sleep because I know I can't. The clouds look like dreams and the drops on the windows make me sleepy, very sleepy but I can't sleep. The noise of my classmates sounds like a bee humming, and it makes me sleepy, very sleepy but I can't sleep. Tick-tick goes the pens. It makes me sleepy, very sleepy but I can't sleep.

"I don't know why, but I just kept on," Esther said. That is exactly what she did. She kept on. She kept on past:

> It's a rainy day and I am in the fourth floor of my school. I look out the window and I see the clouds.

She kept on past the conventional stopping places, past the places of firm footing where she could record what she knew. She kept on into the unknown territory of associations, thoughts, and feelings as they were happening to her. Joshua Bazán kept on, too, past the relationship between himself and his brother that he understands and onto the relationship between his mother and his father that he doesn't. Rafaela Villar kept on, past the nice smell of a Caribbean flower and on to her mother, all dressed up with perfume behind her ears. Chris Ralph, too, kept on. He kept on past the sun, which seemed to shine with every last ounce of light it had left, past the building, a giant that gradually became smaller, to his father, who stood over him and woke him up to talk about another job interview and the prospect of moving. Isoke Nia kept on, too, past open house night and into all of her life until she came to Day 3 and Day 4, when she gave birth and was loved and loved and loved . . . and made biscuits on Sundays.

6

From Notebooks to Projects

When the circle of fifth graders grew quiet, Michelle Eisner spoke. "Do you know how, when we spoon tiny, yellow kernels of popcorn into the bottom of our popcorn poppers, many of them turn into big, perfect pieces of buttery popcorn while others remain as little yellow kernels? Well, the same is true, I find, of entries in my notebook. Some of them turn into big, important writing projects—letters, picture books, petitions, songs—and some remain as they are."

Meanwhile, across the city in Brooklyn, Sharon Taberski found another way to talk about the same process. "When Theodore Giesel wrote *Horton Hatches the Egg,*" she said, "he did not begin by creating in his imagination the story line of a moose giving birth in a palm tree. Instead, a sketch he'd made of a moose accidently slipped up against an entirely separate sketch of a palm tree, and Giesel found himself looking right at the idea for his book. All he had to do was find how it happened that a moose was nesting in a palm tree . . . and what happened next."

Sharon continued, "The same thing happens sometimes when I get ideas from my writer's notebook. I had two separate entries. One was about the calmness I feel folding laundry and the other was about my mother's death last fall . . . and all of a sudden I realized they needed to come together into a story of how, when I was a child, the laundry was a frightening thing for me. I used to be the one to go into the dark, cold basement to get clothes out of the washing machine. All the way down the stairs, I would call up to my mom, 'Mom, are you still there? Mom, can you hear me? Mom, Mom?' We'd continue talking back and forth until I got the clothes moved out of the dryer and into the hamper and carried the hamper up the stairs to where I felt safe again." Then Sharon said, "Now my mother is gone, and when I call, 'Mom, Mom, are you still there?' no one answers me." Sharon continued, "I need to explore the question of what it's like for me to face my fears alone now, without my mother at the top of the stairs, and so I'm going to do more entries about that."

Meanwhile, Joanne Hindley, who is one of my closest colleagues in the Project, said to the writers at P.S. 173, "When I read over my notebook entries, sometimes several of them make a sound in my heart. Katherine Paterson once said that her writing comes from ideas that make a sound in her heart, and that's true for me as well." Joanne went on to say, "When I read over my entries, they sometimes move me in ways I don't expect. I thought this one was about how I looked as a child, but when I reread it, it filled me with memories of being shy, and I realized all of a sudden that the feeling—the heart-sound—that threads through many of my entries was that as a child I grew up desperately trying to find ways to blend into the crowd, to not be noticed." The children listened as Joanne read her entry aloud:

> When I was a child, I wanted nothing more than to be the kid with long, straight, mousy brown hair. Instead, I had red, unruly hair. I wanted to pull my hair back in a ponytail or to wear it loose and free. Instead I wore thick braids—anything to control its stubbornness. I hated my hair and what it did to me.
>
> Whenever I had an argument with someone, I knew their retaliation would be to tease me—and always the teasing was about my hair. "Red!" "Carrot-top!"
>
> One time I sat at the kitchen table while my mother washed the dishes and I cried about an incident that happened on the school bus. Much more upsetting than the teasing, though, was the realization that, as I retold it, my mother was crying.

"I have other entries about not wanting to be noticed, too," Joanne said, "so I said to myself, 'How could these puzzle pieces fit together into one picture?' I could put the entries beside each other in a book with different scenes of growing up, but I try to do new things in my writing. I've decided instead to experiment with writing a fictional story, only I've started the story with the truth. It begins with a young girl who often used to sit in the back of the limo that her grandfather drove, feeling the eyes of the world looking in on her."

In each of these stories something significant happens: kernels become popcorn, two separate sketches become the story line for a beloved tale, a series of separate entries becomes a work of fiction. Michelle Eisner, Sharon Taberski, and Joanne Hindley know that as their young writers move between notebooks and projects, transformations such as these will not always occur. Sometimes the process of moving from notebooks to projects will be more like stringing favorite beads together than popping popcorn kernels. Other writers in Joanne Hindley's shoes might have decided to combine entries into chapters in a book entitled *Growing Up Shy* rather than turn them into a fictional story. When children do this kind of cut-and-paste transition from notebook to project, the resulting work is sometimes very fine indeed. But it is no accident that Michelle, Sharon, and Joanne have talked about and demonstrated a composing process in which something new happens in that space between the notebook and the writing project. Behind all our talk about the stages and processes in the composing process, it is perhaps fair to say, is our hope that significant things will happen all along the way as we and our youngsters compose.

Finding and Pursuing the Meaning in the Moments

The focus of this chapter becomes "How do writers grow as they move from notebooks to projects?" and "How can our teaching support this growth?" First, in order for us as writers to shift from gathering to making, and from a wide-angle to a telephoto lens, from following the flow of our thoughts to deliberately crafting a piece of literature, we must select. "Of all that I have said and noticed and questioned and imagined . . . what will I pursue?" "Of all the patterns that intrigue me, the unanswered questions and undeveloped fragments . . . what feels most promising?"

It is important to notice that when I wrote *The Art of Teaching Writing* five years ago, I phrased the questions we asked in choosing topics differently. My emphasis then was on finding an incident to record or a subject to teach others, not on finding topics to explore. The young writers in *The Art of Teaching Writing* asked, "What are my areas of authority?" "What are the topics I could teach others about?" "What have I been doing?" Back then, I shared mini-lessons and conferences that were meant to reassure teachers and children that topics as small as "jumping on Mama's bed" were worth writing about. I encouraged young writers to fill long strips of adding machine paper with hundreds of possible topics until they finally realized that anything and everything could be a good topic.

The fact that this approach made topic choice easier and more accessible to children was important. As long as responsibility for choosing topics remained in the teacher's hands, and as long as all students were writing together, entire classrooms of children moved in a lockstep fashion through a single, uniform process. Then, too, as long as teachers controlled topics, children tended to write on generic themes that weren't particularly pressing for them. So it was important in the field of writing to argue that topic choice is easy and that we are each surrounded by hundreds of potential topics.

I now realize that this line of thought is only half true. We are each surrounded by potential topics, but a certain combination of factors makes some of those topics stand out from the rest. "Jumping on Mama's bed" may indeed be a very good topic—or it may not be very good. But the challenge of topic choice goes beyond determining whether something is or is not a good topic; it also involves determining what the topic *may be good for.* Let me explain. What I'm saying is that the challenge of topic choice doesn't end with the decision to write a story about jumping on Mama's bed. Such a story could be written in countless different ways. It could, like Joanne's story about having red hair, be the story about a child's self-image, but it could also be a story of defiance or of sisters playing together or of summertime or of the differences between Mom and Dad or of one's childhood home. When a writer decides jumping on mama's bed is an image worth pursuing, the writer needs to write more in order to explore questions such as "What draws me to this topic? What's its significance for me?" "What other images connect with this one?" Composing a text has everything to do with finding the meaning in the moments, and then with deliberately shaping a text that conveys that meaning to readers.

Once Joanne Hindley recognized the undercurrent of bashfulness in her entries and decided to build on that, she began to write with an organizing intention. If she hadn't decided to use the entries as a seed for a fictional story, she might have rewritten or combined the entries in ways that highlighted her bashfulness. She might also have prefaced these entries with some thoughts about why it was so important to her that she blend in with the crowd. All of this involves retelling the anecdotes in ways that bring meaning to those moments. Such deliberate crafting is essential to the process of composing.

Conferences That Nudge Youngsters over the Threshold Between Notebooks and Projects

If we return to the questions "How do writers grow as they move from note-books to projects?" and "How can our teaching support this growth?" we have one obvious answer: when writers keep notebooks, topic choice no longer consists of conjuring up something to write about. Instead, it implies a larger decision—selecting a topic, angle, or plan that feels significant and promising. Topic choice becomes more difficult and yet more important. There will be times in our conferences when we will nudge youngsters over the threshold between notebooks and projects, but we want to do this in ways that help youngsters begin to make this transition on their own.

Seven-year-old Ilana Goldberg looked up from her notebook and, before I had asked anything, said in a voice I had to stoop to hear that yes, one part of her notebook mattered most. "When I had to let my hamster go in the park." Again sensing my unspoken question, the quiet, dark-eyed girl whispered, "because then I had no one to come home to."

"Are there any other entries, Ilana, that have to do with that?"

"Um . . . um. . . . " Ilana was clearly surprised by the question and unsure of what to say.

I asked it again, this time explaining myself in hopes that Ilana would soon internalize this question as she had the others. "When I have something big to say, like having to let my hamster go and not having anyone to come home to," I said, "sometimes I find that other entries speak about that same topic. You might look at your notebook and see if other entries connect with this one."

Ilana nodded and quietly turned to a particular page. Stroking the page, she said, "This does, about my grandmother. Because before she died, I had someone." When the workshop ended, Ilana had dedicated a portion of her notebook to this topic. A few days later, after writing more entries on the topic, Ilana moved onto rough-draft paper. Eventually, after peer conferences and share meetings and more conferences with her teacher, Ilana published a book, *Alone in a February Park,* which was about far more than a hamster. In her book, Ilana told the story of losing her grandmother, of coming home each day to only a hamster, and of letting that hamster loose in a cold February park. The final scene has everything to do with a little girl who, like her hamster, feels cold and alone.

Once Ilana had found the entry that mattered most and seen another entry that connected to it, she was well on her way to composing a piece of writing with more scope than those she'd written before. As soon as she connected the loss of her hamster with the loss of her grandmother, something new began to happen in both her writing process and her written product.

A similar thing happened when Gene Blackmond, a struggling writer from P.S. 206, made a connection between two entries in his notebook, which resulted in the picture book shown in Figure 6–1:

My Sweater
by Gene Blackmond

Dedication: To the memory of my brother, Mickey, and my sister who helped me put it into words.

It's red and warm.
I feel good and warm when I wear it.
I love my sweater.
When I don't have my sweater on . . .
I really miss it!
It was my brother's.
He gave it to me.
And that's why I love it!
I had it for a long time.
He died.
That was . . .
Eight years ago.
All I have left to remember him by
Is my red sweater.

In their writing, both children shift between telling about something that has happened to them and placing that event in a larger framework that reveals what it means to them. By combining the red sweater with the brother's death, the loss of a hamster with the loss of a grandmother, Gene and

Figure 6–1   *"My Sweater" by Gene Blackmond*

Ilana have given their writing point and counterpoint, a depth of vision, but they have also given their writing process life. As they moved between notebook and rough draft, and between one rough draft and another, they weren't just doctoring up their entries to make them suitable for public appearances. Instead, they were exploring the central questions of their lives.

In the beginning, it will probably be our conferences that help writers like Ilana and Gene to ask, "What is important to me?" "Are there other entries that speak to this?," questions they can later ask of their work themselves.

Lydia Bellino often holds a sample conference with a single writer in order to demonstrate conferring and then asks her class to engage in similar sorts of conferences. She suggests that class members group themselves in clusters of four and that one person in each cluster then read his or her entire notebook aloud. The others write—or talk—back, responding the best an outsider can to the question "In this notebook, what are the themes, the connections between entries, the ways of writing, or the interests that thread through many of the entries?"

When ten-year-old Chris Ralph read his notebook to a small cluster of children, he was surprised by the connections his classmates saw. "Now I can see what they're saying," Chris said later to me. "I thought they were about different things, about this book or that one, but now I see they are all in a way about my mother." Chris showed me these entries as examples:

The book *Walkaround* was very good, but I didn't feel that it related to me very much. There were a few places that the book related to me. One of the lines was when Mary and the bush boy were staring each other down. Peter was standing next to Mary. Suddenly he sneezed. That's like me—always sneezing.

There was another part. When the bush boy had died and the two kids were searching for food, the book said, "And the ghost of the bush boy was with them in every passing plant and stone. For both children had fallen into his ways." That reminded me of when I came to live with my dad. My mom said that I would always be with her in mind and heart.

When, in *Swiss Family Robinson*, they went back to visit the ship to get stuff after they left, it was like last year when I went to Ohio to get stuff. When I was taking certain things it reminded me of when they were going around the ship taking only the things they needed. I wasn't as desperate as they were to take things, but I still had to choose. Certain things I would take and certain things I would leave.

Today, in *88 Steps to September* when they were coming to the farm and everyone was quiet it reminded me of when I came to live with my dad. Although on the trip we were noisy for most of the way, when we got to Massachusetts the car was suddenly quiet. I don't know why. Maybe I was quiet because I was anticipating seeing my dad but already missing my mom. I knew that I was going to live a much different life like in the book when Bob locked himself in the car. They knew it was going to be much different. They didn't want to face it. I guess I didn't either. I overcame it just like he probably will.

Today I noticed a suitcase floating down the East River. When that happened I felt like, "Ha, ha, you lost your bag," but now when I think of it I feel very sorry for them. It was like when my hamster died. They were probably feeling the same thing. Now I think we're even.

Chris decided that he would write more entries about leaving Ohio, and that to begin he would let the suitcase remind him of leaving his mother, which it probably did anyhow. Then he'd try a draft that would bring together all the entries about leaving his mother, combining them in a form that felt like literature.

For Anna Gay, who is seven, it wasn't a conference, response group, or a mini-lesson but rubber stamps, bought during a Saturday morning visit to the Museum of Natural History with her father, that initiated the idea for her project. Anna couldn't have such glorious rubber stamps without also having a table-top printing house and a publication. She arrived at school on Monday announcing that she would produce a class anthology of poems and stories. Because the stamps were pictures of fish, and perhaps because the anthology combined an odd assortment of items, Anna named her publication *Fish Chowder*. Her first step was to make the cover (Figure 6–2). After that, Anna began studying *Cricket* and *Highlights* magazines and filling her notebook with notes on review boards and tables of contents and indexes and the like.

Anna's story may seem totally idiosyncratic, but it's actually not uncommon that the inspiration for a project comes from life, not from the notebook. Whether the writer wants to toast a birthday, mourn a death, protest plans to drain wetlands, say good-bye to a friend or mend the breach in a relationship, there's usually enough raw material in a notebook to launch almost any imaginable project. When Edwin decided he would gather photographs and writing together to make a memory book of the house he's leaving behind when he moves, he searched through his notebook. When Mary Beth volunteered to teach youngsters from another classroom about writers' notebooks, she, too, searched through her notebook.

Sometimes none of this works. Palak Shah, a ten-year-old boy from India, for example, was stuck. "I'm just trying to think of a project," he said when Shelley approached him. "Everybody at my table is doing one and I want to do one too."

Before Shelley approached Palak, she had already learned from his teacher that he wrote quickly and that, until this year, he expected to publish whatever he'd written immediately. Palak boasted that last year he'd published sixteen stories and three poems. This year he had already written a great deal

Figure 6–2   Anna's "Fish Chowder" Cover

in his notebook, and clearly he was itching to see his entries culminate in publications . . . and for good reason.

"Palak, it's great you care so much about your writing," Shelley said, "but a project is a big commitment. Sometimes I think that we don't choose our projects; they choose us. It's as if an entry or a line says to us, 'I'm so important. Please do something with me.' Do you get that feeling when you reread your notebook?"

"Yeah," Palak said with great seriousness. "But the problem is, everything is important."

Shelley nodded, and after asking Palak's permission, she began to leaf through his pages, hoping to see his eyes light up or his expression change. When this didn't happen, Shelley switched her line of thinking and tried a different tack. "Palak, I'm wondering what kind of writing you'd be most proud to publish," she asked.

"Scary stuff," he responded quickly. "I love Alfred Hitchcock and Alvin Schwartz's scary stories and adventure stories, too." The rapid clip of Palak's words and the eager look on his face told Shelley she had hit gold.

"Have you ever tried to do the kind of writing you admire?"

"Nope," Palak answered, pushing back the wedge of straight, black hair that had fallen over his forehead. "It's too hard. I wouldn't know how to begin."

"Well, my guess is that you might begin by looking through your notebooks again, searching for the seed of some scary story."

Figure 6–3 Palak's Spooky Story

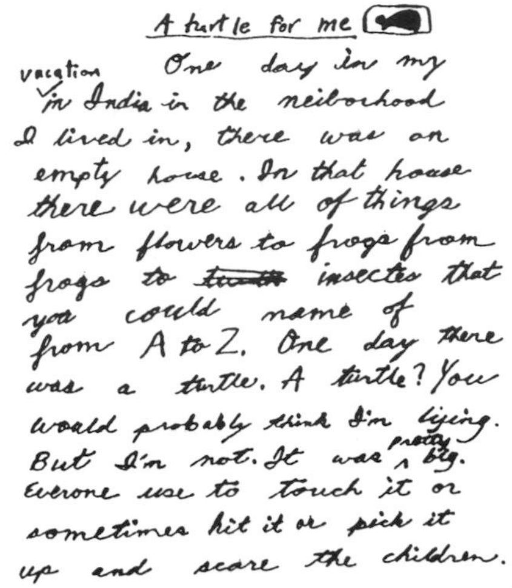

> A turtle for me
>
> vacation One day in my
> 'in India in the neiborhood
> I lived in, there was an
> empty house. In that house
> there were all of things
> from flowers to frogs from
> frogs to ~~truth~~ insects that
> you could name of
> from A to Z. One day there
> was a turtle. A turtle? You
> would probably think I'm lying.
> But I'm not. It was pretty big.
> Everone use to touch it or
> sometimes hit it or pick it
> up and scare the children.

"That's easy," Palak said. On the very first page of his notebook he'd written a true story that was spooky. He showed Shelley the entry (Figure 6–3), describing a scene from a family visit to India, where there was an abandoned house filled with treasures, including a huge turtle that scared little children:

A Turtle for Me

One day in my vacation in India in the neighborhood I lived in there was a empty house. In that house there were all [sorts] of things from flowers to frogs, from frogs to insects that you could name of from A to Z. One day there was a turtle. A turtle? You would probably think I'm lying. But I'm not. It was pretty big. Everyone used to touch it or sometimes hit it or pick it up and scare the children.

Shelley was about to ask Palak if any other entries had a similar mood when he added, "I think my Halloween piece is spooky too, and so is the one about sleeping on the couch." Flipping through his notebook, Palak pulled out the two entries shown in Figure 6–4:

Ghosts
     Bones
          Skeletons
BOO
That all makes up to Halloween
WOO
    BOO
       Turtle Stew
It's all a part of Halloween.

Figure 6–4   Palak's Other Entries

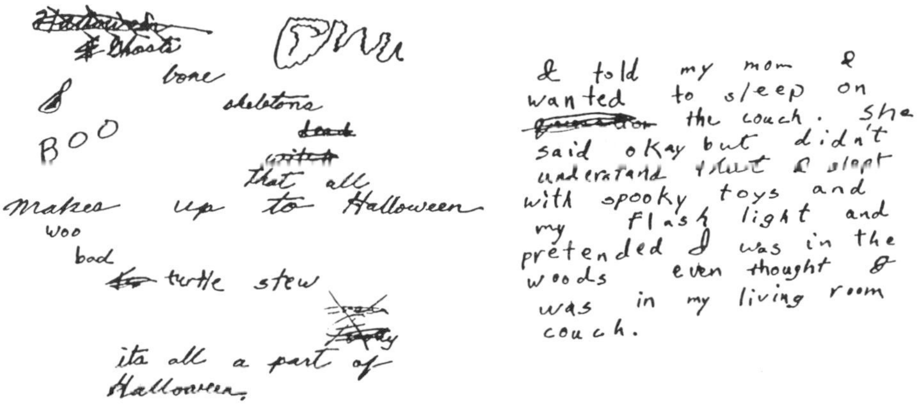

I told my mom I wanted to sleep on the couch. She said okay but
didn't understand that I slept with spooky toys and my flashlight and
pretended I was in the woods even though I was on my living room
couch.

He read all three aloud. "It's interesting, Palak," Shelley began. "I get a
very different feel from the Halloween poem than from the other two entries.
Which kind of writing feels closer to Hitchcock and Schwartz?"

"I guess the turtle and the spooky toys one," Palak said.

Shelley nodded. "There are real people in those entries and real feelings in
them, so the scariness matters; it's somebody *particular* getting scared," she
said, adding, "I guess the challenge now will be to think through what you
might do with those entries."

Palak looked confused. "You mean I should write a whole bunch of scary
stories, like Alvin Schwartz does, like *Palak's Scary Stories to Tell in the Dark?*"
he asked.

"You might," Shelley answered, but in her mind she was not thinking that
each entry would become a separate story. "You might write a whole collection of scary stories," she said, "or you might try to write just one wonderful
one. You might, in fact, combine the best parts of what you've got."

"Like write fiction?" Palak asked. "Like a kid falls asleep with his spooky
toys and has a dream about a scary house filled with turtles? Or maybe the
kid's in India and his friends make him sleep in this empty house?" Palak
didn't need Shelley anymore, and so she continued on her rounds.

In each of these conferences, the writer—Ilana, Chris, Anna, Palak—has
not chosen a topic he or she wants to publish a piece about as much as a topic
he or she wants to pursue. These children are now launched onto what we call
"projects." We use this word not because we envision yarn bindings, dedications,

marker pen drawings and accompanying dioramas, but because these young-sters are, we hope, working on endeavors of scope and significance. Over the course of the year, children, the classroom community, and the resources in the room will all grow into the challenge of these projects. In September, when youngsters may not know the procedure for securing various kinds of paper, or for going to the library, or for editing their work, or for holding peer conferences, it's important to remember that, just as parents buy clothes children will grow into over time, we can teach in ways young writers will grow into over time.

In September, children will write collections of poetry without necessarily knowing anything about white space or visual imagery, and in the same way they'll merely recopy five entries about being alone into a chapter book. We can and must watch all this writing without needing to "make it right" or "to teach it all," knowing that we will have a whole year together with these youngsters and that, for now, what we really need to celebrate is their ambi-tion to do something big with their writing, their steadfastness in pursuing something over a period of time, and their growing comfortableness with new tools and habits of thought.

Predictable Problems in Early Drafts

It's essential, above all, to protect ourselves and our youngsters from feelings of failure. Among the Project staff when one of us says, "I'm leading a staff development course on moving from notebooks to projects," someone else will invariably respond, "Can I come to the last few sessions?" or "Let me know when you get to the projects part." The jesting reflects some real issues that come up for us at the project juncture in the writing process.

One problem is that many of us are so enchanted by the process of keep-ing and rereading and reflecting on our notebooks that we unintentionally delay moving to projects until it becomes clear that the energy for the note-books is diminishing. Suddenly it becomes urgent that everyone immediately have a project, and, because this can't happen instantly, the workshop runs into trouble. It's equally (or more) problematic if a teacher never finds it necessary to move from notebooks towards projects. If teachers and children are not pursuing their writing beyond the level of collecting entries, then there is often no reason to confer, no need for share sessions, no occasions for re-vision, no intention to craft literature, no opportunity to make reading-writing connections—and the classroom doesn't feel like a writing workshop at all.

We need to avoid these problems by being sure that early in the work-shop—by the second or third week of notebooks—we are already helping children move from notebooks to projects. Some teachers set deadlines, say-ing, "By September 22 let's all choose a topic to pursue in our notebooks." Other teachers confer with youngsters in such a way that six or eight children find a focus early on. The rest of the class will still be well ensconced in the notebook, but by the time they have spent another week generating entries, the six children can begin to act as starter dough helping the others move into projects.

For me projects are also hard because as the work turns the corner toward publication, I am apt to return to my deeply entrenched instinct to evaluate. I can teach myself to read notebook entries without necessarily demanding that the writing be beautiful, clear, moving and wise, but rough drafts are approximations of a goal in a way that notebook entries are not, and it's hard to resist thinking, "Is this rough draft worth all the hard work, all the entries, all the weeks of gathering?" "Does it validate the process of keeping a notebook?"

But these questions are unfair. The learning and living and growing that happen as youngsters and teachers notice raindrops and old ladies talking and suitcases floating down the East River cannot be on trial whenever a child attempts to produce a piece of literature, nor can the yearning to do something big—to edit an anthology or combine pages of entries into a single story—be questioned simply because the first results are clumsy.

In the bath tonight my three-year-old son Miles sailed his little boat closer and closer to the frothing white water under the faucet, and as he did, he said, "Into the embers of waterfall you go!" I laughed in delight at his wonderful "rough draft" language. I rejoiced just as much in Miles's misshapen valentine, soggy with glue, and in the self-rigged basket he uses to pull books up and down from the top level of his new bunk bed. Whether or not I teach Miles that embers are most often found by a fire and that glue goes *between* things rather than on top of them is unimportant compared to the absolutely essential fact that I must tolerate—and indeed delight in—my son's awkward, all-wrong early "drafts."

I need to remember all this when I'm confronted with the drafts that Ilana, Chris, Anna and the others produce as they attempt their projects. Sometimes we'll look at their drafts and think, "Their entries were better," or "This is identical to the first entry." But if we find ourselves testing the idea of notebooks, for example, by looking to see if there is great insight and power in children's early drafts, children will think that it is they who are on trial . . . and no one who feels on trial can write or live well. The drafts children produce, especially early in the year, will probably be like misshapen, gluey valentines, and we need to respond to them with the same warmth and trust.

Notebooks, Literature, and Conferences Nourish Rough Draft Writing

It's no accident that I am talking about responding to writing in the middle of my discussion of students' transition from notebooks to rough drafts. Finished writing can get up and demand its own response, but early drafts require teachers and fellow writers who have the eyes to see what is not yet there.

When I was partway into this book, I was blessed with readers who loved what I was saying and believed the book was going to be significant. Now, looking back on the partial manuscript they read, I realize what an act of trust and love it was on their part to say this, but at the time I drank in their words of support and let myself risk becoming deeply involved with the book. Because of those readers and their responses to my early efforts, I began to believe in this book and to bring all my life to the writing of it. Later, when these same readers and a number of new ones gave me criticisms and suggestions, I was able to hear them only because those early responses gave me the faith and the courage to bond with my text.

When Lydia Bellino, the teacher of teachers I mentioned in Chapter 2 who found ways to immerse children in the books she read aloud, first learned that Miranda's project would center around a little notebook entry about the day she threw broccoli out the window and it hit her landlord on the head, Lydia was surprised. Of all the fourth graders in this classroom, Miranda had always seemed more serious and more grown up than the others. She was taller, more mature looking, and wore her long hair pulled back in a grown-up style. Lydia couldn't help wondering, "What does she see in this silly little broccoli entry?" but deliberately phrased her question differently.

"Miranda," she said, "I'm wondering how you went about deciding to write on this topic. Of all that's in your notebook, what drew you to this entry? Was it an easy decision or a hard one?" These are essential questions.

Miranda's response was instant. "I picked it because it reminds me of Patricia MacLachlan, and she's my favorite writer. In the book I'm reading (*Seven Kisses in a Row*) she has a whole chapter on broccoli and I thought it was amazing that I had an entry on the same thing. But now I don't know what to do. I guess I'll try to fix my entry up . . . ?" From her intonation, it was clear that she wanted her teacher to offer her direction for the next phase of her writing.

Miranda's vague charge to herself, "I guess I'll try to fix my entry up," is not unlike the charge many youngsters give themselves. Then they sit for days looking at the entry—pushing it around and sometimes nibbling at it as if it were rejected broccoli, grown cold in front of them—until finally someone says, "This is good enough. You can go on to something else."

It's no wonder that Miranda and the other youngsters who say, "I have to fix up my entry," have very little energy for the task. The process of writing, at its most fundamental level, requires an act of intention, of hope, of reaching for a dream. Fixing something up is far from answering a call to create literature. Writers must also be reaching to convey a belief, to make something lovely, to affect a reader, to hold a moment or a world in their hands. That sense of possibility was there for Miranda; she felt it when she read MacLachlan's chapter but she forgot it when she looked at her own few lines and at the daunting challenge of doing something with them.

In the conference, Lydia touched Miranda's face and looked for a moment into her big, sad eyes. "Can you back up, Miranda, and tell me about MacLachlan's chapter and about the miracle of finding you'd written on exactly the same topic she had?" Miranda opened the book, and they looked at the chapter with great excitement. Miranda was one of the children who'd been swept up by Lydia's reading of *A Taste of Blackberries,* and she was thrilled when Lydia asked to borrow Miranda's book. Soon Miranda agreed that yes, she'd go back and fill herself with the feeling of that chapter and then look over her entry while thinking, "If MacLachlan were my teacher, and if I really did want this entry to grow into a piece of writing like this chapter, what would MacLachlan suggest I do?" Miranda eventually decided her broccoli story needed to be longer and funnier and more full of dialogue if it were to become anywhere near as good as MacLachlan's chapter.

When Lydia heard Miranda's assessment in passing, she nodded her head in great seriousness and said, "I can't wait to see how you do it—how you make it longer, funnier, and with more dialogue." Then Lydia moved on to another youngster, leaving the challenge in Miranda's lap.

Miranda seemed a bit surprised to face the task alone again, but this time she had an idea. She would interview her mother and, if she dared, her landlord.

The idea came because Miranda had conferred earlier with Lydia in a small group. "Would those of you who are into projects come to the back of the room to talk?" Lydia had said, adding, "Bring everything with you." When the group formed at the back of the room, everyone brought their project containers—the folder or portfolio or box that contained what they needed to write their rough drafts. Lydia looked through the containers and noticed that most held one thing only: a page or a half-page of writing. She said, "You can't write empty-handed," and devoted the meeting that day to talking about how important it is to have the books that influence our writing with us, as well as our notebooks. Then Lydia showed the children some ways in which notebooks could continue to be useful once they were working on projects. Melissa, for example, had been writing about a family barbecue, and Lydia encouraged her to interview others and record the interviews in her notebook. "What do you like about being at a barbecue? Why do you think we have a barbecue only once a year?" she could ask her mother and her sister.

That discussion between Melissa and Lydia planted a seed in Miranda's mind, and the next day Miranda's notebook and MacLachlan's book were both out on Miranda's desk while she worked on draft number two of the broccoli catastrophe. Miranda had inserted book markers into her notebook. One indicated a line she'd created once to use when the time was right (Figure 6–5, A). The other page marker (Figure 6–5, B) called attention to the notes Miranda had made the night before as a result of her interviews.

In the draft she wrote that day, Miranda drew on both the interviews and the lines she'd collected in her notebook, but she drew most of all on her sense of what Patricia MacLachlan had done in her chapter. MacLachlan's slapstick humor, her play on words, and the sound of talking around the kitchen table are all evident in Miranda's entry:

When I was eating broccoli, rice and chicken, I said to my mother, "I like broccoli all right, but my taste buds don't like it."

"Just eat it. It's good for you," my mother said.

We were eating while the phone was ringing, the front doorbell was chiming, the dryer was buzzing and the oven was dinging. My mother went to get the door, answer the phone, take the clothes out

Figure 6–5   Miranda's Page Markers

A   The phone was ∧ringing, the front
doorbell was ∧chiming, the dryer was ∧buzzing
and the oven dinging. | Put in |
                          | to a |
                          | story |

B   Interview

Mon   My mother remembers when I
through the brocoli that it fell
on the landlord's head and
he got furious. His face
looked like a red apple.

landlord   He felt disgusting because it felt
gooky and it fell right on his head.

---

of the dryer and take the muffins out of the oven. Meanwhile, I went to the window and threw out the broccoli. Then it landed on the superintendent's head.

I said, "I'm in troubbble trouble." We heard some lady calling up at us.

My mother quickly ran to the kitchen window and asked, "What is it, Steven?"

The super replied, "Your daughter threw broccoli down the window and it landed on my head." My super was furious, and his face turned red like an apple. He went to his apartment downstairs in the basement and started cleaning the broccoli off his head.

My mother asked me, "Why did you throw the broccoli out the window?"

"I didn't want it," I replied.

"Well," my mother said, "it was really my fault. I shouldn't have forced you anyway. But you should not have thrown it out the window. You should have eaten a little bit."

The doorbell rang, "Ding, dong, ding, dong." When my mother answered the door it was my super. He said, "If you or your daughter throw food out of the window again, I will raise your rent $10 more."

Our rent was already $350. If he put $10 more it would be $360 for my mother to pay. Today I learned my lesson not to throw food out the window. You would get in big trouble. I'm never going to throw anything out the window again.

When this draft was completed, Miranda brought it to her response group. One of her classmates asked a wonderful question: "What will you do with this? Is it a beginning of a longer story, part of a book about what to do when you don't want to eat your food, or what?" The question led Miranda to decide that she wanted her story to become a picture book, and so, not surprisingly, she piled a whole new set of books on her desk when she returned to her draft to ask, "How can I make this into an effective picture book?"

Lydia knew that Miranda and her classmates would probably study the genre of picture books in greater depth later in the year, but she didn't suggest that Miranda postpone the genre until then. Instead she made a mental note that when the class turned to an intense study of picture books, Miranda might want to reread her picture book in that context.

This time it was Crescent Dragonwagon's picture book *Diana, Maybe* that became important to Miranda. Miranda had already read the book countless times; this, I find, is true of almost any book that affects our writing. Now, looking back through the book, Miranda said, "I think my first page can be a little like the first page of *Diana, Maybe.*" Crescent Dragonwagon's book begins:

> On Sunday mornings,
> when my father stands at the stove
> wearing his blue bathrobe
> and flipping over the blueberry pancakes,
> he sings a song that goes
> "Hey, good-lookin',
> what you got cookin'?"
> while my mother,
> in a red caftan,
> squeezes the oranges
> for juice and sings along.
> As I put out the syrup and butter
> and the special Sunday-morning plates
> with the flowers at the edge
> for my mother and father and me,
> I wish I could put out another plate,
> for Diana.

"If you want to create a scene like Crescent Dragonwagon's opening scene," Lydia Bellino said later in a conference, "you may have to pay attention to the details at the dinner table with your family." Then Lydia wisely added, "But be careful not to add so much detail to the dinner table scene that the broccoli incident no longer seems important. If you're going to spread parts of the book out into scenes, you need to be sure to do this with whatever scenes matter most."

Once again Miranda turned to her notebook as a place to record, observe, and gather information. She wrote:

> When my mother went to throw out the garbage, I tiptoed to the kitchen window. I took my spoon and scraped it out of my plate. When I was throwing the broccoli out, I looked around to make sure my mother wouldn't catch me. I was very afraid to do it. My landlord was sweeping the sidewalk downstairs and the broccoli fell on his head. His face turned like a red apple.

The next day when Miranda worked on her picture book, she again drew on her notebook and her previous draft, but she also incorporated what she had learned from *Diana, Maybe*. In Miranda's new draft, she deletes the slow, careful description of spooning broccoli from the bowl. "It should happen faster than that," she explained. This is her final draft:

> When I set the table, I put a fork, a knife, and a spoon on each napkin. I put a cup next to each plate. Then I put a water pitcher, an orange juice pitcher and a milk pitcher. I put salt and pepper shakers. I set the table real nice.
>
> When the food was ready my mother put rice and chicken in her bowl and then in my bowl. My mother put an extra bowl in the middle of the table. I asked my mother, "What is that bowl for?"
>
> My mother replied, "You'll see." I waited until she put something in that bowl in the middle of the table. I wondered if it was jello dessert. Then I said, "Nah."
>
> When my mother came out of the kitchen she put broccoli in the bowl. She put a lot of broccoli on my plate and she put broccoli on her plate. I said, "I like broccoli, but my taste buds don't like it."
>
> My mother said, "Just eat it." When my mother went to the bathroom, I went to the kitchen window and threw broccoli out the window.
>
> When my mother came back, she heard somebody yelling up at us. When she looked out the window, the landlord had broccoli on his head. The landlord said, "Your daughter threw broccoli out the window and it landed on my head." Then the landlord went to his house and cleaned the broccoli off his head.
>
> When he came back, he said, "I will put $10 on your rent for littering."
>
> My mother told me to say I was sorry. I said, "Sorry, Steven."
>
> My mother said, "You are punished for a week." She gave me another bowl of broccoli. I had to eat it. I learned my lesson.

Miranda and her teacher worked hard on Miranda's succession of drafts. But Miranda is not the only child in this classroom. Imagine the scene: Ilana has brought in old photographs and letters and is using them to remind her of how her grandmother looked and the things she did to make Ilana feel loved. Two other girls are looking through books of folksongs to help them understand what to do to turn a notebook entry into a song. Palak has used fasteners and ditto paper to make himself a blank book, and on each page he's sketched notes about what that page should contain. In doing so he has realized that he needs more images from his early childhood in India, and so he has returned to his notebook to gather them. Anna has been holding "editorial conferences" with each of her classmates to determine what, if anything, they want to submit to *Fish Chowder*. Add to these the twenty-eight other writers in the room, each with his or her own plans and problems and ideas that make a sound in the heart.

The prospect of helping each of these youngsters as Lydia Bellino has helped Miranda is a daunting one. "How can I possibly be there every step of the way for each of my children?" teachers ask. But the good news is that we not only *cannot* be there every step of the way, we *should not* be there every step of the way for every piece of writing. When I wrote *The Art of Teaching Writing*, I said, "Our job in a conference is to put ourselves out of a job." How true those words are. "Our job," I said then, "is to ask questions of children so that children internalize these questions and ask them of themselves and their own emerging drafts" (1986, 120).

The important thing is that, after all their good work together, Lydia Bellino and Miranda need to look back and say, "What have I learned that can help me another day with another piece of writing?" We so rarely do this. Children don't look back in this kind of reflective way because there's almost nothing in school or out of school that invites them to do so. And the same is true for teachers. We're always rushing on to the next writing conference, the next child who needs us, the next week, the next unit, the next test, the next staff development session, the next deadline, the next group of young people . . . who has the time to look back and ask, "What have I and this young writer done together?" Then, too, even a teacher as wonderful as Lydia doesn't look back to reflect because by now she is probably feeling guilty for having spent so much time with one child. And she's probably questioning whether the final product is better than the early draft and is she a good teacher of writing and do her methods work and were her conferences appropriate and did anything happen that was worthwhile. . . .

The final product does seem belabored. It sounds as if Miranda is trying too hard or as if she's dressed up in someone's high heels and is stumbling a bit as a result. But shouldn't we expect this kind of thing along the path of learning to write? When a young writer deliberately tries to create an effect, the result is often a little self-conscious and overdone. But why is it so hard for us to glory in what the writer has tried to do, or even in the very fact that the writer has deliberately tried to do something?

Miranda's experience offers many potential lessons, but unless Miranda and Lydia Bellino look back to name and revel in and remember those lessons, they may slip away. Imagine how important it would be for Miranda, and for the classroom community, if she moves on from this one writing experience knowing

- That it is not enough to just assign oneself to "fix up" an entry. In moving from a notebook to a project, writers need a sense of vision, of goals.
- That it helps to have books we're learning from on our desks as we write.
- That you can pretend a favorite author is your teacher and try to imagine the suggestions he or she might make to you.
- That notebooks can be used for recording interviews and that this is especially helpful when we want to expand entries into projects and when we want to include other peoples' voices in our writing.
- That effective lines or phrases collected in a notebook can sometimes be woven into a draft.
- That picture books—and indeed most narrative writing—are written with scenes . . . and that it is especially important to turn key events and moments into scenes.
- That writing scenes slows down a piece of writing, and that sometimes it's more important to let things happen as quickly on paper as they do in real life.

I can imagine that when Miranda and Lydia have looked back and reflected on the work they've done together, Miranda might make a list, in her notebook or inside her project folder, of strategies she'd used to turn a five-line entry about broccoli into a significant piece of writing. She might talk with other writers about the time line and the tools of her writing. She might also be challenged to find another seed idea—a connection between entries, a bit of beautiful language, a perplexing question—and to pursue this project entirely on her own. "Just keep track of what you decide to do along the way," Lydia might tell her. "Take notes on the tasks you set for yourself and the challenges you take on, so that later you can help me and the rest of the class know the story behind your writing." Finally, Miranda might meet and compare notes with other writers who have also, in their own ways, moved from notebooks to projects. These youngsters might ask themselves, "What did all of us do in common? What did only some of us do? What can we learn from hearing about each other's processes?"

If Miranda had this kind of debriefing session with the group of classmates that originally met with Lydia Bellino, she'd find that Melissa did indeed interview her parents about the family barbecues. Melissa's original draft was long enough and good enough, however, that Melissa ran into problems Miranda didn't encounter. For Melissa, the challenge was deciding how to integrate the new material gathered from the interview with the old personal narrative account of the family barbecue. Melissa at first added her mother's reactions to the picnic onto the end of a paper so that she told her own experiences at the picnic first, then her mother's. In a conference with Lydia Bellino,

Melissa was challenged to consider other options. In the end, she decided that instead of writing one section of her story about everything she liked and didn't like about the picnic and then doing the same for her mother, she would intersperse her mother's ideas in with her own. Melissa had written, for example, that she liked the pool because she had to get her hand stamped and because she got to watch her older cousin diving. After interviewing her mother for a second time, now on targeted subjects such as "Why do *you* like the pool?," Melissa added that her mother liked the pool because it kept the children busy. Similarly, Melissa had already said she liked the barbecue because while the hot dogs were cooling, she and her cousin sat on the seesaw and this gave them a chance to talk. After interviewing her mother, Melissa used codes to add that her mother liked the barbecue because there were paper plates so no one had to wash dishes and because she got to see all the new babies in the family.

Of course, many children didn't do any interviewing at all as they moved from notebooks to projects. Leo Soto had written two entries in his notebook about his brother, but he didn't want to bring them together into a single story. Instead, these entries made Leo care all over again about the fact that his brother hadn't invited him to be in his wedding, and so Leo's project was a letter to his brother, as shown in Figure 6–6:

Figure 6–6 Leo's Letter

Dear Pito

    I love you Pito. I hope you come soon. I don't miss you that much because you didn't put me in the wedding. You put everybody in the family in the wedding except me. I'm not as mad because me and mom had a talk. You are coming back in December because you are going to get married to Sandra. I'll do anything to be in the wedding. I just want to be in it.

    In marias wedding I carried her train and I'll carry Sandra's train, just to be in the wedding. I saw Nelida's dress it was very nice. Now all you gotta do is get me a tuxedo so I can be in the wedding.

Love Leo

The End

Dear Pito,

I love you, Pito. I hope you come soon. I don't miss you that much because you didn't put me in the wedding. You put everybody in the family in the wedding except me. I'm not as mad because me and Mom had a talk. You are coming back in December because you are going to get married to Sandra. I'll do anything to be in the wedding. I just want to be in it.

In Maria's wedding I carried her train and I'll carry Sandra's train, just to be in the wedding. I saw Nelida's dress; it was very nice. Now all you gotta do is get me a tuxedo so I can be in the wedding.

Love, Leo

Orlando Fernandez, like Leo, had written for real-world purposes. He'd brought his early and subsequent drafts to the debriefing session, but it was only later, from Lydia Bellino, that we learned the story behind his work. Orlando was the class jokester and the class spokesperson, and so when Shelley Harwayne offered to hold public conferences with a few young writers in the school library and to talk afterwards with teachers and children about the process of moving from notebooks to projects, Orlando was the first to volunteer. He arrived in the library proudly carrying his first draft of "Rules to Go to the Bathroom." When Shelley peeked over Orlando's shoulder and saw what he was working on, it was all she could do to keep her face from betraying the sinking feeling she experienced. How could she help this class jokester improve the quality of his writing about bathroom rules? She spoke briefly with Orlando's teacher, and then decided to begin by telling him the truth. "Orlando, when I saw your title, I wondered if you were just fooling around. But your teacher told me you take your comedy writing very seriously. Is this a piece of writing you want to work hard on and make your best?"

"Of course," Orlando answered as he leaned back, stretching out in his chair. "I love to be funny."

Shelley decided to continue being honest. "Orlando, I'm not sure I know much about comedy writing. All I guess I can do is read it and tell you if I find it funny. Would that be helpful?"

Orlando agreed, and as Shelley read his draft he watched her face closely. This was his draft:

I wonder why I have to go to the bathroom everyday? I hold it in till either past eleven o'clock, lunch (hardly) or the afternoon. Here are some rules to follow if you want to go to the bathroom safe and proud:

1. *Never* ask before eleven o'clock.

2. *Always* ask after eleven o'clock.

3. *Always* ask at quarter to eleven o'clock.

4. Never ask first (before anyone else).

5. Always let he/she ask before you. If he/she gets in trouble, then ask like one hour later or don't ask at all. If he/she doesn't get in trouble, well, ask like five minutes later.
6. Never ever ask the teacher if he/she is in a bad mood. NEVER.

So if you want to go to the bathroom just follow the rules above.
NOTE: Always approach the teacher in a calm, orderly fashion.

"Well, Orlando," Shelley began, "I certainly do think you're a funny writer. Can you guess which lines I find especially funny?"

Orlando skimmed the page and selected Rules 1, 5, and 6.

"You've got a good eye for comedy!" Shelley said. "Those are exactly the lines that made me laugh the most. What do you think you might do with this list of rules once you're finished?"

"I've already copied them out of my notebook onto a separate sheet of paper to make them neater. Maybe I could hang the rules on the bathroom door or make copies and give it out to the kids in the class," he said.

Shelley knew that Orlando rarely revised his writing, but instead copied favorite entries into a final form. "Well then," Shelley said, "if it's to be published in a way that does a real-world job, your challenge is to make each and every line your best. Perhaps you need to try another draft. Why not take a fresh sheet of paper and jot down those three strong lines, and then try to build on that good beginning?"

"Should I leave out this stuff about me going to the bathroom?"

"It's up to you, Orlando. You could decide to have an introduction to the rules, or begin right with the rules themselves. It's up to you."

This is the revised draft Orlando shared when he met with Lydia Bellino and his classmates:

1. Always approach the teacher in a calm, orderly fashion.
2. Never, ever ask the teacher to go to the bathroom if he/she is in a bad mood.
3. Never ask to go to the bathroom in a cool way.
4. Never ask to go to the bathroom if you are in trouble, until it looks like the teacher forgot about you getting in trouble.
5. Never ask before 11:00 unless it's an emergency.
6. Never ask to go to the bathroom if a child asked before you and the teacher said NO.
7. Never fool around in the bathroom when the Principal is hanging around.
8. Always raise your hand to ask to go to the bathroom, never call out (or say OO, OO, OO!)
9. Never ask to go to the bathroom more than three times in one day.
10. Never fight with an older boy/girl in the bathroom.

11. Never ask the teacher to go to the bathroom if you're in the middle of a test or if you got a bad test score.
12. Never ask the teacher to go to the bathroom if she has a lot of desk work.
13. Always, always, ALWAYS follow the rules above.

Tomas Esparra's process was probably the one most used by children. Before beginning his project, he reread his entire notebook and selected the entry shown in Figure 6–7 as the most important one:

The Man with the Smile

My grandfather is a good man. Every time I used to go to his house he would take my hat and run to the kitchen and hide it. Then I would start screaming, "Where's my hat? Where's my hat?" My grandfather was great at hiding things and having fun with me. Only one day he didn't take my hat and he was not there. My grandmother came out of the room and said he died. I did not know what death was, but now I do.

"What I do when I find a topic or two that matters a lot to me," Lydia had said to him, "is that I start a section in my notebook for each of these topics." Lydia had used little plastic tabs to divide her notebook into sections and was collecting entries on two topics. Tomas decided he'd adopt the same strategy, only instead of adding a tab to his notebook indicating "grandfather entries," he decided to collect them on the back few pages.

"Just write anything that comes to your mind about your grandfather," Lydia said to him. Tomas, meanwhile, decided he'd read anything he could find about grandparents, and he used the books to jog his own memories. For

Figure 6–7 Tomas's Entry

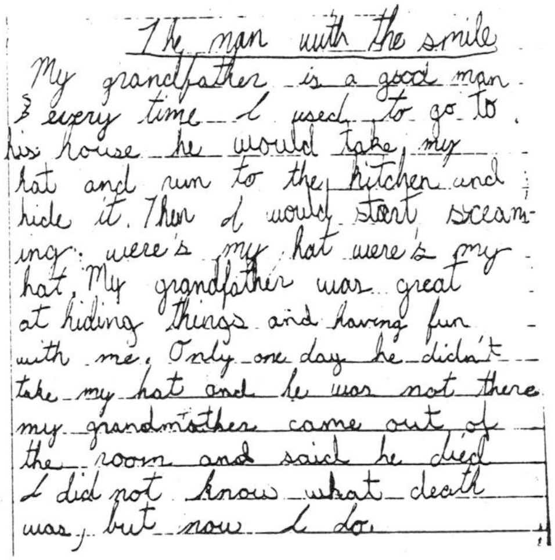
The man with the smile
My grandfather is a good man.
& every time I used to go to
his house he would take my
hat and run to the kitchen and
hide it. Then I would start screaming: were's my hat were's my
hat, My grandfather was great
at hiding things and having fun
with me. Only one day he didn't
take my hat and he was not there.
my grandmother came out of
the room and said he died
I did not know what death
was, but now I do.

about two weeks, he collected entries. Some were short, a few words indicating worlds of memory. Some clearly came from talking with others about his grandfather. One was an expanded version of an earlier entry. Then one day Tomas took out clean notebook paper, and without a word of help from anyone and without any rough drafts or revisions, he wrote the book shown in Figure 6–8.

Now that Tomas, Miranda, Palak, and the others have discovered the growth that can happen in themselves and their texts as they move from notebook entries towards literature, these youngsters can become teachers of writing. When their classmates gather in a circle, they can hear stories not only of the teacher's writing but also of their friends' writing. And when Tomas, Miranda, and the others tell the stories of how their writing grew, these stories will benefit not only those who hear them but also those who tell them.

Figure 6–8 Tomas's Book

① My grandfather was a good man. Whenever I went to his house he would take my hat and trot off to the kitchen as confident as he could be and hide my hat. Then I would start screaming at the top of my lungs "where's my hat, where's my hat." My grandfather would say, I'm surprised he didn't break the windows." But my father would just chuckle. My grandfather was good at hiding things like my football. He would put it down his back and when I looked it was in his big round hands. Only one day he didn't take my hat or my football and he was not there in the living room studying the 1978 Sony T.V. My mother came out of the room and said he had died. I was puzzled. I thought I was on a different planet with the same people speaking a different language. I did not know what the word death was then, but now I do.

② My grandfather used to to take me to baseball games with 20 thousand other enthusiastic people. Then my grandfather would sit me on his lap. He would put his arms around me and rest his chin on my head. I would just cuddle up closer. Then I could smell the fine aroma of the P.R. soap which smelled like spring roses blooming. Then he would tell who was next to bat. When he would tell me Reggie Jocson was up to bat my eye's would sparkle and I would clap. Every time one of the teams would hit a homerun, I would fly of his lap and clap with my chubby hands. He would just chuckle. Everybody in the row that we were sitting in wanted to strangle me, kill me with one glance but my grandfather would just smile with his firm face and hug me.

Figure 6–8 Continued

③ My grandfather would say,"lets play some baseball."When we used to get to the park I used to get to think I was the only one there with my grandfather teaching me the principles of baseball. He would pitch me the ball to me I would twist around and fall. Every body around us would giggle and point but my grandfather would pick me up and say"try it again." My grandfather would get someone to pitch the ball so he could get behind me and help me swing the bat. "I hit it, I hit it," I would say. He would smile and open his arms and hug me and say "you're going to the majors son, you are, you are."

④ My father woke me up one morning and said "you're abuelo (Grandfather) is here. I jumped out of bed and went to the living room. There it was. The bike of my dreams. It was yellow with black pipe lines to the back of it and it was my own.

I was so happy that when my grandfather saw my happiness he started to cry and then hugged me and laughed his heart away.

⑤ I was looking forward to going to the park with my father but he had some business to take care of. But I did not lose hope yet. I asked my grandfather. He laughed and said "I will take you." I grabbed my bike and started riding it out the house. My grandfather was jogging with a dazzling grace behind me but every time I looked back it looked like a baren field with one person on it, me. I looked to the right. He was not there. I looked to the left There he was right beside me. When we got to the park. We raced and he would beat me and say "it dosen't matter who win's. It matters if you have fun". I told him I had fun and hug him and felt so secure and safe and raced again.

⑥ My grandfather and I went to the beach and we had lots of fun. It was fun because when I used to want to go into the water, he used to put me on his broad shoulders. I used to feel I was in the clouds looking down on everyone. Then he would run and jump into the water with me on his shoulders. He would let me bury him in sand. But every time I used to put some sand on him, he would knock some off. Then he would get out and say "next time son, next time". But Know I now, there will never be a next time.

7

Revision of Teaching

Magical writing is contagious. Stories of particular children, children like Tomas and Miranda and the others, are told and retold, cherished and remembered. In them we see what is possible for all children. But good writing classrooms are not filled with success stories alone; they are also filled with heartache and struggle, with bravado and jealousy, with students who think they have nothing to say and with students who spend more time on their margins and handwriting than on the content of their writing. Whether or not students keep notebooks, whether or not we confer wisely and well, some of our children will still lean over their desks to hide their tiny, tottering row of letters. Some will still ask, "How long does it have to be?" and complain that their hands hurt, their pens are dry, their memories are empty, their notebooks or their projects are lost or stupid or boring.

We all have these children, but we each tend to believe we alone have these students, and that we have them because we are inadequate as teachers. And so we put construction paper over the windows on our classroom doors, and when people ask, "How's it going?" we manage a weak smile and say, "Fine." But if we can learn to trust in ourselves enough to take the construction paper down from our windows and say to each other, "Things aren't perfect in my workshop," we will quickly realize that the problems do not exist in our classroom alone, nor are they a reflection of our personal failings. We are all struggling with the same problems.

The idea that our students should carry on sustained work on particular writing projects makes us feel especially inadequate. In many classrooms, experienced writing workshop teachers have found that, although we've already been giving students the long blocks of time they need to delve deeply into their writing, many students seem to write only in seven-minute dabs spread out over the hour-long workshop. In between their fleeting moments of writing, they sprawl across their desks to gossip with each other and lean back in their chairs to chat about this and that. They meander about the room, checking out every conversation. On their way to get another sheet of paper, they stop to plan their weekend.

We see this, and our stomachs tighten. We try to talk sweetly and listen well in conferences, but the truth is that when we ask, "What are you up to, Andre?" we often mean, "Would you sit down and work?" When we ask, "How can I help?" we often mean, "Have you made any progress?"

"Will the idea of going from notebooks to projects help students sustain work on something?" we wonder. "Will notebooks increase the level of productivity in my workshop?" In some ways, notebooks make matters seem worse. When writers worked on rough drafts, it was easy for us to focus on the work in progress and not see its place within the cumulative collection of a child's work. Although children are probably no less productive when they write in notebooks, the fact that their writing is dated and collected sequentially makes it hard for us to avoid confronting the issue of productivity in the writing workshop. Because we are no longer conferring over single pieces in isolation, the big picture of the child's writing is always painfully evident. Andre wrote a wonderful three-page entry last Friday . . . but there have been three days of writing workshop since then, and what has he done?

We, as good teachers, need to trust our instincts. If we look around the classroom and the noise and congestion feel chaotic, if the environment feels unproductive, if we yearn to ask for silent writing, if we find ourselves making mini-lessons and share sessions longer because at least then we feel on top of what's happening in the classroom, we need to listen to ourselves. This doesn't mean we should clamp down on talking in the classroom. The biggest problem of all in schools may be that children are silent. Gordon Wells points out that even children from severely language deprived homes have richer language experiences at home than they have at school. Eighty percent of the talking in schools is done by teachers. When children do talk, they are usually restricted to providing short answers to the questions teachers ask at the rate of one question every eleven seconds (1986, 87).

Clearly, the answer is not to clamp down on students' talk. If we were designing schools from start to finish, clearly we'd build in hours and hours of interactive learning. Youngsters need to talk about books, molecules, the Civil War, and current events . . . and they also need to talk about their writing. But it's an odd thing to have school days, as some of us do, in which the primary— and, in some instances, the only—time for talking is the reading-writing workshop, for in a sense, writing and reading are among the relatively few activities that require concentrated silence as well as talk. In some ways it would make more sense to reverse matters and have the entire school day brim over with talk and the reading-writing workshop center around a shared silence (with time to talk, too).

If we are going to listen to our anxieties about the talking in our classrooms, then we need to recognize that, although some talking supports reading and writing, some of it also interferes. Writing requires an amazing amount of focused mental activity. "I spend a great deal of time simply walking around," Joyce Carol Oates says, "sitting, daydreaming, going through the motions of an ordinary life with—I suspect—an abstracted, dreaming, rather blank expression on my face" (Murray 1989, 35). Charles Dickens described his writing as a similar patchwork of self-absorbed activities. He recalled "prowling about the rooms, sitting down, getting up, stirring the fire, looking out the window, tearing my hair, sitting down to write, writing nothing, writing something and tearing it up, going out and coming in" (Parini 1989). In the transitions between this mosaic of activities, even professional writers find it all too easy to be detoured from their writing.

If professional writers who work alone in an office or study with no incoming phone calls and no distracting noises still invent or find ways to be distracted from their writing, should we be surprised that our youngsters tend to be lured away from writing? This is especially understandable when youngsters are writing in a room filled with thirty friends, half of whom are talking. It is particularly easy for youngsters to be distracted because they grow up conditioned to the piecemeal curriculum of schools and to the seven-minute intervals between television commercials. For youngsters, work usually happens in little dribs and drabs. Until they enter a writing workshop, many youngsters have never been asked to follow the train of their own thought, to pursue and flesh out, refine and critique their own ideas. Suddenly they're expected to follow an idea through all the various writing activities—jotting in a notebook, rereading, drafting, talking, reading, planning, hearing from an author, editing—and so instead they take the normal seven-minute dab of writing and spread it out over the hour-long workshop.

The problem is that writing well has everything to do with giving sustained, focused attention to a project. In chapter 1, I quoted Richard Wilbur's poem "The Writer," with its beautiful description of the urgency and stillness that surrounds a young girl as she writes. Wilbur pauses in the stairwell hearing the clatter of typewriter keys. "A stillness greatens," he says, "in which the whole house seems to be thinking."

In talking about the essential ingredients of creative thought, Vera John-Steiner, author of *Notebooks of the Mind,* says, "There are differences among human beings in their willingness to pursue and hold the power of ideas" (1985, 9). John-Steiner goes on to say that the willingness to hold an idea long enough to unlock and shape its power is the single characteristic that separates creative from mundane thinkers.

If our children are going to learn to do this, it may be necessary for a stillness to greaten in their classrooms. They may need for a while to be encased in a bubble of stillness in which the whole writing workshop seems to be thinking (we will discuss this more in chapter 9). But silence won't create intensity. In Wilbur's poem, the daughter's room is filled with "a commotion of typewriter-keys / Like a chain hauled over a gunwale," not because she's writing in a quiet place at the prow of the house but because her writing reaches into the quiet places within her. The girl's intensity comes from the fact that writing for her is a way to haul up the anchor and head off on new passages, that in her writing she clears the sill of the world. The question of our next two chapters, then, is how we can establish environments in our writing workshops that invite this kind of intensity and commitment.

8

When Writers Clear the Sills of Their World

Shafts of sunlight streamed into Room 211, dancing over the shoulders and hair of the youngsters who sat closely together on the floor near the window. They listened raptly, their eyes and bodies motionless, to the quavering voice of Yolanda.

Dark-eyed Yolanda looked up only once from her paper. Watching, one felt that if she looked again into the eyes of her listeners, she would not be able to hold back her tears. And so she continued, quietly sharing the story of her little brother's debilitating disease, which she said is slowly distorting his features, turning him bit by bit into a freak. The doctor had given Yolanda's parents a photograph showing the full horror of what the boy would become, and recently Yolanda's cousin, in an act of anger, got hold of the photograph and showed it to the boy, taunting him with it.

When Yolanda finished reading, a "stillness greatened" in the room. Then, in quiet voices, the children and their teacher, Pazcual Villaronga, began telling their own stories in response. One child spoke of how she sometimes looks in the mirror and sees in her mind a picture of what she's becoming. Another added that she sometimes feels that she's changing into a freak, too, only it's not her looks that are changing but her feelings. A tiny boy with huge brown eyes talked with enormous empathy about how the cousin probably didn't mean to be so hurtful, and the boy said he is sometimes jealous of his little brother who gets attention because he has asthma. "What do you do with feelings like these?" the children asked themselves.

As Yolanda heard her friends empathizing with "the cousin," tears streamed down her face. When I watch moments such as this, I cannot help but think, "God, do we need stories." Stories can change the world. Early people told stories to explain the glowing embers of fire, the moon, the birds,

105

the fish, and the feelings inside them. They told stories that pushed back the darkness and bound them together into a community.

Stories still push back the darkness and bind us together into communities. The respect that was in Room 211 that day—respect for the goodness of people and for the fullness of our lives and for the power of stories—made that classroom a good place for writing. There are aquariums in that classroom and plants and bulletin boards and a corner for author studies, but that classroom is a good place for writing because stories—and poems and letters and memoirs and songs—are doing their work in the world of those children.

Yolanda's story opened everyone in that room up to life. That is the power of literature. To read literature well, whether it's Yolanda's story or a Robert Frost poem—is to be moved by the dust of snow from a hemlock tree and by the drama of other lives. Yolanda's story affected that classroom like Toni Morrison's *Beloved* and Wallace Stegner's *Crossing to Safety* have affected teachers who gather in reading groups throughout New York City. When stories such as these are on the desk beside us as we teach and learn, we live our lives differently. We are reminded of what matters most. When stories and poems and songs are doing their work in the world of classrooms, then teaching, learning, and living become graced with a larger perspective.

The moment in which Yolanda shared her story brought the community in Room 211 together, filling the room with compassion, but it also gave writers in that classroom an image of what writing can do. The community witnessed the power words can have, and they will see writing and treat it differently because of it.

When We Tap into Real Reasons to Write

A stillness will greaten in our writing workshops when teachers and children experience for themselves the real-world power of writing. We write to plan, to remember, to schedule, to arrange, and to correspond, but more fundamentally, we write to survive. In Lawrence Thornton's *Imagining Argentina*, the imprisoned Cecilia finds that not having pens and paper with which to write is almost as bad as torture itself. Carlos, Cecilia's husband, puts her pain into words:

> From the first morning after she had been taken from our house Cecilia longed for paper and a pen, the crudest paper, the cheapest ballpoint. She would have been delighted to have pieces of torn sacks, pencils worn down within two inches of their erasers, so long as she could write. She knew better than to ask any of the guards, and for months she grieved for the absence of writing materials. . . . In Cecilia's mind what she feels and the ability to write about it are not separate, and there has always been an interplay between her writing and her life, almost as if, in writing, she were checking on the progress of her own emotions . . . (1987, 178)

To survive, Cecilia must find a way to record her pain and outrage, and eventually she does. By imagining the ridged swipes of plaster on her prison wall as lines, she uses the invisible ink of her mind to record her story onto the walls around her.

"Why do I write?" Elie Wiesel says. "Perhaps in order not to go mad. Or, on the contrary, to touch the bottom of madness. Having survived by chance, I am duty-bound to give meaning to my survival" (1986).

Shelley Harwayne shared the story of Cecilia and that of Elie Wiesel with 150 black teacher-educators who came together from throughout South Africa to a writing institute in Soweto. Before Shelley and her daughter left America, they searched for South African literature and found little. Then, as they traveled among village schools in South Africa, they found that in school after school the library shelves were bare. Classrooms filled with sixty black children would typically have only three or four I-Can-Read versions of *Goldilocks* or *Puss-in-Boots*. And so Shelley said to the educators who had gathered in Soweto to learn about the teaching of writing, "You, like Elie Wiesel, are duty-bound to give meaning to your survival. It's your responsibility and your children's to fill those library shelves with the stories that no one else is writing. You need to write for yourselves, and for the children of South Africa, and for the teachers and children of the world who need to hear you."

A stillness greatened in that room as the South African teachers wrote about a father detained in prison for eight years. They wrote of urine trickling down their legs because no nearby shopkeeper would allow them to use the toilet. They wrote poems about a brother disabled in a mining accident and folktales about beasts and jungle boys, wise men and witch doctors. They wrote poems and chants and shows, too, for the market theater, and they wrote an Izibonga song, a South African song of praise performed at funerals and workers' rallies and on other special occasions. They wrote with urgency and rigor because they wrote about topics that matter and they wrote for people and occasions and causes that matter.

Rigor in the writing workshop comes from response. Rigor, intensity, and hard work—and, sometimes, writer's block—come from the memory of past responses and the expectation of future responses.

As teachers of writing we know the importance of response. That is why we agonize over what to say in conferences, carry lists of good conference questions with us, and monitor every sentence out of our mouths lest we commit the dreaded sin of "taking away ownership." And it's why we give the same scrutiny to peer conferences. But the problem is that when we are consumed with worry over our responses and our children's responses we tend to forget that writers need real responses from the real world. We need people to listen through our writing to our ideas. We need people to hear our stories and recall their own. We need people to laugh, to cry, to agree or disagree, to question or argue. We need to send our writing out into the world.

And so when Shelley was in South Africa, she talked with teachers and children about toasts they wanted to give, speeches they wanted to make, causes they wanted to address, and events they wanted to celebrate. She told students about Barbara Marin-Rivas, a twelve-year-old girl whose poem is now used on the stationery of anti-apartheid workers all over the world:

The Sound of Freedom

The sound of freedom
Hear it
It is coming
It is coming slowly
But it's surely on its way

Hear it.
It is almost here
Soon it will be here
Soon we will be free
We will be free
We will love our freedom

If we want freedom
We must fight for it
We must study for it
We must work for it
But we will get our freedom
The freedom that we want.

Shelley also told students that Malissa Taylor, a white high school student, had written and circulated a petition to integrate the whites-only Johannesburg High School for Girls. She told about students who gathered at a local youth club to shape stories and songs into shows for the market theater. This is one of their chants, in which these young people lament what happens when tribal customs are lost to big city ways:

Bring the Cattle Home

Mzilikazi bring the cattle home
Shaka bring the cattle home
Moshoeshoe bring the cattle home

They are eating the wrong food
Drinking wrong waters
Speaking in foreign tongues
Shaka bring the cattle home

They took marimba and brought piano
They took the land and brought in plots
They took the huts and brought in hostels
Mzilikazi bring the cattle home

They took the horn and brought the trumpet
They took Indlamo and brought disco
They took lobola and brought the rings
They took the gods and brought the Bible
Moshoeshoe bring the cattle home
They took the songs and brought in doe, tee, la,
so, far, me, ray, doe
Shaka bring the cattle home

They took poetry and brought Twinkle Twinkle
Little Star
How I wonder what you are
Like a diamond in the sky
Mzilikazi bring the cattle home

They talk different, they wear different
They walk different
Moshoeshoe bring the cattle home

THE KISHILE POETS
UPH'U VAN DER MERWE

In New York City, too, we tell young people about the real-world purposes of writing. We tell them about the letter-writing campaign that forced Roald Dahl to revise a book. He received so much criticism for his references to Oompa Loompas in *Charlie and the Chocolate Factory* that in the 1973 edition, they are no longer black and they are no longer from Africa. Hundreds of people had written Dahl to protest the fact that the owner of the chocolate factory was like a Great White Father who takes pity on a tribe of pygmies starving to death in darkest Africa and imports them to England to work in his factory. Dahl had described the black pygmies as infantile, musical, and satisfied with candy for meals and wages. Because people put their anger and dismay into writing, Dahl changed his words.

In New York City and in writing workshops throughout the country, young writers write with urgency and rigor when they anticipate a real-world response. How crucial these responses are to those of us who are learning to write.

When one of Liz Dolan's seventh graders shares his written reflections about participating in a reading group with senior citizens, he learns from seeing stern Mr. McKenzie's face soften as he hears the story, and he learns from Mrs. Colonzo rapping his hands angrily at the way he described her. When fourth graders from P.S. 321 hung signs on the hundred-year-old elms on their block, "Save Our Trees. Don't Kill the Trees. Don't Kill Nature," they learn from seeing the saws biting into those trees and from seeing that signs alone weren't enough.

When one of Jane Kearn's eighth-grade students wrote to the company that makes Bic pens protesting their decision to stop manufacturing a certain kind of mechanical pencil, that youngster didn't need a conference with his teacher in order to learn the effectiveness of his letter. The crates full of mechanical pencils that arrived at his door—a lifetime supply—did more than any writing conference could have done to convince him that his letter had been effective. The same was true when a fourth grader's letter to Harper and Row—"We love your books, but now we want to write our own. We have no paper"—brought a truckload of paper to a New York City school.

Publishing Puts Demands on Writing

How far our thinking about publications has come! Four years ago when we were making our videotape, *The Writing Workshop: A World of Difference,* we illustrated the importance of publication with a scene showing youngsters mounting their finished writing in a photograph album and lucite frames. Now we want to replace those scenes with that of a twelve-year-old boy in the library searching through special education journals and then returning to his piece about his Down's syndrome sister and rewriting it toward publication. We want to replace the lucite frames and photograph albums with scenes of a third-grade teacher standing in her bridal gown in front of the altar at her wedding, reading to the groom and to the congregation, "I give you my tomorrows." We want to replace the old video scenes with new ones in which Beverly Cleary and Russell Baker and other writers talk about the turning point in each of their lives as writers occurring when a teacher read their writing aloud. In *Growing Up,* Baker describes what it meant to see his words moving an audience.

> "Now boys," he [Mr. Feagle] said, "I want to read you an essay. This is titled 'The Art of Eating Spaghetti.' "
>
> And he started to read. My words! He was reading *my words* out loud to the entire class. . . . Then somebody laughed, then the entire class was laughing, and not in contempt and ridicule, but with open-hearted enjoyment. Even Mr. Feagle stopped two or three times to repress a small prim smile.
>
> I did my best to avoid showing pleasure, but what I was feeling was pure ecstasy for at this startling demonstration that my words had the power to make people laugh. . . . I had discovered a calling. It was the happiest moment of my entire school career. (1982, 239)

Publication is not a prize for writing so much as it is a part of the process of writing. The reason our young people need to publish their writing, then, has everything to do with the fact that when we write for readers and for causes, it puts demands on our writing. A writer asks, "Will the rhythm of this song catch hold at the worker's rally?" She imagines voices raised together singing her words in unison, and suddenly she hears the words that feel out of step with the others.

A writer wonders, "Will the National Down's Syndrome Society use this writing in a brochure or a journal?" and looking with this lens, he decides to crop all but the very best parts. These deliberations represent an entirely different aspect of authorship than what we experience as we record and muse in our notebooks. During notebook writing we ask, "Where does this trail of thought lead me?" and "Why am I thinking of this?" and "How do I feel about this?" Now we ask, "How can I make readers, listeners, workers at the rally feel what I want them to feel?" and "Is this good enough? Is this the best I can do? How can I do better?"

When Frank Smith says,

> Written language is for stories to be read, songs to be sung, newspapers to be shared, letters to be mailed, jokes to be told . . . recipes to be cooked, messages to be exchanged. . . . It is not for having your ignorance exposed, your sensibility destroyed or your ability assessed. (1986, 179)

he is saying something crucial. Yes, writing is first for reading and singing and mailing and exchanging and cooking rather than for correcting and grading. But the process doesn't end there. The world itself asks for rigor. At New York's Natural Museum of History, there is a showcase filled with handcrafted items made by Eskimos. Beside a perfectly stitched sealskin parka a plaque explains that the women who sew such parkas use tiny, close, even stitches to protect the lives of their husbands, who hunt in temperatures as low as 60 degrees below zero. Near a group of intricately woven baskets, a plaque reports that these baskets are made with such care because they're used to carry boiling water. When baskets and parkas and stories and poems are attached to the important people and the important passions in our lives, then we have reasons to care enough to become craftspeople.

Teachers of writing would be wise to devote less time to mounting children's writing onto bulletin boards and more time to helping children find real-world audiences for their writing. Older students can make tapes to accompany their writing to provide read-along experiences for younger children. A child who has written about learning to play baseball can be a resource for another child who wants to make the baseball team. Children in one class can attend seminars given by children, teachers, and parents from another class. Youngsters who are inspired by a book in the school library can borrow Charlotte Huck's idea and slide their writing under the book's jacket flap. The school can schedule public readings for the first Friday of each month, and children from all classes can be asked to submit writing that fits that month's topic. Groups of young authors can give seminars in which they talk with other students and with parents about their writing processes. The music teacher can help children choreograph melodies to accompany their words. When schools become richly literate communities, teachers and children write differently.

When writing is for books to be read, poems to be recited, songs to be sung, letters to be mailed—when we can remember and imagine response—we are more apt to write, and to read our writing, with an outsider's eyes, asking ourselves, "What effect will this text create? How can I be certain these words will really be heard? How can I be sure they will matter to readers?" Writing for readers is important. Having readers who sigh and laugh and remember and cry and wince and argue is what compels reading-writing connections, and the kinds of revisions we do for an audience.

By Responding to the World, Writers Enrich It

Sending writing out into the world is important for what it does to writers. But it is equally important for what it does to the world. Recently, there has been a lot of discussion about the fact that the "best and brightest" of our young people are not choosing to devote themselves to public service. It's not difficult to imagine why. The world's problems are so gigantic it's sometimes hard for any of us to think that our best efforts could make a difference. But the writing workshop can change this. When five-year-old Emanuella Grinberg wrote a letter to the school custodian

> Dear Mr. Beiter,
>
> Two girls were bothering me in the bathroom in the lunchroom. Me and my friends want doors in the bathroom.
>
> Thank you.

that led to new bathroom doors, this young girl must have learned that she can make a difference in the world. When six-year-old Allen Jones wrote a letter (Figure 8–1) that altered an entire school's practices, he learned that his words can matter in the world. This is his letter:

> Dear Mr. Romano,
>
> I want to help our school. But I don't want to let balloons go up in the air. I love birds. Birds like to eat. If they eat the balloons they will choke and die. And when the balloons break and fall to earth, who will clean up the mess? I hope we can spend the money on good stuff. Please teach us to SAVE THE BIRDS AND NOT TO LITTER.
>
> Maybe we can plant flowers, buy water to keep the park grass green, have a picnic for all the families to meet, give money to animals [or] give money for the poor.

By Responding to the World, Writers Enrich It

Figure 8–1 Allen's Letter

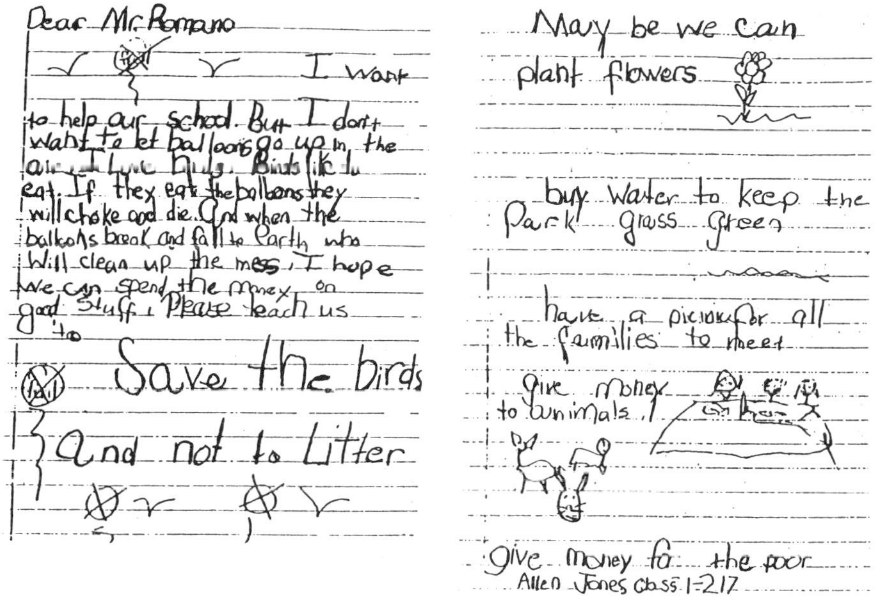

In the writing workshop, we have for a long while talked in terms that are political. We've talked about enfranchising our students, about empowerment and giving voice to young writers and letting youngsters claim their authority. But sometimes it has seemed that by enfranchising students we have meant only that the writer decides when to add a detail or fix the ending of a story. Empowerment must also mean that children learn that their words can make a difference in the world.

It's not coincidental that 70 percent of the people who are jailed as political prisoners, whose dissent so upsets political systems that they are put in jail, are writers. The pen is indeed mightier than the sword. But sometimes we don't let kids know this. When we tell kids about great writers, we don't include Martin Luther King. Many of our youngsters know Margaret Wise Brown's *Goodnight Moon* by heart, but they don't know King's words by heart:

> I have a dream that one day on the red hills of Georgia the sons of former slaves and the sons of former slaveowners will be able to sit down together at the table of brotherhood. . . . I have a dream that my four little children will one day live in a nation where they will not be judged by the color of their skin but by the content of their character. I have a dream today. (1963)

Then, too, when we talk about reasons to write, we need to let our young people know that writing gives a voice to the historian, the scientist, the lawyer, and the ecologist. It's not coincidental that when we're asked to think of a great physician, we think of Lewis Thomas, or that when we're asked to think of a great veterinarian we think of James Herriot. Writing gives people voices in the world.

Primary teachers everywhere have already been showing their young writers that writing can reach into the world and make a difference. In kindergarten and first grade, children use whatever sound-letter correspondences they have to write posters of class rules. "No pushing at the drinking fountain. No fooling around," a child writes. And when she sees classmates wrestling, she runs to get the rules, shakes them in front of the tussle of misbehaving children, and calls out, "Can't you read? It says, 'No fooling around.' " Five-year-olds hang signs on the playground slides pleading for kids to stop putting mud on the slide, and they hang posters on their building saying, "Stop putting graffiti on my building." But in many schools, when children like five-year-old Emanuella move beyond the primary grades, chances are they will no longer write for real-world reasons. Once children move up in the grades, they don't very often write posters, signs, demands, or requests. Instead, fourth graders and tenth graders tend to write pieces for bulletin boards and photo albums and lucite frames. Yet all children deserve to know the real-world power of print. If our words can make a difference in the world, so also can our lives.

"When writing is fed by the world," Don Murray has said, "it may in turn feed the world" (1986, 149). Cannot we also say, "When writing is fed by the world, it *must* in turn feed the world." Ultimately and finally, the reason our writing and our children's writing needs to be sent into the world is that when this happens, we will not only write differently; we will also live differently.

9

Silent Spaces and Study Groups in the Reading and Writing Workshop

When nine-year-old Susie Sible was asked to think of an image of herself writing, she said, "I am alone in the woods, with no one around, and I put my hand on the rough tree and I say, 'Tree, you are mine. You are in my story,' and I lie back against the rock and pretend the whole world is mine and I am the author."

When the poet William Stafford tried to capture the moment in which he first became a writer, he said,

> Once in the evening in the library something happened. . . . It was winter; a strange, violet light was in the sky. . . . Something about the light, and the quiet library, and my being away from home . . . made me sit and dream in a special way. I began to write. . . . I was as if in a shell that glowed. All the big, dim reading room became more itself and had more meaning because of what I was writing. The alcove . . . was darker and more velvety. (1986, 9–10)

The moment in which Beverly Cleary, author of the *Ramona* books, began to write was saturated with a deep, peaceful solitude. "As the rain beat against the windows," she recalls, "a feeling of peace came over me. . . . To this day, whenever it rains, I feel the urge to write" (1988, 146).

Georgia Heard, author of *For the Good of the Earth and Sun* and a longtime member of the Project staff, describes settings for writing as places that give her the excited urge to write, as places that are rich and warm, where time slows down, where whatever she wants to do is possible. "Sometimes when I was a girl," she recalls, "my mother would cook a turkey on Sunday; the smells permeated the house as I lay upstairs on my bed reading and gave me a feeling of peace" (1989, 22–23).

When our writing responds to the beauty and horror of the world, when we write for people and passions and occasions that matter, when we write within a community of writers and our words are shared, heard, questioned, discussed, and celebrated, we need solitude and stillness and the luxury of time in order to feel the urge to write welling up inside ourselves. We need places and moments in which we can come home to ourselves.

When we as teachers look out at our writing workshops and ask, "Could I write here?" we aren't asking only, "Could I fill a few pages with print in this room?" We are also asking, "Could I have that sense of yes-ness, of empowerment, of having something to say in this room? Could this room be charged with the significance that William Stafford felt in that winter library? Could I, in this room, have that feeling of expansiveness and power that Susie Sible spoke of when she lay back on the rock, and looked at the sky, pretending the world was hers and she was its author?"

The environment in a writing workshop will not create the urge to write but it can either invite or dissipate reflectiveness. When Antoinette Ciano, who teaches alongside Laurie Pessah, Anne Gianatiempo, Eileen Braghieri, and others at P.S. 148, began drafting a book of childhood memories to give her father, with whom she'd been fighting, Antoinette realized that she needed quietness and solitude in order to dig back into her memories and find moments of tenderness. She needed a focused, quiet space in order to recall not only the events but also the feelings during her Sunday morning bike rides with her father across the Brooklyn Bridge and into Little Italy to get real mozzarella cheese.

Antoinette first wrote about that memory in the midst of the bustle of her classroom. As kids conferred along the edges of the room and leaned back in their chairs talking, Antoinette wrote down just the facts of the story. Then at home, sitting in front of the fire, she wrote about how, when she was a small and vulnerable little girl on her battered yellow two-wheeler, her father sometimes tied a rope between his bike and hers, towing her along. But now, although she still feels small and vulnerable, he's not there to help on the uphill roads.

"When I reread what I had written in front of the fire I realized that I couldn't have dug that deep if I'd been writing in my classroom workshop," Antoinette said, and she began to join Shelley, me, Laurie Pessah, the staff developer from her building, and other Project teachers in reexamining the assumptions that had guided much of our thinking about the structure of writing workshops. We thought first about the value of silence. When we say that writers need time to write, time to remember, time to imagine and dream and rewrite, are we also saying that most writers need uninterrupted silent time to write? We think perhaps this is so. When we write within a bubble of silence, we turn inward, into ourselves. We finish a passage of writing and put the pen down. We're done. But no one draws our attention away, no one lures us into something new. And so we sit with our writing, and we find that although we thought we'd said it all, new thoughts begin to form, and we're off again. . . .

William Sloane's advice to writers may have relevance for some writing workshops, especially in grades two and above:

Shun the impulse that diminishes the tension inside you while you are writing. Don't talk about your novel to other people. Don't read sample sections to your Aunt Minnie or your best friend or anybody else. (1983, 106–7)

For several months now, Antoinette's workshop has begun with thirty minutes of the hustle and laughter of interactive study groups. Then it has moved into thirty to forty minutes of writing in a bubble of silent intensity in which the whole classroom seems to be thinking. The silence (at its best) is respectful and generous. It is closer to the silence one experiences in a beautiful wood-paneled and well-carpeted library than the silence that results after the teacher has flicked the lights on and off and demanded ten minutes of silent writing time.

Antoinette is not the first Writing Project teacher to institute a period of silent writing time, but she and the others who have joined her in this recent venture are vastly happier with the results than they were with their earlier efforts to do this. The difference comes in part because Antoinette's primary intent is not to discipline students who are gossiping and talking throughout the workshop, nor is it to crack down on unproductive students. Her goal is not to set limits, nor is it to manage the chaos. It is instead to create a space for solitude and stillness so that writers can listen to themselves. And so Antoinette doesn't reprimand and scold; she invites. She doesn't tower over the silence; she participates in it.

It is important that Antoinette is a part of the intensity she tries to create. It makes a big difference that Antoinette participates in the silence, writing quietly and personally alongside her students, rather than clicking her way among the desks, supervising and checking to make sure her writers are productive. In the same way, when adults are sitting on the living room floor talking together in a group and a powerful person enters the configuration, it makes a big difference whether that person joins people sitting cross-legged on the floor or towers above them. "I try not to silence the kids at all. I just sit among them and try to create around me the mental space I need to think," Antoinette says. "On good days, that mental space spreads out into the classroom."

Once the bubble of silence is established, Antoinette usually shifts from writing to conferring. Instead of moving from desk to desk during this silent writing time, giving all students the impression that she is on call, Antoinette is apt to devote most of her attention to three or four leisurely reading-writing conferences. Generally she does this by sitting with one child at a time, talking quietly in the carpeted library area.

Another difference between this and previous efforts at establishing a silent writing time is that now solitude and silence are set against a large, generous time for talking, shared study, and laughter. When Antoinette began to think of the writing workshop as having two halves—a time for study groups and a time for solitude—she thought that all she was doing was corralling the talk that had been there all along into an enclosed space. But when she deliberately gave part of her workshop over to talk, Antoinette was surprised to discover that it was an entirely new thing for her to really and truly feel unambivalently positive about talk. "I realized that only now that I had a time for silent writing could I also truly have a time for talking," Antoinette says. It was a new feeling for Antoinette to enjoy, participate in, and nurture her students' interactions with each other. It was a new experience for her not to feel as if her head was a rotating fan turning this way and that to check whether the room was quiet enough for writing and silent thought.

Freed from this sort of vigilance and worry, Antoinette and the other teachers and Project staff members who have been exploring this structure for their writing workshops have begun to give new attention to the kind of talking that can surround and support writing. Over the past few years, Antoinette's students, like students the world over, have experienced mixed success with peer conferring. They know the logistics of peer conferences. The unstated rule has always been that it is okay to banter quietly back and forth with someone as you work at your desk, but if you really want help revising a draft, you can ask a friend seated anywhere in the room for a conference and sit together on the edges of the classroom in conference alley. "I need help with this draft," a child will say as she sits with her friend, because that is how many children think a conference should begin. Often, however, the child's real purpose may not be to get help in revising a draft but to get a response. (Not many of us actually look for people to tell us to rewrite our manuscripts.) Because revision was the only sanctioned, approved purpose for peer conferences, no one ever gave a lot of thought to nurturing alternative reasons to talk during a writing workshop. Until Antoinette instituted a time for study groups and a time for silent writing in her workshop and consequently began to think seriously about the purposes of extended talk, the attention that she'd given to peer conferences had gone either toward containing talk so that writing could coexist alongside it, or toward teaching students the questions they could ask and the suggestions they could make in order to solicit revision.

It was a breakthrough, therefore, when Antoinette gave herself and her students time to talk about writing and then asked, "What kinds of talk might happen during this time and space?"

The best description of what happens now in the writing workshop in Antoinette's classroom is that for thirty minutes each day, the room is filled with a sea of talk about writing. John and Omar are sitting on top of a cluster of desks with an overhead projector between them, intently discussing a typed text of Cynthia Rylant's *The Relatives Came* that is projected onto the screen in front of them. They each have their notebooks in hand and are writing down and trying to understand the examples of repetition they find in the text. In the back corner of the room, four boys are clustered on the floor at the listening center. Apparently they've just heard a tape-recorded rendition of Esphyr

Slobodkina's *Caps for Sale* and are now poring over a copy of Vera B. Williams's *A Chair for My Mother* trying to determine how they will make an equally fine recording of it. At a cluster of desks, Samantha is reading her entire notebook aloud to several friends. Together they are trying to identify patterns and recurring topics. Irene and Tientien each have a copy of a page from Georgia Heard's book *For the Good of the Earth and Sun,* and they are looking through their writing folders to find bits of writing that could benefit from Georgia's advice. Outside the classroom door, youngsters have arranged the duplicated pages of several picture books into long columns that stretch down the corridor. They are talking among themselves as they lean over the line of pages, scanning them to see the different ways authors have structured their texts. There are many other clusters at work as well; and, of course, each day the endeavors of each group turn new corners.

One of Antoinette's roles in this happy, thriving community is to help groups recognize and respond to their need to turn those corners. By the time Antoinette joined Edwin Echeverry and Wilfredo Moya, for example, they'd already copied all the beautiful language they could find in Kathryn Lasky's *Sea Swan* into their notebooks. "It helped me because I want to write with beautiful language like this story. So I jotted down every single part of beautiful writing that I saw and I thought, 'How can I write that kind of language in my own writing?' " Edwin explained, showing Antoinette his notes. They began like this (see also Figure 9–1):

To see the deadly nightshade that bloomed in darkness.
Where the children swam and ducked and leaped over, under and
    through the curling surf.
Elizabeth thought only a fish could.
Last tour of the garden.
As they made wishes on night-blooming flowers and first stars.

Antoinette was probably tempted to respond by dreaming up the next step for Edwin and Wilfredo. But she has learned to resist her urge to jump quickly to solutions and next steps. Instead, she first tries to take a little extra time to understand the situation. She asked Edwin and Wilfredo to back up for a moment and explain exactly how they worked together. "Do your notes on Lasky's language match?" she wondered, and when a glance at their notebooks showed that they did not, Antoinette asked, "Did you talk as you did this?" They hadn't. It's not hard to guess the reason. It would have taken a fair amount of forethought for Edwin and Wilfredo to arrange a way of proceeding on a task that called for real collaboration. Because each of them had a copy of the book, the easiest way was for each boy to open his copy and begin recording the nice language, which is exactly what they did. Now they were done and ready for their teacher to tell them what to do next. Instead, Antoinette asked what had never been asked before in that writing workshop. "How can you two work together and learn together? How can you two use

Figure 9–1 Edwin's Notes

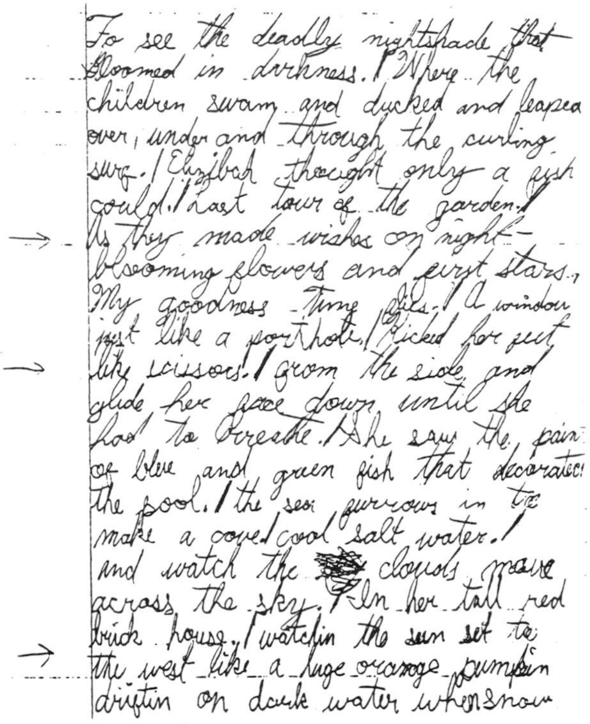

Lasky's book and your writing to learn *together?*" The question has emotional valences that are very different from those that used to surround the questions Antoinette (and the rest of us) generally asked about peer conferring. Then the question often was, bluntly put, "How can one of you help the other add onto or improve his or her draft?" That old question put youngsters in an odd one-up, one-down relationship with each other and inferred a single-mindedness toward revision that wasn't always there. The new question, although still a challenging one, issues a more generous and natural invitation.

It's exciting to look together at the language of a book. It's not that different from sitting with someone on a rocky ridgeline and passing binoculars back and forth trying to determine if the bird soaring overhead is really a hawk. "Did you see his beak? It's a hawk all right." "No, there are no hawks around here. It's probably a crow." "It's too big for a crow." Edwin and Wilfredo hadn't talked in this way about Lasky's language, but it was within their reach to do so. When Antoinette left them, they decided they'd each reread their notes, choosing the bits of *Sea Swan* they liked best, and then they'd try to decide together what the best parts of her book were and what those parts had to teach them about beautiful language.

This was only one of several corners Edwin and Wilfredo were to turn during the next few days. Later, when Antoinette challenged them to move back and forth between reading and writing, they searched through their own notebooks for beautiful language in the same way they had searched through Lasky's book, only they agreed to do this collaboratively, each writer reading his notebook aloud and the other helping to listen for good language. Wilfredo went first, but he only read a few pages of his notebook before he stopped and said, "None of this is like literature. I was just putting it down. I wasn't making it beautiful." Then Wilfredo said, "When I hear it now, memories keep popping into my head. I'm going to write them like literature." This is what Wilfredo wrote:

> In a small area of Lima, Peru, there was a river
> Where my cousin and I would play all day.
> The water was calm and blue.
> The rocks were soft and shiny
> from water that only the river could bring.
> At night the stars would come out and play.
> At daylight they would hide.
> My cousin and I would lie next to the river
> And watch the clouds drift by.
> We loved that river
> And it loved us.

"You're like me," Edwin said. "I like to write about the earth, too, about the stars and sun and sea." Then Edwin read his friend's words again, and this time he said, "What I notice is the way you make the stars do what you do. You come out and play, and then you have the stars come out and play, too."

And so it continued, with Edwin and Wilfredo swapping ideas and sharing satisfactions, and the other clusters of children shifting in similar ways between parallel and shared work. The children who had begun by examining the structure of predictable picture books shifted toward looking at the structure of their textbook, their novels, and their own writing. The group that had been working on an oral reading of *A Chair for My Mother* brought in props and arranged for keys to jingle, water to run, and coins to clink at the appropriate moments. They also wrote the music teacher a long, pleading letter asking if she would provide accompaniment for their reading. While they waited to hear from her, they paired off and worked in twos to begin considering how they could invest equal care in doing readings of their own texts. Omar and John soon had two overhead projectors and were comparing two texts with each other; eventually they brought out their own writing and pored over it as if it, too, were projected onto a giant screen.

The energy, excitement, and investment in that classroom, during the hubbub of study groups and later during the silent intensity of "the writing bubble," provided concrete evidence that these youngsters had become insiders in the reading-writing process because they had discovered the delight in written language that draws people to write and read. Annie Dillard says it well:

> There's a common notion that self-discipline is a freakish peculiarity of writers—that writers . . . grit their powerful teeth and go into their little rooms. I think that's a bad misunderstanding of what impels the writer. What impels the writer is a deep love for and respect for language, for literary forms, for books. It's a privilege to muck about in sentences all morning. It's a challenge to bring off a powerful effect, or to tell the truth about something. You don't do it from willpower; you do it from an abiding passion. . . .
>
> Writing a book is like rearing children—willpower has very little to do with it. If you have a little baby crying in the middle of the night, and if you depend only on willpower to get you out of bed to feed the baby, that baby will starve. You do it out of love. . . . You go to the baby out of love for that particular baby. That's the same way you go to your desk. There's nothing freakish about it. Caring passionately about something isn't against nature, and it isn't against human nature. It's what we're here to do. (1987, 75–76)

10

New Frontiers

When Writing Project teachers began to hear about the idea of study groups and silent spaces, they had questions: "How can I be sure the work in study groups will connect to writing?" "Are the groups permanent?" "When does the work of a study group end?" "Do I initiate the activity of a study group or do the kids?" "Does all this become a substitute for mini-lessons?" "How much time a day is devoted to the study group?" "How can I . . . ?" "When should I . . . ?" "Do I . . . ?" "Can I . . . ?" "Should I . . . ?" At its best, our response has been, "What do you think?" and "That's a good question" and "Let's watch and see."

Teachers have also come to us with reservations. "If we tell kids when they can and cannot talk, aren't we boxing them in?" "Are the activities as arbitrary as they sound?" "Does it really make sense to tell kids they can't get help in the midst of silent writing?" At its best, our response has been "Maybe you're right" and "That's a good question" and "What do you think?"

It would be a shame if thousands of teachers throughout the country hurried to install the structure of Antoinette's classroom in their writing workshops. There is nothing magical about the idea of dividing the workshop into a time for silent writing and a time for interactive study. The idea represents a trade-off, and there is loss as well as gain in this (and any) management system.

But there is something very magical about the way Antoinette has joined with other teachers in order to look at the rough drafts of her teaching and ask hard questions. Together, these teachers have asked, "What has been working that I can build on?" "What hasn't worked that I can delete or change?" "What am I really trying to say?" "How else could I say this?" "What am I discovering?" "When is my energy high (or low) and what might this mean?"

In order to rethink her teaching, Antoinette has drawn on the wells of her own reading and writing. She has reached into herself and once again asked the question she has asked over and over: "What is it that I, as a writer, need in order to write well and with fulfillment?" Antoinette knows that when she asks that question of herself, it doesn't yield tricks and strategies and activities as much as an organizing image, but it is that image that she values and searches for most. Altering the organizing image of our classroom alters everything about our teaching. In *The Art of Teaching Writing*, I stress,

> As teachers we are called upon to be artists. We must remember that artistry does not come from the quantity of red, green, and yellow paint, or from the amount of clay or marble, but from the organizing vision that shapes the use of these materials. It comes from a sense of priority and design.
>
> If our teaching is to be an art, we must remember that it is not the number of good ideas that turns our work into an art, but the selection, balance, and design of those ideas. (1986, 9)

Antoinette was wise to know that instead of trying to patch up her existing writing workshop with a new motivator, or a new system of accountability, or a new push toward publication and the like, she needed to rethink the organic whole of what she had been doing. Instead of piling more and more new teaching ideas into her classroom, she needed to step back and draw on all she knew and felt and believed in order to create something beautiful. All too often, when we revise our classrooms, we do so in a piecemeal and timid fashion, adding a little of this and a little of that without asking whether the ideas fit together into an organic whole. Sven Birkerts was speaking not only about reading but also about teaching and living when he said, "We expect, to be sure, that the novel will have a dramatically satisfying shape. But do we finally hope for anything less with regard to our own lives?" (1989, 358). Good teaching comes not from the quantity of good ideas, but from the way those ideas fit together into a dramatically satisfying whole.

Even when a classroom management system feels balanced and alive, it probably cannot guide our teaching forever. It is not necessarily the youngsters who need us to venture toward new frontiers; we as teachers need this pioneering spirit to keep our teaching alive. At a National Council of Teachers of English conference, Donald Murray looked out at a crowd of writing-process people and said, "As we begin to fill auditoriums, to influence curriculum, to sell books, we need to be careful lest we get fat. When you feel you know how to teach a writing process workshop, watch out. When you feel it is easy to answer other people's questions about your teaching, watch out. When you feel others are wrong, wrong, wrong, watch out." Then he added, "We need to watch out lest we lose the pioneer spirit which had made this field great in the first place. We need to watch out lest we suffer hardening of the ideologies" (1985).

Murray could have been talking directly to those of us who staff the Teachers College Writing Project. Success—even moderate, occasional success—is dangerous stuff. It can suck us in. We end up believing there is no other way. We end up being afraid to deviate from what we are doing for fear our hard-won successes will vanish.

One of the most helpful things about introducing notebooks was that when we loosened the screws of our existing workshop, moved it about to incorporate notebooks, and saw things change as a result, not just a little, but a lot, we learned that the writing workshop, as we'd always known it, could be altered to incorporate new ideas. The most hopeful thing about notebooks is not that they turned writing into lifework or that they invited writers to turn back and reflect on their writing. Notebooks, we found, are crucial because they remind us that they are not crucial. They are just one more idea, one more rough draft. Writing workshops were alive and well before notebooks, and they will be alive and well after them. But notebooks showed us that writing workshops could be altered to incorporate a new tool, a new way of regarding writing. And this meant workshops could be altered in other ways.

The most hopeful thing about notebooks is that they were, for us, the final proof that there is no Wizard of Oz behind writing-process teaching methods. Our methods come from mere people, from each of us and our colleagues and students and the folks who question us. All we can do is live out our current beliefs as best we can . . . and continue learning.

We are drawn to the idea of dividing the writing workshop into a time for silent writing and a time for study groups partly because this is our newest and freshest idea. It is so new for us that it hasn't even been well integrated into the teaching described elsewhere in this book. The idea makes theoretical sense to us, answers some of our questions, and feels workable enough to make a difference in our crowded New York City classrooms. But more than this, it's fresh and new, and therefore it is bringing the Writing Project staff and teachers together in much the same way that it is bringing students together.

Our best new ideas for classrooms are valuable because they help us stay alive and awake as professionals and as people. Our best ideas for classrooms help us listen with new attentiveness to the voices and passions of our youngsters and our colleagues. The idea behind Antoinette's classroom is only one among many that have caught hold in Writing Project classrooms over the last ten years, and although some of these ideas have come and gone, they have left a legacy. Those of us in New York City who are very involved in the teaching of writing and reading place great emphasis on developing new ideas and on our own ongoing study. Neither staff development nor self-development is regarded as a one-time thing. Teachers meet together in study groups over lunchtime and after school, and we regularly observe in each other's classrooms. There have been many new frontiers: new forms of celebrations, variations on mini-lessons, schoolwide literacy projects, service work in the City, tutorials and case-study research between upper-grade children and kindergartners, choral readings and jazz chants, and linkages with art and music. Most of all, these new ideas have helped us approach the teaching of writing and reading with a spirit of adventure.

It was the first graders in Dora's classroom, rather than Joanne Hindley and first-grade teacher Dora Ferraiuolo, who invented the idea of a grandparent course of study. The children were already writing a great deal about their grandparents, and whenever a child read or told a story about a grandparent, everyone seemed to have related stories to tell. Dora and Joanne decided only to seize the moment by naming and celebrating and extending the trend.

Although our kindergarten and first-grade children don't generally keep notebooks, these children did. They brought in blank notebooks because they wanted special containers for this study. They stapled into these books the writing they'd already done about their grandparents. They also began carrying these notebooks with them everywhere in order to collect a great deal more.

Sara had never met her Grandma Rose, but she realized that, through her parents' stories, she could come to know this special person. She returned from a long weekend with a notebook that brimmed with anecdotes and memories. Soon Sara's classmates were following her lead, and they, too, were interviewing parents and other relatives in order to learn about their grandparents.

Another day, Joanne entered the classroom to find Dora's children clustered around her, listening raptly to letters Neha and Shannon had received from their grandmothers. Soon many more children were mailing and receiving letters.

Similarly, after Allison recorded the words to a German folksong her grandfather had sung to her when she was a baby, other children throughout the classroom began recording songs and sayings in their notebooks as well. When Allison returned from a spring vacation visit with her grandfather in Florida, she had with her an audio tape of him singing and translating that song. Soon other children had their own audio tapes.

What the children and their teacher eventually collected in their notebooks was as diverse as the reading they were doing on grandparents. They read picture books like Vaunda Nelson's *Always Gramma*, Patricia MacLachlan's *Through Grandpa's Eyes*, Eve Bunting's *The Wednesday Surprise*, excerpts from novels such as Lois Lowry's *Autumn Street*, and poems and songs and letters.

All of this culminated in a special day when the children's grandparents came to school and listened as their grandchildren read aloud the stories they'd written about them. Erin's grandfather seemed uncomfortable in the classroom, unsure of how to act properly in this setting. But all of his restlessness left when six-year-old Erin Taylor Glynn stood, proud and tall in her party dress, and read the entry in Figure 10–1 aloud:

I remember my grandfather's most beautiful garden in the world. He said a long time ago, "Come Erin, come see the rose bush I planted for you."

Figure 10–1   Erin's Entry

So I came and saw the rose bushes. They were full of love. He came with me. He said, "The one on the right is Grandma's, the one on the left is mine, the rose bush in the middle is yours."

When all of the children had read, Dora Ferraiuolo stood, her hands shaking just a little and her eyes still shining with tears from the sight of these grandparents, sitting so attentively watching the fresh, alive faces of their grandchildren with such tenderness. "My grandmother is here in my memories," Dora said, "and I read this in her honor" (see Figure 10–2):

We had a garden in our backyard. Each year it bloomed with the roses, carnations, lilacs and other flowers my father would plant. My grandmother lived with us. She was always in the garden. She loved it there. At each flower's last bloom you would see her carefully pick the loveliest one. She would then press it and save it in a special glass jar.

Whenever she was invited to a wedding, she would go to her glass jar and remove one of the dried petals. She would put it in the card to the couple. "It is right for a young bride to start life on a fragrant note. This petal will bring her luck," she would say.

When it was my turn to get married years later, Grandma again went to her flower jar. And along with her gift, out tumbled rose petals, bits of carnations, lilacs and all the variety of beautiful flowers she had kept and pressed over the years. The card said, "For you, Dora, the whole garden."

Figure 10–2   Dora's Piece

> We had a garden in our backyard. Each year it bloomed with the roses, carnations, lilacs and other flowers my father would plant. My grandmother lived with us. She was always in the garden. She loved it there. At each flower's last bloom you would see her carefully pick the lovliest one She would then press it and save it in a special glass jar.
>
> Whenever she was invited to a wedding, she would go to her glass jar and remove one of the dried petals. She would put it in the card to the couple. "It is right for a young bride to start life on a fragrant note. This petal will bring her luck," she would say.
>
> When it was my turn to get married years later, Grandma again went to her flower jar. And along with her gift, out tumbled rose petals, bits of carnations, lilacs and all the variety of beautiful flowers she had kept and pressed over the years. The card said – "For you, Dora, the whole garden."

Sometimes the new, organizing ideas behind our classrooms come not from children, as in Dora's classroom, but from other Writing Project sites around the country. Jerry Harste recently brought me to Gloria Kauffman's extraordinary fourth-grade classroom at Millersberg Elementary School in Goshen, Indiana, and my visit to that classroom has led New York City teachers to experiment with the idea of text-sets. As part of her literature program, Gloria's children gather in small ad hoc groups to read and discuss clusters of books. When I was in the classroom, Gloria's children were divided among five text-sets, each text-set loosely fitting under the umbrella topic of pioneer life. Several children were reading copies of Patricia MacLachlan's *Sarah, Plain and Tall.* Another cluster of children was reading picture books about quilts, including Patricia Polacco's *The Keeping Quilt,* Tony Johnston's *The Quilt Story,* and Valerie Flournoy's *The Patchwork Quilt.* Still other clusters were reading about early immigration to this country, pioneer families, and family traditions. In each instance, the first task of the cluster was for each member to read all the books. Then the cluster members would gather to brainstorm all the ways they might talk about their shared texts. On huge sheets of newsprint or on the chalkboard, each group made itself a web of possible angles for discussion. One group, for example, decided they could compare the families in the different books, or discuss the various roles the quilt played in each of the stories, or look at the various techniques used by the illustrators, or discuss differences in authors' styles. "Combining the books into text-sets seems to provide edges of difference that make it easier for youngsters to have good book talks," Jerry Harste said during the visit. And from the easy energy in Gloria's classroom, it seemed his point was well taken.

When teachers in our Writing Project learned about Gloria's success with text-sets, many began incorporating text-sets into their own classrooms. It has been exciting to borrow someone else's idea (the idea of text-sets originates with the thought-collective that surrounds Jerry Harste and Gloria Kauffman) and to invent our own ways of extending that idea. After Judy Davis participated in a text-set discussion at a Writing Project staff development session, she organized a text-set party for Writing Project colleagues. "Come . . . and bring a text-set," her invitation to teachers said. Some of the text-sets that were brought involved several works by a single author. Others had a common topic.

At the text-set party, almost all the text-sets people brought contained a marvelous diversity of genres. A grouping around islands, for example, included Rachel Field's poem "If Once You Have Slept on an Island," an excerpt from Johann Wyss's *Swiss Family Robinson,* and the song "No Man Is an Island," as well as Kathryn Lasky's *My Island Grandma,* Barbara Cooney's *Island Boy,* Robert McCloskey's *Time of Wonder,* and Carol Carrick's *Lost in the Storm.* These were some of the other text-sets that were assembled that day:

OLD PERSON/YOUNG PERSON RELATIONSHIPS
Penny Pollard's Diary by Robin Klein
In *Hey World, Here I Am!* by Jean Little: "Mrs. Bull," "About the People," "Mrs. Thurston"
Wilfred Gordon McDonald Partridge by Mem Fox
In *Children of Christmas* by Cynthia Rylant: "For Being Good"
The Two of Them by Aliki
How Does It Feel to Be Old by Norma Farber
Tomas Esparra's story about his grandfather (see Chapter 6)

A CHARACTER STUDY
Crow Boy by Taro Yashima
Madeline by Ludwig Bemelmans

Miss Rumphius by Barbara Cooney
Miss Maggie by Cynthia Rylant
I Know a Lady by Charlotte Zolotow
Wilfrid Gordon McDonald Partridge by Mem Fox
The Story of Ferdinand by Munro Leaf
Lentel by Robert McCloskey

NUCLEAR WAR
Hiroshima No Pika by Toshi Maruki
Sadako and the Thousand Paper Cranes by Eleanor B. Coerr
The Wall by Eve Bunting
The Butter Battle Book by Dr. Seuss
Faithful Elephants by Yukio Tsuchiya
A letter to a Hewlett-Woodmere child from Yukio Tsuchiya

Irene Tully, a first-grade teacher on Long Island, has added an interesting twist to the idea of text-sets. Long ago, she remembers hearing that an educator named Jane Baskwill sent book-packs home with her rural youngsters. And so Irene now has twenty knapsacks hanging on hooks in her classroom, each knapsack holding a different text-set. She has also added response logs and puppets, small figures, or hats to each knapsack in order to give students ways to respond to the stories by reenacting and inhabiting the world they create. The local community in which Irene teaches has donated funds for many of these text-sets. The last time I saw Irene, she was searching for nonfiction books, poems, and stories about big machinery for a text-set knapsack financed by the local builders' union.

Like the idea of dividing writing into silent writing and study groups, the concept of text-sets suggests broad and encompassing changes in reading-writing workshops. It isn't just one more jazzy new strategy to be wedged in with all the rest. Instead, it's an idea that challenges us to let go of (at least for a time) some of our old methods and to give this new idea the life space it requires. For Project teachers who have been dissatisfied with what happens when reading response groups are comprised of readers who have each read his or her own self-chosen book or when the entire class reads copies of a single text chosen by the teacher, text-sets provide a step halfway between. Of course, teachers needn't choose between text-sets, whole-class books, and individually chosen books. In many classrooms, readers are often involved with several different kinds of reading. They read text-sets and short shared texts—poems or articles that are duplicated for the entire class and discussed under the teacher's direction—in order to develop lenses for looking at books and ways of talking about books. They also read their own independently chosen text. Finally, the teacher reads aloud to them.

The idea of text-sets has brought some of us—teachers, Project staff, local authors, parents, and children—together with great energy. The grandparent study did the same thing with a different configuration of people. We've had equal fun with service projects that turn buildings inside out and help us remember the needs of the world around us. Even the "simple" task of trying to supply our classrooms with books, paper, writing utensils, and publication materials has brought us together. Schools have organized Bottles-for-Books recycling centers, and children have written eloquent appeals to publishers for books. More recently, we've begun to build alliances with art and music teachers, and to see countless possibilities in those collaborations. But for us, the most fruitful projects have been those that fall under the general rubric of "genre studies."

In many of our classrooms, we think of seasons of the year not as autumn, winter, and spring but as poetry, memoir, and nonfiction writing, or as journalism, fiction, and picture books. In many classrooms, teachers and children are apt to alternate between times when everyone pursues the full diversity of genres and times when the entire community in a classroom (and sometimes in a building) gathers to read and write within a particular genre. Genre studies have taken different shapes in different places. In a few classrooms, the seasons of study are long, and a child's entire year is devoted to deep exploration of a genre or two. In still other classrooms, genre studies occur in centers and study groups, so that at any one time, there might be several simultaneous genre studies going on. But most often, genre studies last about two months. The genre studies in kindergarten and first grade include specialized genres; very young children may gather as a class to read and write not only poetry and plays but also alphabet books, wordless books, list books, scratch-and-smell books, songs, recipes, and how-to books. In our upper-grade (2–12) classrooms, we have had special success with genre studies in poetry, nonfiction, memoir, and picture books, and we are deeply involved with the challenge of fiction. Since Georgia Heard's recent book, *For the Good of the Earth and Sun*, beautifully conveys the ways Writing Project classrooms work with poetry, in this book I will share our adventures with three other genres.

I hope that the chapters that follow invite readers to tackle genre studies and similar projects of their own choosing. Picture books, memoir, and nonfiction writing have been rich frontiers for us in part because our Project staff includes writers who live and work within the worlds of these particular genres. Readers will want to use their own resources: for example, a spouse who is a scientist, a longtime dream of becoming a storyteller, or a connection with a local journalist. The important thing is that we use whatever we have on hand in order to stay alive and inquiring.

11

Picture Books and the Magic of "Once upon a Time"

$\mathbf{A}$nita Silvey, editor-in-chief of *The Horn Book*, paused in the middle of her speech on trends in children's literature. "For those of you who have always wanted to write a picture book, there has never been a better time," she said. "Publishers are searching everywhere for new picture book manuscripts" (1988). There was a quickening in the room. It was as if all of us paused, looked up to meet each other's eyes, and smiled shyly, heady with the sense of possibility that danced in the air. It wouldn't have happened had Anita Silvey said, "There has never been a better time for those of you wanting to write short stories . . . or sonnets . . . or science fiction." The quickening in that room came because in every aisle, one of us, and another, and another, had long held the secret dream of someday writing our very own picture book.

We have, after all, been cocreators of picture books all along. Anthony Browne and Bill Martin and Jane Yolen may have written the words, but we've written the music to make those words sing. We've invented our own haunting lyrics to Bill Martin and John Archambault's *The Ghost-Eye Tree*, we've added in the long pauses, lowered our voices in slow quiet sections, quickened them in the places where words tumble quickly, one against the next. Our voices have highlighted the cyclical gathering of phrases in Tony Johnston's *Yonder*, and we've spotted Mike Mulligan's Mary Ann, digging outside Virginia Lee Burton's *The Little House*. We've not only brought picture books to life, we've also moseyed about in the field long enough to know our way around. The classics aren't imposing books we ought to have read. Instead, they're the books of our childhood, the books our grandpa read to us, the books we know by heart. We know what works in picture books because we've lived our lives with them. We know endings that loop back to beginnings, creating stories that circle back like the seasons and the moon and the stars. We know the lasting quality of language like "Little pig, little pig, let me come in." We know refrains and repetitions like "Oooo . . . the halfway tree . . . the Ghost-Eye tree . . . was feared by all . . . the great and small . . ." that gather together all the voices, all the pages into a culminating chorus. When we look out over the field of picture-book writing, we do so with the comfortable feeling of recognizing landmarks and being able to read the lay of the land.

Then, too, we can imagine writing picture books because all the magic wouldn't have to come from our sentences alone. Our words would be made elegant by a backdrop of gorgeous art, smooth paper, and the smells and textures of a book. And our story would be read by co-creators, by teachers who sit in cozy circles with children or by fathers who sprawl on living room floors with kids and blankets and pillows on all sides. And so when Anita Silvey said, "For those of you wanting to write picture books, there has never been a better time," the room was filled with a sense of possibility and hope.

If an invitation to write picture books calls forth a quickening of spirit in us, how much more so does it in young people. This is the genre they've lived with the longest. These are the books they've carried home from libraries and received as birthday presents. These are the books they've owned for years and years, the books they've gathered together around a teacher to hear, the books they've sprawled on the living room floor to read with Dad. The idea of writing picture books fills young people—especially, I suspect, those between the ages of seven and fourteen—with a sense of possibility. And no wonder.

Seven-year-old Sharon Arana had been in a writing workshop during first and second grades, and she'd written often about her weekend activities before she attempted a picture book. A few of her stories had been tacked onto the bulletin board, but from the start, *Where Are the Dinosaurs?* was different. It was to be a book, a real book for the library with a call number and a dedication and, best of all, readers. Sharon worked on this picture book and others during a four-week course of study that culminated in a ceremony during which Sharon and her classmates read their books aloud to smaller children seated on their laps. Figure 11–1 shows the picture book Sharon shared that day.

The Contribution of This Course of Study

It's easy to lose sight of the fact that this picture book was written by a second grader. When I read *Where Are the Dinosaurs?* I think, "I'd love a copy for my library," and this is my response not only to Sharon's book but to many of the picture books our children write. It is for just this reason that young people need to write in this genre: their writing will belong in libraries and alongside their reading, and they will, therefore, learn to make reading-writing connections.

When young people write mostly half-page narratives but read mostly book-length novels, it takes a big act of imagination on everyone's part to regard their writing as similar to their reading. Of course, youngsters are great pretenders. They are happy to pretend they are authors, dressing up their

Figure 11–1   Sharon's Picture Book

"published" writing with the names of make-believe publishing companies, copyright dates, dedications, and "about the author" blurbs. But for a lot of children, the reading-writing connection feels like pretending. All too often, when our children write, "Yesterday I went to the park and played games and then came home," the problem is not that their text is unsuccessful as literature but that they don't seriously intend to write literature. Instead, they view the writing workshop as a time for written-down show-and-tell.

It's easy to see why. In the past, many of us tended to introduce writing by suggesting that children choose something important that has happened to them and then tell it to a neighbor. "Now, write it down," we used to say.

Later, classmates asked questions about the event, and we would encourage the writer to add missing details and tell more about the episode. But where in this introduction of the art of writing did we convey that the challenge of writing is to tell a wonderful story? In what way did we suggest that an author needs to tell the story so well that readers will be moved by it? When a child writes the heading at the top of a sheet of lined yellow paper and then begins a draft, how often does that youngster have an image of good literature in mind? Intention is crucial.

Shelley Harwayne recalls the terrible problems she had in learning to drive. Her instructor tried everything—endless pointers, step-by-step instructions, and criticism—but nothing helped. Then one day he said, "Shelley, you're paying attention to everything around you—the steering wheel, the dashboard, the roads to your right and left—but in order to drive, you need to keep your eyes on where you want to go." Picture books help us keep our eyes on where we want to go. Because of their brevity and apparent simplicity, children can learn, in a picture book course of study, what it means to sit down with paper and pen, intending to render a story, an image, an idea into literature.

Each literary genre teaches lessons that pertain to all genres. Nonfiction writing can teach the power of research and the value of filling a text with surprising and pertinent information. Poetry can teach playfulness, respect for language, and the ways form can support content. Picture books can teach us to listen to the sounds of language, to feel for the structure of stories, to explore the relationships between form and content. But above all, picture books can teach us how to learn from our reading.

Structuring a Reading Workshop to Support the Picture Book Writing Workshop

"It's easy to underread picture books," a teacher, Kathy Harwood, recently observed, and we have found this to be true. It's easy to think we can brush up on the genre by glancing through a stack of picture books from the library. The problem is, first, that picture books are meant to be read aloud, with others, and over and over; and, second, that in order for any text to imprint itself on us so deeply that it affects even our writing, we need to know, internalize, and love that text.

If we're going to read picture books and ask our students to read picture books in such a way that the books actually affect how we write, we need to establish reading environments that encourage us all to talk, reread, memorize, read aloud, and reenact picture books. That is, we need to organize reading workshops that invite us to live our way into these books.

Some readers may question the notion of an entire class of fourth graders—or seventh graders—poring over picture books. "What about the idea that readers should choose their genre as well as their book?" these teachers may ask, or they may say, "Picture books may be well-matched with my children's writing, but they are not well-matched with my children's reading level." We had the same concerns. Over time, we've become comfortable with the trade-offs we make by occasionally replacing independent reading with a genre study, and we've come to think that picture books, like poetry, can offer far richer reading than many people might suspect.

Each teacher will design a reading workshop differently, but probably all of us will include the kinds of reading involvement shown in Figure 11–2.

Many of us will want to begin a picture book course of study by filling the classroom with crates of wonderful picture books. Before long, the room will brim over with exclamations of "Listen to this!" or "This book is great!" For many reasons, I find it important to accompany independent reading with reading aloud. I want to demonstrate that picture books are written to be read aloud and to be heard, and I want children to know they will be expected to read books aloud to each other during the reading workshop. When reviewers at *The Horn Book* and Greenwillow Books gather together to review manuscripts of picture books, they always begin by asking someone to read the text aloud. In a similar way, some teachers introduce picture books by asking each child to bring a cherished picture book to class to read aloud. At P.S. 7, Wiletha Cunningham invited a custodian, the superintendent, a parent, and the art teacher from her district to share one of their own favorite picture books with her children. Only after this opening session did she bring cartons of picture books into the classroom, and even then the children joined her in upgrading and organizing their new library before she gave them the long-anticipated signal, "Go to it!"

It is bound to happen that teachers and children will choose books to read aloud that are already familiar to some class members. "Oh, I know that one," children will say, and this becomes an opportunity to tell children that picture

Figure 11–2   Reading Involvement

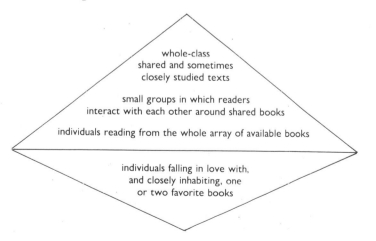

books are written not only to be read aloud but also to be read over and over. Like songs, picture books become more important to us as they become more familiar. The preschooler who comes to know a book so well that she brags, "I can read it with my eyes closed," is revealing something about young children as readers, but she is also revealing something about picture books as a genre. Susan Hirschman, the editor-in-chief at Greenwillow Books and a leading authority on children's literature, says, "In a good picture book, one reads the final page and longs to start over, reading it from the beginning again." It makes sense, then, that in the picture book course of study, some of the books that are read to the whole class will be read aloud several times.

Teachers will also want to use reading aloud as a way of guiding children into territory they would not travel on their own. It might be important, for example, to share wonderful nonfiction books, such as Karla Kuskin's *Jerusalem, Shining Still* and Ronald Himler's *Nettie's Trip South*. It might also be important to read aloud several different versions of the same story, reading, for example, *Cinderella* alongside Charlotte Huck's *Princess Furball*, a wonderful new rendition of this familiar tale, and reading Jon Scieszka's version of *The Three Little Pigs* as told from the point of view of the well-intentioned and innocent wolf alongside more traditional versions of the story.

But the most important thing is that the books we read aloud must be the books we know and love dearly. Listeners will be drawn in by the books themselves but more so by our relationships with the books. No one who has ever heard Don Holdaway's reading of Jill Bennet's *The Teeny-Tiny Woman*, for example, will ever encounter that book without reexperiencing Holdaway's delight over it, and the same is true for Donald Graves's reading of Jane Yolen's *Owl Moon* and Adrian Peetom's reading of Mary Ann Hoberman's *A House Is a House for Me*.

Then, too, especially in the beginning of a course of study on picture books, it will be important to read aloud books that have the power to stop us in our tracks—to slow us down, shake us, move us, and change us as readers. *The Two of Them*, Aliki's poignant story of the relationship between a girl and her aging grandfather, is such a book, as are two books about the agonies of war, Yukio Tsuchiya's *Faithful Elephants* and Toshi Maruki's *Hiroshima No Pika*. Books such as these bring weight and significance to the entire genre and dispel any lingering sense that picture books are "baby books."

The reading that has seemed to help New York City's young writers the most has been the reading done when small groups of children gather to study sets of shared books. We've seen various ways of organizing this work. In some classrooms, children work in small groups with text-sets gathered together by the teacher. This method often begins with youngsters browsing through all the text-sets and then forming groups as each individual selects one set of books to settle into. One group, for example, worked with five books about children growing into an understanding of their parents' careers, another with five books about children who have newly arrived younger brothers and sisters, another with five books about going to bed, another with five stories of a quest for treasure. Most of the themes were broad enough that teachers could include folk and fairy tales, books with sparse, simple texts, books that are in fact poetry, and longer story books. The presence of a shared reading topic—careers, siblings, going to bed, a quest—does not mean that members of a group will write about that topic. Instead, the groups exist because they facilitate talking and allow youngsters to see the different approaches writers can take toward the same subject. Clustering the books around a shared topic seems to highlight for children the range of variations and options available to them. In other classrooms, members of each group don't begin with a text-set but rather with the challenge to gather together such a set. The sets need not have a shared topic; each set may simply be a collection of favorites.

The Story of One Picture Book Reading Workshop

In Eileen Braghieri's fourth-grade classroom at P.S. 148, members of each group searched through public and school libraries and asked everyone they knew for recommendations, negotiated at length with each other, and finally agreed upon a collection of ten "all-star" books. One of the groups in Eileen's class selected

I'm in Charge of Celebrations by Byrd Baylor
Gorilla by Anthony Browne
Night Noises by Mem Fox
In Coal Country by Judith Hendershot
A House Is a House for Me by Mary Ann Hoberman
Make Way for Ducklings by Robert McCloskey
Love You Forever by Robert Munsch
Where the Wild Things Are by Maurice Sendak
Grandma Remembers by Ben Shecter
Owl Moon by Jane Yolen

Once the group members had all read, exclaimed over, and shared their books, Eileen began suggesting ways they might interact with the books. One day early on, she challenged each group to act as a review board and jointly determine which of their books deserved what they called "the Caldecott Award."

Another day, Eileen asked group members to think about the fact that some of the books they were reading are probably not true picture books but are technically called story books. The difference is that in story books, the story can be fully understood through the words alone. In true picture books, a minimum of words is used and the pictures carry much of the meaning. In Maurice Sendak's *Where the Wild Things Are,* for example, after Max cries, "Now let the wild rumpus begin!," there are no words at all but only splendid pictures to convey what happens. "Which of your books are true picture books?" Eileen asked. "What can you learn from studying the artwork in both the picture books and the story books?" It was important for Eileen to raise the issue of artwork early in the course of study, because her students would need to think about illustrations when they wrote their own picture books. Eileen reminded them that they would probably want to find spaces in the text in which the pictures could do the work. They would certainly want to include "dummies" of the art with their manuscripts. Eileen also mentioned in passing that even in story books, the illustrations extend the text in as many ways as possible, sometimes adding hidden messages and meanings.

After hearing all of this, members of each reading group sorted their books into categories and examined them closely to see if they could discover ways in which the artwork added meaning. When Eileen came to talk to each group, the children reported that sometimes the artists and techniques—collage, pen sketches, watercolors, and so forth—seemed well-matched to the story and at other times less so. But above all, children pored over the artwork looking for hidden meanings. With their teacher's help, they saw the journey of the flea and the mouse and the changing colors of the sky in Audrey Wood's *The Napping House*. They noticed that in the final dark scene of *Goodnight Moon* they could see the dim outlines of a mother rabbit fishing in a stream with carrot bait, hoping to catch her child, a picture originally appearing in Margaret Wise Brown's earlier book, *The Runaway Bunny*. They noticed that when Willy, Anthony Browne's hero in *Willy the Wimp*, returns at the end of the book to being the skinny, frail boy he was at the start, his colors are brighter, conveying the impression that perhaps his body-building, confidence-boosting work had done some good.

The reading group members also spent quite a few days studying the structure of their books. Laurie Pessah, the staff developer at P.S. 148, introduced this idea in Eileen's classroom by saying, "Just as beaded necklaces have patterns, perhaps two small red beads followed by a big blue one, then two more small red beads and another big blue one, so, too, books often have patterns." In their reading circles, children could quickly see that some of their ten books were circular, with endings that circled back to the beginning. A few children gathered a collection of circular picture books from across the different reading groups: Donald Hall's *Ox-cart Man*, Cynthia Rylant's *The Relatives Came*, Uri Shulevitz's *The Treasure*, Rosemary Wells's *Max's Chocolate Chicken*, and so forth. These children took this collection of books and looked at them carefully, studying the various ways the authors had constructed a circular structure. They noticed, for example, that whereas in *Ox-cart Man* almost every page in the beginning is brought around full circle by the end, in other books, like *Max's Chocolate Chicken* and *The Relatives Came*, it is only in the very last few pages that a loop appears, taking readers back to the beginning.

Meanwhile, children also found other entirely different structures. Some of their picture books—Cynthia Rylant's *When I Was Young in the Mountains* and Charlotte Zolotow's *I Like to Be Little*, for example—are composed of a series of snapshots. Again, one group took this category of books and studied it to see whether they could identify the particular logic behind the way the snapshots were sequenced in each book.

Still other books have what Laurie Pessah called a cumulative structure, each page adding something more (often quite literally) to a growing collection of items. The group that took these books—Margaret Wise Brown's *Goodnight Moon*, Eric Carle's *The Very Hungry Caterpillar*, Barbara Emberley's *Drummer Hoff*, and Audrey Wood's *The Napping House*—tried to find a unifying link in each. Usually, in books of this kind, a common element, like the string that turns beads into a necklace, turns a list into a story: without the caterpillar, which devours everything in sight, readers would find *The Very Hungry Caterpillar* rather like reading the telephone book (Shulevitz 1985, 41).

Some books contain two contrasting sections. Judy Blume's *The Pain and the Great One* begins with a sister complaining because her brother is a pain; then the point of view switches, and the brother complains that his sister thinks she is such a "Great One." Similarly, Marlene Shyer's *Here I Am, an Only Child* begins with all the bad things about being an only child and ends with all the good things.

Finally, the children found that many books have a typical story structure. Fairy tales always fit into this category, and so do many story books. These books tend to open with a description of a situation; then something happens to change that situation, a conflict is introduced, and eventually it is resolved. *The Gingerbread Boy*, for example, opens with a description of a situation: a childless old man and woman make a gingerbread cookie. The conflict is introduced when the cookie comes alive and runs away from them and from everyone else. Eventually, a fox resolves the problem by eating the cookie, and the tale ends with the fox licking his chops, and the old couple, the horse, the cow, the threshers, and the mowers all returning home.

It was Martha Horn, a former member of the Project staff, who first helped us think about the architecture of picture books. We were filled with excitement over this new lens for looking at these well-loved books. We would read them aloud at dinner parties and meetings and decide which category suited a particular title. When the children learned about this structural way of looking at books, they were equally intrigued. Now they had something to do with the books other than just laughing and sighing over them. Categories made the field seem more manageable. Children could slot some books into one category, others into another. When we learn that trees can be sorted into sugar maples, oaks, elms, and the like, we often become more observant of trees in general because we have something to notice. The same thing happened when the children began realizing that picture books could be categorized according to shape. Only later, when all of us were deeply involved in writing picture books, did we recognize that although labels helped us to see some things, they also limited our perception. This problem became clear when children in the writing workshop began coming to us saying things like, "I'm not sure if I should write this book so it's all the good, then all the bad things." When we responded, "What's your topic?" they'd say, "I don't know." We realized then that, although categories can be helpful, the really crucial thing for a writer to consider is the match between form and content. Children need to know this. Cynthia Rylant's *This Year's Garden*, for example, has a circular shape because the circular pattern of the seasons is what her book is all about. If we give too much attention to labeling picture books according to form, we run the risk of conveying to children the mistaken idea that authors merely pour their content into preset, easily defined formats (the five-paragraph essay, the "research paper," the circular picture book).

The reading workshop continued, in any case, with Eileen and Laurie Pessah suggesting ways in which readers might interact with their picture books, and with the groups negotiating exactly how they would proceed with the challenges set before them. Over time, the composition of Eileen's reading workshop changed. Because she believes that reading-writing connections happen when a text matters to a reader so much that it even affects that person's writing, one of Eileen's goals for the reading-writing workshop was for each of her students to fall in love with a single book. In the adult reading-writing group that meets for two hours every Friday morning at P.S. 148, Eileen learned from the inside that when we fall in love with a book, it goes a long way toward guaranteeing that the book will affect us deeply enough to make a difference in our writing. The books we love become such a part of us that the lilt of their language and the pacing of their plots are in our minds as we write. "How do you learn to write?" Hemingway asked, and then answered his own question: "Read *Anna Karenina*, read *Anna Karenina*, read *Anna Karenina*."

At P.S. 148, Eileen and Laurie knew from the start that at some point the reading groups would dissolve and each child would begin living his or her way into a particular book. Once a child found a book he or she loved, that child read the book aloud over and over to different audiences. The child took the book home and shared it with parents. The child read it to brothers and sisters and cousins and neighbors and grandparents and friends. The child read the book to several senior citizens at a home for the aged and then to first graders, sometimes individually, one first grader after another, and sometimes in small groups. "If a reader cares enough for a poem," John Ciardi once said, "he would never have to study it. He would live his way into it." In Eileen's classroom, Ciardi's words proved true. Eventually children began anticipating responses to their books and became cocreators, heightening the cyclical gathering of phrases, pointing out the hidden messages in the artwork, varying their pace as they read. Finally, some of Eileen's youngsters formed drama teams and puppeteer guilds, and, with sock puppets and paper bag people and choral reading groups, they brought their stories to life in classrooms up and down the halls of P.S. 148. But most of all, children kept their chosen book(s) out on the desk as they wrote.

Study Groups That Involve Young Writers in the Essential Challenges of Picture Books

For the four upper-grade teachers at P.S. 148 who were working together on the six-week-long picture book course of study, this was their first foray into the idea of silent writing time and study groups. They'd seen the structure operating in Antoinette Ciano's classroom and had heard from her and from Shelley, me, and Laurie Pessah about the things we had learned from the earliest drafts of this teaching idea. But they still had lots of questions and felt lots of trepidation, and they were glad for each other's support.

When the four teachers first met with Laurie Pessah and me to plan the study groups, their first questions were wise ones: "Where are our kids as writers these days?" "What are the biggest issues for them now?" In talking, the teachers realized that even as they started the picture book course of study, their children's needs were already widely divergent. Because this genre study was growing out of ongoing writing workshops, some of the writers in their classrooms had already begun moving, quite independently, from their notebooks into drafts of picture books. Other children would enter the picture book units with notebooks that contained rich repositories of material for picture books. Still others needed more time for generating notebook entries that might eventually contain the seeds of a picture book.

The teachers decided that they would work together to plan possible starting points for study groups and that they would try to think of several study groups for each stage of progress they had identified. As the teachers envisioned it, in each classroom during the half hour a day set aside for study groups, each child would hang his or her name tag on a choice board that listed optional activities. Since there would only be a certain number of hooks under each study group, the chart itself would help direct the flow of children and curtail the size of each group.

When Children Need to Generate Notebook Entries

For children who needed to generate more notebook entries, the teachers devised a number of activities meant to trigger associations and memories. In one study group, each child read an especially loved picture book aloud to the other members of the study group. Then, fast and furiously, they all wrote and wrote and wrote notebook entries that came from their listening. Later, the members of this study group would go to the library together and gather a list of the topics addressed in picture books, and again, they would let those topics evoke in them their own list of possible topics. In the same way, they also read picture books written by classmates and by other young writers from around New York City for inspiration.

Other children who needed more time for generating notebook entries gathered in a different study group. Their first task was to learn about ways authors find "seed ideas" for stories and explore whether the same strategies might help them find their own seed ideas. These children were given pamphlets and blurbs about authors and names of people who were knowledgeable about authors to interview. They quickly learned, for example, that the topic for Anthony Browne's *Gorilla* came from his longtime passion for gorillas. Then they wrote in their notebooks and talked with each other about their own longtime passions and asked each other whether seeds for picture books might be hidden in these. Might Benny write a story about racing cars? Could Collette's picture book grow out of the sewing projects she does with her grandmother? These youngsters also learned that *Make Way for Ducklings* emerged from a scene Robert McCloskey saw each morning on his way to work, and again they asked, "What scenes do I see often, and what possible texts might those scenes contain?" Could Sonya write about the peaceful scene of her cats, curled together on her bed? This same study group also learned that Byrd Baylor's writing comes from collections she keeps, that Dr. Seuss's *Horton Hatches the Egg* began as a doodle, and that the Babar books grew out of bedtime stories the de Brunhoffs told their two small boys. Each of these anecdotes led the children into new ways of generating notebook entries.

In both study groups, children spent most of their time writing, sharing, and celebrating their notebooks. They found treasures in the notebook entries they were generating together, but they also attended to the notebook entries they'd gathered throughout the year. For members of both groups, the presence of the study groups meant that someone was keeping tabs on what they did and did not write in their notebooks, and this attentiveness fostered a new level of involvement.

When Children Begin Developing Seed Ideas for Picture Books

Students with brimming notebooks needed to find and develop seed ideas for picture books. In order to design study groups to help with this, the teachers and I felt we needed to re-create for ourselves the *process* of writing a picture book. We needed to think together about how this kind of literature comes to life. If picture books start with a well-crafted lead sentence, it's still not at all clear that the process of writing picture books should begin by fiddling with optional lead sentences. What then are the fundamental dynamics behind writing picture books? Do these texts usually ride on images and scenes . . . or what? If there are correct answers, we were not sure what they are, and we were especially unclear about instances in which the artwork leads the way in picture books. But despite these uncertainties and questions, we were quite sure that the text of picture books is carried to a major degree by the melody and rhythm of the words.

Cynthia Rylant describes how she writes picture books by saying, "I'm listening in my head to the tune, to the rhythm, to the poetry. Picture books should sing" (Silvey 1987, 702). Uri Shulevitz says, "A picture book is like a musical score for reading aloud to a child who doesn't know how to read yet. The printed words in a picture book are intended not only to be seen and read, but to be spoken aloud as well" (Silvey 1985, 58). Jane Yolen advises writers of picture books, "Read each of your sentences aloud as you write."

The primacy of language in picture books is obvious to any parent. Even when my sons were too young to understand the words in their books, they remembered them. When Miles reenacts *Jack and the Beanstalk*, his favorite part is when the giant strides into the kitchen bellowing,

> Fee, fi, fo, fum,
> I smell the blood of an Englishman.
> Be he alive or be he dead
> I'll grind his bones to make my bread.

And the line Miles quotes most frequently from *The Three Little Pigs* is the little pig's response to the wolf, "Not by the hair of my chinny-chin-chin." In Jane Yolen's *Owl Moon*, Miles especially loves "For one minute, three minutes, a hundred minutes, we stared at each other."

It's one thing to appreciate the language in finished picture books, and it's another thing to produce such language yourself. To help youngsters do the latter, the four classrooms at P.S. 148 each instituted an enormously successful storytelling study group. After children hang their name tags on the hooks for this group, they are given an activity card stating, up front, that their beloved author, Robert Munsch, tells a story hundreds of times before he writes it. Students are then urged to find something they've written in their notebooks or to choose an idea for a picture book that is still in their minds, and, without any further preparation, to take a turn at storytelling. The storytellers are given a sense of occasion in that they are asked either to sit on top of a desk or in a chair while the rest of their group sits on the floor at their feet. "Wait until everyone is listening!" youngsters say to each other. This admonition comes in part because when a teacher works with this group, she gives the children lessons in storytelling. Children have learned the importance of having their audience as close as possible in an effort to re-create the around-the-fire, in the cave feeling. They know that the Australian storyteller and author Mem Fox advises storytellers to begin telling a story by sweeping the group with their eyes as if to say to each person, "Welcome," and that she thinks it is vitally important for storytellers to see scenes in their mind's eye. "If you don't see the story in pictures, how can your lips paint a picture for the audience?" she asks (1988b). Mem's advice is very helpful for people who are retelling a familiar story, but it is essential for people who are telling stories as a way of drafting and redrafting their own story. The children at P.S. 148 also learned that it is the quality of language that holds people's attention in a story. Mem Fox urges storytellers to let their voices go fast and slow, loud and soft, high and low, and to pause. "I drag the last line out," she says. "I may end the story with, 'I lay down beside him and we—both—went—to—sleep.' The contentment of that last line makes the magic of the story."

In her study group, Esther Portela volunteered to go first. She started hesitantly, with long pauses, as if she were planning each word before she said it. Before long, however, her voice was clearly leading the way, showing her the possibilities for her story. This is what Esther said that day:

Once it was the day I had to come [to New York City] and I was looking all around at all the animals in Spain, and I saw this leaf and knew

I wouldn't see it any more once I left Spain. I picked it up and thought, "I hope I can see the country when I'm in America."

I left that little leaf alone on a rock there, and I knew if I went back to Spain, I would find it.

When I came to America, to New York City, I opened the window, and there were leaves there. I carefully picked one up and brought it into the apartment and laid it on a tissue. My mother said, "Why do you have those leaves in here? They're messing up the house. Throw them out." I shook my head.

"I can't throw them away. They make me think of Spain."

When I returned to Spain, the leaf was still there, dry. And I was happy because instead of saying goodbye to the animals, I was saying hello.

Esther's success with storytelling was instantaneous and almost miraculous. When called upon to create a unified story, she had drawn upon several bits from her notebook, embellishing them and linking them together into a tightly woven, well-paced narrative.

Ben didn't have Esther's instinct for storytelling. When he climbed onto the table and began to talk, there wasn't the same lilt of a story in his voice. Instead, he talked as if he were participating in an awkward conversation with an adult. "See, I like baseball cards. Sometimes I get a whole lot from a friend." At this point, I touched Ben's arm and quietly interjected, "Ben, can I ask you a favor? Would you start your story, 'There was once a boy who liked baseball cards.' " Ben backed up and began again. This time, he assumed the stance of a storyteller, and his words gathered momentum.

There was once a boy who liked baseball cards. He bought a whole mess of them, two hundred and fifty for one dollar, from his friend. He bought four packs, five packs, six packs, until he was building a baseball card empire. Then, one day, he took his baseball cards and started slinging them across the room into the garbage can. His mom came into the room and handed him a book, Barron's *SSAT Exams*. "Write down the sentences," she said.

When Ben, Esther, and the others finished storytelling, they weren't urged to put the stories they had told into writing. The intention had not necessarily been for them to produce an oral draft, but rather for them to see how a sense of occasion and audience can invigorate whatever they choose to write.

In another study group designed for children with rich, well-filled notebooks, youngsters divided themselves into pairs, and one member of each pair read his or her notebook aloud while the other listened. From James Merrill, they had learned that sometimes they could find just an ordinary passage in their notebook that nevertheless had the potential to become much more.

"The words that come first," Merrill says, "are anybody's. . . . You have to make them your own" (quoted in Heard 1989, 42). Together, the children looked for places with potential. They ask, "Where are the places in which I've written something that is really very personal and important, even though it may not seem so to anyone else?" Once the children located places of potential in their notebooks, they talked about them with each other, articulating what they thought and felt and imagined that connected to the entry. In her study group, Annette decided she had more to say about horses than this entry reveals:

> My favorite horses are Apple Jack, Truman, Mo, and Junior. They are brown with a black mane. Horses are very useful animals. They help farmers pull things, carry people and logs, and help people get faster to where they are going. The hooves of the horse need to be sanded so they don't get ruined.

After talking about the story that underlies that entry, Annette wrote a second entry, this one stretching over several pages. Here is an excerpt:

> I used to know these two horses named Apple Jack and George. They were in the same age group and they were both sold to the Gold Coast. One time Apple Jack had a heart attack doing a jump. He collapsed. Gold Coast retired him, and sold him to a place where old horses stay. George got colic over the summer and the veterinarian said, "There's nothing we can do except put him to sleep" . . . so they put him to sleep.
> I think a lot about horses. There are many kinds of horses, like thoroughbreds. This breed was developed especially for racing. American Quarterhorses star at rodeos, and they are the tallest horses in the world. . . .
> When I'm near horses, I feel so good that I wish I owned one . . .

When Annette's teacher saw the way she had taken a short, generic entry written in anybody's words and turned it into such a long, vigorous, and personal entry, she included a copy of what Annette had done with the laminated card introducing future members of this study group to possible ways they might proceed.

While Annette developed the seed idea for her picture book by making her topic more specific and more personal, some children found a story kernel they felt could be expanded, and their stories grew from that kernel. Etasha Gonzalez read a few lines from her notebook over and over to herself, almost as if they were the words of a song, and then let those words lead her further. Figure 11–3 is her picture book.

Picture Books and the Magic of "Once upon a Time"

Figure 11–3   Etasha's Picture Book

Figure 11–3 Continued

In designing yet another study group for children with rich notebooks, the teachers wanted to help youngsters think about the shape of a picture book story. If language is one of the two essential elements in a picture book, form is probably the other. In picture books, as in poetry, both language and form are bottom-line ingredients. "There has to be a weave and a cross-weave in order to make cloth," poet Stanley Kunitz says (quoted in Heard 1989, 75). When the teachers first designed activities for this group, one activity referred children back to the work they had done in their reading groups. "As you expand your writing from a seed idea toward a whole book, how do you think you will shape your story? Will it be circular, cumulative, a series of snapshots . . . or what?" But as I mentioned earlier, odd things happened. Children began assigning themselves forms and then writing in an almost fill-in-the-blank fashion. This is not a productive way to go about writing. Had Annette, the child who wrote about horses, tried to produce a story structured around all the good things and then all the bad things about horses, she would probably never have seen the stories that emerged in her long entry. Once she has written the entry, however, it would probably help her to look back and ask "How is this entry shaped?" and to notice the section on retiring horses, the one on kinds of horses, and the one on her love of horses. A knowledge of story structure might help Annette realize that if she decides to craft a piece of literature based on her horse entry, she has more options than simply dividing the entry into three chapters or three stories. If Annette has a feel for story structure, her teacher might help her realize that she could combine two of her sections in an interesting way. She could, for example, insert her feelings about loving horses into the story about the retired horses she knows. She could write about retirement in general, and the mixed feelings people and horses experience when this time comes. She could also create a character, perhaps a young girl like herself, who is filled with questions about horses that are answered as the book progresses.

In thinking now about what the writers at P.S. 148 did with structure and what we've learned about inviting youngsters to build their seed ideas into well-shaped texts, I would probably want to put my faith in developing and tapping into writers' intuitive feel for a well-structured story. Teachers and children both tend to feel threatened by considerations of form, and yet all of us have an intuitive sense of form and story structure. When my son Miles was two, he used to climb onto my lap and say, "Tell me a story," and then he would start the story off for me by saying, with just the proper lilt, "Once there was. . . . " After just the right interval, in which I would introduce the characters, Miles would interject, "And then what happened?" Even in his make-believe play, Miles demonstrated a knowledge of story structure. He would build a fire department, decide which chairs would be the buildings, set his fire trucks in place, and then, when the situation was established, he would make something happen to change things by setting off the pretend fire alarm. One truck, then another and another and another would rush to the scene of the blaze, squirt the water, and save the people. Then, as Miles drove the last truck back to the garage, he would say, "That's all. The fire is over. The dark sky's coming. Good night fire trucks. Good night."

Although we, as teachers, sometimes feel unsure of ourselves when talk turns to the structure of texts, like Miles, we have a finely developed intuition for form. At a recent workshop on picture books, participating teachers cut and folded paper to make blank books for themselves and then had about ten minutes to produce an instant draft of a picture book. All the books we wrote that day were rough and incomplete. Yet most of them, like Mimi Aronson's book, *Lost*, sounded like literature and had the shape of literature.

Lost

Once upon a time
There was a little boy playing . . .
No one noticed him wandering off.
His mother looked and looked
and she looked
and she looked.
Frantic now, she asked for help.
Everyone looked
and looked
and looked.
Is the boy lost? Taken?
The mother retraced her steps
and looked
and looked.
Then, behind a rubber raft, she saw a foot . . .

> Looking up at her, the little boy said,
> "Did I win, Mom? Did I win at Hide and Go Seek?"

How did Mimi and the rest of us develop such a feel for form? How can we help students develop and use their instincts for shaping a text?

Instruction in circular or cumulative texts alone will not help youngsters look through their lives and find bits that have the shape and weight and feel of a picture book. But it probably would be helpful for members of a study group to spend time reading and rereading, and maybe even analyzing, the structures of some of the simplest and most classic picture books of all. *Goodnight Moon* by Margaret Wise Brown is one example. *The Carrot Seed* and *The Happy Day* by Ruth Krauss are others. A more recent example is *Max's Chocolate Chicken* by Rosemary Wells. Each of these books has been heralded as one of the finest picture books of all, yet each of them has only fifty or so words. Because they've been pared down to just the essentials, the structure of each is very clear. In *Goodnight Moon,* for example, everything introduced in the first half of the book reappears in the closing goodnights. Similarly, *The Happy Day* has no loose ends. The book opens with a catalog of all the animals asleep in the winter, and then each of the animals sniffs spring and joins the circle of celebration around a single flower in the snow (Shulevitz 1985, 55).

Then, too, we can encourage young writers to look for and share those bits of their lives that have the feel of picture book stories. Shelley Harwayne recently came into the Project office saying, "I have an idea for a picture book." Her husband, Neil, in his fastidiousness about finances, has filed every receipt from twenty-two years of marriage in oak files in their attic. Now a squirrel seems to have made its way into their attic. Walking across the lawn that morning, Neil stooped to pick a bit of paper off the grass and found that it was a slightly chewed receipt dated 1968 for $13.86 for books. "That happens a lot now," Shelley said. "My husband is being outwitted by a squirrel."

Just as the journalist lives with an eye for fast-breaking news, so, too, the picture book writer stands back from the war of wits between Neil and the squirrel and says, "That would make a good story." Stories are everywhere: in childhood memories, in the tales people tell us, in our areas of expertise, in our imaginations. The challenge is to find an idea that has a shape, that has a beginning and a middle and an end, that adds up.

It maybe hard at first for youngsters to identify and select the bits of their lives that, when set alongside each other or re-created, will work as a story. It may be easier to *recognize* such moments than to create them. After the members of this study group read and talk about the architecture of some very simple, classic texts, it might be helpful if they are then invited to look at a familiar novel or memoir like Laura Ingalls Wilder's *Little House on the Prairie,* Patricia MacLachlan's *Sarah, Plain and Tall*, or Jean Fritz's *Homesick,* and (for fun) to select and perhaps combine moments to create possible picture book texts. In each of these books, readers could cup their hands around countless such moments. Similarly, the writers could all reread someone else's notebook, cupping their hands around the bits that might have the weight and shape to become picture book texts.

But perhaps the most important thing children can do is to study the structures that emerge in their own picture books. Writing well has everything to do with being able to read one's own work with an eye toward the unmet possibilities that are there. In almost any draft of a picture book, an embryonic structure will be evident to those who have the eyes to see. If children can see these structures in their own and one another's texts, they then can write their way into them. Sometimes during study-group time children would rewrite their entries and drafts to highlight and build on a structure that was already there. More often, they would tell their stories to each other over and over in different ways, knowing that later in the day there would be time for silent writing. Then they would bring what they had written to the study group the next day.

All of these instructions for a study group might sound too complicated to fit onto a task card. Some teachers use these cards only to *remind* group members of activities the entire class learns about together. In these classrooms, teachers give all the children an overview of every group when they introduce the chart that lists optional activities.

When Children Are Drafting and Revising Picture Books

Let us look finally at the study groups that pertain to children who are well embarked on drafts of picture books. Once children are working on emerging drafts, there are endless ways in which they can go about extending or critiquing and revising them. Mostly, of course, these children need to write, but all of these writing workshop classes gave children about forty minutes for silent writing before or after their study groups. In study groups, then, children who are writing leads or endings could benefit from looking at, ranking, and categorizing the lead sentences or endings in the books they are studying in their reading groups. They could look again at the ways illustrations carry information and then consider whether information is now carried by their texts that might better be conveyed through their artwork. They could examine the ways the books they read have used scenes, and they could consider whether scenes need to be more important in some parts or in all of their writing.

Rather than forming groups around specific endeavors such as these, the teachers at P.S. 148 wanted to suggest activities that were broad and flexible enough to allow writers to deal with whatever concerns were important to them at that moment in their writing. For this reason, one of the study groups was organized like a typical writing response group. Each day, two writers received help. At the beginning of the response group, the members would determine which of them would receive help first, and then that writer would say what he or she had been doing and thinking and what kinds of help he or she wanted. The listeners responded to the rough drafts in the ways I describe in *The Art of Teaching Writing*.

The teachers also wanted to highlight the reading-writing connections that are such an integral part of this course of study. For this reason, they organized another study group that was also structured like a writing response group, only in this group, writers came not only with drafts in progress, but also with picture books from which they wanted to learn. Conversations often moved between writing and reading. With help from the teacher, children learned to follow questions such as, "What problems are you having with your writing?" with questions such as, "How do you think the author you're reading would do that?" and "Do you think you could give that a try?" They have also asked, "Have you seen other authors who do it differently?" and "What do you think you should do next?"

It was no surprise that Jane brought *The Relatives Came* with her to the study group. Jane's love of Cynthia Rylant had clearly been part of her motivation for writing her own book filled with *When I Was Young in the Mountains*-like vignettes about when her relatives came to visit. Everyone in the group liked Jane's original draft, but when they asked her, "How would Cynthia Rylant improve on this?" Jane found herself answering that her book didn't have a feeling, a mood, like Rylant's did. Jane wasn't sure what to do about this problem, but in a later conference with her teacher, she recognized that if she wanted to convey a clear mood to her readers she needed to establish one overarching mood in her mind's eye. Because she'd been thinking of a lot of different visits from her relatives, some in the summer and some in the winter, the mood of the book wasn't any clearer to her than to her reader. In Jane's next draft of her picture book, every vignette came from summertime visits:

> I remember summers when our cousins came with laughter in their eyes and with their California wrinkled clothes.
> I remember sitting together in a circle talking and the smell of my mom's cooking. She made huge salads of fresh vegetables and hamburgers and hot dogs and jello for dessert because ice cream would have melted.
> I remember those summer nights when my cousins and I would play outside late. The mosquitos bit us and the ice cream man would come.

In still other groups, writers followed up on their concern with language and form. They listened to language by reading their drafts aloud as if they were the most wonderful literature in the world. This didn't happen without some cajoling. When Tomas Esparra first read his draft aloud to a study group, he read it without much energy or intonation. His teacher, who was in the group at the time, interrupted to say, "Tomas, this is literature." She suggested he go out into the hall to practice reading it well so that he could give his text the reading it deserved. When Tomas returned and read the draft aloud to group members, he'd improved not only the expression in his voice but also the language in his draft. Notice the revisions on the page shown in Figure 11–4.

Figure 11–4   Tomas's Piece

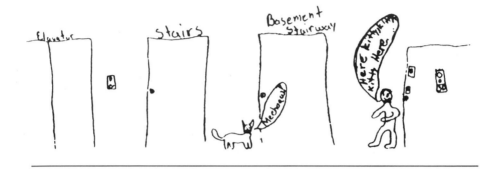

In this same study group, children read their drafts aloud into a micro-phone in the empty auditorium as a way of attending to their language. The idea for this had come from Cynthia Rylant, who once said, "I've always said to myself, 'If I can't read my picture book text by myself to an auditorium full of people, and live by it, then I don't have a good text'" (1987, 702).

After working on language for a while, Laurie Pessah and I turned the group's attention to the form of their drafts. The children read their drafts to friends and asked them to talk about the structures they noticed in the drafts. Because the children had already been looking at structure in published picture books, they were able to do this to some degree with each other's drafts. Still, it was a challenge, and the main benefit was simply the fact that the writer and at least one reader gave careful attention to the organization of the writer's work. Often, we found that children were not able to see the loose ends and detours in each other's writing or to envision structures that could bring shape to texts. Time and time again Laurie and I found that although structures seemed to be evident in writers' first drafts, as children elaborated on their stories, adding more details and trying to write scenes, they lost the tongue-and-groove tightness of those early drafts. Revision of picture-book drafts must involve subtraction. This is true as well in poetry, and the similar-ities between the two genres are worth noticing. Whereas the novelist enlarges and expands on experience, both the poet and the picture book writer chip away at it as if they were sculptors working at blocks of marble, trying to clear away everything extraneous in order to expose the most significant issues, emotions, and events. Author Jean Little says, "For me, the hardest thing about writing a picture book is that it keeps trying to become a novel." She adds, "It helps if I can find an ending. You need the right ending in a picture book, and you need to reach it right away."

The other lesson we learned about form was that when children write with a sense of balance and wholeness, it is usually a result not of extensive revision but of having made several different attempts at a topic. Often, the best way to improve the form of a story is simply for a youngster to read his or her draft aloud, listening especially for the section that sings, and then to write the story fresh, beginning with, or at least building upon, that section and using as few words as possible. Both of the following picture book texts emerged in such a fashion. They do not represent the first writing the child ever produced on the topic, but they did emerge in one swoop after several other less successful drafts had been discarded.

Too Many Books
by Gretchen

Joi has too many books. But she can't get rid of them because she loves them and she reads them over and over again.

On her birthday she gets books, on Christmas she gets books, she gets books from everybody for everything.

Joi has books everywhere; on the coffee table, on the television. She even has books on the refrigerator.

Every week she returns books to the library and takes more out.

Everybody looks at her funny because she takes so many.

And it was true she did have a lot, so she decided to give some away.

She gave one to a little boy on his way to school. She gave some to a bunch of kids at the library. She left some in the dentist's office . . .

And soon the whole town was reading books!

But she didn't notice. She just sat in the library reading a book.

Gretchen's story has a satisfying ending, and this is crucial in a picture book, although a satisfying ending is not necessarily a happy one. In this story, ten-year-old Warnell Holmes doesn't resolve his problem, yet he does bring the story to completion. When readers reach the final line, they know it has a sense of finality. Its ending functions as an "Amen."

Me and Grandma
by Warnell Holmes

Sometimes when I go to visit my grandma, she doesn't have time for me. I get really angry when she comes home from the park and plays with my sister. Then I feel left out.

But when we are alone, we go out to the back yard, and she makes me sweaters and reads me books.

When she reads books to me, I feel so close to her, and when we go to sleep she tucks me into bed.

I give her a big kiss and a huge hug, and we all say good night.

Then morning comes, and she fixes me a big breakfast before she goes to work.

I feel angry because I can't have those last minutes with her, to go to the back yard and hug and kiss her just one more time.

So I sit on the porch waiting for my mother, with my bags packed, ready to travel back home.

I wish she could have been there when I left.

Finding a Satisfying Ending for the Story and for the Course of Study

Although Warnell's story has already achieved a level of completeness, one of the ways he might grow as a writer is to decide that, rather than tackle a whole new topic in his next picture book, he will linger with the images and themes of this story for a while and see if there are other moments or images or memories or dreams that somehow relate to this book. In the upcoming chapter on memoir, Judy Davis could have ended her story with the scene in which she drops the birthday cake and runs into the woods to escape her father and his certain wrath. Instead, she ends it "and now I hear myself telling my daughter that she's not doing well enough . . . and I wonder if I hear my father." Esther Portela could have ended her storytelling with the episode of putting a leaf on the rock in Spain and thinking, "I'll be back, someday, and I'll see this again." Instead, she jumps ahead to a rainy day in New York City when she brings a leaf in from the windowsill and it, too, becomes a monument to her memories of Spain. Both of these writers juxtapose a seemingly different and separate image with the main narrative of the story to add another layer of meaning.

This is one—and only one—way to end a story. It is, in some ways, what Mark Graña has done in his picture book, "The Best Rock in the World." This story was initially a straightforward narrative about finding a pretty rock, but when Mark reread the first draft, he asked himself, "Why did the rock matter so much to me?" Then he added the references to his dog and in this way made his story add up to something far bigger than it had initially.

The Best Rock in the World
by Mark Graña

There was a boy who loved collecting rocks from a riverbank because they looked beautiful and because his dog was killed by one.

One day he went to the riverbank to get some rocks for memory. He rolled up his sleeves and dunked his arm into the water. SPLASH!

When he took his hand out there were five rocks in his hand, but there was one that was black, white, and pink.

It was so pretty he took it home. When he got home, he showed it to his mother. She said, "Put it away."

He thought, Why? This is the most beautiful rock in the world! But why bother explaining, again thinking about his dog who was killed.

His mother called, "Dinnertime." The boy took the rock and slipped it into his sock.

"Hurry up," his mother called.

"I'm coming, I'm coming," he called.

After dinner he took a hammer and cracked the rock open. It looked like vanilla and chocolate swirls. That night, before he went to sleep, he thought about looking for more rocks tomorrow.

And he's kept that rock forever for its beauty, and for the memory of his dog.

Mark's earlier draft about a rock had a beginning, a middle, and an end. He could have declared it done and put it away. But time and again we find that when writers take the opportunity to circle around a subject, to linger with a moment, to let one scene connect with another . . . all of a sudden a new insight or memory emerges and brings a new dimension to the initial text. We saw this when Ilana Goldberg realized that her sadness over letting her hamster go, cold and alone in a February park, had everything to do with the fact that since her grandmother died, she, too, felt cold and alone. We saw this when Isoke Nia realized at the Open House that the memory of her mother's hands linked with other very different memories of her mother's hands as she kneaded white, shapeless dough.

Of course, circling back and seeing a subject in a new light is important in written texts, but it is also important in life. It's not only in our writing but also in our living that we need to linger for a moment, to let one scene, one lesson, one adventure connect with another.

How crucial it is that children reassemble in their reading groups, only this time, to read and share and learn from the work of their own hands. They can read their own books aloud to each other and hear the memories and associations and feelings these stories evoke. They can read their own books, and the books of their classmates, to brothers and sisters and cousins and neighbors and grandparents and friends. They can read their book to first graders, and form puppeteer guilds and choral reading groups to make their books come alive. We learn to write not only by reading, rereading, and inhabiting *Anna Karenina*, but by doing the same with our own writing.

It is fitting, therefore, that this chapter ends where it begins, with the reading of wonderful picture books. *Retta and Me* and *The Great Antique Room* were both written by fifth graders.

Retta and Me
By Danisa Colic

Retta and me are best friends. I like green lollipops, she likes pink. My hair is brown and straight, hers is blond and curly. I like teddy bears, she likes baby dolls. Retta and me are different but we're still best friends.

Sometimes when Retta and me come home from the first grade, we go to the newspaper stand and get lollipops. Then she comes to my house and we eat graham crackers and apple juice. It's our favorite thing to eat.

Together.

Every Friday, Retta and me go to the park with our mommies. Then we run down the big hill and spread our arms out. Like the sparrows that fly through my back yard.

Sometimes I go to Retta's house and then we play dress-up in the attic. There are lots of old clothes up there. Hats with feathers, smooth long scarves, long gloves made of beads, and lots of necklaces. We look like grownups in the clothes. Then we pretend we're having a tea party and have graham crackers and apple juice.

But now Retta always gets tired when we run on the hill. She always is too tired to come to my house. She says graham crackers make her stomach feel icky.

Then one day my mommy told me that Retta was sick. She was in the hospital. Mommy said she had a disease. I decided I wanted to visit her.

So Mommy took me to visit Retta. I took her my most favorite teddy bear. But when I got there the doctor didn't want to let me go into her room. I thought that was mean. He said I was too little; but really I'm pretty big. He did let me look through a huge window into her room though.

Then I looked through the window. All I saw was a little cot and a fluffy white pillow with a skinny little girl who was as white as this paper laying on it. She had her blond hair cut very very short and she had a needle in her arm and a tube in her mouth.

"That's not Retta," I said.

"Yes, that is Retta," the doctor said.

Then I cried and cried into my mommy's lap.

One day Retta came back to her house. She was still skinny and still had short hair. She also had a wheelchair 'cause she couldn't walk. She was too weak.

On Friday Retta's mommy let me push her wheelchair up the big hill all by myself, with nobody around. When I pushed Retta to the very tip-top of the hill I looked at her for a long time. Then I couldn't see Retta clearly 'cause I had some tears in my eyes.

I started to cry. Retta did too. Then we gave each other a big hug.

Maybe someday Retta will get better and we can both run up the big hill. But if she doesn't, I'll always be happy to push her wheelchair.

The Great Antique Room
By Sharif Abou-Taleb

Dedicated to my mother and her dream.

Once upon a time there was a sparkling, eye-catching living room filled with priceless antiques.

It belonged to a sparkling family of three. One of them was a young boy who loved the antique room. But his parents wouldn't let him in because they were afraid he would break something.

And to make matters worse, it was also his living and dining room. He had to eat in the kitchen and he hated it, for although the kitchen was beautiful, it was the dining room that intrigued him.

One day his mother made the living room area into a magnificent antique store.

He got more and more excited about the antique store because he thought for sure he would be able to go in since it was now a store. But instead, the rules got much stricter.

So for many years he stayed away. He got older and older and always stayed away.

Then one momentous day he was accepted into the fifth grade baseball team.

He practiced around the house. He practiced until his mother saw him and screamed as loud as the fans singing the "Star Spangled Banner" at Yankee Stadium. She said, "If you dare practice with a tennis ball or any other type of ball, I'll take you off the team."

After she cooled off she said, "Use a sock if you have to!"

He agreed but he really wanted to use a tennis ball.

So when his mother went to the supermarket, he broke the rule.

He played for hours and hours and, as luck would have it, he broke his mother's favorite vase called the Great Crystal Vase.

He tried to glue the vase but with no success.

So he did what any red-blooded boy would do, he hid it.

Day after day, he was nervous. He felt so guilty he told his mother. She was so proud that she didn't make him leave the baseball team.

So he and his mother fixed the vase. When they were fixing the vase, he found out a shocking secret. His mother also restored antiques.

After the vase was repaired, it was put up with all his fifth grade baseball team trophies that he won. Although it could never be sold, it rests on a shelf forever with all the baseball awards that he would win in the major leagues in the future.

─── 12 ───

Memoir:
Reading and Writing the
Story of Our Lives

Several times a year, I return with my sons to the large brick farmhouse in which I grew up. We collect still-warm eggs, skip stones across Eighteen Mile Creek and, above all, visit with my parents. There has been a new poignancy to those visits lately. My parents are growing older. Topics of conversation have changed to include hearing aids, lifts in the shoe, and electric blankets that warm the bones. My mother's horses have always been her first love, but now, as arthritis stiffens her joints, she wonders how much longer she'll be able to ride. I can't imagine a time when her day doesn't begin with throwing sections of hay in for her girls and swinging the barn doors open wide. My father's knees are feeble. He still insists on doing the farm chores, but when we do fence posts together and he gives me a turn at the sledgehammer, it isn't a joke anymore.

Although my parents don't like the slick, suburban look of newly paved blacktop, they've decided to repave the gravel driveway. "It's good for resale," they say. And when I described a woman I know as old, they responded with studied casualness, "Oh, how old is she?" The question says everything. "How old is old?"

My father wants to write his memoirs. His father, before him, wrote an autobiographical memoir entitled *The Log of a Long Journey,* which he passed on to his children. Now my father is beginning to think about writing his own. He will write in order to find the plot line in his life, its themes and turning points and larger meanings. Ernst Becker has said, "What human beings fear is not growing old, but growing old without things adding up." And so we write our memoirs.

Why Write Memoir?

Memoir has become the genre of our decade. Each week *The New York Times Book Review* demonstrates again that memoir is what authors are writing

165

and what reviewers are reading. At least, it's what grown-up authors are writing.

Until recently, our children have not tended to write memoirs. They have tended instead to write personal narratives. They've written about single moments rather than about the plot lines or patterns that bind those moments together. Instead of finding threads that weave the stories of their lives into statements of "this is who I am," they've remembered fun times or shared weekend adventures. They've written about their day at the amusement park, about teaching their dog to sit, stay, and heel, about leaving for a family trip to Canada. The purpose of their personal narratives has been to report the chronological details of an event. But the purpose of memoir is to explore the significance of those events. Virginia Woolf says, "A memoir is not what happens, but the person to whom things happen."

Rory remembers that when she was a little girl, her father once got out his tools to fix the sink and asked her brother to be his assistant. "Can I be your assistant?" she had asked, and he had replied, "You're too little." Now, as a writer of memoir, Rory asks, "Why do I remember that moment? What does it say about my whole life?" Do young children need to think in these ways about the plot line in their lives? Do they have the impulse for memoir? I think so.

I think of ten-year-old Sandra Bazelais, who has recently moved from Haiti to New York City, and from Brooklyn to the Bronx. Does she need to look back and think, "How do the pieces of my life fit together?" I think so. She writes:

When I was in Haiti, I liked to lie among the soft grass and daze up into the dark, dazzling sky. I liked to get some peace and quiet away from my noisy, scattering house.

Sometimes when I was feeling lonely I'd climb high, rough mountains almost to the top just so people would say what a brave girl I was. Instead they said, "Are you out of your mind?" "Are you crazy?" "You could have been killed."

When I was high up on the rough mountains, I got most of the view of Haiti, and I said to myself, 'The Country of Sun,' what a perfect name for Haiti, because the sun gets everything right: it makes the birds happy, the flowers blossom, the roses smell sweetly.

Playing by myself is actually not fun, but when I lived in Haiti I tried to make it fun by picking roses and climbing rough mountains.

In *Self-Consciousness*, a memoir, John Updike says that as we age, we leave behind a litter of old selves. Sandra is only ten, but she has already left behind old selves. Updike looks back at himself as a little, unwilling 4-H member with a strawberry project, and as a skinny, scabby, frantic-to-be-noticed high school student relentlessly pushing his cartoons, posters, and jokes, and finds himself "tenderly taken . . . with those selves, with their diligence, and their hopefulness" (1989, 222). When I hear Sandra talking about that barefoot girl in Haiti who used to lie in the soft grass and gaze up at the dark, dazzling sky, who used to climb rough mountains so people would say, "What a brave girl you are," I can't help but think she knows what Updike is talking about when he describes learning to love the old selves we've left behind. Is this important? At a time when the rate of child suicide has increased threefold in a decade, and when more than half the children entering kindergarten in New York City will not graduate from high school, I think it is.

The careful, caring thought about oneself that goes into memoir writing is important not only for adults but for youngsters as well. When we hear Updike talking about learning to love the selves we leave behind, when we hear Becker saying that what humans fear is not growing old but growing old without things adding up, we, in our egocentricity, tend to forget that no one is growing old faster than children. It's children who know the glee, and the sadness, of finding they can no longer squeeze through the gap in the backyard fence. It's children who find their voices changing, their legs getting longer, and hair growing in places it never did before. It's children who constantly outgrow trousers and shirts, expectations and roles. Do children need to look back with tenderness on their lives? I think so.

Some children know what it is to page through an old photograph album with their mothers, hearing stories of the olden days. Some children know that when they return to well-worn, well-loved books, they meet again the child who believed in those stories: in trolls under the bridge, and magic beans, and a boy who could tame the Wild Things by saying, "Be still," and staring into the yellow of their eyes without blinking even once. Some children have rummaged through trunks of baby clothes, hearing stories of how they wore this funny little hat to bed and spilled grape juice on that coat. This is the very stuff of memoir . . . and it is the stuff of faith and self-esteem and hope. Children who reread their lives bring a sense of that story to all they do.

The act of rereading our lives, like the act of rereading a text, propels us forward with a sense of direction and momentum. When David Booth (1989) says, "All we can give our children is a sense of story, of something caring and committed to carrying them through their lives," he is talking not only about trusting that books tell stories, but also about trusting that there is a story line to our lives, that the moments of our lives fit together, that there is movement forward, that the pieces add up to something satisfying and whole.

The Essential Characteristics of Memoir

In New York City, memoir has become the genre of the decade for children as well as for adults. Courses of study in reading and writing memoir go forward against the backdrop of the wonderful diversity of topics, genres, and reasons for writing that exist in the world and in the writing workshop. When children devote some time to writing memoir, it doesn't mean they are writing "My Life Story: From Diapers to Dances"; but it does mean that when Sandra Bazelais writes about childhood moments in Haiti, she is encouraged to tell not only what she did during those moments, but also what she thought and felt, and in this way, to make the moments add up, to make them reveal her life as a whole.

Tiffany Wooten's memoir, like Sandra's, places moments and events in the context of a life. It is a collection of incidents and, at a deeper level, of relationships. It opens like this:

> When it's just finished raining, and I'm standing on the sidewalk waiting for a bus and a car rushes by, splashing me with mud from knee to ankles, I wish I was in North Carolina, safe on a porch. You can hear frogs croaking, fireflies are lighting their tails, and the stars twinkle down at you and the sky is as clear as the sea. In North Carolina, everyone in my family has heart to heart talks, and we share secrets.

Later, Tiffany wrote about her cat and, through her cat, herself:

> I'm sort of glad my cat Toby died, because if he didn't I would have never known how death works. It comes to you when you're happy, loving and holding someone. Then that someone is gone. Death has taken them.
>
> Toby and I were best of friends. I bathed him slowly so he wouldn't be frightened, and then dried him with the blow-drier so he wouldn't be cold. I watched scary movies with him, so I could hug him when I was scared, and I let him cuddle like a little ball at the edge of my bed. In the mornings he'd lick my face.
>
> When Toby died, a part of my heart split apart. I lost my only true friend. That night, the sky seemed to close around me, letting me have no air. I went out on the terrace, and in the faded blue sky I saw the stars and clouds and wondered if they were making the shape of my Toby.

The story of Tiffany and her thirty classmates is first the story of their teacher, Judy Davis. On a cold December morning, Judy joined 150 other upper-grade Project teachers for a day-long workshop on autobiography. Dorothy Barnhouse, the person who introduced me to memoir and is my mentor in it, began the workshop by plunging everyone into the act: "Let's take five minutes, or a single piece of notebook paper, whichever comes first," Dorothy said, "and write our autobiographies." Then she took up a pad, lowered her eyes, and without so much as a glance up, began to write.

"She had some gall," Judy says now, recalling the way the entire audience hung for a moment, on the brink of revolt. "Had she policed the room, we'd never have written. But there was something in her implicit faith that made us take her seriously."

When five minutes were over, people looked up, ready to hear why we'd been asked to produce instant autobiographies. Dorothy said, "Listen to this excerpt from Vivian Gornick's autobiography, *Fierce Attachments.* " And then, as all of us in that room held our page-long overviews of our birth, childhood, and schooling, we listened to Vivian Gornick who chose, instead, to reveal her life through this passage about her best friend Marilyn's mother:

> I preferred spending the afternoon in the Kerner apartment to spending it anywhere else. It was like having no parent in the house. Mrs. Kerner might be masquerading as an adult out on the street, but Marilyn and I knew better. . . .
>
> My mother's presence was powerful, but Mrs. Kerner's was touching. Her distress was so open, so palpable. . . .
>
> She was a terrible housekeeper who never stopped keeping house. At all times she had a rag tied around her head, a feather duster in her hand, and an expression of confusion in her eyes. She would wander around the house, aimlessly flicking the duster here and there. Or she'd drag out an iron monster of a vacuum cleaner, start it up with a terrific whining noise that made you think a plane was about to land in the living room, push it across the threadbare carpet a few times, lose interest, and leave the vacuum cleaner standing where she turned it off, sometimes for two or three days. . . .
>
> She never finished vacuuming because halfway through a push across the rug she would stop, jerk about (sometimes forgetting to turn off the machine), rush into the bedroom or the kitchen, where Marilyn and I were reading or drawing, and, with her hands on her face and her eyes shining, exclaim, "Oy, girls! Only this afternoon I was reading a story in the paper. A woman—poor, good, beautiful— was rushing across the street, her last penny in her hand to buy milk for a sick child she left upstairs . . . a car comes rushing around the corner, hits her, knocks her down, crushes and destroys her. . . . People come running. Blood everywhere! The world is drenched in her blood. They take her away. And guess what? You'll never believe this. . . . An hour later they find her hand in the gutter. Still clutching the penny."
>
> My heart would beat faster as she spoke. Mrs. Kerner was a spellbinder. Hers was the power of a born storyteller. (1987, 26–28)

The juxtaposition of our writing and Vivian Gornick's writing said it all. We don't have to scavenge through our lives looking for the big events—our twelfth birthday, graduation—we can write about our best friend's mother and her vacuuming. Writing memoir has everything to do with rendering the ordinariness of our lives so that it becomes significant. Then, too, when we write, rather than recalling facts, we need to re-create worlds. Rather than writing with statistics, we need to write with scenes. Rather then reporting on our time line, we need to explore the truths that underlie it.

We listened that day to other memoirs—to Beverly Cleary's description of Thanksgiving, and the relatives coming, and the oak table stretched to its limit under the smooth white cloth, the sight of which filled Beverly Cleary with longing. She got out a bottle of blue ink, poured it out at one end of the table, dipped her hands into it, and pit-a-pat, pit-a-pat around the table she went, inking handprints on that smooth, white surface (1988, 7).

We listened also to the beginning of Jean Little's *Little by Little* and to an excerpt from Zora Neal Hurston's *Dust Tracks on a Road.* At the end of the workshop, when Dorothy said, "Now let's take five minutes, or a single piece of notebook paper, whichever comes first, and write or rewrite our autobiographies," everyone in that room knew, as we knew nothing else, that writing autobiography or memoir is not an act of recording one's life story but of composing it—of creating it. We understood why William Zinsser titles his wonderful book on memoir *Inventing the Truth.* This time when the five minutes were over we talked in pairs about the choices we had just made and how they differed from those we had made earlier. Then several of us read our writing aloud, filling the room with our stories. Judy Davis's voice was strong and clear, cracking only once, when she stood to read:

> My memories are shattered by a father who frightened me. I could never do things right in his eyes. I could never please him. My birthdays were always celebrated in the Catskill Mountain bungalow colony in which we spent our summers. My father brought a cake from the City, and this year as always, when I wanted to carry the cake to the casino by myself, he warned me that I wouldn't be able to do it.
>
> I was determined. I had to. Carefully I balanced the cake on my outstretched arm. It was heavier than I had imagined and I concentrated intently on holding it. Suddenly, I lost my footing in a muddy area, and the cake flew face down into the mud. I ran, muddy, crying, into the woods to hide from my father and his certain wrath, and now I hear myself telling my daughter she's not doing well enough . . . and I wonder if I hear my father.

Launching a Course of Study on Memoir Writing

When Judy returned to P.S. 183 the next day she carried with her a new respect for the lessons that can only be learned about writing and reading from the inside. We often return from staff development sessions that way. The yearning to write usually lasts until we stop for a moment at our school mailbox and find it full of memos: two kids will be pulled out for this, three for that, one for this, one for that, and in addition to the MAT, the CAT, the SAT, the PSAT, the DRP, there'll be yet one more addition to the alphabet soup of tests. Hemingway has said that what a writer needs above all is a "built-in shockproof Crap Detector," but this is even more true for teachers who want to write. Judy, however, was determined. If she was going to help her children write and study memoir, she needed to do the same. And so Judy and a cluster of colleagues began working with Joanne Hindley and me on their memoirs and on the teaching of memoir. Other teams of teachers and other Project staff members around New York City decided to work in similar ways.

Because all of us—teachers, Project members, and children—have been both participants and curriculum developers in the course of study on memoir, we have encountered the challenges of this genre together as a team. And so when our children have said, "I can't remember that much of my past," and "Nothing has happened in my life," we haven't dreamed of dismissing their fears. We've shared them. Everyone, it seems, approaches autobiography saying, "I have this memory problem." We're each convinced that no one could have a memory bank as empty as our own. By talking and writing together we discover that no one comes to writing with ready-made memories lined up on the shelves of the mind, ready to be taken down and put onto paper. Memories aren't found; they're composed and invented. And that happens when we talk, and listen, and read and write, and through all of this, unpack our childhoods.

In Judy Davis's classroom, as in many other classrooms around New York City, children had been periodically pushing their desks out to the edges of the classroom, clearing the space for a storytelling circle. At the beginning of the year, after her visit in Anne Gianatiempo's classroom, Judy had led a storytelling circle in her classroom, inviting children to tell each other the stories that are told over and over in their families, to exchange the stories that are often buried with the treasures stored in shoeboxes under the beds and in drawers full of "private stuff." By the time Judy and her students approached their course of study in memoir, they had already been sharing stories such as these for a long time, and so Judy, Joanne, and I decided we would build upon what Judy's youngsters had already done by asking them to select images, events, and treasures that reveal important things about themselves. "Let's see if we can find one or two photographs that convey what we were like at different ages when we were little," Judy suggested. The next day the room was filled with the hubbub of small groups passing around each other's photographs. "Is there something you can bring from home that will give us a feeling for the uniqueness of your history, your growing up?" Judy asked. Judy and the children also created individual time lines on long strips of adding-machine paper, which they eventually draped onto the classroom walls. There was a time line tracing one child's changing involvement with piano, and another showing the main events in a relationship between two brothers, and a third showing one child's changing taste in toys. Groups of children gathered around these time lines to hear each other's stories about the big moments, the turning points, the saddest and happiest times of their lives. Over time, some—but not all—of these stories and memories were added to children's notebooks.

Reading Memoir

As the classroom filled with storytelling, shared memories, and notebook writing Judy introduced examples of published memoirs. Judy wanted to do something dramatic: push desks to the margins of the room, pile lots and lots and lots of books on the floor, and then invite students to spend an hour or two browsing and glorying in the books. But this is not easily done with memoir. It is easier to fill classrooms with poetry or picture books or nonfiction than with memoir. Although new and wonderful memoirs for adult readers tumble off the printing presses every day (Paul Auster's *The Invention of Solitude*, Gretel Ehrlich's *The Solace of Open Spaces*, Maxine Kingston's *The Woman Warrior*, Robert MacNeil's *Wordstruck*, Irina Ratushinskaya's *Grey is the Color of Hope*, Richard Rodriguez's *Hunger of Memory*, John Updike's *Self-Consciousness*, Tobias Wolff's *This Boy's Life*, and so on), there are fewer memoirs for young readers.

But obstacles can become opportunities. Instead of spending our weekends wracking our brains over how to get around the dearth of memoirs, we can bring the problem to the classroom community and enlist everyone in a literary search. Sabrina had never been inside the cool, towering stacks of the library until she went there in search of autobiographies. Miguel never met Mrs. Titus, the gentle, grey-haired librarian at the branch library near him, until he timidly asked if she knew of any memoirs for children. Parents sent books in, and many members of the school staff joined in, including the principal, Tanya Kaufman, who is both a fabulous administrator and an expert on whole language education.

The important thing is that when youngsters are invited into the search, the question of what memoir is becomes interesting to them. Every book will have its champion. Jerry was sure that even though Richard Margolis's *Secrets of a Small Brother* is an anthology of poems, it can also be classified as memoir. "Listen to the author's note," he said.

> I have one sibling, an older brother, and as kids we were inseparable.
> The fact that my own two children are both boys revived my memory
> of what it was like to be a small brother.

Avril argued that in a similar way, Cynthia Rylant's *Waiting to Waltz*, an anthology of autobiographical poems about her adolescence in Beaver, North Carolina, deserved a place in the growing library of memoirs. Several novels that are written in the third person but are in fact autobiographical were included: Mollie Hunter's *A Sound of Chariots* and Mildred Taylor's *Roll of Thunder, Hear My Cry*. Excerpts from Anna Quinlen's *Living Out Loud* and Sandra Cisneros's *The House on Mango Street* were included, as were excerpts from other adult memoirs. Several young adult books, Maya Angelou's *I Know Why the Caged Bird Sings*, Dick Gregory and Robert Lipsyte's *Nigger*, Jamaica Kincaid's *Annie John*, and Bette B. Lord's *In the Year of the Boar and Jackie Robinson*, were also included. But the most important memoirs were those written by the children's best-loved authors: Beverly Cleary's *A Girl from Yamhill*, Roald Dahl's *Boy*, Jean Fritz's *Homesick*, Eloise Greenfield's *Childtimes*, Madeleine L'Engle's trilogy, beginning with *A Circle of Quiet*, Jean Little's *Little by Little*, Bill Peet's *Bill Peet: An Autobiography*, and Cynthia Rylant's *But I'll Be Back Again*.

In addition, a number of beloved picture books seemed to fit into the category of memoir: Byrd Baylor's *The Best Town in the World*, Beverly and David Fiday's *Time to Go*, Eloise Greenfield's *Grandpa's Face*, Judith Hendershot's *In Coal Country*, Charlotte Pomerantz's *The Chalk Doll*, Cynthia Rylant's *The Relatives Came* and *When I Was Young and in the Mountains*, Ben Shecter's *Grandma Remembers*, Anna E. Smucker's *No Star Nights*, James Stevenson's *When I Was Nine*, and Jane Yolen's *Owl Moon*.

During this early phase of the memoir-reading workshop, when children were independently doing lots of wide-ranging reading and were also listening together to Fritz's *Homesick*, I think the most important thing was that they were moved by the stories of other people's lives. Later, there was time to return to these books in order to admire and study the author's craft. Even Robert Cormier, who says, "Reading is the most important thing I do, besides the actual writing," describes his reading by saying, "I'm always asking as I read, 'How did the writer do this? Why do I suddenly have tears in my eyes?' " (Silvey 1985, 289). Cormier is first moved to tears and only then asks, "How did the writer do this?" Too often, in trying to make reading-writing connections, we approach texts with dissecting kits, so intent on separating out the qualities of good writing that we forget why we read and write in the first place.

Ring Lardner has said, "If you can't cry, how can you write?" We might add, "If you can't cry, how can you read?" If we read *Homesick* and don't remember our own loneliness, we haven't really read it.

Touching *Homesick*, Avril Estime-Darnell said, "This book is giving me my own story. I kept thinking, Jean Fritz felt out of place in China, but me, I feel out of place with my own father." Avril's memoir, "The Wonders of a Little Girl's Heart," begins with a preface:

I would like to show you the wonders, glory, and darkness between my father and me.

And it ends,

I wish that I had a father that I saw more than twice a month. I wish I had a father that was there when I needed him. I wish I had a father that understood my feelings and knew me. I love my father, but deep down inside, he's a stranger to me.

Adrian Peetom, a Canadian whole language educator, once told us, "If I could say one thing to teachers of reading, I'd say, 'Trust the books. Trust the books, and stay out of their way.' " His advice is equally good for teachers of writing. Trust the books. Trust that Eloise Greenfield, Jean Little, Roald Dahl, Cynthia Rylant, and the others can do a splendid job of introducing children and adults to the genre of memoir.

Generating the Raw Materials for Memoir

When all of us, children and adults alike, are reading and writing memoirs, the memoirs we read will spark memories in us. They will turn on the lights in forgotten rooms of thought. Some of Judy Davis's students found that Jean Fritz's stories about her first name reminded them of their own stories. In *Homesick,* Fritz writes:

> The name Jean was so short, there didn't seem to be enough room in it for all the things I wanted to do, all the ways I wanted to be. Sometimes I wondered if my mother had picked a short name because she had her heart set on my being just one kind of a person. (1982, 30)

Sandra Cisneros, author of the extraordinary memoir *The House on Mango Street,* also reflects on the story behind her first name. She writes:

> In English my name means hope. In Spanish it means too many letters. It means sadness, it means waiting. . . .
>
> It was my great-grandmother's name and now it is mine. She was a horse woman too, born like me in the Chinese year of the horse— which is supposed to be bad luck if you're born female—but I think this is a Chinese lie because the Chinese, like the Mexicans, don't like their women strong.
>
> My great-grandmother. I would've liked to have known her, a wild horse of a woman, so wild she wouldn't marry until my great-grandfather threw a sack over her head and carried her off. Just like that, as if she were a fancy chandelier. That's the way he did it.
>
> And the story goes she never forgave him. She looked out the window all her life, the way so many women sit their sadness on an elbow. I wonder if she made the best of what she got or was she sorry because she couldn't be all the things she wanted to be. Esperanza. I have inherited her name, but I don't want to inherit her place by the window. (1986, 12)

Judy didn't tell the children to write the story behind their names; she only mentioned this in passing as an option. But many of the children who did choose to do so were eventually able to weave these entries into their finished memoir, bringing an added dimension to their writing. A memoir that focuses on climbing rough mountains in Haiti or dropping a birthday cake in the mud can hold a number of rich subtexts, and for some children the story behind their name can become such a subtext.

When we read published memoirs, we are reminded also of the places in which we grew up. It's hard not to notice that writers of memoir usually begin by placing themselves in the context of their childhood homes. For Madeleine L'Engle, Beverly Cleary, and Vivian Gornick, home is a house. For John Updike, it's a town, for Jean Fritz, a country, for Robert MacNeil, the seashore. But for all of these authors, the sense of place is crucial. Knowing this, children can take time in their notebooks to reflect on the places in their lives that matter most: their bedrooms, their apartments, their alleys, their streets, the rock overhang where they go to be alone. Because these entries are written within a course of study on memoir, the writers will want to describe places, but they will also want to describe themselves within those places. "How did I feel there?" "What did I do there?" "How is this room, this home, this country, a reflection of me?" "How is this place part of the whole story of who I am?"

When ten-year-old Naomi Cruz wrote about moving from one apartment to another, her entries revealed not only the places in her life, but also the person who lived in them. One entry began:

> In Brooklyn, I had my own room. I had a closet, a window that I could open any time I felt like it and most of all I had privacy.
>
> Then, news came. We had to move. I thought I'd still have my own room, but when we got there I saw only two bedrooms, and my mother said I'd have to sleep with my brothers.
>
> I had to say bye-bye closet, bye-bye windows, bye-bye privacy, bye-bye room. I had to say bye-bye to the 'No Boys Allowed' sign. I loved that sign. It kept dirty boys out of my room.
>
> Now this room with my brothers makes me vomit. I never vomited in my precious Brooklyn room. It gave me happy feelings and a good life. That room was my life. It will always be my life. I know it haunts me right now.

In a similar way, memoirs such as *Little by Little* and *A Girl from Yamhill* remind us that imaginary play can also be crucial to our memoirs. Jean Little tells how she used to make the piano keys talk. The deep notes demanded, in a giant's voice, "Little girl, who are yooouuu?" With the help of the pedal, it growled on and on. Then Jean's right hand made the little girl answer in the quavering voice of the high notes, "Oh, a giant is coming!" Then the giant's footsteps would go "Boom! Boom!" up the keyboard (1987, 8).

Jean Fritz describes how, in church, whenever the minister, Dr. Carhart, began a sermon, she'd play an imaginary climbing game, shinnying up the columns and working her way from rafter to rafter. "Today I was balancing myself just above the altar," Fritz writes, "when I heard Dr. Carhart say that he knew what death was like. I hung tight to the rafter" (1982, 60).

When young readers drew attention to these sections in published memoirs, it was as if they opened a floodgate. Fifth grader Jamie Bakaroudis, for example, wrote the piece in Figure 12–1:

What Tomorrow Brings

One evening a little boy named John was looking out of his bedroom window. He saw the moon rising. The boy imagined if the moon was the Queen of the sky and owned it. He was thinking about the stars and how they sway left to right. Then John's mom came into his room. His mom said, "John, go in bed and I'll tuck you in." So she

Figure 12–1 Jamie's Piece

What Tommorrow Brings
by: Jamie
Baharoudis

One Evening a little boy named John was looking out of his bedroom window. He saw the moon rising. The boy imagind if the moon was the Queen of the sky & owned it. He was thinking about the stars & how they sway left to right. Then johns mom came into his room. He's mom said "John go in bed & Ill tuck you in". So she did. After johns mom tucked him in she was going to put john's night light on but he said "Dont worry mom the moon is my night light tonight". So his mom creeped out the door. The stars are performing a show While little john was tucked in bed
He thought about Tommorrow.

---

did. After John's mom tucked him in, she was going to put John's night light on, but he said, "Don't worry, Mom, the moon is my night light tonight." So his mom creeped out the door. The stars are performing a show. While little John was tucked in bed . . . he thought about tomorrow.

Ten-year-old Ilana Goldberg also poured a long, detailed description of her imaginary play onto the pages of her notebook. She wrote:

When I was young, I went to my great-grandma's apartment at least once a week. It was a magical place, her apartment. Going there was the nicest thing in the world.

In Grandma's apartment, everything was pretend except the pictures I brought her every week. She had a carpet decorated with fake roses that became real in her apartment, her magical apartment.

I used to wash, style and cut Grandma's hair (pretend, of course) and grandma used to pay with pretend money, but give me a real 50 cent tip.

I baked blueberry pies on Grandma's chairs. No one else could see them but Grandma and she always told me they were the best pies she ever tasted.

Not every child or every teacher wanted to re-create and explore their imaginary play, but many did, and these entries, like the entries about names and places, helped bring added dimensions to their memoirs.

Finding New Meanings in the Moments

When teachers work together within a genre-based course of study, one of the questions we ask ourselves is "What are the special challenges of this genre?" Writers of memoir, it seems, usually approach the genre feeling that they don't have many memories. This problem becomes far less pressing once we begin to hear the stories of other lives, as we read them in published memoirs and hear them being shared in our classrooms. Every time someone describes anything—a bedtime television show, a New Year's Eve tradition, the scene when a parent comes home from work—we find ourselves flooded with our own memories.

The challenge of memoir, then, quickly moves from the issue of having enough memories to the more complicated one of knowing what the memories reveal about who we are. The central challenge then becomes finding out how particular moments fit into the plot lines of our lives. When we write memoir, we must discover not only the moments of our lives but the meanings in those moments.

It is also tempting to retell the old stories we've been told about our lives rather than to invent new ones. Our first tendency is to write prepackaged memories. As a child, I was nicknamed Bright Eyes because I found a lost watch and often spotted turtles before they slipped from their lily pads. That is, in any case, how the story of Bright Eyes goes. But if I probe a little more deeply, I find myself wondering whether the nickname was part of my father's campaign to boost my self-image. The challenge of memoir is to discover memories that no one talks about, to document stories that haven't been told, and to draw conclusions that haven't been drawn.

One powerful way to invent new memories (rather than merely taking precomposed memories off our mental shelves) is to carry our notebooks with us everywhere, recording in them whatever we notice. This may seem like strange advice for writers of memoir. Memoir is about our past, not our present. Or is it? One of the essential lessons we have learned from Vicki Vinton and Dorothy Barnhouse is that memoir is always double-edged. Unlike fiction, in memoir the unfolding story is always being remembered by a writer who is now older and wiser. Interestingly enough, whenever there is a "then" and a "now" in memoir, there seem to be both moments and meanings.

One way to find moments from our personal histories that speak in important ways to who we are today is to jot down whatever impresses itself upon our attention today, letting that observation act as a plumb line. Whatever we notice today, whatever we feel today, whatever bobs on the surface of our attention today is often deeply anchored in our histories.

Recently, feeling confined and restless after a morning at my desk, I decided to go for a jog, the first since I gave birth to my older son three years ago. When I reached a hill halfway along the route, I slowed to a walk. As I strode along the shoulder of the road, I was acutely conscious that the drivers of passing cars were no doubt looking at me. "Look down," I said to myself. "If your eyes don't meet theirs, they won't honk." Then, as I walked along intently staring at my feet, I suddenly felt silly. "Who am I trying to kid?" I thought with a start. "They won't honk at me anyhow. Those were the good old days, Lucy, before the kids . . . that was ten years ago when you ran in your little red shorts." I looked up, and this time, I tried to catch the eyes of each driver who passed. "Honk, please honk," I thought.

The moment was a fleeting one, but because I was keeping a notebook, I recorded it. Later, within the context of my work on memoir, I began to follow the chain of associations back into my childhood. "Why am I so self-conscious?" I asked myself. "Was I always?" Forgotten memories surfaced. As a child, my eight brothers and sisters and I used to go through the pasture behind our house to a swimming hole in the Eighteen Mile Creek. Returning, we would all take our bathing suits off outside, hang them on the line, and run into the house naked. This way we wouldn't traipse mud and wetness throughout the house. Later, when we were older, each of us staked out a bit of territory in the labyrinth of the dark, cobwebbed cellar rooms and changed into our bathing suits there among the dusty bird cages and aquariums and racks of old skis. There may be nothing very significant in those memories, but they are new ones; they haven't been pasted into photograph albums or talked about over the Thanksgiving dinner table, and therefore they offer space for new meaning-making.

Young people can follow a similar process of thought. Sandra Bazelais stares at a crack in the ceiling and remembers other times when she has done this. It is a simple turn of thought, but if she hadn't been attending to what she was noticing, she would never have recalled other times she stared at the ceiling. Now, in her notebook, she writes:

> I remember one rainy day when I had nothing to do so I started humming. My mother asked me to stop and I went to my room, lay on my bed, and just looked up at the ceiling and started thinking. I was thinking about my house. I wished my house was made out of glass, and I could look out the glass windows and see robins going into their houses to comfort the baby eggs.

Similarly, the simple act of watching an old movie on television led Yasmin Melendez to write:

> Every time I watch an old western movie or the Lone Ranger, it reminds me of when me and my brother used to play cowboys. We even dressed up like cowboys. We had cowboy boots, a pair of jeans, a plaid shirt and a cowboy hat. We had fun. We used old broomsticks as horses and hopped around all day. Once it was summer and my mother took us out. While my brother was running, the wind blew his cowboy hat away in the streets. When my father went to get it, it was smashed. A car just ran over it. My father couldn't find another hat like that one. Since that day my brother and I never played cowboy again.
>
> But our relationship has changed a whole lot since that day. We never do anything together because any time we play we get into a fight. We can't even play a game of Monopoly without him accusing me of cheating (which I don't). He's only interested in his Nintendo and television.
>
> I wished we had a better relationship. I think that's why I always scream at my brother when my father and I are playing cards or dominoes.

Another way to invent new insights about our lives is to stand on the shoulders of old insights. In the memoir-writing workshop, we need to join our students in rereading the pieces of writing and the notebook entries we've written over the years and ask, "Can these be windows into my life?" Megan discovered an old notebook entry in which she described accidentally shaving off one of her eyebrows. Her sister, offering to help, proceded to shave off Megan's other eyebrow. When Megan reread the entry in the context of the memoir workshop, she wrote in the margin, "I do lots of things like this. Why? I do really weird things all the time. Why?"

In her notebook, Betty Sullivan, a fourth-grade teacher, realized that, although her father had gone to great lengths to give her elaborate gifts on her birthday, the gift she remembers most is the little bit of shaving cream he used to put in the bathtub for her to play with. Reading this entry, Betty wrote, "I need to think whether my daughter will have little gifts like this to remember."

When Betty and Megan let their old notebook entries prompt new entries, they were letting themselves be affected by their lives. Writers of memoir struggle with the thought "I'm not famous. Why would anyone want to read the details of my life?" The answer is that readers can be moved and touched by someone else's life. The laws of physics (and of human nature) are such that a reader is apt to be affected by a writer's life only if the writer has also been affected by that life. If we allow ourselves to be moved by particular moments in our lives, then we stand a chance of carrying readers along on our journey. And the process of being moved by our own writing (and living) can happen not just with very old entries but even with what we have just written.

Whatever we've just written can prompt new ideas. So we reread our writing, reread our lives, and say, "Why am I such a weird kid?" "Was I always this way?" "What other weird things have I done?"

We move from remembering old moments toward inventing new meanings then, when we let whatever occurs to us today act as a plumb line into our past and when we probe and question the thoughts and memories we have recalled. Another way to bring significance to the attic full of memories is to turn vague, incomplete memories into richly sensory ones. At a recent Writing Project conference, Vicki Vinton spoke on the importance of the imagination within the genre of memoir. "We need to make the past real and vivid and compelling, as if it happened yesterday. To do that, we attach sensory information—particular smells and sounds from other times in our lives—to the memory in order to develop rich, evocative writing." Vicki described her process of "stalking a memory." She recalls an image of her father, sitting alone in the basement in front of his fish tank, staring into it. "The truth is that he couldn't have been alone if I can picture him sitting there," Vicki says. "So where was I? I don't know, but in my writing I put myself sitting on the stairs, looking at him, because that is true to my emotional recollection if not to the 'facts.' " Then Vicki said, "The other question is *why?* Why was he sitting there and why do I remember the image? Does it have anything to do with the fact that as he sat watching that carefully controlled little world of the fish tank, chaos reigned in the house above him?"

As Vicki stalks her memories adding sensory details, she supplies tone and nuance and meaning to those moments. To do this for ourselves, we need to take time to recall—and to interrogate—a few particular moments in our lives rather than rushing to summarize many moments. Judy Davis's memoir might revolve around the single scene of dropping the birthday cake in the mud, Betty Sullivan's around shaving cream in the bathtub, Megan's around shaving off her eyebrows. William Blake once spoke of seeing the world in a grain of sand, and truly there are worlds in those moments. Betty could shape a memoir around that bathtub scene if she used her notebook to explore what she and that little girl in the tub saw and did and thought and felt and remembered and hoped. She might recall the early morning smells or the rumpled look of her father. She might question why her mother has no place in those memories. She might imagine the way she probably played with those puffs of shaving cream. Betty and Megan and Judy might linger a while longer in a single moment or they might first collect more scenes, finding in them questions they've never asked and patterns they've never noticed. In either instance, the challenge is to move beyond reporting, beyond the solid ground of what we already know to the edge of dawning realization and wonder.

Shaping a Finished Memoir

Once seed ideas and memories have accumulated in notebooks and growth rings of meaning have formed around them, writers begin to imagine ways to proceed toward a finished memoir. The process of moving from a collection of memories, some of which have been fleshed out with details, toward a crafted, shaped memoir involves a new set of challenges. This in and of itself can be problematic. In some of our classrooms, by the time children get around to shaping a completed memoir, they are so pleased with what they have written and so tired from the intensity and emotion of the genre, they are eager for a quick exit. Often there is such power and intimacy in some of the notebook entries that neither teachers nor children can imagine doing more than selecting their best entries, refining them, giving them titles, and then sequencing them under a general title that is encompassing enough to include them all.

It's important for us to recognize that this earliest and easiest kind of shaping is viable and worthy of respect. It may be that a writer needs to choose and combine his or her best entries first and consider new challenges and new possibilities later. But it's also helpful to think of ways we can encourage young writers to do more than cut and paste to shape a finished memoir. There will come a time, for example, when we can encourage writers to move beyond the idea of a chapter book in which each entry remains in its separate box toward a single integrated piece. To do this, we as writers and teachers of writing will need to ask, "How do the moments and the images combine?" and "How does this entry fit with the next one, and how do they fit into the whole of my life?"

Sometimes we can help youngsters find one unified thing to say about their lives by posing a question for freewriting or discussion: "What has been the most surprising thing that you've realized about your life?" "If you were to pick a single moment that acted as a turning point in your life, what would it be?" "What are the themes of your life?" "If you were to pick two objects that are central to your whole life, what would they be?"

These questions may conceivably help writers determine the shape as well as the content of their memoirs. The way we organize memoir should reflect what we want to say. If we find three themes in our life, our memoirs will probably have three thematic sections. If there is a single turning point in our life, our memoirs will probably center around a moment that is revealed in great detail.

With our students we can also discover ways to organize memoir by learning from what others have done. Sometimes authors have gathered a series of images or anecdotes. One of the most accessible examples is Cynthia Rylant's *When I Was Young in the Mountains*. This picture book is organized almost like a series of photographs, each illustrating the broad theme of Rylant's childhood in the mountains. Other memoirs are structured similarly, although often a more focused theme strings together the seemingly separate beads of memory. In Sandra Cisneros's *The House on Mango Street*, for example, each vignette illustrates her yearning to break away from the street (and the ethos) in which she lived as a child.

Eloise Greenfield's memoir, *Childtimes*, is divided into three parts: the first contains vignettes that form the grandmother's story, the second vignettes that reveal the mother's story, and the third Eloise Greenfield's own story. Each of the generational sections begins with a page called "Landscapes," which provides a context for the life that follows. Taken as a whole, the book is about black people struggling not just to stay alive but to live.

There are still other ways to organize memoir. In *But I'll Be Back Again*, Cynthia Rylant writes about three elements that were particularly important in her growing up: music, kissing, and heroes. Each element becomes the title of a section of the book, and they are woven together at the end of her text and again in the photographs that follow the text.

Other writers of memoir take one event or several—or perhaps one event that happened over and over in their childhood—and convey a sense of their lives through the details of that event. Rylant's *The Relatives Came* does this, as do many of the poems in Rylant's *Waiting to Waltz* and Richard Margolis's *Secrets of a Small Brother*. In these instances, one of the challenges the writer faces is that of making a small moment reveal something bigger and more universal. In her poems, Rylant often does this by having two parts: first she describes an incident, then she turns back to reflect on it. In so doing she shows how the incident reveals her as a person. She shows herself as a young adolescent, bravely leading home by the hand a younger child who is frightened by the thunder and lightning of a storm, then turning to walk home alone, brave and strong on the outside but inside, a little girl crying.

In some writing workshops, teachers illustrate these ways to structure memoir through share sessions. In other workshops, children work in small clusters, and each cluster has a set of memoirs (or excerpts) that they read, reread, and examine for different things. In still other workshops, children who need help in structuring memoir work together in a study group devoted to that challenge. The most important thing is that youngsters are reading and talking about memoir while they write in this genre.

In Judy Davis's classroom, children gained new lenses for looking at memoir through broad, independent reading of memoirs and through a close study of several texts. In particular, they studied Jean Fritz's *Homesick*, a marvelous example of the memoir genre. The entire class looked closely at the opening page (Figure 12–2).

"In this beginning part," Raymond said, "it's not like a prologue, but it's like Jean Fritz is saying to the readers, 'Wait, you need to know this first.' "

Stephanie nodded. "Sometimes there are parts that hold the whole book together. These first few sentences are like that. So is the title."

Raymond listened, puzzled. "I thought the book was about here, at the bottom of the page where it said she was born on the wrong side of the world. She gets to the river, and you think, 'Why is this important about the river?' But I think she says this because it's a seed. She thought of the river, and then her thinking grew to her grandmother, and that led to the part about being on the wrong side of the world. And that's when the seed has grown into a tree. That's what the book is all about."

"It's funny, isn't it," Kenny said, "how she spends so much of her time on the maps, and the river, but what the book is all about is just that little line on the bottom of the page."

Figure 12–2 Page from Jean Fritz, Homesick

1

In my father's study there was a large globe with all the countries of the world running around it. I could put my finger on the exact spot where I was and had been ever since I'd been born. And I was on the wrong side of the globe. I was in China in a city named Hankow, a dot on a crooked line that seemed to break the country right in two. The line was really the Yangtse River, but who would know by looking at a map what the Yangtse River really was?

Orange-brown, muddy mustard-colored. And wide, wide, wide. With a river smell that was old and came all the way up from the bottom. Sometimes old women knelt on the riverbank, begging the River God to return a son or grandson who may have drowned. They would wail and beat the earth to make the River God pay attention, but I knew how busy the River God must be. All those people on the Yangtse River! Coolies hauling water. Women washing clothes. Houseboats swarming with old people and young, chickens and pigs. Big crooked-sailed junks with eyes painted on their prows so they could see where they were going. I loved the Yangtse River, but, of course, I belonged on the other side of the world. In America with my grandmother.

Twenty-five fluffy little yellow chicks hatched from our eggs today, my grandmother wrote.

I wrote my grandmother that I had watched a Chinese magician swallow three yards of fire.

Avril didn't agree. "I think the river's important, because I think the book's about a place, and she talks about the place and she makes China real, not by talking about the Great Wall, but by talking about everyday life."

At this point, Sabrina interjected, "Do you notice how she puts things together that don't really go? The river, the letter. When one thing leads to another thing, it's like a path you walk down. She's thinking about China, but then she thinks about America, and the letter . . . it's like a path you walk down."

Scott said, "There's a letter inside. I never realized you could do that."

Then Tiffany added, "The book clashes. Twenty-five chicks—that's America. The magician swallowing fire—that's China. She clashes it. There are things you can say about America and China that are the same—I wake up and have breakfast—but she wrote two different things, two things that are not the same. She clashes them."

Conferring with Drafts of Memoir

The process of reading memoir, then, is very much like the process of writing memoir. When these young people read Jean Fritz together, they found growth rings of meaning in her life story. In conferences, one of the things that happens is that the scenes and moments writers have collected in their notebooks gather growth rings of meaning around them. Another thing that happens is that writers begin to envision possible ways of structuring their completed memoir. When the Writing Project staff spent a day in Judy Davis's classroom, the first youngster who came to us for a conference was Raymond MacLeish.

"I just wrote this entry," Raymond said. "Do you want to hear it?" He then proceded to read "The Bite":

The Bite
by Raymond MacLeish

When I went to Jamaica there were four dogs. The most ferocious was called "Lion." He always bothered me. So I got angry and hit him with a stick. Wrong move. The little puppy called "Lion" jumped up and bit me in the arm. Boy did I yell! In came my grandma, with a stick. Fwap! Out went the dog. The bite started to sting. My grandma put some cream or something on it.

I opened the conference by saying, "Raymond, in my writing class, we've been reading a book that's the life story of a person named Annie Dillard, and my teacher, Dorothy Barnhouse, asked us one question about the book. She said, 'What's it about?' I want to ask you that same question, What's your entry about?"

Raymond didn't pause for an instant before answering. "A relationship. A relationship between my grandmother and me."

Impressed, I responded, "That's so interesting, Raymond. I think most kids would say that the entry was about some dogs biting you, but you know that a story can really be two stories. That on one level, this can be about dogs in Jamaica biting you and your grandmother hitting them, and that on another level, it can be the story of the relationship with your grandmother. Congratulations for knowing that." Then I continued, "But you know, Raymond, as I run my hand down the page, I'm just trying to see how much of your writing involves the relationship."

Raymond watched over my shoulder as I moved my finger down through the lines of his entry. "There, that line," he said. "That's the part about my grandmother." He read, "In came my grandmother with a stick. Fwap!"

"Oh," I said. "So that's the part about the relationship. Raymond, why didn't you build the relationship up more if it's the main thing for you?"

"Well, I didn't know when I wrote it that the relationship would be important," Raymond said.

"As you were writing and reading the draft you realized that your relationship with your grandmother seemed to be the important thing?" I asked, nodding. "I understand. That happens to me, too. Sometimes it not until I'm halfway done with a draft that I begin to realize why the topic's important."

"I could add some more sentences," Raymond interrupted to say, "to this bottom part, telling how I was feeling."

At this point, Vicki Vinton, who had been among the people listening to the conference, joined in to say, "What I do that might work for you, Raymond, is that if I realized at this point that I wanted to write about my grandmother, I'd try to really concentrate on that, filling myself with the feelings I had about my grandmother when I was little. Then in my notebook I'd write all that I could remember about my grandmother, keeping my pen on the paper and seeing if I could surprise myself by remembering things I didn't even know I remembered. The way she looked, the songs she used to sing to me. Anything. You might want to do that."

Another conference was with Kenny, who announced that his memoir was about seeing his father. He had written, "I saw my father. We had Coke, and then we had a hot dog," and he was done.

"Kenny," I said, "I know that you have a lot more to say about seeing your father. I know it was really an important time. Could you tell me what happened? What happened when you got together?"

"We had Coke," Kenny said, as if exasperated because he'd already written all about the meeting with his father. He looked at us and paused, and I looked at him, and then he spoke. "Then we were walking along, and my father put his arm around my shoulder, and, and, and . . . he started pointing out buildings to me, and I wished that he wouldn't take his arm down. I could remember when I'd walked around and seen other kids with their fathers and wished me and my father would be like that." Again Kenny paused, and again I simply looked at him and waited. Kenny said, "Then he started telling me that when you get old, the way to earn money is to have a lot of money and lend it," Kenny said, "and I felt big and important, the way he was talking to me."

Listening to Kenny and watching as he found his story, I knew that the reason I care about writing memoir—and about writing in general—is that for all of us, the life we're given amounts to "We had Coke, and then we had a hot dog." The rest depends on what we make of it. Being human means we can remember and tell stories and pretend and write and hope and share, and in this way add growth rings of meaning to our lives. Being human means that in addition to going through the motions of our lives, we need to turn back and celebrate our lives. We need to paint and map and write and make believe and tell stories and represent and reminisce. We need to develop the eyes to see. What human beings fear is not growing old, but growing old without things adding up.

— 13 —

And the Walls Come Tumbling Down: Bringing Our Lives to Nonfiction Research

Debbie's father detoured to avoid the unshaven man who stood near the shadowy entrance to Ray's Pizzaria. Inside, ten-year-old Debbie, her sisters, and her father settled themselves down with pizza, salads, and sodas. Through the window, they could see the silhouette of the homeless man, his shoulders hunched against the wind and his arms buried under his overcoat. Then Debbie's father seemed to change his mind. He stood up from the table, walked abruptly to the counter, ordered a slice of pizza and a soda, and took them outside to the homeless man.

"My father is the one who has influenced me most in my life," Debbie says. "But this time I could tell I had influenced him. My study of homelessness affected him because it has affected me, too. I used to crush empty cans of soda, but now I look at the cans and think, ''Someone could get a five-cent refund.' Five cents isn't that big," she says, "but I've been affected by this project and that's big."

The research Debbie and her classmates have done on the homeless has not led to reports pasted onto manila paper or bound with yarn. Instead, it has led Debbie's father to give pizza to a homeless man, and it has led Debbie to live her life conscious of what an empty soda can could mean to another person. And yes, Debbie, that's big.

The research has led Sabrina to recruit fifth graders from classrooms throughout the district to join a clothing drive, it has led Raymond to work with a cluster of classmates on a nonfiction book for kids, and it has led Billy Cherry to deliver a speech to the congregation at his Baptist church:

In the Bible it says, "Do unto others as you would like them to do unto you," and I'm doing that. But money isn't what homeless people need the most. They need faith.

187

I wonder if I was homeless and I prayed every night saying, "Dear Lord, please help me and my family get an apartment and some clothes," and after I prayed, God still didn't bless me, would I still believe in him? Would I have the faith to go on with life?

I notice that every time a homeless person comes to my classroom, I always ask him, "Was there a time in your life you felt like giving up?" I wonder what I would say if I were homeless and a kid asked me the same question. . . .

I can imagine being homeless. The other day I saw a rat in the apartment and I only had a dollar, not three or five dollars, and the rent was overdue . . . and now I know I went through homelessness in my own little way. But that's my secret . . .

When Annie Dillard was Billy's age, her research was not on homelessness but on the war, on Hitler, on the concentration camps. She read nonfiction articles from *Time, Life,* and *Look,* and she read Anne Frank's *The Diary of a Young Girl* and *Thirty Seconds over Tokyo* and *To Hell and Back.* It was as if, as she read, she herself was marching from Moscow to Poland and losing her legs in the cold, growing up in a Warsaw ghetto, and kayaking in Antarctic seas. Looking back on her adolescent reading and imagining and studying, Dillard says,

Those of us who read carried around with us like martyrs a secret knowledge, a secret joy, and a secret hope: There is a life worth living where history is still taking place; there are ideas worth dying for, and circumstances where courage is still prized. This life could be found and joined, like the Resistance. I kept this exhilarating faith alive in myself. . . . I would not be parted from it. (1989b, 46)

When I think of Annie Dillard's introduction to nonfiction reading and writing and of Raymond's, Billy's, and Debbie's, I'm filled with an overwhelming sense of regret over my own introduction to nonfiction research. Like grown-ups who caution youngsters to color within the lines, to make sure the grass is green and the sky blue, my teachers taught me the etiquette, the posturing, and the packaging of scholarship, but they did not teach me that ideas can change the world.

I remember the weekend I began my first real research report. I was so ready to do important work. I was ten, and I loved the grown-up feeling of a Saturday afternoon in the library. I remember with goose bumps the smells of paper and books and wooden tables, and I remember the significance and urgency of whispered voices and quiet steps. I remember how scholarly I felt turning the tissue-thin pages of the *Encyclopaedia Britannica,* copying down facts onto my index cards. And oh, the index cards; how I loved the concreteness and weight of them, that mounting physical evidence of my labors, and how I loved the deliberateness with which I unzipped my new pencil case, choosing from it a blue pen for notes and a green pen for book titles.

But that is all I remember. For me, reading and writing nonfiction centered around pencil cases and tracing paper, index cards and bibliographies. I learned to underline book titles, but I did not learn that research can give us hobbies, passions, and a sense of mission. I did not learn that communities form around shared ideas, communities of people who read, listen, watch, and write in order to outgrow themselves.

When my father was ten, he fell in love with research. It did not happen as he copied facts from the encyclopedia onto index cards. Instead, it happened during a long summer at Camp Merryweather. "It was an old-fashioned sort of a camp," Dad recalls. "Every afternoon we had rest time; we'd lie on our cots and the camp director's wife would read to us. I remember lying there on my cot, with one of those green Army-Navy blankets over me, looking up at the rafters and listening as she read *The Microbe Hunters*. I remember being filled with so much excitement I could hardly bear it." Dad explained, "My father's job was like a banker's; it was a job, nine to five, and when the job was over, he had his fun. Lying on that cot, I realized it didn't have to be that way. I vowed, right then and there, that when I grew up, I'd know the passion, the teamwork, the drama that those microbe hunters knew."

My father and Annie Dillard had each discovered something about research that is far more important than outlines and citations. They learned why Cynthia Moss, a researcher who lived in Kenya for ten years studying the behavior of elephants, compares it to reading a very good book about a family saga. "You get so involved," she says, "you don't want to put it down." Anne Roe, who studied sixty-four scientists in order to write *The Making of a Scientist*, found that these researchers all shared, above all, an intensity, an absorption.

How different my Saturday afternoons in the library would have been had my teachers told me that what mattered most in research was my absorption, my fascination with a subject. "The best writers of nonfiction," Milton Meltzer says, "put their hearts and minds into their work. In the writer who cares, there is a pressure of feeling which emerges in the rhythm of the sentences, in the choice of details, in the color of the language" (1976, 21). The strongest testimony to the importance of passion in nonfiction writing comes from the texts themselves. When I read Lewis Thomas, Byrd Baylor, Nancie Atwell, or Martin Luther King, I know the challenge of writing nonfiction has everything to do with the fact that when a person cares deeply about a subject, that caring draws not only the writer but also the reader into a lived relationship with that subject.

The fact that Byrd Baylor loves the desert so much she lives in a rough-hewn cabin and donates her royalties to a Save-the-Desert foundation is not just a cute author anecdote. It is a lesson—*the* lesson—of good nonfiction writing. I am affected by hawks and desert canyons in Byrd Baylor's books because she herself has been affected by them. And yes, Debbie, that's big.

In *The Art of Teaching Writing* I argued that youngsters need invitations to research things they know and care about: Yugoslavian traditions, gymnastics, the process of being adopted. As a parent, I am discovering all over again the power of these personal projects. My sons, Miles and Evan, and I are totally immersed in the challenge of choosing a puppy. We've got books about dogs and lists on the refrigerator of dog names and of Bearded Collie kennels. We've been pursuing ads in the newspaper and attending dog shows. Both boys have made a dog bed—one out of blocks, the other out of a cardboard box.

The richly literate life, it seems to me, has everything to do with knowing that the process of choosing a puppy—or hatching frog eggs, or fixing mopeds—can be the door to worlds as rich as the world behind C. S. Lewis's wardrobe. I couldn't bear it if, when my boys grow up and go to kindergarten, their teachers do not recognize that interests are entryways into research.

Despite the value I place on my sons' dog research or on another child's collection of sea glass or love of Shetland ponies, still, when a group of teachers and I formed a study group on nonfiction reading and writing, we were certain that this time we wanted to call children together to study a shared topic.

The Value of Whole-Class Topics

Our interest in whole-class topics did not arise only from the fact that we knew it would be easier to gather resources and scaffold research for one topic than for thirty. It was also influenced by escalating racial violence, the growing threat of acid rain, the changing boundaries of Europe. The well-being of our planet seems too precarious and the needs of our neighbors too urgent for us to be satisfied with simply researching topics as personally important as choosing a puppy. We also want to help students care about topics outside themselves. We want to help students read, study, and live their way outside their own lives and their own worlds. And we want this not only for our children but for ourselves.

A few years ago, many of us heard my colleague Ann Lieberman tell about a kindergarten teacher who found herself skipping out of the school building. "That teacher is indicative of the profession," Ann said, and she proceeded to talk about how elementary school teachers sometimes live in a naive, childlike way, hanging stuffed ghosts around their homes on Halloween and singing "The wheels on the car go splish, splish, splish" as they drive through the town on their Saturday errands.

Listening to Ann, I was offended. I wanted to sing Peter Pan's refrain, "If growing up means it would be beneath my dignity to climb a tree, I'll never grow up . . . not me." But I also wanted to hide from the shock of recognition. I can get so absorbed in my teaching that the dimensions of my world get narrow. Often over the last eight years, several thousand educators have gathered in the huge auditorium at Teachers College for Writing Project reunions. As I've looked out at that room brimming full of black, white, Asian, and Hispanic teachers, I've known that we represent children who have nannies, chauffeurs, and $300 sweaters . . . and children who live six to a room and eat from a tin of baked beans warmed on a hot plate. Until recently, I've never mentioned what I saw. It was safer, somehow, to talk about putting poems to music and drafting alternate lead sentences. And so, listening to Ann, I wondered if my immersion in the world of teaching had led me to live my life like an ostrich, not seeing what I didn't want to see.

But the world is changing too quickly, too radically, to keep our heads in the sand. Yesterday in the hall of a school building, I chatted with a colleague who was about to drive her daughter's computer to Johns Hopkins University. Before she left, she was going to call from the classroom's computer to find out the weather in Maryland. Meanwhile, the cover of *Time* magazine says, "In 1492, Europe discovered America. In 1992, Europe discovers itself."

Young people feel the changes in the world. They feel the changes and they worry. They are worried about beaches closing down because of pollution, about lakes and rivers becoming dry, about friends abusing drugs. When children carry notebooks with them everywhere, they are all the more apt to see and question and wonder. They see the rich patrons of Manhattan's Tavern on the Green restaurant walking past the hungry and the poor. They see the old woman from their apartment building who sets newspapers and paper plates out on the stone wall each morning and feeds the swarms of homeless cats that have come to depend on her. They see the customers who come and go from the alley beside their apartment. They see these things and they worry.

And so children in Judy Davis's P.S. 183 Manhattan classroom embarked on their study of homelessness, and children in P.S. 148 began researching the assimilation of new immigrants into their school and their borough. Students in another classroom decided they would deviate from their school's long-standing tradition of the third-grade "animal report" and do research instead about ecological and environmental issues in their township. Children in other classrooms decided to study heroes with learning disabilities, the New York City public library system, and the issues surrounding deaf education.

Launching Whole-Class Research Projects

Whenever my husband, John, and I watch television together, he is apt at some point to mutter, "She's going to switch from a fake gun to a real one," or "He's not the loving son-in-law she expects." I'm always caught off guard by these dire predictions. I usually eye him curiously, then shrug and continue watching. Yet almost inevitably, within a few minutes, the woman will indeed switch guns and the son-in-law will emerge as a scoundrel.

Astonished, I turn to him and ask, "Did you watch this before? How did you know?"

Usually, John dismisses my question, "It was obvious, Lucy." But a while ago, he peered at me for a moment and then pressed on. "Lucy," he said, "When you watch television, what are you doing?"

"I'm watching television," I answered, a touch of sarcasm in my voice. It seemed an obvious answer. But in retrospect, I realize that John is doing something very different. He is asking questions, searching for answers, building hypotheses, and looking for clues and confirmation. Meanwhile, I am waiting for things to happen.

Often, it seems to me that our students sit in front of their nonfiction texts the way I sit in front of the television. They wait for information to come to them. They wait for books and teachers to "learn them." This is not only bad grammar; it's impossible. Learning requires an act of initiative on the learner's part. No one can learn for us. Learning, by definition, is something we must do for ourselves.

When our study group began talking about ways to launch whole-class research topics, we knew that instead of delivering an overview of the topic to passive listeners, we wanted to begin by inspiring students to take the initiative. We wanted to help them forge their own trails of thought. We tried to learn everything we could from others who had already found ways to do this. Susan Radley began her course of study on seashells by giving each of her second graders a packet wrapped in tissue paper. She had never mentioned that they'd be studying shells, and she certainly didn't tell them that she had put a different shell inside each packet. "How can you determine what's in your packet?" Susan asked. Soon these seven-year-olds were feeling scalloped edges and testing the brittleness of their wrapped objects, hypothesizing about them and drawing what they imagined was inside. The research continued after the children finally opened their packets, for then they began categorizing their shells according to size, color, and whether the edges were rounded, sharp, or very sharp. Soon each child was thumbing through a book and scanning a chart in order to find the name of his or her shell. Questions about shells were gathered on a huge sheet of paper, and the research project was launched.

When Mary Winsky and her student teacher, Rebecca Sheridan, helped their junior-high students study Japan, each cluster of adolescents examined one or two artifacts Rebecca had brought back from her travels and surmised from those artifacts all they could about Japan. The next day the students, working in pairs, began leafing through an assortment of current publications—*The New York Times*, *The Wall Street Journal*, and an odd assortment of magazines and catalogs—in a clue-seeking expedition. "From what is right around us, what can we surmise about Japan? What questions do we have?" Rebecca asked.

In *The Art of Teaching Writing* I suggest that we can help students to be active, alert learners if we invite them to list all they know about a topic in one column and then, in a second column, all they want to know. Recently, Di Snowball, a former president of the Australian Reading Association, led Writing Project teachers through a variation on this kind of list-making. She began by writing "Life Cycle of Insects" on the chalkboard and then asked us to call out any words that came to mind. Soon her chalkboard looked like Figure 13–1.

"Let's classify what you know," Di Snowball said, and we found four categories: where they live, what they look like, what they do, and their life

Figure 13–1 Di's Writing

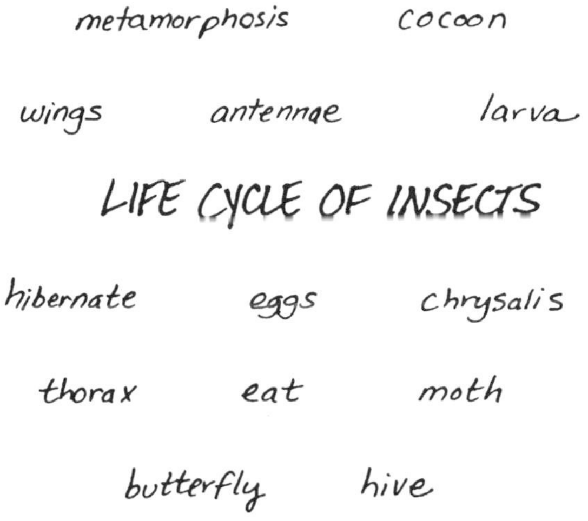

metamorphosis   cocoon

wings   antennae   larva

LIFE CYCLE OF INSECTS

hibernate   eggs   chrysalis

thorax   eat   moth

butterfly   hive

---

cycle. Focusing on the "life cycle" category, we selected the relevant words
and talked about them in order to inventory our existing knowledge. We
knew the word *chrysalis* but were unclear about the differences between a
chrysalis and a cocoon. By checking the indexes in several resource books, we
found the sections in each that could clarify our confusion, and skimmed
through them. "Look at how much we've accomplished in just fifteen minutes," Di exclaimed. "We've found a direction to our research—and we've
found it not by listing what we don't know but by gathering together and
discussing what we thought we knew. We've developed four categories, which
should give us each a framework—hooks on which to hang information—to
use as we continue reading. Finally, we've demonstrated that when we turn
to resource books, we read them very differently than we read narratives."

In the end, most of the teachers in our study group decided to launch their
research simply by gathering their children together to swap stories and questions and memories about the whole-class topic. Since these circles had
become a ritual in these classrooms, when children gathered, their attention
was not on choreography and on questions such as "Where do we sit?" but on
the subject at hand. And because the sharing circle belonged to the ongoing
writing workshops, children learned that their research would be an extension of what they had been doing all year in reading and writing.

Much later, I would regard the decision to launch our research work with
a storytelling circle rather than flow charts and categories as emblematic of all
that Judy, the other teachers, and I did. Over the next six weeks, we would
stress the importance of anecdotes, quotations, empathy, and personal stories
and inadvertently give less attention to charts, maps, categories, and debates.
I didn't realize until the written products began emerging that, although we

were preparing children for one important kind of nonfiction writing (we helped them write the nonfiction we liked to read best), we did not lay the groundwork for expository writing, the kinds of nonfiction that involve bullets and charts, subheadings and statistics. In retrospect, the teachers and I now know we could have done more in this area, but we wonder whether such an emphasis should have been woven into the work we did or whether it belongs in our next research project, our next unit of study.

In any case, Judy Davis and many of the other teachers began by gathering children together to swap stories and questions, and this conveyed to them that our work with nonfiction would be similar in some ways to that with other genres and different in others. In all the classrooms, the challenge to gather resources and learn new information became one of the unique challenges of the genre.

Gathering Resources

"I told my kids this project was going to be *ours*, that we'd gather the resources together," Judy says, "and that it wouldn't be easy because there aren't a lot of nonfiction books for kids on homelessness." The class rose to the challenge. They brainstormed ways to generate resources, and each child promised to do something each night for the project. They started bringing newspapers, magazine articles, and pamphlets into the classroom as well as information they had transcribed from radio and television programs. Everyone pitched in to write parents, district office staff, agencies, and journalists for more information. Soon the classroom was awash in a sea of names and numbers, facts, and quotations.

"I knew we needed a way to coordinate all this," Judy said, "so we met on the rug." By ten o'clock that morning, several youngsters were wrapping burlap around a piece of cardboard in order to make a "Facts Sheet." Others were stapling construction paper over a closet door in order to make a contacts board, and another child was cutting out letters to label the board with the acronym SCRATCH—Students Committed to Researching All the City's Homeless. A cluster of youngsters met to decide on categories for the contacts board: People to Call, Places to Write, Trips to Take, Waiting for Responses, Our Calendar. By the time I arrived in the classroom two days later, there were already over forty yellow stick-ems on the board. As Ja-keeya explained to me, when someone thought of a contact, he or she would write it on a yellow stick-em. When someone assumed responsibility for that contact, he or she initialed the stick-em. Once calls had been made and letters written, the stick-em was moved to the Waiting for Response column; once plans were confirmed, details were added to the calendar.

"If something happened and we had to end this whole thing right now," Judy said to me that day, "I'd still look back—even on just this week of research—and think of this as one of the best parts of our year." I could sense what Judy was talking about when I realized that each of the stick-ems crowded onto the SCRATCH board represented another person venturing into the world. Behind one was the story of Reginald, who'd been a disengaged student most of the year, walking half a mile to the police station each day after school until finally, on a Saturday, he tracked down a policeman whose beat included several areas in which homeless people gathered. Reginald ended up by mounting a New York City street map onto poster board, using pins to indicate those gathering places, and writing a piece titled "Why Here?"

Behind other stick-ems was the story of Judy Davis spending a Saturday at the Donnell Library, of Chris asking his father's friend whether an eleven-year-old could volunteer in a soup kitchen, and of Sabrina phoning the runaway hotline and saying her name was Lisa. "What's your last name?" the person queried. When Sabrina responded, "I'd rather not say," the person hung up the telephone. Undaunted, Sabrina resolved to try again, this time with a full pseudonym in hand. "I'm going to say I haven't run away yet but I'm thinking of it," Sabrina said, "and I'll write down how she advises me." Sabrina's *chutzpah*— the Yiddish word for gall or guts—may lead her into lots of awkward predicaments, but it will also help her to do some very fine research.

As Shelley Harwayne has pointed out, all too often it's only the packaging around a child's report that has chutzpah. The titles of Larissa's, Yoonmee's, Luis's, and Dorothea's reports (Figure 13–2) are bold and presumptuous, but the texts themselves read like an encyclopedia. Stephanie's quirky and delightful preface (Figure 13–3) gives way to a bland and voiceless collection of facts. These youngsters need to bring the confidence and pride that is evident in their titles and prefaces into their information-gathering process. Research—like entering a competition, applying for a job, establishing a new family ritual, or forming a support group—involves chutzpah.

It took chutzpah for a cluster of Mona Castanza's fourth graders to walk the block surrounding their school building surveying everyone they encountered about their immigration status. "What country are you from?" they asked each passing person, each shopkeeper, each customer. When people

Figure 13–2   Title Pages (L to R): Larissa's; Yoonmee's; Luis's; Dorothea's.

Figure 13–3   Stephanie's Preface

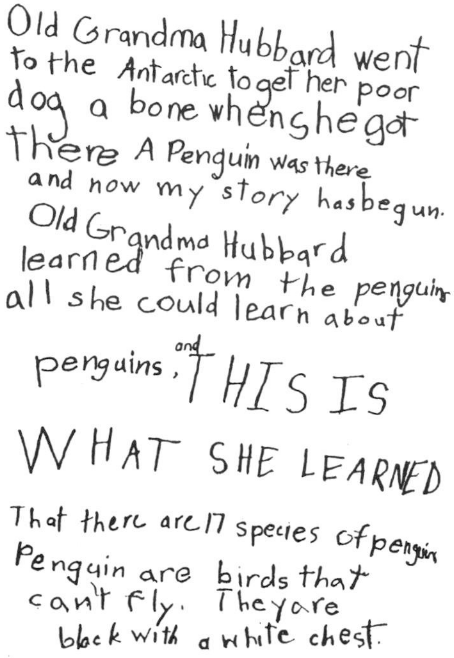

> Old Grandma Hubbard went
> to the Antarctic to get her poor
> dog a bone when she got
> there. A Penguin was there
> and now my story has begun.
> Old Grandma Hubbard
> learned from the penguin
> all she could learn about
>
> penguins, and THIS IS
>
> WHAT SHE LEARNED
>
> That there are 17 species of penguin
> Penguin are birds that
> can't fly. They are
> black with a white chest.

responded, as they often did, by turning the other way and brushing the question aside with a "No hablo ingles," "Wo bu hui shuo ying yu," or "Je ne parle pas l'anglais," it took chutzpah to push the fourth grader who spoke the necessary language to the front of the group. One third of the people the children spoke with that day were illegal aliens.

Of course, it would have been vastly more efficient had Judy, Mona, and the other teachers chosen topics like dinosaurs or dogs, about which there are lots of nonfiction books. By the second day of research, children could have been busily taking their notes. It would also have been more efficient if the teachers had done all the legwork, gathering together the newspaper articles, maps, and picture books, creating resource libraries, and arranging for field trips and guest speakers. But oh, the lessons that would never have been learned!

In fact, the challenge of nonfiction had as much to do with using the yellow pages as anything else. What a lesson it was for children to phone agencies designed to serve newly arrived immigrants and find that the phone would ring and ring and ring, often with no answer at all. Eventually, these children began charting the number of phone calls they had to make before they reached anyone who could answer even their simplest questions . . . and this chart helped explain why so many people are illegal aliens.

But the lessons were even more universal. To me, it felt enormously important that classrooms were filled with phone directories, files of addresses, brochures, newspapers, subway maps, and graph paper. It felt important that children were listening to the news with pen in hand and phoning each other afterward to ask, "Did you get that reporter's name? We should write to her." It felt important that every morning in Judy's classroom there was a mail call and that the teacher across the hall, whose classroom held the fifth-floor extension telephone, would often stick her head into Judy's room to say, "Sabrina, a woman named Susan Martin phoned to say she's bringing two homeless people in tomorrow for you to interview. She'll call you at home tonight," and, "Anabelle, you have a phone call in the office." And it was absolutely extraordinary to have Anabelle return to the classroom flushed with excitement saying, "I've got a speaker for us. His name is Mr. Wilkerson and he runs a family shelter and he's coming next Thursday at one o'clock."

When Mr. Wilkerson did arrive, the first of many authorities who would eventually visit the classroom, it was Anabelle who introduced him. "As director of a shelter, I don't usually have time to speak at schools," Mr. Wilkerson said. "But I kept getting these phone calls. Day after day my secretary would say, ''It's that little voice from York Avenue again.' When I finally spoke with Miss Freedman . . . well, how could I say no to that little voice from York Avenue?" That day, Anabelle and her classmates learned about the homeless, but they also learned about the power of little voices.

Children were also learning about the writing process. They were learning that the writing process doesn't necessarily involve sitting down and pouring our hearts and thoughts onto paper. All the wisdom of the world is not carried inside ourselves. As Roy Peter Clark points out, if our topic is water pollution, we would be wise to interview an industrial polluter, to stand on the shore and look at dead fish, to ride a boat with fishermen who fish the polluted waters. Writing will be a different proposition altogether for people who have done this kind of living.

Interviewing

While Judy Davis's children were preparing for their interview with Ron Wilkerson, youngsters in other classes were planning for interviews as well. In our study group, we reviewed what we knew about interviewing, fully expecting that each of us would confirm and extend everyone else's ideas. To our surprise, while some members of the study group assumed that children would need to prepare a list of questions to ask in an interview, others among us felt that predetermined questions would prevent listeners from following the speaker's lead. And while some assumed that children should be encouraged to take abbreviated notes summarizing the facts they were learning, others felt that it was crucial to record direct quotations. Thinking back, I realize that our disagreement echoed the age-old differences between experimental and ethnographic research. While experimental researchers tend to value the objectivity that comes from preset questions, more ethnographically oriented researchers tend to believe that the informant must have a major role in determining the course of an interview. "I need to understand your work," the ethnographer might say. "Let's see . . . Would you walk me through a typical workday from the beginning, explaining what you do and think?" Especially if this interviewer knows how to extend what the informant says, she will probably learn a great deal more from this interview than she would have learned had she peppered the informant with questions. When we talked in our study group, we realized that our differences of opinion existed because many of us held assumptions about our children's research that had been shaped by the experimental, quantitative research paradigm we, as teachers and teacher-researchers, had grown to distrust.

In order to unlearn some of the existing canon about interviewing, we tried to remember that everything we knew about conferring also applied to interviewing. We read James Spradley's *The Ethnographic Interview*, Michael Agar's *The Professional Stranger*, and William Zinsser's chapter "The Interview" from *On Writing Well*. We learned from journalists, too, beginning with my brother Geoff. Several years ago, when Geoff had just graduated from college, I received a frantic phone call. "Lucy," he said, "I'm being interviewed tomorrow for a job with the *Detroit Free Press*. What will they ask? How can I prepare myself?" The next morning Geoff flew to Detroit and met one junior reporter after another until finally, in the late afternoon, he was brought to the office of the senior writer. The moment for Geoff's interview had arrived. Geoff took a seat, anxious and eager. The senior writer pulled his chair closer, but before they could speak there was a knock on the door. One of the junior reporters looked in, gestured a greeting to Geoff, apologized for the interruption, and then left. "What a good fellow he is," Geoff said. "I enjoyed talking with him this morning."

"Yes . . . and what's that good fellow's name?" the senior writer asked. Geoff snapped his fingers, reaching back in his mind for the name. "Ummmm," he said. "Uh . . . uh. . . . "

The senior writer didn't supply the name. Instead he asked, "What did you think of that photograph on his desk? Surprising, isn't it?"

"The photo?" Geoff said. "I don't believe I saw that."

"And that paperweight. Interesting, isn't it?"

"Was it a rock?" Geoff asked. Then, looking at his watch, Geoff said, "We should probably start the interview. I have a plane. . . . "

"The interview is over," the writer said, and walked my brother to the door.

The study group realized we can learn from the *context* as well as the *content* of an interview, especially when we are conducting interviews in the informant's own territory. If, for example, the interview is interrupted by ten phone calls, that's revealing. If the informant introduces us to the custodian, the secretaries, and the community members who come and go, that's revealing. Then, too, we learned that although we and our students would probably not approach interviews with lists of fill-in-the-blank questions, we do need to come knowing everything possible about our informant and his or her topic. Journalists know that an interview should give access to information we cannot get another way, that it's a waste of time to ask a veterinarian, "How many years does it take to become a vet?"

Shelley Harwayne was in the classroom on the day that Ron Wilkerson came, and she and Judy joined the children in taking notes as he explained his job at the Third Street Family Shelter for the Homeless. After ten minutes, Shelley intervened to suggest that listeners talk about what they were hearing and learning. This pause for active listening, this "I hear you saying . . . ," helps listeners stay on top of what we are hearing and invites the informant to expand upon and clarify what he or she has said. In this instance, Shelley especially wanted to invite youngsters to hear and think and question and marvel at all that Ron was saying. Because she knows that interviewing well requires us to think on our feet, following leads, noticing contradictions, anticipating the questions our readers will want to ask, eliciting more anecdotes and more examples, Shelley wanted to attend to and value children's thoughts and observations. The secret of a good interview has very little to do with forming a list of preset questions but a great deal to do with listening well.

"It was striking to compare the kids' and Judy's notes with my own," Shelley said. "They had written down the statistics—the date Ron's center opened, the date it was expanded—and I'd written down that during Open House week Ron went to seventeen different Open School meetings, that he refers to the kids at the Center as "my kids'. . . . "

The difference between what the children and their teacher had recorded and what Shelley had recorded again echoes differences between experimental and ethnographic research paradigms. Experimental researchers "write down the facts," valuing, above all, statistics, dates, and key names. More ethnographically oriented researchers tend to place more trust in anecdotes, images, observations, and people's own stories told in their own voices.

Once Judy and her students began noticing anecdotes and revealing details along with "the facts," they began to interject comments such as, "Can you give another example?" and "Were there other times you got emotionally involved?" These "tell me more" nudges are trademarks of a good interview. Informants almost invariably begin by talking in generalities. "We have so many crises at our center that it's hard to get away," Ron said. When students wisely responded, "Tell us about the crises," they signaled to Ron that, yes, they were interested and yes, they wanted specifics. Later, when Anabelle conducted her follow-up interview with Ron, he said, "I'm a casual sort of administrator." Anabelle asked, "What do you mean by that?" and Wilkerson answered with a story. Because Anabelle had ingeniously arranged to phone him from a telephone that had a long-running answering machine attached, she was able to use his exact words as the lead to her profile of him. It begins:

"In the job previous to this one, I was an assistant to a Commissioner. I had to write a lot and no one can write with their shoes on. So I'd take my shoes off and get comfortable. One day my boss, who's a very demanding man, told me to get into his office immediately. I went right in without my shoes, and while he gave me an assignment the big boss came in. I didn't want the boss to see my toes sticking out of my socks, so I tried to keep my feet under the table. From then on, I threw out all the socks I had with holes in them."

"I like to keep a comical side to things," says Ron Wilkerson, Director of the Third Street Family Shelter for the Homeless. Mr. Wilkerson also describes himself as a concerned person. Some people turn off their jobs but Mr. Wilkerson has a beeper because he has one job you can't turn off—the problem of homelessness.

I found it pretty amazing when Mr. Wilkerson said to me, "If you had told me I'd become the director of a homeless shelter when I was in college, I wouldn't have believed you." His major was political science and he wanted to become a great lawyer or a politician. "Never did it cross my mind that I might go into service work," he said.

Mr. Wilkerson has seven godchildren, but all the residents of the shelter are like his family. "It's a good feeling to know you're in the helping business . . . and that I'm helping others," he said. Eight-year-old Freddy moved with Mr. Wilkerson from the Forbell Family Shelter to the Third Street Family Shelter. Freddy calls Mr. Wilkerson's mother every day after school and chats with her about what he's doing. During Open School night Mr. Wilkerson went to open school for Freddy and for sixteen other children. Mr. Wilkerson told me once that when he was visiting a school he was deeply hurt when a principal said, "All homeless children go to the homeless table."

"Write It in Your Own Words": Bringing Our Lives to Research
Anabelle's profile of Ron Wilkerson emerged long after she introduced him to her classmates. Her earlier notes had none of the fluency and detail of the profile, and this was true not only for Anabelle but for the other children as well.

"How can we help kids write in their own voices?" we asked during our study group meetings. This is the age-old question of the research report. When I was ten, I knew more about plagiarism than about research. Over and over I'd been told, "It's against the law to copy. It's stealing." I imagined the police coming with handcuffs to carry off anyone who forgot to change the big words into smaller ones. I remember explaining to my younger brothers and sisters, "You can get kicked out of college for plagiarism." I still recall our solemn, big-eyed awe at the thought that there could be criminals right in our own classrooms . . . and I recall my own private unspoken fear that I myself might be caught.

To this day, most teachers introduce the research report with admonitions about not copying. Some of us begin the research unit by reading sourcebooks aloud to students or showing filmstrips in order to be certain that students don't copy. Other teachers have rules: "Your books must be closed during note-taking." "Only when the reading is done do you take notes." "Never write in whole sentences; use brief phrases so you won't be tempted to copy."

But *my* notes are filled with direct quotations. I cannot imagine putting books aside before I take notes. If I did, my notes would be filled with vague summaries, paraphrased references, and distilled facts instead of details, surprising language, and observations. "Caress the detail," Nabokov said, "the divine detail." I want my notes to be tools to think with, and so they must be very particular. Then too, often what I value most are the words someone has used; the words aren't disposable peanut shells that carry extractable kernels of meaning. I don't want my notes to be filled with summaries any more than I want my library filled with plot outlines.

The more important quarrel I have with all the well-intended rules and admonitions against "copying" is that if our purpose is for all of us to write about research in our own voices, then rules against copying are not the issue. The issue is, how do we help ourselves read and interview and learn our way out of our own lives? The issue is, how do we let people like Ron Wilkerson affect us? How do we let census figures and news stories and radio broadcasts about the homeless connect with our own experience? Writing with voice means writing with one's life. We will write with voice when we have read, questioned, dreamed, argued, worried, wept, gossiped, and laughed over a topic.

We helped some students write in their own voices by arranging for them to become mentors for newly arrived immigrant children or volunteers at a shelter. But we wanted to help the entire classroom community live into a relationship with our topic. In Judy's classroom we longed to climb aboard the subway and bring the class to interview homeless people at Grand Central Station. Judy worried—and wisely so—about permission slips and safety, so we were relieved when Perdita Finn, a student of mine who was visiting the classroom, suggested an alternative. We gathered on the rug for a guided imagery exercise that turned out to be one of the most extraordinary experiences of my life.

Perdita began by saying, "Yesterday, when I gave this homeless person in my neighborhood some money, she took my hands and held them for a moment. I looked down at her hands holding mine, and I noticed that her skin was thick from being outside for so long without any mittens. My glasses were dirty that day, and she always gives me a tissue to clean them. As she rummaged in her pocket, I could tell her hands hurt, that it was hard for her to move her fingers. That night, as I was putting cream on my own hands, I thought of what it would be like to have hands that hurt so much."

Then Perdita asked if we had moments in which we thought about being homeless. Billy said, "This man on First Avenue was sitting on a crate and his leg was dirty and had bumps on it and the skin was coming off." Perdita nodded and said, "I wonder how that would change your day, if you had those bumps on your leg?"

We talked for a while before Perdita said, "Let's see if we can think of this classroom as a place for the homeless. We'll each need to find a spot in which to sleep. Spread out." As we settled ourselves on the cold tile floor, we giggled and role played. "You touched me. Get away!" one person said dramatically. "I want this," another called out.

Perdita quietly intervened. "I think we're keeping what it's like to be homeless on the outside of our skin. We don't want to let it inside us. Let's lie still on the floor and imagine where we are." Perdita's voice grew quiet, and so did the classroom. "Are you on the sidewalk or in a homeless shelter? Maybe you're sitting up because it's a little warmer that way. Think of those bumps on your feet that we talked about."

I shifted around on the floor trying to get comfortable and reached down to rub my sore feet. "Don't worry about letting me know what you're doing," Perdita said. "Keep your eyes closed." The room grew quieter. "What's it like to have people you don't know breathing near you?"

After a long silence, Perdita said, "What worries are on your mind?" She paused and then asked, "Where's your stuff? Are your belongings near you? Are they safe?"

After a while, Perdita shifted to new kinds of questions. "Are you wearing more than you'd like to? Does anything hurt or itch?" "What are you thinking about, dreaming about?" She paused. "I'm going to touch someone on the shoulder, and when I do, tell me how you feel right now."

For the next few minutes, one after another, we spoke into the space of that classroom. Later, pretending it was morning, we stretched the kinks out of our bodies and went outside to see the familiar block around the school through the eyes of a homeless person. Many of us were in our shirtsleeves, and we shivered in the wind and looked longingly into the parked cars. In some cars, blankets and extra coats were bunched casually on back seats. I found myself noticing that, yes, the car doors seemed to be locked. A few of us spotted a recessed doorway just below street level. We huddled in it just to feel its warm arms, and then, miraculously, we saw a huge slab of cardboard—a makeshift roof. When we peered into a garbage can, I was for a moment hungrily hopeful, nudging open the pizza box just enough to see what it held. Many of us found a place to sleep—a hidden roof, a warm grating, and an alley. Chris noticed some magazines and remarked that they'd make an adequate pillow.

Back in the quiet of the classroom, we wrote. Sofia Gonzales wrote,

The world seemed so big today and I felt so small when I was out, cold on the street. I looked for a place to get warm and maybe a place to get food. Everything reminded me of the home I didn't have, and I was angry at the people who looked at me and smirked because they had their fur coats and diamond rings and fancy beds.

Geirthrudur Finnbogadottir wrote,

I noticed a difference as soon as I walked outside. The trees looked bigger because there wasn't any certain place to go. It wasn't that cold but roaming around knowing there isn't a warmer place makes you colder. There were a lot of possibilities for food and shelter that I hadn't noticed before, and there seemed to be more food in the stores than I'd seen before.

I felt like sitting in a corner and huddling myself, and I thought about how I'm often self-conscious about the smallest things. I don't think I could stand it if I were homeless. People would assume things.

In all my years as an educator, I'd never before participated in an activity like this one, and I was moved to tears by the power of it. *"This* is research," I thought to myself as I listened to children putting into words what I had also experienced. How could a single hour so affect me? I too had found my mouth watering as I looked into the garbage can. I too had regarded that stairwell as cozy. Surely, learning to care in this way about a subject is an essential research skill.

I sat on the corner rug surrounded by Judy's students and waited until the silence in the room was full. Then, looking at each child as a way of gathering that child into the circle, I told the youngsters that the classroom had been feeling like a busy newsroom, with all the excitement of fast-breaking news, of reporters running about with clipboards scooping up stories, of investigators following up on leads. "In this unit of study, we will be writing nonfiction literature," I said. "In order to write nonfiction well, we need to have a space in the day in which the classroom feels like a library." I talked about the notion of "a stillness gathering in which the whole house seems to be thinking" and about creating a bubble of silence and intensity in which we could put our minds and hearts onto paper.

Then I told the youngsters that one reason I was saying all this was that, once the unit on homelessness had begun, instead of writing long, meandering, and thoughtful entries about their lives, they had been writing clipped and abbreviated entries about their research. "Let's all of us write in silence for forty-five minutes," I said. Before we began writing, I reminded students that our notes, thoughts, and questions about the homeless had been gathered alongside entries about our birthdays, families, and fears for a reason. I suggested that we each take time to reread our entire notebook, thinking whether "unrelated" entries might not connect to the topic of homelessness in surprising ways. The room grew quiet, and a stillness gathered in which the whole classroom seemed to be thinking.

After about twenty minutes, I spoke into the silence. "Sometimes it helps to share in the middle of writing time," I said. "This is what I've written so far." And I read this entry:

Homelessness

I begin by thinking of my childhood home, of the great oak Old Lean-over that stretched across Eighteen Mile Creek and of the make-believe classes I would teach to the creek underneath Old Leanover's webbed roots, which clutched at dirt. I think of Gut Smasher Hill and how proud I was to have the steepest, most treacherous tobogganing hill right in our backyard, and I think of my room, too, and how I would kneel under the window beneath the house's eaves and pray to God for someone to choose me as their partner in gym or to invite me to the sophomore prom or to tap my shoulder at the Honor Society induction.

Home was more than home. It was a world, and inside that world I built myself. I am who I became in my house. I am the girl who taught the creek, who braved the Gut Smasher, who prayed to be included. How could I have built myself if I didn't have a home around me? How could I define myself if I didn't have Susie, that giant bear with flattened fur who'd been with me since I was six? How could I define myself if I didn't have my window, the stairway up to my room, the stair that creaked and gave me away? How could I define who I was if I didn't have a shelf of favorite books that said, "I'm the kind of person who loves *Lad: A Dog* and *Exodus*"?

When I was young, the project of my life was finding and making me into me. I had so many decisions. Was I going to be the kind of girl who . . . ? Somehow that search for who I was going to be had to do with what I wore, with what I hung on my walls, with what wallpaper I chose for my bedroom.

I suppose all of this feels far from the issue of homelessness. I can't imagine what it would be like to live in a shelter, but I suppose the more important thing is to imagine what it would be like to live my life cognizant of the fact that people near me and like me do live in shelters. If I really let in the world's sadness, how would I live differently?

That morning Marion Misilim read:

Once I made a little basket for my teddy, with a pillow and a blanket. Some people don't even have what my teddy had, and that's sad.

Chris Ralph read:

My Mom and Dad divorced when I was very young, and I moved to Ohio with my Mom. I started building my life around my friends and my Mom . . . then, when I had to move from one parent to the other, the feeling I got was like the side of me that was going at average speed with my friends had fallen down and crumbled away and I was homeless from all that.

Geirthrudur, whose parents were at that time planning to move to Connecticut, read:

Yesterday night before dozing off to sleep I thought of moving. . . . I looked around the room and wondered what it would look like without any furniture. I remembered the last time we moved, the nakedness of the apartment. . . . It's really all the furniture and small things that makes it home. When I thought of leaving the snug apartment, I just wanted to pull the apartment together like a blanket and squeeze it tight.

Sabrina recalled her birthday party and realized that homeless children don't have a place to hold birthday parties. Chris thought about the necklace Nick gave him before he moved. "When I wear it, I feel that Nick is with me, like his characteristics are in me. Do homeless people have a place to keep special belongings like this necklace?" Billy wondered how long a rich and elegant person would last if he or she were homeless. Soon everyone began finding connections between their early or "unrelated" entries and the topic of homelessness. Of course, the connections were not really between old and new entries but between our lives, dreams, and feelings and the man in the oversized overcoat who stood in the shadows outside Ray's Pizzaria.

Looking back now, it seems to Judy and me that the class had crossed a threshold. For most of us, everything we'd been learning all year about notebooks became directly relevant to our work on the homeless. We were able to push ourselves to generate words about a statistic or quotation even when we thought we had nothing to say because all year we'd been taking single lines from our notebooks and trying to say a great deal more about them. We were able to take two separate entries—one about a necklace and one about shelters for the homeless—and write into the gap between them. We were able to take a small, specific moment and ask, "How does this fit into the whole of my subject?" We were able to reread our entries, making marginal notes. We could do all of this because we'd done it before, and the payoffs were astonishing.

Once youngsters understood that the memory of a bed they'd made once for a teddy bear could be the seed idea for a thought about homelessness, it wasn't difficult for them to see that facts and statistics could also launch trains of thought. During another interval of silent writing, we each put something we'd learned from our research at the top of a notebook page and then filled that page with our thinking about that bit of information.

That morning, at the top of a new page Debbie Ulloa wrote, "By June 30, 1990, all the hotels for the homeless in New York City will be closed" and then went on to recall all the distressing things she'd heard about hotels for the homeless. Chris Ralph wrote, "President Bush has only reduced the defense budget by 3 percent" and then mused about why, considering the changes in Europe and the Soviet Union, Bush wasn't moving more money from defense to social causes. Once youngsters knew they had a place for their opinions, they had opinions on almost everything. Liz Halem wrote:

I'm reading this Covenant House book. When Tim and his friends couldn't get drugs they shot oven cleaner into their veins. I may be Catholic, but when Father Ritter said God helped Tim out of the darkness, I think it was Tim who helped himself.

Anabelle Freedman wrote:

Beth just told me about a place called Calcutta in India. It's a place of poverty and that's where Mother Teresa spends most of her time. Mothers in Calcutta are willing to cut off their children's arms so the children can look like they are in greater need when they beg on the streets.

Then Anabelle skipped a line in her notebook and with beautiful cursive writing tried to craft a lead sentence for her profile on Ron Wilkerson. She wrote: "Is America becoming like Calcutta? With the help of people like Ron Wilkerson, it won't."

Once children became accustomed to seeing ideas grow from their kernels of information, they began finding that almost everything in their lives could become seeds of thought. Avdo inventoried the contents of his refrigerator and then wondered what homeless people ate. Vivian Gornick describes this absorption:

Whatever a scientist is doing—reading, cooking, talking, playing— science thoughts are always there at the edge of the mind. They are the way the world is taken in; all that is seen is filtered through an ever-present scientific musing. . . . The natural biologist walks through a city park, across a suburban lawn, past an open shopping mall, and is half-consciously wondering: Why two leaves instead of three? Why pink flowers instead of white? (1983, 38)

When Avdo and some of the others began showing this kind of lifelong absorption in their research, it seemed to me a startling and significant thing. "How true it is," I thought, "that when I'm deep into my research, everything nurtures it." When I went on a week's vacation with my family this spring, I couldn't help but regard my tennis coach's methods as a lens for thinking about writing conferences. I viewed each "memory rock" Miles and I collected as containing a story. When I'm deep into research, everything in my life nourishes my writing. As Gornick says, "It is from this continuousness of thought and perception that the scientist, like the writer, receives the crucial flash of insight out of which a piece of work is conceived and executed" (1983, 39).

Finding and Nurturing the Seeds of Writing

Although it was true in Judy Davis's classroom that small flashes of insight often generated major pieces of writing, this happened only for children who were willing to let go of some of the good material they'd collected in order to put their faith—and their energy—into developing their most promising seed ideas. In nonfiction writing, as in memoirs, for some youngsters the move from notebooks to projects involves merely selecting, combining, and sequencing their best entries. For others, the process involves finding a small image or idea with the potential to become much more and then living with that idea for a long while before eventually writing about it.

Helping children make these choices, helping them imagine possibilities for future research and writing, was more intellectually taxing than any work Judy and I could remember doing. Part of the challenge was the sheer volume of the notebooks. The children had written so much and thought so much about the homeless that any decisions they now made as writers were almost inevitably difficult. Author Gail Godwin says that in writing, "the choice is always a killing one. One option must die so that another may live. I do little murders in my workroom every day" (1980, 254). In order for Debbie to focus on her comparison of hotels for the homeless and the glitzy hotel next door to her apartment building, she had to postpone or abandon work she'd done on the legality of begging in subways. In order for Billy to focus on his speech, he had to leave a number of splendid rough-draft poems undeveloped in the compost pile of his notebook.

Because these were decisions that writers needed to make on their own and because the decisions often required a great deal of thought, Judy and I insisted that, before conferring with one of us, children needed to reread their notebooks looking for themes, for sections that seemed to be entryways into further research, for questions that lingered, for insights that commanded attention. Often they did this in pairs, each child taking most of one workshop to read and discuss his or her entries and quotes. Sometimes this process of rereading and rethinking yielded ambitions and plans for more focused writing and research. When this didn't happen, it sometimes seemed that our conferences couldn't proceed until children had done more thinking about their notebooks. In these instances, we sometimes asked them to borrow a strategy ethnographers often use: "cooking one's field notes." This meant that, as an intermediary step between notebooks and projects, they wrote long, rambling pieces in which they mused about selected ideas and images collected from their notebooks, forming trails of thought from one to another.

Eventually, children in Judy Davis's classroom fashioned plans for their future research. Debbie decided to research the differences between fancy hotels like the one next door to her apartment and hotels for the homeless. Alex found himself empathizing with homeless people who had been separated from their family members, and he decided to research separation as he'd experienced it when he left his brother in Yugoslavia, as classmates from split families had experienced it, as the homeless sometimes experience it. Angelica decided to try her hand at journalism, writing and submitting articles about their class's research, about how children could help the homeless, about the people they'd interviewed. Jon decided to write about his own journey: in

October he had called homeless people "bums," but after doing some research he'd written a caring, generous poem dedicated to the homeless.

Meanwhile, in Mona Castanza's classroom, Mona and Laurie Pessah urged children early on to choose a focused subtopic rather than staying for a long while with the generic topic of immigration. They did this because when the children researched the umbrella topic of immigration, they tended simply to circle again and again around the idea that it was hard for immigrants to leave their homelands and that they felt dislocated in America. Mona realized that, ironically, limiting the size of her children's topics would open up new possibilities for their research. Soon one group began researching the process of becoming a citizen and another focused on the process of teaching and learning a second language. A fair number of children decided to work on subtopics that did not necessarily emerge from the particulars of their own notebooks. The power of Yurak's firsthand narratives about her early experiences in an American classroom led Mona to suspect that it would be worthwhile for a group of children to study the experiences of newly arrived immigrants at P.S. 148. "Do any of you want to form a study group around this topic?" Mona asked, and soon a small group responded. Because Mona's children had been involved in study groups during their work with picture books, it wasn't difficult for them to work in this way. Yurak's group began brainstorming ways they might gather entries and learn about the newly arrived immigrants at P.S. 148, and Mona, meanwhile, moved through the classroom helping children form groups and then helping the groups define productive goals and activities for themselves.

In both cases, by the time Alex had decided to focus on issues of separation and Yurak had chosen to research newly arrived immigrants at P.S. 148, the dynamics in each of their classrooms had changed. It was almost as if each child needed to make his or her own "Contacts Board." The image of thirty-two Contacts Boards, each covered with yellow stick-ems, each representing another individual's forays out from the classroom, aptly conveys the richness and possibilities for chaos in these classrooms once projects are under way.

In classrooms such as these, teachers will need to invent ways of staying in touch with children's progress. Some teachers have borrowed Nancie Atwell's idea of beginning a workshop with a "status of the class" conference in which they call off the name of each student and then record on a grid what that student intends to do that day. Others ask children to take ten minutes each Friday to jot down a memo outlining their progress and their plans. Still other teachers have a schedule so that each day they take home a complete collection of five children's work. Some teachers have a giant chart listing all the possible ways children can pursue their research, and each child checks off what he or she has done on the chart.

It may seem that these forms of record-keeping are important because they allow us to maintain some semblance of order and accountability. But their real value lies in the way they help children to plan, to be deliberate students of their subjects. When pursuing an idea, a researcher needs to look backward and forward constantly, asking, "What am I learning?" "What do I need to learn?" and "How can I learn this?"

Once Yurak and a cluster of other children decided they would study how newly arrived immigrants fared within their school building, they needed to go through the same involved process that stymies a great many doctoral students. They needed first to focus on more specific questions: "Which children maintained traditions from their homelands and why?" "How do non-English-speaking immigrants learn English?" Then the study group decided to conduct a survey. As inevitably happens in research, each step yielded new problems. How could they survey kindergarten children? Soon the group decided that surveys would be sent home to parents of kindergartners. This meant writing letters of explanation. In this way, as children followed the trail of an idea, they not only drafted and revised; they also surveyed, responded, charted, recorded, interviewed, scheduled, questioned, duplicated, distributed, corresponded, and telephoned.

The challenges of this kind of writing are new ones, and this meant that children who had not until now been regarded as strong writers became leaders. When Judy Davis and I imagined all the benefits of this research, we knew that studying the homeless would help children care about and respect neglected people on the streets . . . but we never anticipated that the research would help children respect neglected members of their own classroom community. How important it was that this unit on nonfiction gave children new ways to be excellent!

In junior high, I was overweight and gawky and self-conscious. I'll never forget sitting in my squad line, in my light blue gym uniform with the boxer shorts and the snaps down the front, with braces on my teeth and large bumps on my head because I'd used rollers for the first time in a desperate effort to fit in, and having Janine Briggs—beautiful, tall, thin Janine Briggs—turn around, look at me, and say, "You have the most beautiful eyes, Lucy." I will never forget those words and the thought, "If *Janine Briggs* said this, it must be true." I sat up and felt my soul gather there in my eyes. After that, I lived through those eyes. I'd walk down the hallway in my hand-me-down dresses and my braces and my all-wrong hair styles, and I'd think, "I have beautiful eyes." If I heard someone call my name, I'd turn my best feature towards them. Everyone deserves at least to have beautiful eyes. The wonderful thing about a course of study in nonfiction is that it gives more people a chance to be excellent.

In order to allow children who thrived on nonfiction to assist those who struggled, Judy encouraged children to meet regularly in response groups for the purpose of planning their research. Our colleague, Pat Wilk, suggests children in these groups might find it helpful to study attributions in published pieces of journalism. They might, for example, underline all the attributions in an article on Oreo cookies in order to answer the question "Where did the author get this information?" When children see that a researcher learned about Oreos from a person at Nabisco, from the National Bakery Board, from previous articles on Oreo cookies, and from tellers at the grocery store, they can envision a wider range of sources for their own subjects.

On the Trail of an Idea: Research, Reading, and Observation

Once Marion decided to research teenage runaways and Avdo to gather people's recommendations for what Mayor Dinkins could do about New York's homeless, each read with a new and important sense of direction. Previously, Judy's children had tended to select articles from the reading table almost at random; now they skimmed each one, putting most aside as they searched for those that addressed their concerns. Until now, they'd often collected information from books and articles without stopping to notice if one source contradicted another. Now their reading was more deliberate, as if they had mental pegs on which they could hang much of what they learned.

Children read through their source material as one might expect they would. They copied quotations with our blessings, and with our cajoling they sometimes wrote summaries of what they read. Often they wrote reflective entries based on their reading. They read difficult materials with a partner, and on several occasions, when children came back from the library, we'd say, "Why don't we divide into little groups so we can hear what each of you has learned about your topics?" It is an extraordinary thing to watch children grow into the role of being a teacher. Usually they begin reciting a few facts, and then, as they speak, something interesting or surprising comes to mind and they talk with new energy. Listeners draw in and the "teachers" feel this new attention and find themselves saying things they never knew they knew. "We are the teaching species," Erik Erikson has written. "Human beings are so constituted as to need to teach not only for the sake of those who need to be taught but for the fulfillment of our identities, and because facts are kept alive by being shared, truths by being professed."

I've always known that researchers learn from books, interviews, and especially from the opportunity to teach, but during this project I also realized the importance of learning from observations. Always before, I had tended to think of observation as something that belonged in the hands of scientists or poets. I am neither, and so I have usually learned from talk, activity, and books, but not from closely observing the world around me. I think my biases against observation began way back when I was nine and Mrs. Mitchell taught me "the techniques of close observation." She gave me and each of my classmates an index card. We were to make a pinhole in our card and then study our shoelaces through that pinhole. As I think about it, whenever a teacher has tried to teach me the techniques of close observation, the challenge has been to describe the smallest, most minute details of an already small and, in my eyes, trivial object.

If I were in Mrs. Mitchell's place now, hoping to show fourth graders the power of observation, I would begin by asking them to think of a scene or an image they remember. Or I might help them by asking, "What matters to you lately?" Then I might say, "If it's the tensions in your family, what scenes or images come to mind? Is it the way people's eyes avoid each other at dinner? Write about that. Is it the tightening of your mother's jaw? The way she turns and oh so deliberately scrutinizes each spoonful of peas she eats? Write about that. Begin with what matters and see the scenes and images that come to mind."

The images that matter are the ones that, out of all those in the world, linger for us. Earlier in this chapter, Perdita began her guided imagery experience by sharing an image of a homeless person's hands. An image like this needs to be re-created not by the eye alone but by the heart and mind and imagination.

What I have come to realize is that an image can function as an illustration that a writer provides in order to convey a clearly delineated idea to the reader. But an image becomes extraordinarily life-giving when it also functions as a resource that readers and writers return to again and again, each time knowing that if we look and listen closely the image will yield something new. Joan Didion describes the never-ending generative power of images. She says:

> I write entirely to find out what I'm thinking, what I'm looking at, what I see and what it means. What I want and what I fear. What is going on in these pictures in my mind . . . images that shimmer around the edges. . . . You lie low and let these pictures develop. You stay quiet. (1980, 20)

In describing the process of writing her book, *The Puppeteer*, Kathryn Lasky talks about a single moment that revealed to her everything about making puppets. She describes watching Paul, a master puppeteer, at work, painting faces on the puppets he'd sculpted. Then suddenly Paul sneezed and the puppets shivered and trembled. As Lasky describes it,

> Light and dark played across their faces, and suddenly I could hear the muffled voices deep in their rubber throats trying to get out. Paul's hours of work were instantly thrown into focus for me. These puppets were not facsimiles of life; they were actors waiting for their voices, for their moves, and like the rest of us a chance at that little slip between two eternities that we call life.
>
> From my perspective as a writer, this moment was the single most important thing that happened in the studio that morning. I would devote a few sentences to the facts concerning his painting of the faces, but the real mystery that I would focus on would be the sneeze. What happens when a two-hundred-fifty-pound puppeteer sneezes in his studio? That was where the tension was, the life and death drama, the mystery of a seemingly ordinary morning. (1985b, 530)

When Lasky decides to focus her book around the image of a giant puppet master sneezing in his studio, her intention is not to explain the mystery of that sneeze but to deepen it. Her decision to focus on one image, one scene, is emblematic of a trend in recent nonfiction books for children. Time and again, authors reveal their subjects through a close look at single moments or single scenes. In *Where the Bald Eagles Gather,* Dorothy Hinshaw Patent doesn't write an encyclopedia account of the bald eagle but centers her book instead around the annual autumn gathering of hundreds of eagles at Glacier National Park in Montana. In a similar way, Faith McNulty, in the extraordinary *Peeping in the Shell,* allows readers to join her in learning from the moment-by-moment struggles of a tiny, very precious whooping crane chick as it enters the world. The drama is not only about the struggle of a single chick; it's also the struggle of a tiny band of people who have devoted their lives to ensuring the survival of these endangered birds.

In her writing, Sofia Gonzales plans to discuss the legality of begging in subways and the current furor about benches being removed from the subways "to give them a cleaner image." She plans to discuss whether the violence on subways connects with the homeless who live there. But because she has read and studied nonfiction by Lasky, Patent, and others, she also knows the importance of drawing upon her own firsthand observations. As she waited one day for the subway, she described the scene in a short sketch she later incorporated into a major piece of writing:

> The subway station roars with trains. They pass by like a movie on fast-forward. Everybody rushes about never thinking about anything but catching trains.
>
> There is a man. His beard is matted and dirty. He is in a blanket and he hovers over a cup which he holds in his hand. In his plastic shopping bag there is a broken bottle, a broken umbrella, some soda cans, one glove and mismatched shoes. He has a backpack too; it is black and only a few papers are sticking out of it. He stands up and sits on a bench. I'm not sure but I think he knows I'm observing him. I feel uncomfortable.
>
> Another homeless man comes by. He is strangely dressed and there is something oddly familiar about him. Then I remember. He is the man I usually see in the park.
>
> The two men talk. I can't hear them but they laugh once. The train roars past and the two men get on. I want to follow them but I guess they would know I was following them, plus I don't know where they are going. As the train leaves, I think that in a way, homeless people have lots of houses all over the City.

It's no small thing to say that Sofia eventually incorporates these observations into her piece about the homeless in New York subways. If dramatic scenes and observations are going to be important in research reports, writers need to know how to shift in and out of close-up observations.

Children can study the way other authors shift between telescopic and wide-angle lenses. McNulty begins her book with a close-up description of the whooping crane. "Picture a big, white bird—the biggest bird you have ever seen," she says. "Picture it standing. Its body is balanced on long, thin legs." For the next few pages, McNulty continues building this scene. "Now the bird leans forward, runs a few steps and flaps into the air. It rises slowly, like a plane taking off. Its wings beat in short, strong strokes, lifting the heavy body. In the air it glides easily, now rising, now skimming the marsh grass, searching for the best place to land." Then McNulty makes a transition that Sofia and the others need to study. She shifts from discussing a single whooping crane to say, "One hundred years ago there were a good many places in America where you might have seen whooping cranes. . . . Now . . . whooping cranes are on the list of species that might become extinct."

Although Debbie Ulloa's hotel piece is in some ways a very simple piece of writing, the moves she makes between her observations of New York's Plaza Athenee Hotel and her reading knowledge of the Martinique Hotel for the homeless show a remarkable amount of control. She begins like this:

> I live next to the Plaza Athenee, one of the most beautiful hotels I've ever seen. It's the only connection I've ever made to the word hotel.
>
> But now I realize that hotels mean different things to different people.
>
> To me, the lobby of this glorious hotel means a place of fantasy where I visit and see antique furniture so old I'm afraid to sit on it. There are waxed floors you could see your reflection in and I'm too scared to run because I might put a mark on it. There are marble columns taller than I am, and flowers almost too expensive to smell.
>
> To Rachel and her children the lobby of the Martinique hotel means old cracked tiles popping up if you step wrong, smells of alcohol and beer in the air from the night before, smells of roach spray from an exterminator that recently came.
>
> To me hotel elevators mean clean carpeted places with velvety seats and polished panels that smell like lemon. The ride feels so smooth, it's like the elevator is staying in one place.
>
> To Rachel and her children it means broken down elevators with graffiti and not being able to finish her children's laundry on time because she is too scared to take the elevators and too tired to walk the 13 flights of stairs. . . .

Three Writers and Their Writing

The seed idea for Ja-keeya Toyer's writing emerged before the work on homelessness began. "Mrs. Davis told us to pick out and copy poems we like," Ja-keeya explained. "When I found Myra Cohn Livingston's 'Secrets' I started thinking that Mom has secrets she doesn't tell me. She doesn't tell me anything about her life." A month later when children in the class began searching for resources on the homeless, Ja-keeya's grandmother gave away part of the family's secret. "Why don't you interview your mother about homelessness?" she told Ja-keeya, and Ja-keeya's life changed in that instant:

It all started when my grandma told me that mommy was a runaway. I started walking down the hall to my mother's room. I was doing something I didn't want to do. I was intruding in my mother's business. But I had to find out the truth about my mother for my sake.

I walked down the long hall to her room, feeling like I was surrounded by guns and people were accusing me of murder. Finally, I reached the door. I knocked. No one responded. I thought, "Ja-keeya, have confidence in yourself. You have a right to know." So I opened the door. My mother was getting ready to close her eyes. She was lying on her polka-dot quilt. She looked very pale and sad. What am I doing here? This is my Mother's room. It's like signing a death threat with blood. I know I'm going to hear something I don't want to hear. She won't talk to me.

"Mom, can I ask you a question?" I said.

"What is it?"

"Nana told me you were once a runaway."

She paused. Tears filled her eyes and started coming down her cheeks. Now what do I do? Is she thinking about all the horrible things that happened to her? Her face became sadder, like someone died. I wonder whether she's going to send me out of the room.

"I'm calm now," she said.

"Thank goodness," I thought.

"Mom, I don't want to hurt your feelings, but can I please record what you're saying? Please Mom? Please?" She's going to say "no," I know it. I'm going to get mad and bang my head against the wall. Why does she take so long?

She said, "Get on with it."

This is it. You're in. You're okay. I rushed and got the blank tape. Here we go. Tape on.

The thing my mother said was, "When I was a little girl, I thought my parents didn't care for me. When I was twelve my mother and father would have fights, and every time I was around they would yell at me for no reason."

While I was listening I thought that my grandma and grandpa had been unfair to my mother. Why can't marriage just be happy for all couples?

Then my mother said, "When I [was] thirteen my parents were getting a divorce, so one day I met some friends. They asked if I wanted to run away. That night I said good-bye to my family. Unfortunately my friends left me on the street, a homeless person."

I could tell my mother was scared to say these things because she was playing with her fingers and tapping her toes. What would it be like if I ran away at the age of thirteen? If I were on the streets, I would feel very scared. I would cover my head so no one would see my face.

Then my mom said, "I had messed up my life, Ja-keeya." She told me that when you're at the mercy of other people, they use and abuse you. "When I finally came home, I felt like there was a new beginning in my life. I felt like I was in heaven."

I looked at my mother on the bed and I felt like I was the mother and she was my daughter. . . .

The draft continues for several more pages. Ja-keeya wrote the ending several weeks into the project, when her mother abruptly ran away one more time. Ja-keeya's essay ends:

Stop tape. Eject Tape. I played it all night long. I listened and listened to the tape. Now my mommy is gone again. Now it's just Nana and me.

This is immediately followed by an adapted version of Myra Cohn Livingston's "Secrets." The poem begins: "We don't mention where she went / We don't say that she was sent."

A week after Ja-keeya completed this draft, she failed all the exams for entrance into junior high. To me, it seems almost miraculous that she could write an essay like this one. But when I interviewed her, it was easy to see that Ja-keeya's writing didn't emerge out of thin air. It grew, bit by bit, as plants grow, and people, and good writing.

Initially, Ja-keeya had considered writing a series of publishable entries about discovering her mother's secret. She decided not to do this because her friend Geirthrudur had already embarked on a similar project. "I didn't want to follow in her footsteps," Ja-keeya said. Ja-keeya also tried writing the draft as a first-person story told by her mother, but "something was missing"—Ja-keeya—and so she realized that the story she needed to tell was her own. Once Ja-keeya decided on the plan for her draft, she tried to write each section as well as she could. "I tried to write it as a scene," Ja-keeya said. She also deliberately moves between telling what happened (the external story) and telling how she responded to what happened (the internal story). In her first draft, she skipped a space each time she switched from the events to her response, indenting the lines about her response. "When I was listening to my mother it was like two conversations were going on. She was saying one aloud to me and one was in my mind." Then Ja-keeya added, "The hardest part was being true to my feelings." Ja-keeya explains her growth in writing this way:

I started writing in third grade because my friends would tease me. They called me names, said I'm too young to have women parts, they called me "Bush" because my grandma would give me weird hairstyles with curlers. I started writing about it and I would keep writing until two in the morning at home, but I didn't bring that writing to school. I would just joke around at school and people didn't know I was good at writing.

From third grade until this year, I was not the true me at school. The true me is the part of me that's good at writing. This year I try to be the true me all the time.

When I take my writing out of the notebook, I look at the paper with my eyes real hard and I say, "Ja-keeya, this isn't the real part; it's a fake part," and so I start on scrap and change it and change it.

When I take it out of the notebook it's like magic because I can make it real and true. I start with all the knowledge that any teacher ever gave me about writing. I have all my essays and I take them out and look at them very hard and then I think about when Mr. Wilson said, "You used to be low in writing, but you've changed into a new person and now you're good at writing," and then I write.

When I finish changing it, I go to my dolls and I make believe they are alive and I say, "Can you help me with this?" I put them up and then they say, "This needs a little more work. It's good. You're working hard and you have a lot of good ideas but now you have to get to the big part—how to finish it . . . "

Then I go to my friend Anabelle and I ask, "How do you end a really important story like I'm writing?" She told me, "Think from your heart, not from your mind," and I do.

Geirthrudur Finnbogadottir is such a skittery, shy child that I was in Judy's classroom for several weeks before I even saw her, and then it was her extraordinary writing rather than her actual presence that caught my attention. Her writing leaves me breathless. "I often think my life is like a handful of sand," she wrote on the first day back at school after New Year's. "One by one [the grains of sand] fall. There's nothing you can do about it. It will keep failing until it's all gone, which is why I hate digital watches that count seconds" (Figure 13–4).

I read her notebook over and over, gasping at this child's language and insights. In one entry, she described her fear, as a little child, of waking up in the middle of the night and having to go to the bathroom:

It was terrifying . . . getting closer to the bathroom and feeling like my heart was running to the light switch.

Another time she wrote,

Sometimes I see a child, and I want to be that age again. I remember the smell of my playschool book bag. It almost always smelled of banana and chocolate.

Figure 13–4   Geirthrudur's January 4 Entry

> I often think that my life
> is like a handful of sand, one
> by one ~~they~~ they
> fall, there's nothing you can
> do about it, it will keep falling
> until it's all gone, which
> is why I hate digital watches
> that cout seconds. *

For this strangely quiet and gifted child, it wasn't easy researching the homeless. Geirthrudur had no interest in real estate taxes, statistics about the homeless, laws on begging, and the like, but more than this, she had a hard time feeling empathy for homeless people. On February 20 she wrote an entry that puzzled me (Figure 13–5):

> I imagine what a shelter might look like—rows of beds or empty rooms, but going farther than the outer edge of anybody is something my mind won't let me [do].

"What does she mean?" I wondered. "What is 'going farther than the outer edge of anybody'?" Then I read all her entries and began to see that she was struggling to get inside the skin of a homeless person. Unless Geirthrudur could understand how a homeless person sees the world, she did not know how to write well about the homeless, because for her writing involves locating a feeling within herself and then reaching deeper and deeper in order to find something true to say. Writing about the homeless was hard for her until

Figure 13–5   Geirthrudur's February 20 Entry

> I imagine what a shelter
> might look like, rows of beds
> or emty rooms, but going farther
> then the outer edge of any body
> is something my mind wonnt let
> me .

she could feel something about them. In one entry she wrote:

> When I think of being homeless, my immediate reaction would be to get a job. I figure there's always some way to earn money. I suppose I could never know what homelessness would feel like. I would always have a job and security of knowing there's my family.

Another time, Geirthrudur wrote:

> I have a lot of mixed feelings about being homeless. To simplify them, I think what I would do in the situation is that I wouldn't have any reason to stay on the streets.

It's not coincidental that after Geirthrudur and her classmates watched the movie *Ironweed*, Geirthrudur's one observation was, "It wasn't that much about being homeless but more of his past. It was mostly his choice to stay homeless. He could have stayed sober and worked."

I do not know what happened to change all this. I do know that Geirthrudur learned from her reading that landlords in New York sometimes set fire to their own buildings in order to oust responsible people who depend upon having rent-controlled apartments. Then, the exorbitant cost of rentals in the City makes it difficult for these people to find another low-cost rental. I know that she learned that 30 percent of the adults in shelters hold full-time jobs. Probably more importantly, I know that after Geirthrudur went outside the school and viewed the block around P.S. 183 through the eyes of a homeless person, her notebook contained a tiny seed of empathy. She wrote, "I'm often self-conscious about the smallest things. I don't think I could stand it if I were homeless. People would assume things." And I know that one day she whispered to me, "I'm going to write a likeness of this notebook." This is a selection from what she wrote (Figure 13–6):

> It was Christmas night in the city. It was quiet; Susan was carrying a small candle. There was no one around, and yet she felt small. Maybe you have noticed her, but pretended not to, only because she fell through the cracks of society. It wasn't too cold outside. Store windows were filled with red, green, and white decorations, and the Christmas spirit was in just about everyone. Everyone who knew what coziness and warmth lies inside their homes, instead of the silent and lonely night ahead.
>
> Susan was lucky that night. She had gotten a warm meal from the local soup kitchen, and had set herself down comfortably next to the wall of a restaurant that the hot air came from. Searching under her layers of clothing and blankets, a stream of panic came over her, but quickly faded as she uncovered a book . . .
>
> **9/29**
>
> I'm staying on the streets because I can't bring myself to ask for shelter or to be under the same roof as many other people, so I prefer to not have a roof at all. I wake up at night now; I can't sleep like I

used to. My nightmares are growing. I dreamed I was back home, home with Mother, I had a small, but new, hat on, and then the wind came and blew off the hat, and Mother with it. I still can't get over it, but she was old, she always took care of me. I always wanted a lot of sympathy, especially when I was small; I guess I never outgrew it.

10/5

I never thought of my old home as being big; sometimes I even hated it. Now I resent feeling that way, like having it ripped away from me was the punishment for not appreciating it. I remember just about every detail, and it seems like a castle now. The black-and-white T.V. standing by the basket Wiskers slept in, under the shelves of old books and statues. It seems more like a home now then it ever did before.

10/6

Once, when I was little, I woke up in the middle of the night; my blankets had fallen on the floor. Being too tired to pick them up, I only felt like sinking into the mattress. It reminded me of the hollowness; in everyone, no matter who you are, there is always a space where there's no explanation, because you can't confront it, you disregard it as being a problem and don't want the memories of it, and self-consciously regret not confronting it. There are many holes in the core of my heart, but it'll take a big shovel to bury the feeling of guilt to Mother. Why did I just leave?

10/25

When I was little, I had high hopes. I never dreamed I'd end up less than what I've ever been. I tossed around ideas like being a doctor, a lawyer, or an actor. I often wish I were a child again; just the thought of having someone else take care of me, it sounds so comfortable and simple. Simple pleasures were of more importance than any long-term plan. Almost forgotten smells still inhabit my mind as a symbol of the simplicity of childhood, like the mixed smell of banana and chocolate milk in my playschool book bag.

10/30

The teachers said I had talent for writing; now it's the only way I can make a statement without everyone turning away in disgust. Any anger is neatly bottled up in the core of my heart, not to be tampered with. It was hard at first, but as time goes by it just seems more and more hopeless. I can't soak in self-pity any more, because there's only me.

11/2

I used to like having a space in my mind that assures me that there's space to relax, and that there isn't too tight a schedule of anything. Now I like to pull everything close to me that would be in any way valuable, including time.

Figure 13–6   What Geirthrudur Wrote

It was Christmas night in the city. It was quiet, Susan was carrying a small candle. There was no one around and yet she felt small. Maybe you have noticed her, but pretended not to, only because she fell through the cracks of society. It wasn't too cold outside, store windows were filled with red, green, and white decorations, and the christmas spirit was in just about everyone. Everyone who knew what coziness and warmth lies inside their homes, instead of the silent and lonely night ahead.

Susan was lucky that night, she had gotten a warm meal from the local soup kitchen, and had set herself down comfortably next to the wall of a restaurant that the hot air came from. Searching under her layers of clothings and blankets, a stream of panic came over her, but quickly faded as she uncovers a book...

9/29
I'm staying on the streets, because I can't bring myself to ask for shelter, or to be under the same roof as many other people, so I prefer to not have a roof at all. I wake up at night now, I can't sleep like I used to. My night mares are growing, I dreamed I was back home, home with mother, I had a small, but new hat on and then the wind came and blew off the hat, and mother with it, I still can't get over it, but she was old, she always took care of me. I always wanted alot of sympathy especially when I was small, I guess I never outgrew it.

10/5
I never thought of my old home as being big, sometimes I even hated it. Now I resent feeling that way, like having it ripped away from me was the punishment for not appreciating it. I

remember just about every detail, and it seems like a castle now. The black-and-white T.V. standing by the basket Wiskers slept in, under the shelves of old books and statues. It seems more like a home now then it ever did before.

10/6
Once, when I was little, I woke up in the middle of the night, my blankets had fallen on the floor. Being too tired to pick them up, I only felt like sinking into the mattress. It reminded me of the hollowness, in every one, no matter who you are, there is always a space where there's no explantion, because you can't confront it, you disregard it as being a problem, and don't want the memories of it, and self-consciously regret not confronting it. There are many holes in the core of my heart, but it'll take a big shovel to bury the feeling of guilt to mother, why did I just live?

10/25
When I was little, I had high hopes, I never dreamed I'd end up less then what I've ever been, I tossed around ideas like being a doctor, a lawyer, or a actor. I often wish I were a child again, just the thought of having someone else take care of me, it sounds so comfortable and simple. Simple pleasures were of more importance then any long-term plan. Almost forgotten smells still inhabit my mind as a symbol of the simplicity of childhood, like the smell of banana and choclate milk in my playschool book bag.

Figure 13–6 Continued

10/30

The teachers said I had talent for writing, now it's the only way I can make a statement without everyone turning away in disgust. Any anger is neatly bottled up in the core of my heart, not to be tampered with It was hard at first, but as time goes by it just seems more and more hopeless. I can't soak in self-pity any more, because there's only me.

11/2

I used to like having a space in my mind that assures me that there's space to relax, and that there isn't too tight a schedule of anything. Now I like to pull everything close to me that would be in any way valuble, including time.

11/19

I was at the library today, mostly for the warmth, but you can only stay inside if you're reading, so I started. Alot of them weren't that good, though there were some good ones that I hadn't seen before, and old favorites, mostly in the children's section. There was was a poem book, with old flulla byes I was going to sing to my children and still the dull colors on the pages were as musical as the words in my mind. But being half ashamed of the fact that I'm a slow reader, reading usually less then three books a year, except this year, I've been reading alot more, luckily this was the year they made up the rule of letting homeless people inside the library as long a they're reading. So I took some children's books into the adult section, making sure to hide the covers carefully. Some of the parts in the books I recognize as well as it were my own past, and the charactors were like my only friends. I couldn't finish though; I had fallen asleep, and when it was closing time I was pushed out Maybe I'll write a book, then just maybe I'll be able to climb out of this hole.

11/19

   I was at the library today, mostly for the warmth, but you can only stay inside if you're reading, so I started [looking at books]. A lot of them weren't that good, though there were some good ones that I hadn't seen before, and old favorites, mostly in the children's section. There was a poem book, with old lullabies I was going to sing to my children, and still the dull colors on the pages were as musical as the words in my mind. But being half ashamed of the fact that I'm a slow reader, reading usually less than three books a year, except this year, I've been reading a lot more, luckily this was the year they made up the rule of letting homeless people inside the library as long as they're reading. So I took some children's books into the adult section, making sure to hide the covers carefully. Some of the parts in the books I recognize as well as [if] it were my own past, and the characters were like my only friends. I couldn't finish, though; I had fallen asleep, and when it was closing time I was pushed out. Maybe I'll write a book. Then just maybe I'll be able to climb out of this hole.

Jon Grimke, a boy whose mother recently died and whose father is now very sick, connected to writing for the first time ever during this project. Jon listened raptly as Judy read Jonathan Kozol's *Rachel and Her Children* aloud; then he wrote pages and pages in his notebook about his life in a low-income housing project: about watching a man jump off the roof of a building because of drugs, about knowing a five-year-old whose mother murdered some people, about a lady who was wheeled into an ambulance because of a drug overdose. "There were two sides to Smith Project," Jon said, "the light side and the dark side." Then Jon went on to tell about homeless people near the project who assembled a shelter for themselves and began fixing and selling broken toys.

Looking back on his year, Jon said, "When Mrs. Davis first told me about writing, I was mad. Now no one has to tell me and I write. The notebook is somebody else to talk to, to tell my problems to."

It was not easy for Jon to focus his work on the homeless. His notebook was filled with pages and pages of notes and thoughts about the topic and about himself. Never in his life had he written so much. Each bit seemed precious to him. "I was one of the kids who wandered for an idea," Jon explained to me, and we both recalled his restlessness as one friend after another settled on a topic. "If I had never wrote 'The Bums,' I don't know what I'd be doing. My whole project relates to that one poem I wrote in October. Now I know: off of a few words, you can make a whole book."

Jon's final project chronicles his learning between October, when he wrote "The Bums," and May, when he wrote an entirely different poem about the homeless. When he explained his project to me he said, "Before, when someone is fat, and then they diet . . . Well, before this research, I was fat with fear, and now I'm skinny and I want to help the homeless." Then he explained, "My grandma had always said, 'Don't go near those weirdos. They're bad,' because she didn't want me to get hurt. And the stereotype of them just went onto me. All of this time before I came to this project, I thought they were drunk, alcoholics . . . scary people."

Then Jon told me about the genesis of his writing. As soon as he thought of his topic, he knew he would want to start with a page about the October day in which he'd written his poem. "I couldn't remember the day that well, but my teacher reminded me of Kathryn Lasky's advice." Jon gestured to the framed quote hanging on one wall of the classroom, in which Lasky said, "In my own experience in writing, I have always tried hard to listen, smell, and touch the place that I write about—especially if I am lucky enough to be there" (1985b, 530).

This quote gave Jon permission to invent whatever he couldn't recall, and so he began drawing from every imaginable source. This is the beginning of Jon's paper:

It was a murky October day. The still, warm air blew on my face as I walked on the familiar streets to school. I noticed that the old man with the dirty white beard was sitting on a bench. I knew him. His name was Abe. A few times I saw him digging through a garbage pail that I would never go near. I also saw him just yelling for no reason. I wondered why he would do this but I feared for my safety so I wouldn't go close. Today he was sitting next to another familiar face. I also knew her because she would always rock back and forth. I could tell she was one of the bums because she had thick clothing and two bags. I stared curiously at them. Somehow she looked weak but still scary. Not scary like the men. They're crazy and they're acting drunk and swinging empty bottles of liquor. They petrify me. . . .

In school I was still thinking about that day and I wrote a poem.

Jon and I looked back on the page together and he told me the sources he drew upon in order to write it. As we talked, I was reminded of June Good-field, who describes the process of writing nonfiction in this way:

All scientists have these little pieces of colored glass, intriguing bits of information or facts which they don't quite know what to do with. They leave them lying around until, prompted by a new idea or a new piece of information, they mentally sift them and select the ones that might help the pattern. (1981, 113)

Jon decided to make the October day "murky" when he remembered a reference in his social studies book to the Loch Ness monster, said to live in a "murky" lake of Scotland. He added a detail about two bags because, as Jon said, "You can picture the homeless people in your head. I remember, I saw that guy sitting down and there were bags." Jon added the detail about the homeless person digging through the garbage after a morning when he passed a homeless man he knew doing the same.

Jon's writing included about five sections, each describing a different lesson Jon had learned. "I got the idea for how to put it together from *Living with a Parent Who Takes Drugs*," Jon said. "In that book, there is one main story, and then other parts with more facts. I really like this idea of writing," he explained. "I can fit the puzzle pieces to make it work."

But of course, what really made Jon's writing work was the way he brought his life to the topic. More than anything, this is the story of a boy who learned to walk a mile in someone else's shoes. "When my mother died and I moved and my father went to the hospital and I moved . . . well, sometimes I think I've moved a lot, but it's beyond my imagination what it means when they say that a homeless person often moves forty times. When I was in the office today, I thought about the eyes of a homeless kid looking at this office and wondering if he would get used to this school before he had to leave it." Then Jon said, "When we were studying the homeless, I could see the scenes of *Rachel and Her Children* on one side of my head, and on the other side I saw myself in scenes like those. In this project I learned to write, but mostly I learned to relate." Yes, Jon—and Geirthrudur, Ja-keeya, and Debbie—that's big. That's big enough to live for.

14

Learning to Confer in Ways That Last a Lifetime

When I was new to teaching writing, I used to travel once a month to the University of New Hampshire for a fifteen-minute writing conference with Donald Murray. Readers of *The Art of Teaching Writing* may recall that I began the section of that book on conferring by asking, "What did Murray do in those fifteen-minute conferences that was worth five hours of driving?" Now, as I again approach the subject of conferring, I am still asking that question, and I am more conscious than ever of the way our experiences as students of writing can provide us with wells to draw upon as we teach.

As I recall, Murray would usually begin our conferences by saying something like, "How'd it go this month?" or "What problems are you running into?" Before long I came to these conferences ready for the invitation to muse aloud about my writing. I'd talk, and Murray would finger his mustache, listening intently, and sometimes he'd ask clarifying questions. Often he would reach for the draft, saying, "Let me take a look." Then he'd ask something like, "Is this section one of the places where you struggled?" or "'I noticed your tone changes here." And we'd talk some more. Then there would be a moment of silence when Murray would scan the draft or his bookcase or the scene outside his window. Out of that silence he would quietly and directly teach something. Once Murray said to me, "You can trust that you write well in your own voice. It might be time to begin trusting other people's voices too, letting other people's voices come through in your writing. Perhaps you could go out on the beat like a journalist; write on a subject that you don't know, and let the experts teach you and your reader."

Another time Murray said, "Your piece is titled 'Balance the Basics: Reading and Writing,' but what I'm noticing when I spread out the pages and look at the balance of attention (I do this with my drafts, too) is that you have

225

seven pages on writing and three on reading. You might ask what the imbalance means, and what it means that your architecture doesn't match your content."

Once Murray speculated about why I talk so fast and write so densely, stuffing in information as fast as I can. (Is it because I grew up in a family of nine children and had to compete for air time?) He suggested that I try letting my ideas stretch out and unfold more in my writing, that I take more time to explore nuances and build images.

Now, as I think about it, I realize that these conferences tended to have three parts. They began with research. Sometimes, but not always, this would involve reading the draft and hearing my reading of it and then asking questions, not little questions to show me he was interested in my topic but big questions about my experience and intentions and problems and discoveries in writing this draft and writing in general. Then there would be silence, a moment of decision. During that moment, it was as if he thought, "Of all the ways I could help Lucy, what's the one thing that might make the biggest difference to her now?" And finally, there would be teaching—teaching in a way that commanded attention and made a world of difference. Generally, it was characterized not by a sea of chatter but by Murray saying one thing simply and clearly. He'd usually begin by pointing out what he noticed, what he saw, and then make a suggestion based on that. He would typically say something like, "What I notice is . . . " and then, "One thing you might try is. . . . "

The important thing is that Murray wasn't looking at the text and saying, "This might improve the paragraph." Instead he was looking at me and saying, "'This might improve you as a writer." Many of Murray's conferences still guide my teaching and my living. I think often about the balance of attention I give to things, about the conflicts between my content and my form, about the value of lingering. In those fifteen-minute interactions, Murray gave me insights and suggestions that will last a lifetime, and I cannot help but wonder how often my conferences give children insights and suggestions that will last as long. I cannot help but wonder whether children carry what I say in conferences with them for years and years.

In the movie *Platoon,* during the worst of the Vietnam war, one of the soldiers describes the craziness of the battlefield by saying, "I'm just counting days and seeing four inches in front of my face." Too often in my writing conferences with children, I look only four inches in front of the writer's face. Too often, I suggest that the writer add a detail, fix an ending, clarify a line . . . and two minutes later, when the work is done, the writer can only line up again to ask, "What do I do next?" In contrast, Murray's conferences were far-sighted.

The problem is not in our intentions. We know that in a conference our job is to interact with students so that they can interact with their writing, not just for five minutes but for a lifetime. The problem, instead, is that most of us have not received the help necessary to confer with clarity, vision, and voice. Let me explain.

Why Conferring Remains So Difficult

Several years ago, I was asked by *Ladies Home Journal* to be part of a feature story on young professional women. I was told to report to a photography studio on the corner of Third Avenue and Twenty-fourth Street. Dressed in my best rose-colored suit, I arrived at the designated address and ten flights of stairs later creaked open a door and stepped into a palatial, glistening white loft. One entire wall was draped with a sparkling fabric that fell in folds over the floor. Little men darted here and there all over the room. Hurrying over to me they said, "This way," and steered me by the elbow into a small corner room and onto a chair. Before I could protest, they cranked the chair back and began busily washing my already-washed hair. After my hair was washed, set, and styled, the makeup team moved in. An hour later I was back in the main room, positioned on the sea of fabric. The men backed up and, cocking their heads this way and that, whispered among themselves. Then one darted off for the makeup tray, another took out a comb, and another began to work on my skirt. He surprised me by unbuttoning my waist button and letting my skirt drop down onto my hips. Crouching behind me, he used half a dozen clothespins to resculpt the fullness of my skirt, then turned to loosen my blouse. After a few final strokes with the blusher brush and lipstick pen, the men set to work on my position. "Move your right foot forward. No, not so much. Just a little bit. Even those shoulders, okay? Turn your head now, slightly to the left. No, to the right. The left. That's it. Chin up. Up some more. That's it. Hold still now." Moving at last to the camera, they called out, "Just be yourself. Act natural."

In the field of teaching writing, the same thing has been done to teachers who want to confer wisely and well. Teachers have been shown the proper position: down low, crouching on the floor or sitting on a miniature chair from the kindergarten room, looking up into the student's eyes. They've been reminded to talk quietly, they've heard the advantages of pausing for more than the usual three-second interval, and they've been warned against holding the student's piece or else responsibility for the writing will be, quite literally, in their hands. They've heard that the student must speak first. They've been warned against evaluating the writing—that's the writer's job. They've been reminded again about eye contact. Then, after all this, they're told, "Just be yourself. Act natural."

It's no surprise that in our conferences with young writers many of us feel guilty and inadequate, certain we're doing something wrong. We position ourselves so that we can look into the student's face, we establish eye contact, but all the while the rules of conferring are scrolling past us. There is a heaven and a hell, a right and a wrong way to confer, and we all live in fear of asking the wrong question or taking away ownership. Shelley Harwayne recently asked a group of teachers to divide into pairs and role-play some conferences with each other. As she looked around the room, Shelley realized that the teachers who were not on task, who were perhaps chatting about their weekend plans, looked great, and that the ones who were trying to confer looked awful. With furrowed foreheads and sweaty hands, they worked their way through the conversation.

When we worry so much about our questions, it's easy to forget what we know about teaching. Mary Ellen Giacobbe, a former teacher from Atkinson, New Hampshire, who now consults in school districts around the country, tells of being met at the airport by a group of teachers who confided immediately, and with great desperation, "We're so glad you're here. We've been waiting three months for your advice." "What's the problem?" Mary Ellen asked. "The kids are writing about farts," they answered. "We told them they could choose their own topics, and all over the school, they're writing about farts. What do we do?" "Tell them not to," Mary Ellen said, matter-of-factly. Surprised, the teachers responded, "We can do that?"

We laugh and think, "How silly." But it's not silly. It's sad. The problem is not that kids are writing about farts but that some of us have lost confidence in our ability to think for ourselves within the context of the writing conference. We only feel secure about our conferring when we stay within the conference scripts we know well. When the child writes, "I went to my grandmother's this weekend," we respond, "Oh, you went to your grandmother's? Could you tell me more about it?" After the child talks for a while we say, "That seems really important. How did you feel?" Then, after another interval, we end the conference by concluding, "Why don't you put that down on the paper?" and move on to the next child. After reading the next child's text, we respond, "You've said a lot of things here. You've talked about this, this, this, and this. Of all these things, is there *one* that is particularly important?" Again the child answers, and then we say, "I'm wondering if you might want to write about just that one thing."

We have all learned these scripts from books on teaching writing, and we are comfortable when everything proceeds as the books told us they would. But this rarely happens, and we constantly find ourselves wishing we could ask someone, "What do I say now?" "And now?" "And now?" The problem is not that conferring is ominously difficult, nor is the problem that we must be excellent writers in order to confer well. The problem is that teachers need more help—and a different kind of help—with conferring than they have received.

In staff development workshops I have talked about kinds of conferences. I've shared lists of good conference questions, I've encouraged teachers to practice the skills involved in squeezing as many good conferences as possible into a ten-minute interval, and I've given teachers guidelines for critiquing their conferences. But what I have finally realized is that none of this is what we need in order to confer well.

Conferring well is every bit as challenging as writing well. I wouldn't dream of helping students write well by giving them a list of twenty good things to say in their texts. Writers don't need ditto sheets of tips or lists of what to say. What writers need is time, ownership, reasons to care, responsive readers, and shoulders upon which to stand. Writers need environments that will allow them to grow and improve. In order to learn to confer well, teachers likewise need equally rich, supportive contexts for learning. We need to focus less on the *product* of effective conferences and more on the *process* of learning to confer.

Time: Giving Ourselves Enough "Slow to Grow"

As Donald Murray says, writers need "time for staring out of windows, time for thinking, time for dreaming, time for doodling, time for rehearsing, planning, drafting . . . circling, moving closer, backing off, coming at it from a different angle, circling again, trying a new approach" (1989, 22–23). Yet no one seems to recognize the contradiction when we say that writers need time and in the next breath that teachers must hold frequent short conferences. No one seems to recognize the contradiction when we—when I—give students time for drafting, revising, and responding, and yet in staff development sessions ask teachers to practice the technique of squeezing as many reasonably effective conferences as possible into a ten-minute block of time.

"The notion that teachers can create conditions that are alive and stimulating for children," Seymour Sarason, author of *The Creation of Settings and the Future Societies* (1972) writes, "when those same conditions do not exist for teachers has no warrant in the history of mankind." If we are going to grow in our ability to confer, we, like young writers, need time to stare out windows, time to think about a student, a piece of writing, an emerging pattern. We need time to plan, rehearse, experiment, to follow one tangent, back off, come at a child from a different angle, circle, acquire a new approach.

Eve Merriam has a poem:

A Lazy Thought

There go the grownups
To the office,
To the store.
Subway rush,
Traffic crush;
Hurry, scurry,
Worry, flurry.

No wonder
Grownups
Don't grow up
Any more.

It takes a lot
Of slow
To grow.

If we're going to develop our ability to confer, we need to give ourselves enough "slow to grow." We probably cannot learn to confer as we rush about the room dragging a chair behind us, always conscious of a Pied Piper line of children waiting for help. The question then becomes, "When we're conferring with a class full of young writers, how can we get enough 'slow to grow'?"

I think we need to start by considering whether we've gotten ourselves caught in a treadmill of ineffective conferences. Sometimes, without intending to do so, we buy into the notion that our classrooms will only maintain their workshop hum if we rush from one corner to another like little Pac-men, devouring problems. Our suggestions, especially when we teach in this kind of hurry, all too often lead to three minutes of industriousness that begin to unravel more and more and more until we return, Pac-man style, hurried and breathless, as if our presence is the only thing that holds the body and soul of the writing workshop together. And so we rush faster still and rarely even give ourselves the time to look back.

If this is happening, our conferences are probably carrying more of the weight of our teaching than they can bear. We need to shift our focus temporarily from conferring to establishing rich, productive environments in our classrooms and organizing important courses of study. It's important to remember that the conference method of teaching is based on the metaphor of teacher as coach. When coaches confer with individuals as they work out or play a game, during those brief interactions they don't organize and initiate the game or assign positions. They only comment on, refine, and support the way a person is already performing in an ongoing game. In the same way, much of our teaching will not happen during conferences. Teaching writing also involves creating a richly literate environment, a classroom that brims over with books and poetry, storytelling and songs, and people's lives. Teaching writing involves demonstrating the process of writing and reasons to write. Teaching writing involves designing learning activities, organizing and nurturing response groups and peer conferring, initiating courses of study, building mentor relationships, laughing together, and crying together. It takes all of this to provide the context that makes conferences possible—and powerful. Yet all of this can also make us feel urgently needed and constantly rushed.

The feeling that one must rush from one child to another devouring problems exists in even the most effective writing classrooms. It exists because we teachers, as a profession, buy into the notion that we can give and give and give and give, because we do not really allow ourselves to hear the truth in Seymour Sarason's words. But although Sarason is right when he says that we cannot create conditions for children unless those same conditions exist for us, he needs to go one step further. If we want to work in conditions that are alive and stimulating for us, then we must take responsibility for establishing those conditions in our classrooms. For starters, this means that we must decide that we are not going to feel guilty about giving ourselves the time to learn.

During the last year of teaching before she joined the Project staff, Joanne Hindley decided that in order to learn about reading conferences, she would deliberately change the pace of her conferring. Instead of holding twenty short conferences each day, she would hold about six short conferences and three long, thoughtful ones. "I knew I needed those longer conferences," she said, "just like I needed more time for responding to the reading journals." Joanne had been bringing home thirty-four journals every night. At two in the morning, she'd be saying, "Ten more journals to go." She realized that her responses weren't particularly thoughtful, and she wasn't enjoying the process. So she began bringing home five reading journals each night, taking the time to read and reread all the entries, to think carefully about the child, and to choose her responses.

In the same way, Joanne began taking the time she needed to learn from the reading conferences she and the children held together. Once she had decided to hold three long conferences (as well as many shorter ones) each day, Joanne found that her attitude as she approached a conference was different. Rather than just saying what she'd been taught to say in conferences and not feeling responsible for what happened as a result, she found herself thinking, "This conference is going to matter. It is going to leave a mark." Then she would listen carefully, reflect on and develop a hypothesis about that child, and invest enough of herself in the conference to learn from the interaction. Because Joanne was intent on making her conferences matter, she found herself watching what happened in the wake of the conferences and conducting follow-up conferences that grew out of the initial ones.

We have become convinced that holding longer, slower conferences is necessary in order for us to develop a touch for conferring in ways that make a difference. But it is also true that the conferences in which we as teachers learn the most will, in turn, be conferences in which writers learn the most. When everyone says the central act of conferring is listening, it's a kind of listening that has little to do with striking a responsive pose (head cocked, big eyes turned up) and only something to do with learning from writers about their guinea pig or their first day of school. The listening that helps students the most is a listening that comes, above all, from knowing that if we take our cues from the writer, this conference can be a place for us to learn to confer.

How can we give ourselves the time to learn in this larger way from selected conferences? We can hold long conferences with one or two writers while the rest of the workshop is engaged in silent writing. We can deal with reading as well as writing in our conferences, meeting with some children during silent reading. Perhaps we can even reduce the number of students with whom we have conferences by asking a local writer to confer (for a while) with a third of the class or by suggesting that each month another five students work with each other on writing a novel or a play or a book. We can schedule writing conferences before school or over lunch. And with a different cluster of children each month, we can use dialogue journals rather than conferences.

In addition, we can give ourselves opportunities for long, slow conferences if we also learn to alternate these with conferences that are quick and efficient. Especially when we confer quickly, we will want to invite writers to identify their problem or question. Then we may not always need to read the draft, and we surely don't need to read it unless the writer gives us a job ("Tell me if it's too long." "Do I need to add more to the ending?") It is also important to remember that the purpose of a conference is not to *resolve* the problem but to *identify* it, suggesting resources and ways to proceed. If Rory is losing energy over her seemingly endless fiction story, it is enough to suggest that she needs models of very short fiction and to set her up with Cynthia Rylant's *Every Living Thing* or a magazine. If Sam needs to talk about his topic, it's enough to pair him with a friend. During conferences intended to be quick and efficient, the writing teacher can act as a switchboard that connects writers to each other and to appropriate resources.

Finally, if we want to spend fifteen minutes in quick conferences that give all the children in our workshop a sense of our presence and availability, it's crucial that after we have a conference at one table in the room, we hold our next conference in an entirely different area. This will mean that we must resist the eyes and the fingers that reach out for us and try to keep us conferring with one child after another around the table. One way to resist the child who wants our attention is to say, "Come along with me," and have that child listen as we confer across the room. We might also avoid problems if we open such conferences up to all the interested writers at a table. If we're talking with Rory about her gradual loss of interest in her writing, for example, we can ask, "Do any of you have the same feeling?" and when we suggest that Rory use a book as a resource, we can say, "All of you might, in fact, think about what problem you're having now as a writer. Is there a way a book might help you as it is helping Rory?"

One way or another, we need to give ourselves at least *some* opportunities to confer slowly, and in this way to develop our skills as conferring partners.

Response: Sharing the Thinking Behind Our Conferences

If we're going to develop our ability to confer, we also need response. Time and response are, of course, the two elements all of us need in order to develop as writers, and the similarities that are emerging between learning to write and learning to confer are not accidental. Everything that can be said about learning to write is probably also true of learning to confer.

Just as writing is a dialogue with one's emerging draft, a process of shifting between pulling in to write and pulling back to reflect on one's writing, so, too, conferring involves a process of shifting between being absorbed by the conversation and standing at a distance from it, asking, "What have I said so far?" "What's good here that I can build upon?" "What is surprising me?" Just as writers develop an "other self" by talking with other writers during the writing process, so too, teachers can develop an "other self" if we're able to reflect with someone else about the minute-to-minute decisions we make during the conferring process.

Seven-year-old Rhashida read her story. It is one sentence long: "My dog died." Ralph Fletcher, who was teaching her at the time, responded, "That's terrible. I'm so sorry." Rhashida went on, "And guess what. I have this sandbox in my back yard . . . ? And even though Cleo is dead, her footprints are still in the sand." Ralph's eyes lit up. What a gem of a detail. What a difference it could make in the piece. "Rhashida," Ralph said, "that's so powerful. Are you going to put that into your poem?" But Rhashida shook her head. "Nope," she said firmly, as if to say, "No. I'm done with it. I'm getting a new dog and I don't want to think about the old one *any more*."

Moments like this happen all the time in our conferences, and they make us feel empty-handed, caught off guard, unprepared. Summer institutes and district office workshops and books on teaching writing can provide us with the initial moves, like those Ralph made in his conference with Rhashida, but nothing quite prepares us for the curve balls youngsters throw at us. "Help!" we think. "Do I urge and cajole Rhashida to add her detail about the footprints in the sand, or do I let the detail slip away unwritten?" We need to find ways to share these questions with each other. We need to laugh about the frustration we feel when a writer like Rhashida blatantly discards a brilliant detail. We need to learn about conferring not only at the university and at home from a book but also in our classrooms alongside children like Rhashida. And sometimes we need to share this learning with our colleagues.

The question that then follows from "How can I give myself enough 'slow to grow'?" is "How can I organize my work so that my colleagues and I can share the fleeting, unpredictable challenges of conferring?" In Writing Project schools, most staff development takes place in classrooms, so it has not been logistically difficult for teachers and Project staff members to study conferring within the context of real classroom situations. Because a Project staff member is in a classroom for only about twenty days a year, it has been important for teachers to find ways to continue to study conferring with each other once we've gone. Some principals have given writing workshop teachers a roving substitute teacher who comes once a month—or perhaps every Monday for a month—to free teachers up to attend each other's writing workshops. Some teachers bring their children together to write because they know that this is the only way they'll be able to confer alongside another teacher. Similar arrangements can be made when we, as teachers, recognize that the best way to learn to confer is by working with a colleague, drawing our chairs together alongside a young writer.

Joanne Hindley and the teachers at P.S. 41 and P.S. 220 began their study of conferring by tape-recording their conferences during their writing workshops. This was especially powerful because in a single week these teachers not only listened to and responded to their tapes; they also reread relevant chapters from books and articles on conferring. "We all reread chapters 12 to 16 from *The Art of Teaching Writing*, and Murray's 'Teaching the Other Self,' and Atwell's chapter 5," Joanne Hindley said. "Most of us had read all of these years ago, but in rereading we realized that we are different people now and can take different things from the chapters." Then, too, these teachers found it's an entirely different matter to read chapters on conferring while also listening to a tape recording of one's own conferring. When Joanne and the teachers gathered for lunch, their insights were amazing. One teacher said, "I notice I don't see what the child *has* done. I'm far too critical." Another said, "I do most of the talking." Another said, "One thing I do well is that at the end of a conference, I pull things together and send the child off with a sense of momentum." These comments about conferring may not seem new or inspired. For years now, writing process teachers have known the importance of letting children talk in conferences and of being supportive. But the important thing is that although these teachers had been "in the know" for years—they'd taught *others* about conferring—only now were they discovering that for all their good intentions they still needed to grow in their ability to confer. Listening to themselves on tape, these teachers were able to see things about themselves they hadn't seen before. "And the most exciting thing was that once we really saw what we were doing," Joanne said, "we could, in an instant, change deeply entrenched patterns."

The teachers made new resolutions about their conferring and taped themselves to see if their conferences got any better. Another time they taped themselves conferring in order to see if they held what I describe in *The Art of Teaching Writing* as process and evaluation conferences. They even transcribed their conferences in a double entry log, recording the conference verbatim in one column and alongside it in another column their musings and explanations, questions and feelings. They shared these logs with each other and talked about the insights they'd gained. Later, Joanne raised some questions, and everyone returned to the transcripts with these questions in mind:

- Who generally speaks first in my conferences?
- Is there a pattern to what happens at the beginning and end of my conferences?
- Whose agenda emerges in the conferences?
- Are the conferences aimed more toward improving this piece of writing, or toward giving the writer something he or she can use another day with another piece?
- How many points do I generally make in a conference?
- Whose voice is most predominant on the tape—mine or the child's?
- Is my voice that of a fellow reader and writer or that of a teacher?

At P.S. 148, the teachers decided that in order to become more adept at the three aspects of conferring—research, making a decision, and teaching—they would try for a while to consider each component separately. They started out by devoting two weeks entirely to research. They began holding conferences that were not intended to be teaching episodes at all but research opportunities. They asked youngsters, for example, to rank their notebook entries and pieces, identifying the ones they liked best and second best and explaining their rationale, and they did this not to alter the child's standards of judgment but to understand them. They asked their young writers how they might improve pieces of writing, and the question was meant not as a side road into revision but as another way of understanding the children as writers. Because they were learning a lot about youngsters and because this learning was their main focus, the teachers also began keeping records of what they were learning. These became more significant than any of us anticipated. Tools shape habits of thought. We see children differently once we have devoted several weeks to this kind of research and have begun keeping a notebook that we've sectioned off with space for each child's emerging portrait.

After their two weeks of research, the teachers at P.S. 148 tried to find ways to share the thinking that underlies the decisions they make as they confer. They worked in clusters of three, gathering together to think about a particular conference. Before the conference, a teacher would give her colleagues an overview of the writer and then everyone would listen as the teacher interviewed the writer in order to try to understand the issues and concerns and agendas that were on the child's mind at that moment. Then, when it came time to make a decision, the group of teachers would talk out their options. "Of all we could say to this writer, of all we could suggest, what's the one thing that might make the greatest difference?"

Wells to Draw on When We Confer

As important as it is to slow down the fleeting and unpredictable processes in our conferences, to voice and share our bewilderment and our resolutions, in the end conferring will always challenge us to think quickly on our feet. Conferring will always call us to invent, instantly, altogether new responses to whatever curve balls a child throws at us. Even if we tend to begin conferences on solid ground with strategies that have worked in other conferences, time and again we will reach the place where we say, "Gee, I wasn't expecting this. Where do I go from here?" and this will be the life-giving moment in our conference. In that moment of choice, when we and our young writers invent ways of talking and thinking about writing, and about life, we will learn to confer.

We cannot plan our conferences, yet we must be prepared for them. We prepare for conferring in very much the same way we prepare for writing. In chapter 4, I quoted Katherine Paterson's description of the living that readies her for writing, and now it seems to me that she nurtures her writing in the same ways that we must nurture our conferring:

> I am conscious of feeding the process. . . . I read, I think, I talk, I look,
> I listen, I hate, I fear, I love, I weep, and somehow all of my life gets
> wrapped around the grain. (1981, 26)

Teachers as Researchers

Several years ago the Edwin Gould Foundation came to me with a startling question. "How can we help make your dreams for classrooms come true?" Schuyler Meyer, the director, asked. "We'll support whatever you think would make the biggest difference."

Schuyler's question was a difficult one. "What would make the biggest difference in classrooms?" I thought about it. Books? Writing groups for teachers? Money to support school-based, teacher-led study networks? All of these seemed crucial. But I decided that the first and most important characteristic of good teaching is that we all watch and learn from our children. For six years, the Edwin Gould Foundation has enabled a team of teachers from throughout New York City to come together weekly to develop the habits of inquiry and the stance of classroom researchers. These teachers have been given research grants and opportunities to study with ethnographers, but most of all they've been given the chance to work together.

Although each of these teachers has a different area of study, they sometimes share research methods. Many of them have institutionalized a daily habit of observation. During the interval of silent writing that opens many writing workshops, these teachers walk silently among the writers with a clipboard and observational sheet in hand, noticing everything they can possibly notice. One day Joanne Hindley, who had introduced Rosalie Franzese to this research instrument, noticed as she and Rosalie watched together that Marta reread her piece twice before resuming her writing. They noticed that Russell sat with a blank sheet of paper, staring into space and tapping his pencil. Peter's pages were clipped together with a paper clip, and he began the workshop by rearranging the pages. Mark took a break from his dinosaur report to look at dinosaur flash cards. Sonya's story was titled *Pet Sematary*. Georgia's desk was buried in papers, projects, and books, and her attention seemed to shift constantly. She wrote for a moment, then dug into her pocket for a quarter and carefully aligned it on top a picture of a quarter in her math book, did a math problem or two, read her assignment pad. . . .

Before Rosalie and Joanne began conferring with the children, they spent a moment or two thinking about ways their observations might inform their conferences. If Marta didn't mention any particular concern in their conference with her, they might ask whether she often reread her pieces and whether the second rereading was different than the first. What is the relationship between Sonya's book and the best-seller with the same title? Did Peter need help organizing his bits and pieces into a unified story?

"When we did the observing together," Joanne Hindley, who is co-leader of this year's teacher-as-researcher project, says, "we first reminded ourselves that we weren't going to spend five minutes collecting a list of reprimands and interventions. We didn't want to look for misspellings and messy papers but instead we wanted to watch and admire and learn from young people."

Once the teachers became accustomed to devoting the opening moments of the writing workshop to research, they began to observe more throughout the workshop. James Dickey has defined a poet as "someone who notices and is enormously taken by things that anyone else would walk by," and sometimes it seems that he could also have been talking about teachers. The teacher of writing is someone who notices and is enormously taken by the wads and drafts on Paul's desk, who notices how Austin's eyes follow Jeremy, his ex-best friend, as Jeremy goes off to confer with someone else, who notices when the light in a student's eyes dims during a conference and when Monday's burst of rapid writing is followed by two days of drifting noncommittally over the surface of the same pages.

When she was teaching, Joanne decided she'd learn the most if she selected a small number of children to study throughout the year. Every night she'd look over the reading journals of these students as well as their writing notebooks and drafts, and every night she'd reflect on what they'd said and done during the day. "From those three students," she says now, "I learned ways of looking and developed questions that helped me with everyone." Now when Joanne works with the teacher-researchers from around New York City, she often suggests that they look together at the children who might represent that teacher's new frontiers. "We look at kids the teacher wouldn't ordinarily look at, at kids who pose problems for that teacher."

Elizabeth Servidio, a first-grade teacher at P.S. 41, has looked especially at first graders who struggle. When six-year-old Molly began the year, she had difficulty with everything about writing. She wrote in tiny books so she wouldn't have to write much. She filled the entire page with illustrations so there wouldn't be any room for print. She responded to conferences with "yes" and "no" answers and always had a horrible look of guilt that probably came from knowing the other kids were doing something she couldn't do. Elizabeth recently showed Joanne a piece of writing in which Molly had obviously written some of the words, copied some of them from around the room, and recruited other youngsters to write some of them. "That Molly!" Elizabeth said. "Can you believe how she roped everyone else into her writing? I told her she was the most resourceful child I know. I am so proud of her. She's so determined to write that she's going to find ways to do so, even if it means recruiting others to help."

The way that Elizabeth Servidio has imbued young Molly's writing and copying with such significance is, of course, an important lesson for all of us. How easy it would have been to scold Molly for copying words from the chalkboard rather than congratulate her on her determination and resourcefulness. But there is another level of significance in this story. As important as it is that Elizabeth recognize the significance in what Molly has done, it's equally or more important that Joanne Hindley recognize the significance in what Elizabeth Servidio has done. How rare it is for teachers to be seen and understood and supported. If Joanne had been intent on unloading her own staff development agenda rather than watching and learning from Elizabeth, she might never have noticed in this example how watching children enables us to teach with wisdom.

Because Joanne watched Elizabeth's teaching, she was able to name and celebrate what Elizabeth does intuitively and to show her ways to build on what she does so naturally. Joanne showed her, for example, that research has everything to do with following lines of inquiry. It helps Molly if we notice and support her resourcefulness, but in order for our observations to be of maximum benefit for our teaching we need to follow them as far as we can. Is Molly's resourcefulness a by-product of the fact that she is a struggling writer? Is struggle an important part of learning to write? Which children in the room are attempting things sufficiently difficult to make them feel they are struggling? What resources do these students use? Which students reach to outside resources for help with their writing and which don't? What is the long-term result of the fact that Molly uses the other children and the words around the room to aid her writing?

Another day Joanne was able to point out to Elizabeth that in our investigations we often overlook things we don't want to see. Because a person cannot possibly attend to everything, it's very easy to gather and talk about the things that illustrate what we believe to be true. For example, if Elizabeth wants to believe that Molly learns from working with her peers she may screen out the fact that when Tara writes words onto Molly's draft, Molly often takes this opportunity to roam around the room. If we want to be informed by our research it's important that we learn to look at things we don't want to see.

Our Own Literacy

Our observation of children is one well to draw upon as we confer; our own literacy is another. In the field of English education, we tend to talk a great deal about how children need time to read and write. We do not talk enough about how we also need time to read and write. A wonderful, dedicated teacher recently said to me, "I don't have that much time for my own reading and writing. I spend five hours a night on lesson plans." I looked at her and said, with all the respect in the world, "I think that's unfortunate." If we think of the great teachers in history—Socrates, Jesus, Maimomodes, Montessori— did they spend five hours a night on lesson plans? No. They were great teachers because they were learned people, because they learned through reflection, long walks, reading, solitude, and writing.

Of course, that dedicated teacher who spends five hours a night on lesson plans is not alone. My friend and mentor Don Graves sometimes asks teachers to bring the books they're reading to conferences at which he's speaking. "I don't read books," some teachers respond. "I teach them." One teacher recently heard me recounting this and said, "Oh, I love to read. I keep the entire set of Robert McCloskey's books beside my bed." Other teachers have told Project colleagues, "I mostly read manuals, not books."

When I was trying to select a publisher for *The Art of Teaching Writing*, I decided to walk up and down the long aisles of publishers' booths at the International Reading Association conference just to look over all the possibilities.

In the first aisle, there were no books for teachers. The same was true of the second aisle. That day I walked down every aisle, and the only publishers I found with books for teachers were Heinemann and Oxford. There were necklaces for teachers, umbrellas for teachers, suitcases for teachers, but no books.

Shirley Brice Heath is right. Heath says that the research clearly indicates that if a child is going to become a reader and a writer, that child needs a bonded relationship with a joyfully literate adult. In the end, conferring comes down to a matter of relationship. If we're going to confer well, if we're going to be that joyfully literate adult for our children, we need to give ourselves time to read and write, and we need to give ourselves colleagues with whom to share our reading and writing. It's not easy in the midst of the craziness of the school year to find time for our own reading and writing. It's not easy to look up from lice checks, roll calls, attendance rosters, midterm exams, report cards, PPT meetings, crises about censorship, portfolios, assessments, textbook adoptions—and to write. It's especially hard to do this because there's so little in school life that supports our own learning and our own literacy. This is one of my biggest concerns for the profession. There are all kinds of things in schools to support young people and their learning—books, small group discussions, large group discussions, mentors, time set aside for reading and writing, courses of study, opportunities to perform and display what they know, people to challenge them—but what is there in schools to support us and our learning? Don't we also need libraries and book lists, small group discussions and courses of study? Don't we also need to read and to write and to re-enact and to paint?

When we ourselves write, we react differently to young writers. Lydia Bellino recently encountered a child who had plagiarized part of a poem. Kneeling beside the child's desk, Lydia said, "I think I know how you feel. Sometimes when I read poems that I love, I find myself feeling jealous of the author. I wish I'd written those words. They feel like me. They ring so true for me." Then she said, "What I do is, I copy the words in my notebook and save them, and sometimes I weave them into my own writing, but I always put the author's name with the words so people will know." Lydia's response would have been very different before she began writing. "I would have responded in terms of 'shoulds' and 'shouldn'ts,'" she said. "Now I feel myself empathizing with the writer. Any problem a writer has, I've been there."

When we write, we also talk about writing differently. Recently I found myself expounding with great passion on the joys of editing to a child. "Editing is like waxing cross-country skis," I said, "or grooming my horse after we've ridden across the creek. Editing is a physical thing for me. I run my hands over and over the surface of my text, attending to the draft in the same way I tend to my skis, to my horse." My metaphor may not be the wisest one in the world, but it was real for me then and newly created in that moment when I said it. As I spoke, I think my words commanded the child's attention because they also commanded my own.

I could go on citing countless examples of how the ways we talk about reading and writing change when we are readers and writers, but something has happened recently to alter my thinking on the value of our reading and writing. What has happened is that we're doing it. All over New York City, a precondition of staff development is that teachers must be willing at least to keep a writer's notebook for themselves; there are also ninety adult reading groups, each composed of about seven teachers and administrators, meeting in schools throughout the City.

What I have learned from all this is that as much as we need to read and write for our students we also need to read and write for ourselves. I have already mentioned that these are hard times for our children. I have talked about the thirty thousand teenagers in West Virginia alone who are alcoholics and about the rate of child suicide in this country. And I have quoted Katherine Paterson, who says, "To give the children of the world the words they need is to give them life and growth and refreshment" (1981, 6).

But these are also hard times for teachers. I am thinking, for example, of the loneliness in the profession. My colleague, JoAnn Curtis, recently did some demonstration teaching in a New Jersey classroom. "It didn't seem to go very well," JoAnn said to me, "and so I was astonished when a woman who'd observed came up to me in the lunch line, all teary-eyed, to thank me." JoAnn confided her feeling that the class hadn't gone that well, but the teacher shook her head as if to say, "It doesn't matter." The woman looked at JoAnn and said, "I've been teaching for fifteen years and this is the first time I've seen someone else teach."

The loneliness is there in the staff room as well. Roland Barth likens the relationship between adults in a school to the relationship between three-year-olds in a sand box. "One has a shovel and bucket; one has a rake and hoe. At no time do they borrow each other's toys," he says. "They may inadvertently throw sand in each other's face from time to time, but they seldom interact" (1984, 24).

These are hard times for teachers as well as for children. We, as a profession, need to read and write because words can give us life and growth and refreshment. Good books can pull together a world. They can stretch us and heal us and join us together. They can give us back ourselves; and, ultimately, all we bring to a writing conference or a writing classroom is ourselves.

When we first began inviting teachers throughout New York City to join adult reading groups, I wondered what would lure teachers to attend. What I have found is that reading together within a community of colleagues is a deeply, utterly personal experience. I think of Irene Chen, who has been struggling all year, and perhaps all of her life, with the issue of what it means to be Chinese and yet to be in a world that is not Chinese. She said recently, "These books are giving me my own world. When I read *In the Year of the Boar and Jackie Robinson* I felt so proud to be Chinese. I could hear my father saying to me, 'Be good. Upon your shoulders rests the reputation of all Chinese.' It felt like the author and I were sharing a secret, that to be Chinese is a way of life."

I think of Sharon Taberski, who said, "I've lived forty years in the last four months of reading, and I've lived through every major life issue there is. I thought the books would make me a better reader, but instead they are making me a better person."

I think of Jeanne Rupp, principal of P.S. 138 in the South Bronx, who says that her reading group, composed of paraprofessionals, school secretaries, teachers, and administrators, gives her a well to draw on in her work as an educator.

"The supreme question of a work of art," James Joyce said, and surely our teaching is a work of art, "is out of how deep a life does it spring?"

15

Records of Growth

A five-year-old announced, "I can read this book with my eyes closed." I knew what she meant. I can read Aliki's *The Two of Them* with my eyes closed. Lionel Trilling says there are books that can be read at the age of ten and then annually every year thereafter. In describing one such book, he says, "It will change only in becoming larger. To read it young is like planting a tree young—each new reading adds another growth ring of meaning." For me, *The Two of Them* is one of those books that can be read over and over. In one of my readings, I realized that it is, among other things, the story of growth and assessment.

As the book reminds me, love involves building structures that anticipate growth. The grandfather makes the little girl a ring that will someday fit her finger, a bed she will grow into, and a shelf of books she will someday read.

The book reminds me also that love involves remembering growth. The little girl and her grandfather tell stories of long ago, of hot soup and castles in the air, of floating in cool water on a rubber tire, and because they look back together, the girl learns to do this on her own. Sometimes when she works at her grandfather's store, she gives out the wrong change, but at lunchtime she and the grandfather laugh about it because she is just learning to count. The book reminds me that love includes sharing, laughing even, at mistakes. It reminds me that all of us, grown-ups as well as children, are changing. It's not only the little girl who grows, but the grandfather as well. *The Two of Them* is dedicated to those who remember, and so too is this chapter.

I remember well the insecurities I felt as an adolescent. Walking to the chalkboard, I'd feel everyone's eyes on me and burn with embarrassment. When I emerged from the lunch line and had to stand there holding my tray and wondering where to sit, I was sure the whole world saw me standing exposed and misplaced, without a seat. When I took the bus into Buffalo with my $30-a-month clothing allowance and looked through the tangled racks of bargain clothes, I was looking not only for skirts and sweaters but also for respectability and acceptance. I'll never forget the day that Lee MacCullam, the youth minister at my church, asked for an appointment to talk with me. We talked often in passing, so when I sat formally across from him in his office, the moment was highly charged and significant. He was quiet. The room was silent, and then out of that silence, he said, "I have a question. Do you like Lucy Calkins?" Flustered, I pulled back in my chair and scanned the office. It was full of his books and family pictures. I wanted to talk about them. Lee wanted to talk about me. And we did, and I have never forgotten it.

To me, that story is a parable about evaluation. There are organizing principles and feelings behind who we are. One of the greatest gifts a person can give us is to make an appointment to talk, to go beneath the day-to-day chitchat and help us feel seen and understood.

The Human Need to Be Recognized

Susan Rosengrant just completed her first year as assistant principal at the Katonah-Lewisboro High School. In passing one day, she said to John Chambers, the principal, "What a year! I should write about it. I should do a self-evaluation." "Why don't you?" John said. "Take the morning, close the door to your office, and write it out." Susan wrote a twelve-page letter to John about her year, and John responded in kind with his own letter, in a dialogue with hers. These two letters were filed in the district office as Susan's yearly evaluation. Neither Susan nor John will ever forget the importance of making that time to look back.

Over the years, we've often asked teachers, "If you think of your time line as a teacher, of all the experiences and workshops and courses and books and students you've learned from, what are the particular moments that have mattered most to you?"

What we've learned from this is that when someone from a district office or university arrives in a classroom, briefcase in hand, and ten minutes later begins giving little tips—"Why don't you display the rough drafts as well as the final drafts?" or "Maybe if you divide the writing folders into four boxes and put them in different areas of the room, you could avoid the logjam around the box of folders"—teachers shrug and think, "You want four boxes of folders instead of one? Fine. Why not?" Or teachers think, "You want me to display those messy drafts? Fine. If I get around to it, I will." If someone suggests laying different kinds of paper out in a writing center, or holding conferences at kids' desks rather than at the teacher's desk, teachers accommodate, but they know that none of it matters too much one way or the other, and so most of these "helpful hints" roll off.

The tragedy is that in those few fleeting minutes, the visitor could have made all the difference in the world, had he or she given what all of us need most: recognition. By recognition, I do not mean prizes and trophies. What I do mean is the privilege of being seen and understood. In this lonely profession of ours, it's terribly important for people to see us at work and to help us know and articulate what we are doing and why.

Time after time, when we have asked Writing Project teachers, "Which moment in our work together stands out to you?" people talk about times when they felt as if they were seen, with all their unmet dreams and loose ends.

A first-grade teacher in Queens tells of the day she and Georgia Heard went to the library together and spent a glorious hour sorting through books, looking for examples of genres she could invite her kids to experience. As they piled alphabet books, riddle books, poetry anthologies, and the like into a big plastic basket, the teacher and Georgia laughed and talked and laughed some more. At one point, the teacher stopped and said, "I haven't laughed so hard in years." Georgia looked at her, grew quiet, and said, "You know, sometimes when I'm in your room, I'm aware you don't laugh much and I find myself wondering if you enjoy teaching." The woman's eyes filled with tears and she said, "I haven't enjoyed it in years. I don't know where the joy went." The teacher and Georgia talked a long while that day, and both agreed that somehow, the teacher had to get the joy back, that nothing else mattered as much. Now, years later, that teacher says, "That talk with Georgia meant the world to me. How good it is to be understood."

For several years I've been hearing that teachers in a nearby suburb are angry and frustrated with their superintendent. Because they've had nowhere to take their frustrations, tension has grown. Finally, this spring, the town's educational association requested that an outside consultant be brought in to help. And so a rabbi met with small groups of teachers, then with administrators, and recorded what they said. Soon after, when school ended for that year, a meeting was scheduled so the rabbi could share his written report with the teachers. People suspected that no one would attend the meeting because summer vacation had begun, but the room was crammed full.

"Even though classes were over and school was out, we were all there," a teacher told me. "And when the rabbi told us back our words, and we saw that someone had heard the essence of what we'd been wanting to say for so long, all of us in that room were in tears. This big social studies teacher beside me was crying; we all were." When the rabbi finished reading his report, the teachers rose in a standing ovation. Problems hadn't been solved, but they had been heard. We need to be heard, to be recognized.

A fourth-grade teacher in Brooklyn told me about how Martha Horn, the Project staff person in her building, once suggested that the two of them each take some time to jot down, in two columns, the things she's really good at and the things she struggles with. The teacher said, "After we wrote, I mentioned a couple of things I'm good at. But Martha had so many others, and listening to them was the most incredible gift in the world." Usually our strengths and our weaknesses are the flip sides of each other, and so it was fairly easy for Martha to help the teacher go from "I'm good at supporting and nurturing youngsters" to "I need to be better at nudging youngsters." It wasn't hard to go from "I'm great at creating a rich environment" to "Sometimes the richness is overwhelming and chaotic."

It's not only teachers but also children who yearn to be seen and understood, to be recognized. Often, the most effective teaching in the world simply involves naming the strengths we see, the growth we notice. I think, for example, of this conference between six-year-old Greg Snicer and his extraordinary teacher, Mary Ellen Giacobbe. This conference occurred during my two-year-long study, conducted with Donald Graves and Susan Sowers, of children and their growth as writers.

Greg had been sitting with a bunch of paper for a day and a half when Mary Ellen approached him and asked, "What's up?" Sighing deeply, Greg said,

> I have no idea what to write about. I discussed it with Dr. Graves, but he wasn't much help. If only he'd give me a title. I want to write a make-believe story, but not the same old one. The old version is: they blow something up, have a fight, and that's all. If I went back to the old version, I'd just write up a title and I'd be going. Making a new version . . . I tried to make a list, see. The Martians need a new car . . . I've been thinking for a day and a half and I'm clear out of space stories, clear out of war stories, and clear out of imagination stories. My writing's all bent out of shape. What's the use of being in school, anyway? I might as well be home.

Mary Ellen responded,

> Greg, you're so frustrated and down on yourself. But a couple of months ago, when you didn't have a topic, you used to say, "I'm waiting. I'm waiting for something." This time, you're stuck on what to write about, but look at all the things you've done! You've talked to Dr. Graves, you've decided you didn't want to write about the old version (that would be too easy), you've made a list of possible topics, you've thought about different kinds of stories—space stories, war stories. I think you've come a long way. You know exactly how to go about coming up with a topic, and you're right. Sometimes it just takes time. You're getting a lot better as a writer.

In *The Two of Them,* Aliki's grandfather nurtures the little girl by telling her stories of the olden days, of building sand castles and floating in cool water on a rubber tire. In the same way Mary Ellen Giacobbe nurtures Greg by telling him stories of the olden days when rehearsal meant waiting for a topic. Mary Ellen has supported Greg's expanding repertoire of rehearsal strategies because she notices them. She's given Greg a sense that he is progressing as a writer. She has let Greg know that he's not just composing stories, that he's also composing his own lifeline as a writer. And she's invited Greg to look backward as well as forward; to have hindsight as well as foresight, to tell—and, in so doing, to shape—the story of his growth in writing.

Remembering and anticipating growth are part of what we do when we care for each other.

The Harsh Reality of Assessment and Ability Groupings

It's hard to reconcile this rich, human sense of assessment with the fact that in our schools, assessment is equated with number 2 lead pencils, filled-in bubbles, and remediation. Number 2 pencils, filled-in bubbles and an alphabet soup of tests? It sounds like a game and it is—a deadly one. Ours is a population of severely labeled students: of bluebirds and buzzards, of rainbow kids and LEP kids, of the top class and the bottom class, of the blue reading group and the brown one. David Booth has found a poem written by a second grader who lets us know what these groupings are like for children:

> I am in the slow group in reading.
> My little brother was a Wise Man in the play.
> My sister is a waitress at The Blue Dragon Diner.
> My brother plays on varsity football.
> I am in the slow group in reading.
> That's all I'm in,
> And I hate it.

Stratified classrooms are especially horrifying because of the way children are classified. In observing children during the first several years of school, Ray Rist found that by the eighth day of kindergarten, the teacher had seated children in permanent groups, with, as she put it, the "fast learners" at table 1 and "those who have no idea what they're doing" at tables 2 and 3. Members of the "fast learners" group received more encouragement, had fewer distractions, and enjoyed more personal relationships than did the children in the other groups. Children in this group were well-dressed and clean and, in contrast to children in the other tables, had a better command of standard English. These groups, arranged on the eighth day of kindergarten, remained intact throughout the three years in which the study took place (1973, 7).

We need to look this situation in the eye and know that streaming and assessment can be racist and wrong. As Donald Graves suggests, it's hard to imagine what it would be like for us if, on the eighth day of our first year of teaching, we were grouped, with all the teachers who "have no idea what's going on" teaching in one hallway. Anyone who entered that hallway would hear first, "These are the bottom teachers." Despite how we taught, all of us in the bottom group would remain there year in and year out. It's hard to fathom what it would be like for us to have to take an exam to determine our teaching competence and then have a score—4.2 or 6.4—that represented our teaching and a bar graph that showed the ways we fell short of the norm. It's hard to imagine any of this; yet this happens all the time to our children.

Parents live with the knowledge that their children will be classified into ability groups. So infants in diapers have swimming lessons. Two-year-olds with furrowed brows work their way through flash cards and phonics puzzles and rush from Suzuki music lessons to computer camps. Parents choose pre-schools based on the amount of reading readiness instruction, and they delay their child's entrance into kindergarten in an effort to ensure that their children will be classified as bluebirds, as winners. And we have depression in kids as we've never had it before.

"I'm seeing kids in second and third grade being referred for attention problems and hyperactivitiy as a result of being stressed and being expected to do things they're not ready to do," says Robert Block, a Tulsa, Oklahoma, pediatrician. "They're in a teeth-grinding kind of environment. You see them in class and their mouths are twisted, their tongues are out, and they're sweating a little" (Putka 1988).

"What kind of America do we want?" Donald Graves asks, quoting a Harvard psychologist who talks about children today that are so desperate to scramble their way to the top they're actually happy when their friends do poorly in school.

The tests and ability groups are worrisome to kids. Marissa writes,

> I used to like to play games, but now I've changed my mind. There's this game we play all the time in school. You need pencils, two of them, and you have to look to be sure they say Number 2 on them. You have to be very still during the game. You can't talk, you can't move. We play the game every week, and yesterday we played the game for two hours. But I know a secret—it's not a game. It's a test.

When Michael Harwayne went off to college, his little cousin was amazed to hear he'd be living at school. "You mean they can test him all day and all night?" she said.

But the tests are especially worrisome to teachers. The tests control us. Miles Olson has said, "The examiner pipes and the teacher must dance—and the examiner sticks to the old tune. If the educational reformers really wish the dance altered they must turn their attention from the dancers to the musicians."

In California, there's a new state assessment program, and it is touted as a model. In this program, third graders in 4,500 schools can be compared with each other. Authors of the program give the example of a school called Vista Grande Elementary School. This school, as Frank Smith tells us in *Insult to Intelligence*, receives a report card indicating that the third graders in the school have "relative strengths"—vowels, details from two and three sentences and alphabetizing—and "relative weaknesses"—consonants, analysis of sentences, details from single sentences (1986, 166). I shudder to think how that report card will affect curriculum. Again and again, the tail wags the dog.

Testing, testing, testing. There are tests everywhere. The other day my stepdaughter, Kira, sat her father and me down to test which of us was most likely to have an extramarital affair. She read a whole battery of questions from one of her magazine surveys. "Do you fantasize about someone else every year, month, week, day, hour?" "Who's more attractive, you or your spouse?" We laugh at those tests. We know it's a joke to think those multiple-choice questions could reveal anything significant about a marriage. But no one laughs at the reading tests.

As Graves (1988) notes, because of the tyranny of these reading tests, students can go from kindergarten to their Graduate Record Exams without ever reading anything larger than a paragraph. As teachers we spend so much time practicing for reading tests that some of us forget there are other ways of responding to literature besides short-answer questions. Those tests have the power to take our breath away. Why? Why have we given them so much power?

The Need for Records of Growth

We've given those tests power because human beings need records of growth. When we ask parents if they have a picture of their child, they inevitably produce a whole raft of pictures. If anyone asks to see a photograph of my sons Miles and Evan, I get out the album. It has photos of each of them the day they were born, their first smiles, the first hike they went on. It shows the sequential story of their growth. Watching and recording their growth is important to me. I need to document every breakthrough.

What records do we have of our students' growth? In the reading and writing workshop, we've given up most traditional records of growth. We can no longer say, "I'm on unit 10 out of 23." "I've covered fifteen skills out of twenty-seven." We can no longer open our grade books and say, "Marcella began the year doing well, then had a setback, and now has recovered." Without any of this, we feel as if we're in quicksand. The folders are filling, the process is continuing (rehearse, draft, revise, edit), but are we going anywhere? Is there real and significant progress?

When we have no other records of growth, we give tests inordinate power. And we're vulnerable to any parent or administrator who tries to take the wind out of our sails by saying, "What about the skills? What about the curriculum?"

We need more records of growth. We need to balance the information we receive from test scores with other kinds of information. We need to have firm ground on which to stand. In the remaining pages of this chapter, I will suggest some principles we can draw upon when we design records of growth.

What Do We Record?

As we bring new approaches to reading and writing into our classrooms, it soon becomes clear that conventional forms of assessment don't attend to the behaviors we value. Tests do not reveal whether children show confident, readerlike behavior. They don't show children's book-handling behaviors. They don't reveal whether children have experiences reading and writing a wide range of genres. They don't draw attention to whether children regard themselves as readers and writers, or to children's levels of independence, involvement, confidence, or enjoyment.

Conventional tests are inadequate in part because they do not focus attention on what many of us believe are the most important indicators of a child's growth in reading and writing. Efforts to design new forms of assessment must begin with the question "What constitutes growth in reading and writing?" This is a question that groups of teachers need to study, and in order to wrestle with this question, teachers of reading and writing will want to read and discuss and use and reread *The Primary Language Record* (Inner London Education Authority 1988), an extraordinary developmentally based system for observing, recording, and understanding children's language development. The *Record* is now used in five hundred British schools and is being distributed in Australia and the United States.

The Primary Language Record helps teachers and parents look at a child's growth in reading, writing, and talking as it occurs along developmental continuums. For example, the *Record* incorporates the Vygotsian notion that learning is initially supported and collaborative and that independence grows as a child internalizes the collaboration. Therefore, in observing children's reading and writing, teachers look for whether a child has enough internalized strategies to be independent. Does a young reader rely on another person? Can this reader approach a familiar text with confidence but still need support? It is not difficult to extend these questions into the territory of writing. Does the young writer rely on having another person ask questions of his or her written text? Does the writer reread and question his or her draft independently? Which kinds of questions and revision strategies has the writer internalized? We need to decide what constitutes growth in literacy, and then we need to attend to these things.

When teachers examine *The Primary Language Record,* they will see that this system of evaluation—like all systems of evaluation—reveals the values of those who have designed it. Myra Barrs and her colleagues regard growth in literacy as a developmental process, and this is evident throughout their document. But there are other values that weave through all that they have designed. For example, it is clear that they believe in drawing upon the perspectives of lots of different people. In speaking with us about this, Myra Barrs said, "We wanted our records to help us listen to parents, for example, in recognition that much of a child's literacy happens before and outside school." There are places on the *Record*'s forms for recording conversations—"a language and literacy conference"—with a child's parents and with the child, and for input from every professional who works with the child. Myra Barrs explains, "A picture or a pattern will begin to emerge when we look at the children's behaviors from a variety of different perspectives. If your measures of evaluation are 'soft,' one way to make them convincing is to gather strong, rich evidence from a variety of sources."

Others have developed their own ways of recording growth. At the beginning, middle, and end of every year, Nancie Atwell, author of *In the Middle*, gave her class of eighth graders a survey. "Are you a writer?" "In general, how do you feel about reading?" "Who are your favorite authors?" "How many books would you say you own?" "Have you ever reread a book? If so, can you name it/them here?" "Why do people write?" "In general, how do you feel about what you write?" (1987, 270–72). Nancie's eighth graders scored second highest in the state on their reading tests, but if they hadn't done well on those tests, she would have had other ways of understanding and illustrating their growth. She could have told parents that, in a nation where only 13 percent of eighth graders choose to read, 92 percent of her students say they like to read. In a nation where the average college graduate reads one book a year, her students read an average of thirty-five full-length novels each year (1987, 158). Because Nancie's hope is that her students will be lifelong readers and writers, she is less interested in whether her students can translate the symbol of the light at the end of the dock in *The Great Gatsby* than in whether they choose to read and write independently. It is no accident that in her survey Nancie asks, "How many books do you own?" "What kinds of books do you like to read?" "Are you a writer?" Her goal is that her students know the life of a richly literate person, and her methods of assessment are in step with that goal.

Designing Methods of Evaluation That Support a Teacher's Area of Growth

In designing methods of evaluation, then, we must ask, "What do I value?" But again, we value so many things: independence, laughter, sensitivity to others, the ability to learn from one's reading and one's earlier drafts and one's colleagues. How do we narrow our focus?

Perhaps the most important thing to remember is that evaluation needs to be in the service of learning. Most often it isn't. As University of New Hampshire researcher Jane Hansen points out, "Most evaluation values what you've already done, not what you are learning," and there is a reason for this. Oftentimes, educators regard evaluation as a means of *demonstrating* that teaching methods work, that students are progressing. The purpose of this kind of evaluation is not to guide teaching practices but to validate them. How good it would be if teachers of writing could design methods of evaluation that would also reveal what doesn't work. For this to happen, we need to recognize that methods of evaluation can reflect and accompany not only our students' growth but our own as well.

Glenda Bissex, author of *GNYS AT WRK* and a leader in the teacher-as-researcher movement, has said, "In my ideal school, the principal at the end of the day asks not 'What did you teach today?' but 'What did you learn today?'" (1986). In schools that value teachers as learners, methods of evaluation can reflect each teacher's "curriculum" for herself.

"What do I want to learn this year?" we ask. If one person answers, "I want to focus on reading-writing connections," then that teacher may ask students to document the instances in which they thought about their writing while reading. Later, these students can categorize and talk about the kinds of reading connections they have made. "Do you tend to notice the genre, beautiful language, the content?" the teacher might ask. This teacher might also interview all or selected students at regular intervals. "When you are reading, do you often think about your writing? When can you remember doing so? Tell me about it."

Shelley Harwayne's interest in reading-writing connections has led her to document and study a whole range of topics that fall underneath this rubric. "Are children more apt to emulate other young authors in their classrooms than famous authors?" she wonders. "Do the author studies that fill our classrooms affect the quality of children's writing in obvious ways?" "Is retelling another author's story truly a low-level skill, or are there widely varying levels of sophistication in children's retellings?"

Assessment needn't focus on reading-writing connections, of course. A teacher may care about this topic and yet not choose it as the focus of his or her record keeping. There are thousands of optional areas of focus. We tell students, "Write about something important to you," and the same advice holds true for teachers. Evaluate something that is important to you. Pat Lynch, a talented and innovative first-grade teacher who is one of Judy Davis's colleagues in Manhattan's P. S. 183, has for several years felt that she never managed to design her classroom in such a way that every child received what he or she needs. "If I fill the room with blocks and housekeeping and carpentry and with the kinds of reading and writing opportunities that can be woven into these purposeful activities, the youngsters who need time and space to focus on paperwork and on long, intricate stories miss out . . . or the reverse is true." This year Pat is team-teaching with another first-grade teacher, and their children are moving between two rooms, one filled with blocks and pretend-play, big books and functional writing, and the other filled with response groups, stapled pages for stories, and homemade anthologies of poems. "I need to find real ways to evaluate what this is like for my kids," Pat says.

Helping Students Design Methods of Evaluation to Support Their Areas of Concentration

When designing a system of record-keeping and assessment, it's a mistake to think assessment exists for parents and teachers alone. Children as well as teachers and parents sometimes feel as if they're in quicksand. Children know their folders are filling but, like the teacher, they wonder, "Am I going anywhere?" "Have I made progress as a reader and a writer?" Young people don't want to hang out in the writing workshop, dabbling and chatting and inventing things to do. Instead, they want to take on big projects, to feel that their work adds up, to observe their skills developing, to know that someone sees what they do (or do not) accomplish. They may not want a prescribed curriculum, but they do want a course to run, one that is largely of their own making, and they want to feel as if they're going somewhere. It's not only teachers and parents, but youngsters, also, who want clearly delineated goals, systems for frequent feedback, and records of growth within the reading-writing workshop.

We've learned the importance of this both from our classrooms and from an important study of young people by Mihaly Csikszentmihalyi and Reed Larson (1984). The researchers asked youngsters to carry the electronic pagers that doctors carry and a sheet of self-report forms. At forty randomly chosen moments during a week, the youngsters were beeped, and each time the beeper went off they were asked to answer a series of questions: Where are you? What is the main thing you're doing? Who are you with? As you were beeped, did you wish you were doing something else? What skills, challenges were involved in the activity? What were you thinking about? How would you describe your mood? Your energy level? Interestingly enough, data showed that these students were not particularly happy when watching television or resting or idly chatting. The activities they like best included sports and hobbies. They felt most alive during highly structured activities—like sports and working on their hobbies—in which they used skills to pursue definite goals and in which they received frequent feedback on their progress.

One way to foster a feeling of productiveness and progress in a workshop is to ensure that the school year has seasons, units of study that have beginnings and endings. In a Global Literature course Mary Winsky and Lucretia Penozza are coteaching this year, ninth-grade students read books and essays and poems about Africa, including Mark Mathabane's *Kaffir Boy* and Hazel Rochman's *Somehow Tenderness Survives,* and responded in reading logs. After six weeks, they chose one piece from their logs and worked at shaping and expanding it into a piece of literature.

Students were asked to write a self-evaluation in which they reflected on particular aspects of their work. During the three reading days that followed, everyone, including the teachers, brought in three copies of their completed work and lots of yellow stick-on notes, and read and commented on each other's writing. Each writer was asked to find a way to include these notes in his or her reading journal. Then they were directed back to their original evaluation to reassess what they said about their piece in terms of what they had learned about themselves and their writing, both from reading other people's writing and from reading people's responses to their own writing. One student wrote, "When I saw how perfect other papers were, I was embarrassed that my paper had spelling errors." Another said, "I think I was more critical of myself in my original evaluation than I needed to be. I'd only heard the work of a few classmates and I'd been intimidated by what I heard. In looking at the whole picture of the class, my piece stands strong." A third student had deliberately used profanity in his draft because he thought it made a point, but upon reading the responses from others, who found the profanity jarring and out of place, he decided he'd made a misjudgment. By the time these days of reflection were over, students were ready to move on from their focus on Africa to a new challenge, and they were filled with energy and with hopes for themselves as writers and readers. All too often, children move from one writing project to another without having opportunities such as this for closure, for reflecting on what they've accomplished and what they want to do next.

A reading-writing workshop can have the tenor of an evening spent hanging around the living room . . . or it can feel as purposeful as practicing for a gymnastics event, constructing a treehouse, or planning a march for nuclear disarmament. Workshops become purposeful, in part, when each student has a clear, deep sense of goals and of his or her own progress toward those goals. One child may want to learn from a particular author, another may want to get published in a real-world magazine, another to learn to write funny pieces, another to become a better speller.

The challenge, of course, is for goal-setting to be more than a perfunctory task. No one knows better than teachers that even when a big commotion is made about goals and record-keeping, they can easily amount to nothing at all. Goals for teachers are in fashion these days. In September of every year, we trump up some goals to put onto a sheet of paper. At the end of the year, when a sheet arrives asking us to record what we did to meet those goals, the hardest part is remembering what we originally wrote down as our goals.

One way to avoid this problem is for students and teachers to see goal-setting and record-keeping as something that everyone in the classroom community does. The teacher may have a special interest in helping students care about their language. Students know this is her goal, and they know this is why she reads books and articles on language and asks them to identify and discuss the sections of their reading and their writing they consider especially beautiful or compelling. Meanwhile, students have their own goals. Andy may realize that in the past his energy for writing related to whether he had an audience, and so he decides to find as many ways as possible for his writing to be heard in the world. He brainstorms possible methods of publication and checks off those he has tried. He researches how others in the classroom publish and what they publish, reads articles about the topic, and gives short talks throughout the school on getting published. Cheryl vows to write in a wider range of genres and therefore maintains a chart of her writing (Figure 15–1).

Figure 15–1   Cheryl's Chart

TITLE & DATE	POEM	SONG	STORY	JOKE	SIGNS	ESSAY	MEMOIR	LETTERS	JOURNALISM
Jelly Fish 9/16/90	X								
Growing Up 10/12/90							X		
Christmas 10/13/90	X								

Of course, Andy's list and Cheryl's graph will only be helpful if Andy and Cheryl read and study and discuss them. Among ethnographic researchers, there is a rule of thumb that equal time should be spent on processing and gathering data. Charts and lists and records need to be analyzed. Teachers and children need to ask, "What surprises me?" "What patterns and what breaks in the pattern do I notice?" "What are the unique things I notice about this record sheet as compared to another?" In order for this kind of reflection to happen, the data we collect must be brought into our conferences, mini-lessons, study groups, letters to parents, and notebooks. Then, too, it is important for Cheryl and Andy and all the other writers in the workshop to rethink the goals they've chosen and the kinds of evaluation they are doing at regular intervals. No system of record-keeping will work forever. After a while, Cheryl will no longer be concerned about writing in an ever-widening range of genres, and her teacher may grow less interested in how children learn to be aware of language and more interested in another aspect of writing. It will be important for both Cheryl and her teacher to select new goals periodically and to design new systems for recording progress. Too often, record-keeping systems become dinosaurs that outlive their usefulness. There's nothing inherently worthy about collecting data about one's writing on a chart, graph, or list. These records will only be as valuable as we allow them to be, which means they need to convey information that is timely and important to the concerns and work of those who maintain them.

Reflecting on Our Histories and Our Futures as Readers and Writers

Donna Skolnick, a teacher in Westport, Connecticut, claims that a simple graph did more for her conferences and those of her colleagues than anything else. After finishing a piece of writing, kindergartners and first graders fill in squares to indicate whether they think the piece is not so good, average, good, or very good. When this kind of record is put alongside their draft, it is far less likely that conferences will center around students' subject matter alone—their guinea pigs, their weekend—and more likely that they will revolve around the students' ideas for the piece of writing and its place within the total context of their work.

When Mary Winsky and John Chambers cotaught a writing workshop for high school seniors, they regularly asked students to join them in free writing as a way of reflecting on their growth and progress as writers. Together they wrote and talked about issues such as these:

- What are your goals for this writing workshop?
- How did you use your time today? How did your use of time fit into your goals? How will you use your time over the next week? Why?
- What did you accomplish as a writer this week? What did you accomplish as a reader?
- How do you see your writing changing? What would you consciously like to change?

- What are you learning about yourself as a writer? What are you learning from others about writing?
- If you were to write a letter to someone else in the class about your progress thus far, what would you say?
- What is the hardest part of writing for you? What is the easiest part?
- What are deadlines doing to your writing?
- What did you learn today?
- "Time Out" Day: What do you want from yourself in order to make the most of the next six weeks? What do you want from the group? What will your next piece be?

The teachers and students also took time at the beginning, middle, and end of each semester to think about their lives as writers, their hopes and goals and growth. Notice the student's goals and John Chambers's comments on them, as shown in Figure 15–2. John, of course, made his own list of writing goals (Figure 15–3).

If we're going to help children look forward in this way, it also helps to invite them to look backward, to move between reporting on what they have done and planning what they will do. In some classrooms, a table of contents provides an index for each child's growing writing portfolio. In others, every child lists the titles of finished work on huge pieces of chart paper. In still others, everyone keeps a chart with one column for the day's plan and

Figure 15–2 A Student's Goals and John's Comments on Them

•GOALS•

1. •to get my point across creatively•

2. come up with ideas/ definite topics easier

3. write short fiction pieces with little difficulty

4. to be comfortable with writing college essays creatively

5. to learn how to make "historical" or "scientific" papers creative and interesting

----

•My first 'project' will be to write several short pieces of fiction, getting topics from college essays, thus combining two of my goals.

Wow. These sound very ambitious to me.
Try not to be hard on yourself if you
find them large and difficult.
    I'm glad you know where you want to
start.
            JHC 9/15/88

M.W.
9/19/88

Figure 15–3   John's Own Writing Goals

```
JAC Goals     (for my writing in 8th period WW)


    >   finish stories
          "Billy Ball"
          "The Ice Cream Emporium"
        & "Back from the Bagwan"

    >   letters
          Melissa
          others (Stephen, Mickey, Frank, Terri (2,)
          still others as needed!

    >   poetry
          old ones?
          new ones
```

another for the day's accomplishments. The important thing is that teachers
and children not only keep these records but learn from them. Writers might
study their table of contents and ask, "How much did I write in a month? A
week? Do my better pieces tend to take more or less time? Do I feel better
about my writing when I'm producing a lot or when I'm working a long while
on a single piece?"

We may also want to ask youngsters to bring in all the writing they've
saved through their lives and to talk in pairs or write about what they can
learn by studying these texts. We might ask children to bring in a short stack
of carefully selected books that, taken as a whole, tell the story of their growth
as readers. We might suggest that children research their reading-writing histories by interviewing their parents and in this way learn about very early trips
to the library, reading-aloud times, first letters, early drawings, and emerging
preferences as readers and writers. As I mentioned in chapter 2, we might ask
children to write their reading-writing autobiographies, or we might encourage them to model an author study of themselves after an author study of
someone like Jean Craighead George. More importantly, we might encourage
each child to design ways he or she can build a portfolio that presents himself
or herself as a writer, a reader, and a person.

One of the reasons it is important for all of us, teachers and children, to
look back on our lifelines as readers and writers is that this helps us all cherish
and watch for our own and each other's growth. If eight-year-old Greg looks
back and says, "Three years ago, in first grade, I wrote a hundred pieces about
the good guys and the bad guys," our first instinct is not to reform him but to
understand him. Because first grade is over and because it wasn't our responsibility anyhow, we allow ourselves to simply understand Greg's first-grade
writing strategies rather than rush about altering them. And so we ask him,
"Why do you think you did that?" Then too, when we look back over our
shoulders, it's quite natural for us to talk as much about patterns of growth

as about particular pieces of writing. It's as natural to ask "What does this show about you?" as "How can this piece be improved?"

When we ask young people to join us in sketching their portrait as writers, it changes the way we see our children throughout the year. We get into the habit of allowing ourselves to simply understand a child rather than insisting every moment become an instructional one. Carl Rogers has said,

> I have found it of enormous value when I can permit myself to under-stand another person. The way in which I have worded this statement may sound strange to you. Is it necessary to *permit* oneself to under-stand another? I think that it is. Our first reaction to most of the statements which we hear from other people is an immediate evalua-tion . . . "That's right"; or "That's stupid"; "That's abnormal"; "That's unreasonable." . . . [I]t is not an easy thing to permit oneself to *under-stand* an individual, to enter thoroughly and completely and empath-ically into his frame of reference. (1961, 18)

The more we know a child, the better observers we become. If we know that during first grade Greg wrote many, many pieces on the same topic, then we are more apt to notice when he moves from familiar to unfamiliar territory, as Mary Ellen Giacobbe did at the beginning of this chapter. By telling Greg the growth she saw, she went a long way towards supporting that growth. Finally, this is why we need systems of evaluation. This is why we need to develop and keep records of growth. By noticing growth, we nurture it.

— 16 —

Hopes and Horizons: Understanding Our Children's Images of Good Writing

As Ariel selected one piece of writing and then another from the maze of papers covering the floor around her, she said, "This one can be a present for my dad," and, "These can go together into a book about friendship," and, "This is my best. I want to send it to a magazine." For half an hour, Ariel continued reading her writing and trying to find a home for her most promising pieces. Finally, confident that she'd separated the best pieces of writing from the rest, she looked up. "I can put all these bad pieces of writing together too, any ol' way. It'll be a book like my reader." Joking, she added, "I'll call it *My Collection of Bad Writing.*"

My Collection of Bad Writing is a book that deserves our attention. Too often, I find myself culling the best pieces of writing from classrooms, the pieces that testify to how much our young people can do as writers, and focusing only on these. I carry these pieces around, studying them and sharing them, and I leave the bad pieces behind on the floor. Although I'd like to deny it, those bad pieces of writing exist. Like Ariel, I need to put them into a reader, and I need to study that reader. We all need to do this.

Peter Elbow's advice is wise. He says,

> The mark of the person who can actually make *progress* in thinking— who can sit down at 8:30 with one set of ideas and stand up at 11:00 with better ideas—is a willingness to notice and listen to those inconvenient little details, those annoying loose ends, those embarrassments or puzzles [or, we might add, those bad pieces], instead of impatiently sweeping them under the rug. (1981, 131)

If we take those bad pieces of writing out from under the rug and study them, we'll see that some of them exist because students have very efficiently written and revised toward their sense of good writing—and that their sense of good writing is misinformed.

Nine-year-old Diane drafted four or five leads in a misguided effort to bring a maximum amount of action and sound effects into her piece about sledding. It begins:

> Zoom, zoom. I went down the hill as fast as I could. I could see my father ahead. Boom, bang, crash, boom. My best friend fell off her sled.

Salma's major criterion for good writing is not unlike Diane's. She, too, works hard to make sure her writing begins with action and excitement. Her autobiography begins like this:

> Well, it happened! I came to life! I was very excited. I met my father and mother, the doctors, and my older brother Steve, who was three years old.

Eleven-year-old Jennifer works hard to be sure that her writing is good. For Jennifer, good writing is not filled with sound effects or action but with romance. In this lead to one of her stories, it is evident that teenage romances have left their mark:

> I shook my head. "I'll never believe it!" "But it's true, Helen! Come and see for yourself." I looked at Brian's face. His hazel eyes had a spark of apprehension in them. My pulse quickened. "Prove it!" I tried to keep my voice steady.
>
> Next thing I found myself in the waiting room. I broke out in a cold sweat. "Oh, Snuffy!" I cried softly to myself. "Oh, Snuffy, please don't die!"

It's not only children but teachers as well who sometimes write and revise toward a misguided sense of good writing. During a recent summer institute for teachers, I pulled my chair alongside a teacher's desk and asked, "How's it coming?"

"I wrote this, and I'm pleased with it. It's all there," the teacher answered. "So now I'm trying something else, and I don't know. . . . " I put my hand on her arm. "Can we back up for a minute? You told me that you were pleased with this piece of writing," I said, bringing the first piece back out of the woman's folder. Looking at it, I said, "It seems you have a terrific opportunity. . . . If you *can* look at this and think about ways to make it even better, you might be pushing yourself into whole new frontiers in your writing." Then I suggested that she reread her piece, marking the sections that worked particularly well and those that didn't work as well. I moved on to another conference. After a while, I returned and sat listening as the teacher read her story aloud to a group of colleagues. It began like this:

> I could hear my husband's voice on the other end of the phone. Something was different about it. What was wrong? "Are you okay?" I asked. "I'm fine," he responded, but I was unconvinced. What had I done? Again I pressed him. "Is something wrong?" And this time he answered, "It's cancer."
>
> Sadness, despair, and grief welled up inside of me. Tears brimmed. This was one of my saddest moments. My heart felt heavy, and it felt like it would burst. I thought fondly about the good times we had had.

For a while, the group simply talked with the writer about her topic and her life. Then conversation turned to the text as a piece of writing. "Now, rereading it, I realize that the first part, about the phone call, is awful," the teacher said, adding, "but I like the part about 'grief welled inside of me and tears brimmed.'"

I didn't know what to say. How could I tell the writer that it was the first part I found incredibly alive and compelling? How could I tell her that, for me, the second half felt more clichéd and generalized? Luckily, an entire group of teachers had listened to the woman read her writing and heard her discuss her sense of good writing, and they joined me in addressing the issue.

Afterward, I realized that I could simply have said, "Make your best better," without hearing her evaluation. If this had happened, as it happens whenever people revise alone at their desks, the woman would have expanded her weaker sections, cropped the strong parts of her draft, and ended up with a terrible piece of writing. Students do this all the time. Teachers say, "See if you can improve it," and youngsters add strings of adjectives ("the cute, peppy, frisky little dog"), sound effects ("bang, boom, eek, crash"), and details like "He was 4' 2" and had yellow, two-inch-long hair." If they're adolescent, they also add romance ("I looked into his eyes and knew"). Often, the more they revise, the worse their writing gets.

In the Writing Project we find that our students often revise in ways that reveal their concept of good writing, but too often we don't stop to learn what that concept of good writing is. It is important to ask students to star what they consider the good sections and to check what they consider the less-good sections of their writing and their reading, and for us to use these marks as a way to uncover what a student looks for in writing. "What is it about this paragraph that you like? Could you imagine it being even more well written? Do you always look for that particular quality in writing?" It is terribly important for our students to rank pieces of writing from best to worst and to discuss the criteria they used to determine these rankings. "You like this because it's funny. Can you show me the funny parts? What makes them funny? If you were going to give lessons in how to write funny pieces, what would you say? Could you make these other pieces funnier?" Likewise it is terribly important that students speculate about how they *might* improve a piece of writing (if they were *going* to work on it), and that they select and discuss excerpts from their own writing and that of other authors that seem especially well written.

Children will surprise and entertain us with their ideas about good writing. Six-year-old Greg Snicer, whose troubles in finding a topic I mentioned in the last chapter, once said,

> I'm going to revise my Hermy books because people like them. (The other books were just practice books.) Revised means adding some tips. Revisement. If you read my book and you find a place where nothing makes sense, give me a holler and I'll revise. Or I'll take out that page. It's easier to take a page out than to go through all that trouble just to revise it.

Eight-year-old Birger Dahl, on the other hand, explained why he liked a particular piece of writing by saying, "It starts exciting, ends exciting, and the excitement keeps on going."

It's easy to view Greg's and Birger's comments about their writing as charming and lose sight of their significance. The importance of what Birger has said becomes evident when we consider how "it's good because it starts exciting" connects with other things he says and does as a writer and reader. When we combine the pieces of the puzzle—the way he revises, the questions he asks in share sessions, the books he likes to read, and the patterns in his written products—a portrait of Birger as a writer emerges. It suddenly becomes very clear that we, as writers, don't have a checklist of disparate qualities, but a unified, cohesive image that we work toward in writing.

A portrait of Birger begins to emerge when we combine his interest in excitement with the fact that he has developed a hierarchy of exclamation marks, or "excitement marks" as he calls them. "You use one at the end of every sentence and more if the guy's dying or if it's somebody's birthday." And it's not surprising that when Birger wrote a research report on the gray squirrel, he wrote it as a story and then rewrote it to add excitement. The first draft of Birger Dahl's squirrel report begins:

> I was climbing up a tree. I put my head in the hole. I pulled out a bird's nest. A squirrel sat in it. He had some food with him—nuts, seeds, bird eggs. He flipped his tail. I knew that he was scared.

He says, "I changed that draft, to put more excitement. Like right here." Then Birger read his new version: "He started barking and wriggling his tail. I put him back in the hole and climbed down the tree."

When describing a peer conference, Birger said, "Vinnie and Paul told me to shorten the lead and shorten my 'ands.' They also said, 'You have only one exciting word—splash.'" When Birger was asked to describe a good peer conference, he said, "Like if it's about a tree fort and it's boring, you could ask, 'What happened up there that was exciting? Did you ever get stuck up there?'" Many of Birger's biggest struggles as a writer revolve around finding ways to insert the information necessary to answer his readers' questions without losing the pace and energy that are so important to him in his writing and, one suspects, in his life.

When six-year-old Greg, author of the Hermy books, was asked how a person goes about writing a really good book, he said, "First a guy writes it, then he shows it to about six friends, then he fixes it up like how they say, on the back of the page or up the sides." When we asked Greg, "How do you revise?" he answered, "I pretend that I'm sitting in the author's chair, reading my piece aloud to the kids, and I think about what questions they'll ask. Like, I write, 'My grandparents are very old,' and I know they'll ask, 'How old?' So I've added here, 'fifty-two.'" Because most of Greg's revisions involve adding missing information, it's not surprising that the revision codes he uses most are carets and arrows.

Amy Macrorie, a quiet young artist, has an entirely different sense of good writing. Whereas both Birger and Greg tend to write narratives, Amy instinctively writes in scenes. On the day I first met her, she described her writing topic by making a tiny sketch and saying as she pointed to parts of the drawing,

> I'm going to write about how the man got down here. The shark is going to touch this sailboat. A baby shark is going to help his dad. It's a great white shark. A skeleton. There's a knife stuck in his ribs.

Amy's story line grows only as she, in her mind's eye if not on the page, adds detail and commentary to her initial sketch. Later that day, when asked what a person needs to do to be a good writer, Amy answered, "Know how to spell and draw good, make good pictures."

At the time, I interpreted these references to drawing as an indicator that Amy hadn't yet learned to distinguish drawing from writing, but now I suspect that Amy's response was an accurate reflection of her writing process. To write well, she keeps her attention focused on the scenes she envisions in her mind's eye. Nothing can wrench her focus away from these scenes. Once I tried to interview her about the drafts she'd written about baby chicks running around in the garage.

"How do you like this draft?" I asked.

"It's good. The chicks were all over the place. They were hard to catch. They were fast and hard to catch," Amy responded.

I rephrased my initial question. "What do you think about the draft, not just catching the chicks?"

"When I was catching them," Amy said, "they were all peeping and screaming, flapping and running all over."

"What are some of the things you liked about your writing?" I asked.

"When I peered in, they were all running, and I was making a picture in words. They were running all over the place."

"While you were writing," I said, "what were you doing to get your ideas?"

"I was looking in my mind, and seeing how the chicks were running around."

For Amy, Greg, and Birger, their topics, their ways of conferring, and their revision strategies are all bound together with their sense of what good writing is. Amy almost never revised by looking back and correcting her draft; instead, she typically re-envisioned the scene and wrote an entirely new draft. Greg, on the other hand, was very concerned about hearing his audience's questions, and many of his revisions involved making small additions or deletions based on comments from his peer conferences. Birger revised primarily to add excitement and to shorten boring sections.

Adults, too, tend to have a cohesive sense of what we look for in our writing, and for us, as for our students, this sense of good writing instructs us as we write. My friend Georgia Heard, author of *For the Good of the Earth and Sun*, writes in a way that is marked by a distinct constellation of qualities; her writing is filled with images, rich descriptions, and intimacy. "Growing up," Georgia says in describing her writing, "there were things happening in my family that I didn't understand. In order to understand my childhood, I learned to linger on the faces, to really look into them and try to guess what was going on. I still do that. When I write and live, I try to look very closely in order to really see." Georgia adds, "My family was formal, and I learned the proper protocol for behaving correctly. But often I'd go downstairs to the German family that lived on the floor under us, and Tanta Ellie would fix me a drink made with raw egg mixed with sugar and a sip of cognac, and there, with that 'second family,' I didn't have to think about ways of behaving. When I write, it's like I'm going downstairs . . . and there, I try to write from my soul."

Roy Peter Clark, a journalist and the author of *Free to Write*, has a different writing (and living) style altogether. Roy's writing is marked by diversity. Recently, for example, the religion section of the *St. Petersburg Times* contained a story Roy had written about an author he had loved as a boy. The article, like much of Roy's writing, was a combination of biography, oral history, theological discourse, literary criticism, and autobiography. Diversity has been a feature of Roy's entire life. His mother is Protestant, his father Catholic, his grandmother Jewish. Roy studied at Stony Brook College on Long Island, and although his classmates drew a radius fifty miles around New York City and said, "This is where I'll work," Roy, instead, began his career in Montgomery, Alabama, a Northerner living in the South and writing from the combination of diverse perspectives that has always served him so well.

Energy is one of the important things I look for in my writing. When I write a speech, for example, I read it over to see where I may risk losing my audience's interest, and then I tighten what I have written so that people won't eye each other, look at the clock, and walk out in the middle. In a sense,

I do that same tightening whenever I write anything. Not surprisingly, I fill my notebook with quotes, ideas, and anecdotes that will, I hope, keep my writing densely packed.

Each of us—Birger, Greg, Amy, Georgia, Roy, and I—has a different center of gravity as a writer and as a person. What I have begun to realize about myself is that when I write with densely packed information, it probably has everything to do with the fact that, growing up as one of nine children, I couldn't count on people staying around to hear the end of what I had to say. The pace of my writing probably has to do with the fact that I get speeding tickets, that my sixty-eight-year-old father still administers six programs, that my mother took only a week off from work when she gave birth to each of her nine children. What I have begun to realize is that when someone's writing is marked by a collage of perspectives and by information gathered from very diverse settings, as Roy's is, that also has to do with autobiography. What I have begun to realize is that when someone writes in images as Georgia does, this, too, has everything to do with autobiography. The same is true for Birger and Amy and every other child. What we look for in our writing has a lot to do with what we look for in our lives.

It's clear, then, that a five-minute mini-lesson on "Writing with Images" or even three days in a study group on images will probably not make a fundamental difference in anyone's writing. The big mistake we make when we hang laminated posters that say "Focus," "Show, don't tell," "Trim the clutter," and so forth, is that we forget that the qualities of writing are the qualities of living. If a person is going to enrich his or her vision of good writing, that person will need at the very least to develop new composing strategies, new kinds of questions to ask of his or her draft, new revision strategies, new tastes in reading, new stars to steer by. Clearly it will not be enough to mention these qualities in a mini-lesson, to write them up on a ditto, to hang them up on a chart, or to summarize them in a speech.

It's helpful, when thinking about ways to convey and teach the qualities of good writing, to think about the significant learning we've done in our lives. I have learned some things that have made a dramatic, fundamental difference in much of what I do, but I haven't learned those things by listening to speeches. I have probably never attended a talk and been changed by the words out of somebody else's mouth. Instead, I have learned most from lived chunks of life: from two years as a researcher working alongside my mentors, Donald Graves and Donald Murray; from teaching in a British primary school; from falling in love with the teachers and children of New York City; from being the mother of two young boys.

In the following chapters I do not ask, "How do I tell students about writing with focus and image and detail?" I do not ask, "How can I tell students about good language and about the importance of density and significance in their writing?" Instead I ask, "How can we help our students grow in their understanding of the qualities of good writing?" "How can we give our students the lived chunks of life that will enrich their vision of good writing?"

Density in Writing: When Texts Take Writers and Readers on Significant Journeys

Greg Snicer scowled as he reread his homemade book. "This story should go in the trash can," he muttered. "The kids will have so many questions." He read,

I saw my father's collections. Then we left

"I go through it wicked fast. The kids'll say, 'What were in the collections?'" Greg's voice trailed off as he picked up his pencil and added,

We saw buttons, coins, stamps and other stuff. (Calkins 1986, 20)

Birger Dahl is eight. He, too, rereads his draft, anticipating the questions others will ask. He underlines a sentence and says,

I'm . . . trying to make parts longer like Susie did in her piece. I'm going to add on at this part when I come out of the garage to the accident. I'll tell about when I was walking across the driveway, how I heard sounds, like the vet with the siren, and I smelled the air. It wasn't bad air and I remember thinking, it was hard to believe a part of me had just died, the air smelled so nice and clean. (Calkins 1986, 153)

Birger and Greg are two of the success stories in *The Art of Teaching Writing*. They demonstrate well the methods I once suggested when students showed us underdeveloped, skeletal pieces of writing. With carets and arrows and with slips of paper dangling from the paper's edge like spider legs, Birger,

269

Greg, and children like them inserted information into their drafts. In this way, they anticipated and answered their readers' questions.

The teachers with whom I worked shared my delight in this process. No longer did youngsters view writing as a one-shot deal. No longer did they try to produce finished pieces in an instant. Instead, Greg and Birger and the others wrote rough drafts, read these aloud to friends in share sessions and conferences, and later added clarifying information. Scissors, glue, and Scotch tape were the regular tools of the writing workshop. Children used a variety of strategies for turning little bits of writing into more respectable finished products. A four-sentence piece about going to Macy's, Sears, and Bradlees became a book with a chapter allotted to each store. Older children sometimes circled important passages in their writing and tried to expand them by saying more. Writers read their pieces to one friend after another and then added requested information with arrows.

When I looked at children stapling, inserting, answering questions, and adding details I was right to be pleased. It was radical and new for children to produce rough drafts and to revise and solicit help from readers. It was exciting to know children had a strategy for fleshing out the underdeveloped, skeletal pieces inexperienced writers so commonly produce. Birger and Greg and the others were helping me and my colleagues see that children could do things we'd never dreamed possible. But when I declared proudly that our children were writing "just like real authors," I was not drawing entirely accurate conclusions, and therein lies the story of why our children's written products now seem very different to me than they once did.

Shortly after I sent the manuscript of this book to Heinemann, I received a letter from Philippa Stratton, the editor-in-chief. "What I liked best about the book," the letter began. I eagerly imagined the end of that sentence. Did she like the anecdotes, the density of ideas, the style of writing? No. "What I liked best about the book was the quality of your children's writing."

In thinking about it, however, I realized that Philippa's response matched my own. When we first brought notebooks and genre studies into classrooms, for us, as for Philippa, there was something about the students' writing that surprised, enchanted, and wooed us into continuing to pursue these new ideas. The writing was often rough and chaotic, but one piece of writing after another had a life force, an intensity, and a density we had rarely seen before. Clearly, the written products are different because the writing processes are different. Let me explain.

I realize now, in retrospect, that I used to view writing as a process of producing and then repairing drafts. I talked about fixing leads, inserting details, strengthening weak sections, reworking endings. When the pieces of writing were rich and alive to begin with, these revisions strengthened the pieces. But quite often, the children with whom I worked ended up fiddling with and fixing pieces of writing that weren't alive in the first place. Children would bring their little pieces to conferences and share sessions. After hearing people's questions and comments, they'd insert bits of information. As often as not, these additions, like little P.S.'s, destroyed the natural sense of song and proportion the pieces contained. I sometimes thanked my lucky stars I was focusing on process, not products.

When children's energy for writing faltered, I held celebrations, brought in new kinds of paper, and arranged new forms of publication. Yet despite my bravado and my energetic efforts, it sometimes seemed that folder after folder contained pieces of writing that didn't have much life in them. There were times when I would begin to feel mired in lifeless little ditties. But there were also times when some children would submit poems to contests, turn pieces into big books for kindergartners, or choose topics that were particularly real and alive for them, and a wonderful surge of energy would sweep through our workshops. I lived for those stretches of time, even though these surges of energy occurred against a backdrop of pieces that were cranked out and repaired and left to gather dust in folders.

I needed to listen to the life force I felt in those magical moments when children had energy for writing. I needed to find ways to help more writers have the intensity and urgency that would lead them to write not only more developed pieces but also more alive pieces.

In a sense, everything in this book addresses the issue of how we can help youngsters write with an intensity and life force; genre studies do this, finding purposes for writing do this, and of course, notebooks do this. The notebooks themselves aren't crucial, but they are a concrete manifestation of our new understanding of the writing process, and that new sense of the writing process does seem to me to be crucial. Our children's writing has more density now because their pieces of writing begin as seeds and grow. The important thing is partly that we've devoted more attention to helping children develop strategies and habits of life that allow pieces of writing to accumulate, branch out, and grow. But we're also listening more for the heartbeat in a piece of writing and trusting it when it's there.

Laurie Pessah drew her chair alongside Samantha's desk. "How's it going?" Laurie asked. Samantha told Laurie she had been rereading her notebook looking for an entry that popped out and said, "Write me, write me." Laurie caught the classroom teacher's eye, acknowledging the work this teacher had already done with Samantha. But the teacher's invitation hadn't yielded any results. Samantha hadn't found an entry that stood out from all the rest, so Laurie suggested another way of running a divining rod over the field of one's notebook. "Sometimes I don't look for the entries that are beautifully crafted but just for those that were fun to write," Laurie said to Samantha. "Why not look back over the stuff you've been writing and see if you have an entry that was sort of fun to write?"

Because Laurie uses her own notebook as a quarry from which she mines material for her staff development workshops and professional articles, she knows firsthand about ways to find small bits in her notebook that bristle with significance. She knows there can be a common thread underlying entries that seem to be about very different topics. An entry about Laurie's brother, an entry about her principal, and an entry about her job all spoke to the larger issue of finding her place in the world. "It's not that I choose these themes," Laurie says. "I'm driven by them." Then, too, Laurie knows that two very separate entries can connect, igniting a spark of surprise. As Laurie spoke with Samantha, she drew on her writing experience in order to give Samantha a range of ways to find and develop seed ideas for writing.

Yes, Samantha said, she did have an entry that was especially fun to write (Figure 17–1):

The Beer

When I was four years old I went to a beach. My mother wanted to play volleyball. She left the beer on the table without telling me. I gobbled the can of beer down. It tasted like salt water with lemonade in it. I can hear the sounds of bubbles popping in my mouth. I see it all in my mind popping popping popping popping popping. Smelling like seltzer water with all the lemonade we could get.

Figure 17–1   Samantha's Entry

"Do you have any ideas about why this entry was such fun to write?" Laurie asked as she skimmed it.

"I guess it's because now I like beer," Samantha said, "and I remember that time when I was a baby and I hated it."

"What I also noticed," Laurie wisely said, "is the way you've used wonderful words to capture what that beer felt like in your mouth."

Samantha giggled and wondered if beer popped in Ms. Pessah's mouth as well, and did Ms. Pessah know what she meant about how beer tasted like salt water mixed with lemonade. It was good talk—natural, flowing, full of energy and laughter. But for Laurie, the talk contained an underpinning of anxiety. "Where do I go from here?" she wondered as she and Samantha chattered about the language in the text. "What are the directions this conference might take?"

"I'm still not that good at conferring," Laurie said later in discussing this conference with me. "Things don't flow for me. As I listen, I find myself thinking about what the child is saying but also about my options. I'm listening and all the while I'm thinking, 'What strategy, what tool can I give to this kid?' I know I'm probably taking away ownership and not listening well, but I keep wondering, 'Where do I take this child?'"

What Laurie needs to realize is that the mental sideshow that goes on during her conferences is exactly what happens in the mind of any reflective, inquiring, researching teacher. Every one of us listens to a child who, as in this instance, has found a seed idea for writing, and asks, "Where do I go from here? How do I help this writer develop this idea?"

The important thing is that Laurie needs to voice her thinking so that Samantha can learn from it and participate in it. "What I'm thinking, Samantha, and I bet you are too, is this: Where do you go from here? You've got a few great lines, but how do you build on them?"

Over time, Samantha will need to identify and steer through these junctures in her writing process on her own. Sitting at home, she'll need to assign herself tasks. She'll need to say, "Now the problem is, how do I build these few lines into something bigger?" and she'll need her own tool box of strategies for shaping an image, a question, a line, a memory, or a pattern of entries into something with larger scope and significance.

As Laurie worked to make an article grow out of one of her entries and as Samantha worked to make a story (or a song, a poem, a letter) grow out of her memory of tasting beer, both writers were working on one of the essential and age-old issues of writing well, described in language arts textbooks as "developing one's writing." In *The Art of Teaching Writing*, I described this process as "adding flesh to the bones of skeletal writing" and as "adding enough detail so readers can make movies in their minds." But what these descriptors neglect to address is the fact that there is an enormous difference between adding a bulk of detail and adding the significance and depth that will make readers care.

The difference comes down to an issue of ownership, and by ownership I do not mean that it must be the writer rather than the teacher who initiates the process of developing a seed idea. What I do mean is that Laurie and Samantha will need to develop their ideas for *themselves,* not for their readers. They will need to go on their own journeys toward things that are new and surprising and significant for them. Then their pieces will be able to carry readers to new and surprising and significant territory.

"No surprise for the writer, no surprise for the reader," Robert Frost has said, and his adage is profound. What this means is that yes, Laurie, Samantha, and the rest of us need to have that tool chest of strategies in order to develop a piece of writing, but at a more fundamental level, we also need to approach writing expecting, even hungering, to learn. We need to know that developing our writing is not a matter of recording but of discovering what we know. Learning to develop a piece of writing has less to do with learning to insert information with arrows, carets, and editing codes or with learning to write longer drafts than it has to do with learning to explore hunches, to interrogate images and ideas, and to follow trails of thought and chains of memory. Texts become well developed and alive not so much when writers *say* more as when they *learn* more. We do not write well-developed pieces by trying to instruct readers; we write them by allowing ourselves to be instructed.

To the question "How can Samantha go about filling out and expanding her writing?" we must add the question "How can Samantha go about learning from her writing?"

The answer is simple. Samantha must write. This may seem obvious, but it is nevertheless true. Writing is the most important strategy writers have for developing an idea or image.

But there are ways of writing that nourish learning and then there are the ways most of us were taught to write. When textbooks (and even those of us who teach writing) say, "Begin by choosing a small, focused topic," "Build your case with several supporting examples," and "Add details that make your ideas concrete," they are doing the equivalent of telling human beings that to make a child you must begin by choosing a small, round head, then add a body with four limbs followed by the appropriate number of well-placed fingers and toes. It is true that writing has a focused subject and details, it is true that a human being has a head and ten toes, but you make both a piece of writing and a child with a living seed that gestates and grows in the fullness of time.

Clearly one way to nudge ourselves into new thoughts as we write is to break out of the confining manner in which some of us and some of our students have interpreted what it means to focus one's topic. "Write about just one thing," I have said, and there is wisdom in this advice. When children were writing page-long stories titled "My Trip" in which they listed their entire itinerary, it helped enormously to say, "Focus on one thing." Now, when they write with some detail about topics like raccoons tipping over the garbage cans at their campsite, the pieces are vastly improved. There is wisdom in the admonition, "Focus your topics."

And yet, there is wisdom also in William Sloane's contrary observation: "Almost all effective writing above the level of the soup can label turns out to be about quite a lot of things fused or laced or linked together" (1983, 112). The raccoon incident will be more interesting if the writer weaves this scene into other similar memories, or links it to a childhood dream of capturing and taming a raccoon, or shows how those raccoons called forth an interesting family drama among those who heard the noise.

Dorothy Barnhouse, who cares very much about the writing-to-learn function of notebooks, has helped us realize that teachers—and young writers—need to unlearn old lessons about writing and learn new ones if we are going to think on paper. In most writing workshops, the entries of both teachers and students tend to be confined within the parameters of the initial topic: a good movie, the presidential election, a dream. It is as if people have an internalized rule stating that if their entry begins, "I have a lot of memories about lying on the rooftop of our apartment building," they must produce a list of memories about that rooftop. This internalized rule means that the writer is not apt to turn her attention to other cherished places in her life, or to question why that rooftop has meant so much to her. The problem with this is first, that we can push ourselves into learning more about the rooftop by finding loops of connection between it and other disparate subjects, and second, that the rooftop may not be the writer's real subject any more than the view from the roof is the subject of Geffen Godder's extraordinary entry:

> I am lying on the roof of my 35th story Manhattan building. It is a warm day in June with the sun pressing against my face and I think of Israel when we used to sunbathe on the roof of our houses eating oranges. If there was no one on our neighbor's roof we would walk from roof to roof. Sometimes we would stop and look straight down at the world.
>
> I'm thinking of when I pretended I was a teacher and everything I learned that day came out of my mouth. I got to control the class and make my own rules.
>
> I'm able to do everything in gymnastics. I love gymnastics. It's the funnest thing in the world. It's not the kind of fun of going on a rollercoaster. The fun isn't the scariness. It's the learning something.
>
> I still can't fall asleep so I plan out what I'll do when I get home: I'll go home, walk down the stairs, press the elevator button, go to the fifth floor and so on.
>
> I think of drawing a masterpiece. I love to diddle doodle. From every little design, I make a big picture. When pencil and paper meet, thoughts go through my head.

At first glance it may seem that after Geffen located herself on the top of her thirty-five-story Manhattan apartment building and reminisced about walking from roof to roof in Israel, she then decided not to develop this kernel. She doesn't supply the expected details about either the view or her rooftop activities. Instead, she begins to write about one disparate image after another, about gymnastics and what she plans to do that afternoon, and her drawings.

Her teacher, Judy Davis, almost suggested that Geffen focus her entry, then caught herself. "It's an entry, not a rough draft of a finished piece," she reminded herself, and this allowed her to stop checking whether the writing was focused and organized and to look instead for whether the writing generated thoughts.

Like Judy Davis, once we alter our lens for reading Geffen's entry, once we let go of our almost automatic urge to focus the topic of any text that contains disparate moments, then we can see that Geffen is in fact gathering and exploring the images that develop from her initial feeling of being "on top of the world." For Geffen, it seems that the significance of the rooftop is not the view she gains of the world but the view she gains of herself. She looks out to see not just rooftops and tiny automobiles, but herself as a girl pretending to be the teacher, as a person who can do everything in gymnastics, as someone who is able to turn doodles into masterpieces.

In her entry, Geffen does not spell out the connection between rooftops and gymnastics; instead, she fills her page with related images. Her entry reveals that she has made writing into a learning process because she trusts the associations that happen in her mind enough to put them on paper. The gaps she creates in doing so stimulate readers (and Geffen herself) to make their own bridges of thought.

If Judy Davis had asked Geffen to write down the thoughts and feelings that link the sections of the entry, she might have nudged Geffen to discover and explain why rooftops remind her of gymnastics. But the important thing isn't that gaps are bridged with explanations. The important thing is that when two unlike subjects are juxtaposed like this, their proximity can ignite sparks of insight. The important thing is that because Geffen dared to link her Manhattan rooftop experience with rooftops in Israel and with the sense of competence she feels in gymnastics and drawing, she has created a piece of writing that is not only about a rooftop scene but is also about a young writer who stands on top of the world with windblown hair and sun-warmed skin, swept over by a sense of empowerment and competence.

This book is filled, in a similar way, with odd combinations. In fact, the biggest difference between the writing style in this book and in *Lessons from a Child* and *The Art of Teaching Writing* is that while they were more exclusively about writing, this book is about many things laminated together. Notice, for example, the diverse worlds contained in these excerpts:

- The most hopeful thing about notebooks is that they were, for us, the final proof that there is no Wizard of Oz behind writing-process teaching methods.
- The reason I care about writing memoir—and about writing in general—is that for all of us, the life we're given amounts to "We had Coke, and then we had a hot dog."
- Of course, circling back and seeing a subject in a new light is important in written texts, but it is also important in life.

The writing by teachers and children that I've quoted in this book has also been full of gaps—and connections:

At that moment I felt jealous. Envious of the flour, the shortening, the baking powder, the salt, the milk that formed the white lump my foster mother so carefully carressed. I longed to be a white shapeless lump, instead of a tiny Black child.

ISOKE NIA

It's a rainy day and . . . I see the clouds gray and mean. They seem to come to you and eat you with their big black mouths.

ESTHER PORTELA

My memories are shattered by a father who frightened me. . . . I ran, muddy, crying, into the woods to hide from my father and his certain wrath, and now I hear myself telling my daughter she's not doing well enough . . . and I wonder if I hear my father.

JUDY DAVIS

As the plane took off . . . everything I left behind was now a long memory, my whole life was only a memory. My house, my school, my friends were disappearing in clouds as we went up and up.

LUZ GORDILLO

The payoff for writing about several things at once is not so much in the final layered effect the process yields—as in this book, where issues of parenting, politics, family life, and ecology thread through an exploration of teaching reading and writing. Instead, the payoff comes because disparate topics and fields are brought together so that a combustive spark results, giving new momentum and direction to our thinking.

A second way to nudge ourselves into thinking new thoughts as we write is to devote less time to fixing up, fattening up, and fancying up our early drafts and more time to generating ideas and specifics around our topic. "Producing writing," Peter Elbow says, "is not so much like filling a basin or pool once as it is like getting the water to keep flowing through until it finally runs clear."

Like many teachers of writing, I used to believe that honoring children's drafts meant that I needed to respond to anything they produced with exclamations like "Oh, you're an author!" and "Do you have ideas for how you can make this even better?" and "What do you think is the strongest part?" The problem with responses like these is that they almost guarantee that writers will stay within the general confines of this early draft, fattening it up, fixing it up, and fancying it up.

We need ways in which we can respect early, tentative writing without feeling we must revise it toward publication. Notebooks give us a repertoire of ways to keep ourselves and our students from hovering too long over that basin of water. Where we might once have asked our students, "How can this be fixed up?" we might now try asking, "What are you discovering?" "Where is this leading you?" "What, of all this, stands out as worth exploring?" "As you reread this, does it spark even more ideas?" "Does what you say here connect with anything you've written earlier?" Each of these questions gives a writer a way to value and learn from writing without necessarily staying with it.

Although those of us who keep notebooks and invite students to do the same can feel satisfied because we've given ourselves and our students a vehicle for trying out discovery drafts and generative writing, the notebooks themselves cannot be equated with habits of thought. It's entirely possible to keep a notebook without investing oneself in generative, exploratory writing.

Several warning signs can tip us off that young writers are not using notebooks as tools of thought. If entries typically begin by staking out predictable turf ("I have a lot of memories of Christmas at Grandma's") and if the writer usually stays within that initial focus, then that writer is probably not using the notebook as a tool for standing on the shoulders of his or her own thinking. Similarly, if a writer typically moves from a notebook toward publication by selecting the best entries, fixing them up, and combining them into either a chapter book or a composition, then that writer is probably not using the notebook as a tool for standing on the shoulders of his or her own thinking. On the other hand, if writers are taking lines or paragraphs from their notebooks and producing a page or more about these bits, even if these new pages remain unpublished, they show that notebooks are probably being used to generate new ideas.

So far, then, what I have said is that if we explore the connections between our triggering topic and other seemingly disparate topics, we can nudge ourselves into having new thoughts as we write. If we can regard our early writing as a process of discovery rather than as something to tidy up and tighten toward publication, we can nudge ourselves into having new thoughts as we write. Finally, by working *from* rather than simply *toward* what matters most, we can break new trails of thought. Let me explain. When Isoke recalled her childhood fear of being empty-handed on Open House night, she could have written a nice little composition conveying that experience to readers. She could have begun her piece with a lead sentence such as, "We arrived at the school when the day was just turning into evening" and ended with a poignant punch line about how she felt empty-handed. Instead, Isoke used this absolutely crucial, fundamental memory not as her closing remark but as her pushing off place and wrote from it into unexplored territory. The procedure for writing out from rather than toward what matters most is not difficult; having the courage to do it is difficult.

Psychotherapists have written whole books about the last five minutes of therapy sessions. They know enough to listen well to those final moments because it's often then, just as the session is about to end, that a patient will raise the central question or make the basic connection that needs to be put at the beginning, rather than the close, of a session.

For me, the hardest part about finding a line or an image that matters most and sums everything up and then putting that bit at the top of a large white expanse of empty page is the fear I'll look into myself and find nothing there. But Annie Dillard offers wise advice. She says,

> One of the few things I know about writing is this: spend it all, shoot it, play it, lose it, all, right away, every time. Do not hoard what seems good for a later place in the book, or for another book; give it, give it all, give it now. The impulse to save something good for a better place later is the signal to spend it now. Something more will arise for later, something better. These things fill from behind, from beneath, like well water. (1989a, 78–79)

A final note: although it is important to put whatever is best and most crucial "up front" in our writing, this doesn't mean that we should place our conclusions up front. It's generally wiser to write out from the specific images and details that resonate for us, that feel significant or disturbing. The obvious reason for beginning with the significant scenes and details rather than with sweeping, generic ideas is that if we begin with general ideas and then provide details and examples to illustrate what we have said, we are apt to constrict ourselves into pulling prepackaged thoughts from the shelves of our mind. But if we begin at least the process (if not the product) of our writing with a scene or a detail that bothers or haunts us (as Isoke did with Open House night and as I did with my entries about jogging and growing old), then attending carefully to that scene or detail can lead us toward ideas we've never had before. Most of us have assumed that the reason to write with scenes and images is that these concrete details allow readers to know the fullness of our experience and make their own meaning from it. In fact, however, the reason for putting concrete details on the page and lingering long enough to capture the vivid, sensory particulars of a scene or an experience is that only then will we begin to know the fullness of the experience for ourselves and make our own new meaning from it.

The effort to see and experience the world is what allows us to be affected by it.

> Still—in a way—nobody sees a flower—really—
>   it is so small—we haven't time—
> and to see takes time, like to have a friend takes time.
>
> GEORGIA O'KEEFFE

For years, we have known the importance of writing with "telling detail," with "revealing specifics." But when writers begin with a topic (My Birthday

Party) and then try to supply readers with telling details (chocolate cake with orange flowers on it or pink balloons) what they are, in fact, doing is working backward. Telling details are by definition those that bristled with such significance for us that, as we wrote, they led us to bigger insights.

For reasons I don't entirely understand, when we record the bits of life we hear and see and think about and remember, when we linger with these bits long enough to let one remind us of another, the details are entirely different from those we include when we begin with a generic topic (such as My Sister's Bedroom) and then try to flesh the topic out with details. When Alexis wrote in her notebook about how every night she and her sister lie in bed listening to their radio waiting until the lights in the nearby building go off, and then check the time to see if the lights are going off earlier or later than the day before, she has captured a detail that she would never have produced had she begun instead by trying to write about the fun times she and her sister have together. I suspect that when we put onto paper the pieces of our lives that for some mysterious reason matter to us, we can capture both those moments and the energy around them.

Writers need to begin with a seed idea and write their way into it. Only when a detail is truly generative, when it takes the writer on a journey into new lines of thought and new worlds of feeling, will it do so also for the reader.

On Loving Words

Those of us in the Teachers College Writing Project have learned to watch and listen with care when New York City writers first become involved in our community. We have found it helpful to notice the things these writers question as they encounter our ideas and the things that seem alien and awkward to them. Two years ago, Vicki Vinton was puzzled by what she viewed as a lack of interest on our part in language. "None of you talk about writing that begins with a phrase rather than a topic. Language often comes first for me. I listen to my words knowing they will lead me. I don't always begin with a topic." Vicki Vinton's observation was right on target. Until our recent work with picture books, we tended to treat language as a minor issue, one that should be attended to in the final editing phase of writing.

Until recently, our message to young writers has been, "Decide first on your topic, then write with detail and information," and "Focus on content first. If you're going to fuss over particular words, do that later, after finding and clarifying your meaning."

We have not been alone in emphasizing information and detail and in disregarding language as a generative tool for thought. In *A Writer Teaches Writing*, Donald Murray, who has also written a great deal about language leading toward subject, describes the writer's seven skills—discovering a subject, sensing an audience, searching for specifics, creating a design, writing, developing a critical eye, and rewriting—but does not mention language. For a long while I often quoted a passage from Murray's book:

> Many students have the misconception that writers write with words, language detached from information. They think that words are pretty balloons filled with air. They dance to the sound of their own voices, they substitute style for subject matter. It doesn't work. (1968)

He goes on to say that writing is built with significant facts, revealing details, pertinent quotations, not with mere words strung together like pretty balloons.

Like Ken Macrorie and other early spokespeople for writing as process, Murray was arguing against traditional methods of teaching writing that emphasized putting lovely language into correct, preordained forms. When I was in school, I was taught to fill my poems about spring with pretty descriptions, fancy words, and big adjectives. My teachers introduced writing assignments by posting word lists around the classroom. They taught assonance, alliteration, metaphor, and simile but never mentioned revision or rough drafts. Murray's warning against focusing on words, then, was not unlike Ken Macrorie's argument in *Telling Writing* (1985) against the overblown, pretentious, decorative "Engfish" students use. It's not surprising that in our efforts to put dysfunctional approaches to writing behind us we inadvertently treated language as a minor issue, almost an afterthought, in the writing process.

If young writers have needed their self-confidence buoyed, we've shown them that they do indeed have areas of expertise, memories, and stories to share. But we have only rarely shown children that there is power and music in their voices and in their language. We've often encouraged students to teach us what they know and care about, but we have only rarely valued the lilt and pace and idiom of their language. We have often responded to writers by telling them what we have learned from a piece, but we have only rarely told them about the phrases that have had a musical appeal for us.

Our unintentional bias against language has been even more evident in the rituals that shape our share sessions. Donald Hall says,

> To read literature is to be intimately involved with the words on the page, and to never think of them as embodiments of ideas which can be expressed in other terms. If we read literature properly, we read slowly, and we hear all the words. The muscles in our throats move and come together when we see the word "squeeze."

Yet in many of our share sessions, after the writer has read a draft, listeners retell the draft in paraphrase so that the writer's actual language drops from sight altogether and only the content remains as a subject for discussion. Rather than asking children to read their pieces of writing several times so that we can all hear and rehear the words, rather than recalling exact phrases, we've tended to extract the subject matter and leave the words behind. We have treated language as a disposable container for the more valuable cargo of meaning.

Caring About Language Early in the Writing Process
Vicki Vinton was right to question the way we relegated language to the tail end of the writing process. It is crucial to attend to language early in the composing process, since caring about language has less to do with buffing one's

final product until it shines (although this is important) than with discovering one's meaning. In a *New York Times Book Review* essay, Louis Simpson addresses this issue, suggesting that it is especially important for a writer to reach for exactly the right words, even while recognizing that those words will probably lead to entirely new and surprising meanings and will thus be tools for thought rather than embellishments on a final product. He writes,

> A pressure to say a thing in a certain way and no other drives the poem forward from phrase to phrase and line to line. The idea of perfection—call it an illusion if you will, but a necessary illusion—drives the poem from beginning to end. If poets thought the words could be changed, the rhythm adjusted later, or that they could negotiate endlessly with the muse, they would destroy the sense of urgency that is the very life of the poem.
>
> As you write, every word has to convey the rhythm you want, and no other word will do. . . . Finding the right word cannot be put off for a later time, for the rhythm of the words that will follow depends on the rhythm of this one. If the next word isn't right, everything that follows will be off . . . poets do have to make changes, but they cannot think so; they must think that the next word and phrase will be perfect. (1988, 12)

For me, this has meant a radical revision in my thinking about language. Once upon a time, if I had been writing a chapter on language, I would have filled my pages with examples of fresh, surprising language from books and from children's writing and an analysis of why each excerpt worked. This approach might have encouraged writers to reread their own texts, looking for vivid gems of language and weeding out passive verbs and clichéd phrases. Now I realize that correcting one's inadequate language is not as important as writing with the ancient Native American belief that words have the power to invoke the spirits, to call forth life. What really matters is searching for the exact, true word to say things we've never said. In *The Writing Life*, Annie Dillard notes,

> When you write, you lay out a line of words. The line of words is a miner's pick, a woodcarver's gouge, a surgeon's probe. You wield it, and it digs a path you follow. Soon you find yourself deep in new territory. Is it a dead end, or have you located the real subject? You will know tomorrow, or this time next year. . . . The line of words is a hammer. You hammer against the walls of your house. You tap the walls, lightly, everywhere. After giving many years' attention to these things, you know what to listen for. Some of the walls are bearing walls; they have to stay, or everything will fall down. . . . You write it all, discovering it at the end of the line of words. (1989, 3, 4, 7)

A person need not be the professional writer that Dillard is to know the process she describes. Just as we distinguish the *thwang* of our tennis ball hitting the racket's rim from the deep, satisfying *plunk* it makes when it hits the center of the strings, we know also the difference between the thwang of untrue words and the deep plunk of words that are truer than we ever knew possible. When we linger over words that ring true, when we copy words like these from a notebook entry to the top of a new notebook page or a clean piece of paper and then concentrate on what we want to say next, we experience the surprise of discovering things we've never thought before.

We need to be concerned about language early in the writing process because it is essential to the very act of generating meaning. But what does this really mean for those of us in writing classrooms, with our notebooks and portfolios and plans for publication? How do we care about words in ways that are generative? How can we establish classroom environments that equip writers to use language well? These are big, tough questions.

Classrooms That Value Language

There is no set sequence of steps a writer can follow in order to explore language. Along with our students we can brainstorm and free write and reflect and revise all we want and yet not experience that internal reaching to capture the complexity and power and delicacy of life. We can choose words carefully yet never dare to say something more true than anything we've ever said. At the same time, we can pursue no overt activities at all and still be immersed in this crucial but underground part of writing.

Although we cannot add a step in the writing process called "concern for language," we can fill classrooms with reading and writing that celebrate language; and along with our students we can assume stances that allow us to use language in rich ways. The phrase "assuming a stance" is an important one. I will use language well when I position myself in relation to both my material and my audience in ways that invoke my own muse. This is the reason that, down through the generations, stories told around campfires have begun with the age-old incantation, "There once was" or "Once upon a time, long, long ago." These words position the storyteller and the audience in a way that invokes a certain magic. Writers, too, can invoke this magic, if they have rich storehouses of language to draw on.

One of the goals of our reading-writing workshop, then, must be to help youngsters build rich storehouses of language. In a recent workshop, Mary Ellen Giacobbe cited Don Holdaway, the Australian educator best known for originating the idea of Big Books, who says that by the time children leave the first grade, they need to have heard at least 1500 stories. Some children have shared stories on their mother's and father's laps for years by the time they come to school, but some children need to build their storehouses in the classroom. Many educators, including Gordon Wells, Frank Smith, James Britton, and David Booth, among others, agree that nothing matters more to a child's eventual success as a reader and writer than this storehouse of language. Robert MacNeil, in his memoir *Wordstruck,* says,

> Music heard early in life lays down a rich bed of memories against which you evaluate and absorb music encountered later on. . . . It is so with words and word patterns. . . . Like music, the patterns of melody, rhythm, and quality of voice become templates against which we judge the sweetness and justness of new patterns and rhythms; and the patterns laid down in our memories create expectations and hunger for fulfillment again. It is the same for the bookish person and for the illiterate. Each has a mind programmed with language—from prayers, hymns, verses, jokes, patriotic texts, proverbs, folk sayings, clichés, stories, movies, radio, and television.
>
> I picture each of those layers of experience and language gradually accumulating and thickening to form a kind of living matrix, nourishing like a placenta. (1989, 23–24)

It is worth pausing for a moment to notice that MacNeil's storehouse is filled with the stories and sounds of literature, but it is also filled with hymns, jokes, movies, and folk sayings. It's easy to be elitist about language, to think that honoring language means that the poetic register is the only one that matters. When we care about language, we enjoy the words a friend uses in describing a white-water adventure: eddy turns, running the waterfall, reading the river, keepers, hydraulics, pour-overs. We savor the language of our cookbooks: fold the egg whites, stir the raspberry purée, cut the cake into thin wedges and garnish with fresh raspberries. We record the wonderful expressions children use. Jacqueline Jackson's notebook is full of "caught poems" overheard from children around her. Here's one from *Turn Not Pale, Beloved Snail,* by Elizabeth:

> I shook and shook the ketchup
> But it didn't bloop out
> So I stamped the bottle
> On the table
> And a glob shot up
> And made a big red splat
> On the ceiling.
> "Quick, hold your hamburger under it!"
> Daddy said.
> "Maybe it'll drip."

Robert MacNeil talks about a living matrix of language as if it's something children need, as much as they need carrots and sleep and sunshine. But in the Writing Project, we have found that we can best involve children in this living matrix of language if it is something we, as teachers, also participate in.

In our Thursday study group comprising writing staff developers from around New York City, we have begun reading aloud together, and we have established our own rituals for doing so. One of us brings copies of a "Hers" column from *The New York Times* or an excerpt from Steinbeck or several pages from Forrest Carter's *The Education of Little Tree*. When we all have a copy of the text, someone—anyone—begins to read, pausing after a passage, a line, a section. For an instant, there is silence, then a voice from a far corner of the room comes from among us, and when this reader pauses, another voice picks up the reading, and in this way the text is shared. Sometimes we circle back to reread, and this time we may read just favorite lines, again, without any discussion and without anyone calling, "Next?" Sometimes we choreograph readings, perhaps reading a text from four corners of the room or reading particular sections in unison. Recently, we gave out a sheet filled with poems and divided the group into clusters of four; ten minutes later, each cluster presented a reading of poems taken from the handout. One group, for example, literally wedged the lines of two rain poems between each other and set them against a backdrop of, "It's raining, it's pouring, the old man is snoring."

This year in New York City, ninety groups of teachers congregate every other week to talk about adult literature. Reading aloud is essential to what happens in these book talks. We may read the opening lines of a book as a way of introducing the next week's text, and we may read aloud as a way to begin talking about a book we've just read. Sometimes we open our book talks by asking each person to read and talk about a passage that is especially meaningful to him or her. Sometimes, we read and talk about passages that seem to capture the essence of a book. Sometimes we search for examples of particular things, like the time we shared all the references we could find to a yellow raft in Michael Dorris's *A Yellow Raft in Blue Water*.

We have reading-aloud mentors, too. We know that on the really special occasions, Llewellyn Berk will read aloud to us, or Isoke Nia, or Lettie Smith. Sometimes we study these readers and others—like Don Holdaway and some of the readers on public television's "Reading Rainbow"—in order to learn the art of reading aloud. We talk about the importance of not prefacing or interrupting a reading with lists of vocabulary words or motivating questions. We talk about respecting the mood of a story. We recall Georgia Heard's caution against being too dramatic in our readings, lest we draw attention away from the text to ourselves. "Sometimes it helps to pretend a friend is sitting next to me and I'm speaking the poem to this person," she says. "For me, this helps bring naturalness and intimacy to my voice." (1989, 6)

We've also found it important to keep an ear out for books and poems that sing. During the Writing Project's Thursday study group, a cluster of staff developers—including Lettie Smith from Harlem, Shirley MacPhillips from Tenafly, Kathy Cunningham from Queens, and Shelley Harwayne—discovered a way to help all of us, teachers and children alike, hear the melody of picture books. These educators have begun to put the words of some favorite picture books to music. Now, when any one of us opens Tony Johnston's *Yonder,* we cannot help but hum the words, "Yonder, way over yonder. . . . " We have a song for Audrey Wood's *The Napping House,* too, and a jazz chant for the words to Virginia Griest's *In Between.* The process of turning literature into song is so irresistible, other teachers and children are joining in. Those of us who are less facile with melody are looking through record collections for background music to accompany texts, including texts written by children. We've decided, for example, that the best background music for Cynthia Rylant's *The Relatives Came* is "Turkey in the Straw."

Shelley discovered that one of the best ways to respond to a child's writing in a share session is to try to see in it the potential for a performance. When Samantha took her place in the author's chair, a quiet but unmistakable ripple of discontent spread through the room. The behavior was covert enough— several children rolled their eyes, and others simply looked at each other or away from the group meeting altogether—that Shelley didn't call the share session to a halt. But when Samantha, looking pained, spoke in an almost inaudible whisper, Shelley knew that reminding her to speak up wasn't going to help. Instead, Shelley listened as closely as possible to Samantha's tortured, simple lines.

"It sounds like a jazz chant, doesn't it?" Shelley said, and with an upbeat, swinging rhythm she read,

> I love green,
> I love black,
> I love blue and yellow.
>
> I love green,
> I love black,
> I love blue and yellow.

Soon the entire class was beating the rhythm of Samantha's jazz chant onto the floor in front of them. "Do you have any more pieces like this one?" Shelley asked the bewildered but very delighted Samantha, and out came her portfolio. Soon the class had divided into four teams, and each team was turning a different piece of Samantha's writing into a jazz chant.

Author Mem Fox (1988b) once asked us, "Is your hair carefully coiffured? If it is, ruffle it up, dye it up, be anything but a teacher with carefully coiffured hair when you teach reading." We sing, grunt, and dance to accompany Maurice Sendak's wonderful pictures of Max and the wild things dancing through the pages of *Where the Wild Things Are.* "You can't teach reading or writing," Mem Fox says, "if you're the kind of person who allows Max and the wild things to have a silent wild rumpus." *This* is what caring about language means, and Mem Fox has helped us know it.

In Molly Bang's *The Paper Crane,* a stranger arrives unexpectedly at a quiet little restaurant and shows the people that a folded napkin can become a graceful bird, that the music of a flute can call everyone to dance. It was in just this way that Mem Fox arrived at our Project to participate in our annual Summer Institute on the Teaching of Writing. Mem is an Australian storyteller as well as the author of many well-loved picture books, including *Koala Lou, Wilfrid Gordon McDonald Partridge,* and *Night Noises.* During our two weeks with her, Mem helped us make literature—poems and stories and riddles—dance and sing and live. None of us will ever forget her presence. We remember the first day. We waited, squeezed into those university chairs with the desks attached, for the seminar to begin. Mem raced in with bags and packages, books and papers spilling out of her hands. "Right, then," she said, and projecting a poem onto the wall, she glanced at our chairs and asked, "Can you clap on your knees despite those tables?" We turned our knees out to make more space for clapping. "Let's be sure we can do the clapping Upppp and Downnn," she said, demonstrating as she spoke. "Are you ready? Get your lips ready, your hands ready, so we're all set." Little did we know "We're ready" meant we were ready to read poems up the page as well as down, to create our own refrains, to gather choir-style in order to perform poems, to stand on chairs, to read against a backdrop of "pitter-patter, pitter-patter" and "talk-talk-talk-talk-talk," to tell stories by heart, to recite the rhymes of our childhood.

Another morning, Mem began by saying, "Let's recall our memories of language. Would you think of the earliest bit of rhyme or song you can remember?" Mem went on to read part of her book *Goodnight, Sleep Tight,* in which Vivien Venn coaxes Skinny Doug, her teenage babysitter, into reciting rhymes for her. Each rhyme is followed by the refrain

> "I love it! I love it!" said Vivien Venn.
> "How does it go, will you say it again?"

Soon all of us were clapping on our knees, with one person after another sharing a childhood rhyme and everyone calling out the refrain. Dawn Harris-Martine sang, "And when you're up, you're up, and when you're down, you're down, and when you're only halfway up you're neither up nor down," and we all chanted, "'I love it, I love it,' said Vivien Venn. 'How does it go? Will you say it again?'" Norm Sherman recited, "Star light, star bright, first star I see tonight," and again we called out the refrain.

Still another day we spent the entire two hours choreographing a choral reading of the poem "Sampan." "Let's have the tallest men on these chairs," Mem said, setting out two chairs and not questioning for an instant whether the tall men objected to standing on chairs. The next tallest people formed a row between the chairs. People of medium height formed the next row, women with skirts sat on the next row, and everyone else crowded cross-legged on the floor in front of the configuration so that, all together, we probably looked like a large family squeezed together for a family portrait. Then we read the poem in unison two or three times, trying to capture the light, quick feeling of the gondola paddles. The men on chairs at either end of the group were the polers for our gondola and called out, "Ohe!" whenever it appeared in the poem. During another reading we made sure our voices stretched out "the lo-o-ong green river." Another time, we made sure our voices also brushed lightly on the line "The branches brusshhhed the water." We read the poem, once with one row providing a quiet backdrop of "splash, splash," and again with another row adding the "thwack, thwack" of the boat's sails. Finally, we were ready to present our masterpiece. Mem went out into the hall and with great ceremony came back into the room and seated herself as our audience. Llewellyn walked to the front and, her eyes sweeping the audience (Mem) eloquently introduced the poem, and Dawn raised her imaginary baton to start us off. None of us has ever forgotten the respectful attention we gave that day to the language of a single simple poem.

The two weeks with Mem were like an adventure curriculum. Instead of doing trust-falls into each other's arms, scrambling up sheer walls, and piling more and more people onto tiny wooden platforms, our adventure curriculum was with language. Instead of developing a sense of comfortableness, confidence, and flexibility with our bodies, we developed a sense of comfortableness, confidence, and flexibility with language. Our classrooms have changed as a result.

In our classrooms we have begun to realize that a course of study in language need not involve analyzing effective images and examining powerful lines. Anne Sullivan, in talking about the education of Helen Keller, says it well:

> All that parents and teachers can do for their child is to surround that child with the right conditions. The child will do the rest; the things she will do for herself are the only things that really count in education.

A course of study in language can begin with rediscovering the magic of voices joined together, of caroling at Christmas time or reciting Passover stories, of singing around the campfire or joining other voices at football games to call out "Sound off, one-two, sound off, three-four!" In a course of study on language, teachers and children can read poems up the page as well as down. We can recite favorite lines by heart. We can turn the opening rainstorm in Robert McCloskey's *Time of Wonder* into a score for a choral reading, going to elaborate lengths to be sure that the sound moving between our voices conveys the incoming rains, and the way raindrops turn into a downpour.

Clearly, in a classroom that values language children as well as teachers need opportunities to read aloud. In some Project classrooms, children read poems, stories, and excerpts (their own and some from other authors) aloud to each other in pairs, in small circles, in whole-class meetings. A child's reading may begin a day or launch a field trip or close a math lesson. Readings celebrate birthdays and holidays and the first snowfall and the birth of baby chicks and the return of a long-absent classmate. Eudora Welty's passage about how she grew up reading aloud in every room of her house has implications for classrooms as well as for homes. She writes,

> I learned from the age of two or three that any room in our house, at any time of day, was there to be read in. . . . [My mother] read to me in the big bedroom in the mornings, when we were in her rocker together, which ticked in rhythm as we rocked, as though we had a cricket accompanying the story. She'd read to me in the dining room on winter afternoons in front of the coal fire, with our cuckoo clock ending the story with "Cuckoo." . . . Ever since I was first read to, then started reading to myself, there has never been a line read that I didn't *hear.* As my eyes followed the sentence, a voice was saying it silently to me. It isn't my mother's voice, or the voice of any person I can identify. . . . It is to me the voice of the story or the poem itself. The cadence, whatever it is that asks you to believe, the feeling that resides in the printed word, reaches me through the reader-voice. (1983, 5, 12–13)

Reading aloud, choral readings, reader's theater, and storytelling combine to give all of us—teachers and children alike—layer after layer of experience with language. And this gives us wells to draw on when we write. When poems and riddles and chants and stories dance in our minds; when a gust of wind leads a teacher to recite, "Who has seen the wind, neither you nor I"; when a spider's web is examined for words; when secret lands are named Narnia and Terabithia, then our writing will be filled with the sounds of literature. An ear for the song of literature is indeed, as MacNeil suggests, the placenta out of which writing grows.

The reading-writing connections that matter most are not the dedications or the "about the author" blurbs children include in their published books; instead, they are the times when our children's words call out to be savored. Judah Beck's writing has clearly been nourished by that "living matrix" of language that MacNeil describes. Figure 18–1 is one page of his writing, as I found it, scrawled into his notebook.

Figure 18–1 Judah's Writing

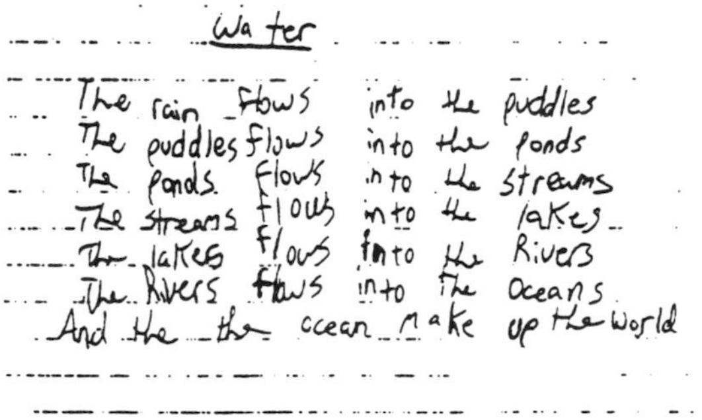
Water

The rain flows into the puddles
The puddles flows into the ponds
The ponds flows into the streams
The streams flows into the lakes
The lakes flows into the Rivers
The Rivers flows into the Oceans
And the the ocean make up the world

Figure 18–1 Continued

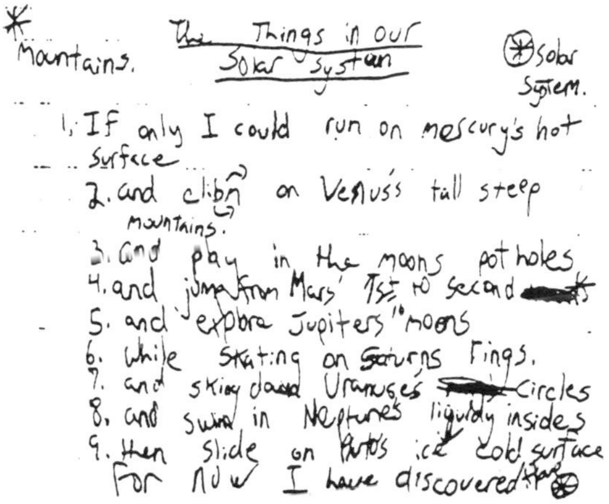
Mountains.
The Things in our Solar System
Solar System.
1. If only I could run on mercury's hot surface
2. and clibm on Venus's tall steep mountains.
3. and play in the moons pot holes
4. and jump from Mars' 1st to second
5. and explore Jupiters moons
6. while skating on Saturns rings.
7. and skiing down Uranuses circles
8. and swim in Neptunes liquidy insides
9. then slide on Pluto's ice cold surface
For now I have discovered

Readers cannot avoid being moved by the voice of Jordana's story about her grandmother. Here is an excerpt:

> When we arrived at the hospital, Uncle Max was waiting for us. Uncle Max was a doctor at that hospital but now he looked like a regular person. He didn't have anything to say. I knew something was terribly wrong.
>
> "How is she?" my dad asked, even before entering through the double doors. My eyes surveyed the hallway of the hospital. Nice hospital, I thought. It's so clean and pretty. Grandma will be fine. They probably have good doctors here.
>
> Suddenly I heard my dad and uncle. "They say it's cancer."
>
> "Oh my God. Help, Mom, help," I whispered. "Is it true?"
>
> "Yes, I'm afraid it is," came my mother's soothing voice.
>
> "I hate cancer, I hate it. I hate cancer with all my heart, with all my soul, with all my might." I had already lost one grandmother to cancer. This was too much.
>
> Later, we left the hospital and went to Grandma's empty house. My mom set the table. All of us sat there eating Grandma's chicken soup, Grandma's chicken, Grandma's salad, Grandma's pudding.
>
> Then I realized that there was one empty seat at the table where Grandma should have sat, one lonely seat with no food, not even a setting. Like there was no setting for life. One empty seat which was

bare. One empty seat which everyone tried to avoid. My dad started crying. I had never seen him cry before. "Suddenly," he said, "everything is so precious."

The process of writing with wonderful language begins to sound like magic. Teachers and children read, climb inside literature, hear the voice of the story, and write literature. That's true. And it *is* magical. But the challenge is to see the literariness, to hear the song, not only in Judah's and Jordana's stories, but in *all* our children's writing. Our colleague, Martha Horn, once came into the Project office with great excitement, saying, "Listen to Wayne's reading connections." Then she passed a page around on which Wayne had written, in wobbly letters,

There once was a dog. He was a little dog with black spots. He was fat. He ate a lot. He had some white on him.

"How nice," we said, nodding politely. Martha was too excited to notice our indifference. She began to read Wayne's text as if the words had been written by Robert Louis Stevenson or D. H. Lawrence. "There once was a dog," she read, and said, "I love that part—'There *once* was a dog.'" This time we heard, and we knew Martha was right. Wayne had not said, "I have a dog." He instead made the crucial shift from recounting information to spinning a story.

The shift Wayne made is the essential, ground-breaking, reading-writing connection. On an unconscious level, if not deliberately, he has made a transition from spewing out material to crafting a work of literature. Hearing his words, we can almost imagine that he paused before he wrote to ask, "How shall I put this?" That pause, that moment of shaping, that intention to create something lovely, is essential.

Children can practice making that shift when they work in notebooks. For many Project teachers, it was startling to see that in the compost heap of notebooks, children were playing with the rhythm and phrasing and sounds of words in ways we hadn't seen before, even in published masterpieces. Notebooks are meant to be places for imperfect writing, and this fact seems to invite writers to be playful and daring with language. Because an entry, like a pencil sketch in an artist's sketch pad, is not intended to be part of a finished masterpiece, notebook writers like Marlene, a student in Randy Bomer's eighth-grade class, give themselves permission to write in imperfect and risky ways:

I am looking at the clouds settling in the valley. To me, it looks like the end of the world. Where does the other part of the world start on the other side?

The trees are wet. It rained, but every morning, rain or not, the clouds settle into the valley. In one place on our bus ride, the clouds hover just above us. Clouds are strange. They have their own mystery.

What is "fine"? When someone asks us how we are, we usually say "fine." Why is this? Are we always fine? I think we say this because we don't want to start a conversation. When you say "fine," people don't say "Why are you fine?" That is what "fine" is all about.

Today is a growling day. You can feel it. It feels like you should be on a hill in a swirling skirt with your hair flying about your face. Growling days are warm, wet, and windy. One day I just made up growlings and fit them to that type of day. Growlings are little red bugs that make low growling sounds and if people hear these they are sucked into the ground . . .

Marlene has used her notebook as a workbench for practicing the shift from spewing out material to crafting language. She and her classmates learned about this shift in part because they have worked within the genres of poetry and picture books. The white space in poems and picture books symbolizes the deliberate shaping all writers must do; since few words are chosen, they are selected with care. From poets and picture-book authors, youngsters learn to ask the question "How can I say this?"

In October, before she'd studied poetry, Mary Lou wrote the prose passage shown in Figure 18–2, about her trip to Ohio:

My Trip to Ohio

I went to Ohio. I went by car there. It took me a long time.
We got there and ate dinner. Me and my little brother played there.
We got presents from our grandma and grandpa.

Then, after working for six weeks on various poems, Mary Lou returned in December to her initial piece about Ohio. This time, she wrote the piece shown in Figure 18–3.

My Trip to Ohio

I go to Ohio every year.
It takes 8 hours to get there.
We passed more than 100 miles.
I get car sick, and I'm the only one!
All my brother does is Sleep! Sleep! Sleep! And he always has to bring his silly toy mutt. He carries him by the tail.
I go by car sometimes and sometimes plane.
I'm always not able to wait so I keep on asking my mother,
"When are we going to get there? When are we going to get there?"
And all my mother says is "Soon! Soon!"
Then my father says, "**Quiet!!**"
Then we're quiet.

Figure 18–2   Mary Lou's Piece   *Figure 18–3   Mary Lou's Rewritten Piece*

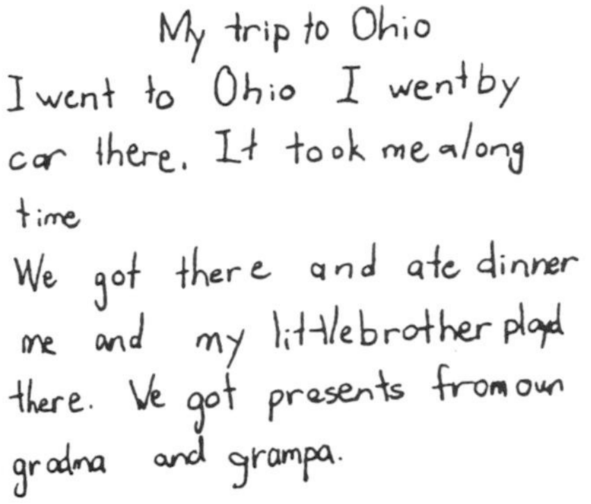

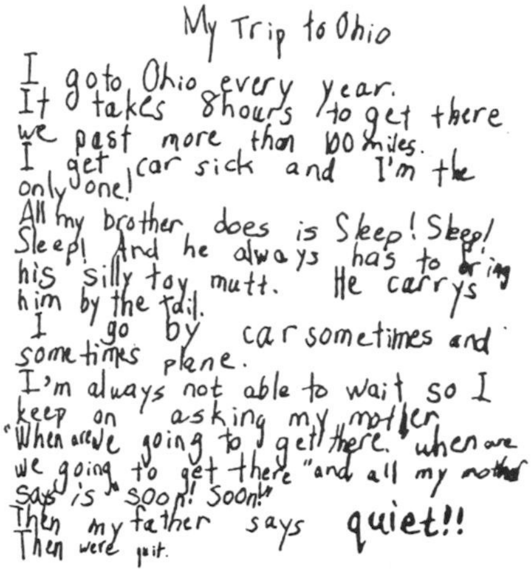

My trip to Ohio
I went to Ohio I went by
car there. It took me a long
time
We got there and ate dinner
me and my little brother plad
there. We got presents from our
gradma and grampa.

My Trip to Ohio
I go to Ohio every year.
It takes 8 hours to get there
we past more than 100 miles.
I get car sick and I'm the
only one!
All my brother does is Sleep! Sleep!
Sleep! And he always has to bring
his silly toy mutt. He carrys
him by the tail.
I go by car sometimes and
sometimes plane.
I'm always not able to wait so I
keep on asking my mother
"When are we going to get there" when are
we going to get there "and all my mother
says is "soon! Soon!"
Then my father says   quiet!!
Then were pit.

In Mary Lou's second version of her Ohio story, it would be hard not to notice the care she has taken with language. But often in our classrooms, children write with only a line or two (hidden in the middle of their prose) that has the ring of literature.

When we read children's writing amidst the hurry of our classrooms, our furrowed foreheads make it easy to overlook lines like "There once was a dog." We cannot scold ourselves into noticing Wayne's line. Eudora Welty, after all, learned to listen to the voice of authors by reading with her mother on winter afternoons in front of the fire, the clock ending the story with "Cuckoo." Eudora Welty did not have to listen to the PA system, the custodian fixing the radiator, the cluster of children talking at the back of the room, the noises from city streets, the paraprofessional who comes to take three youngsters out for tutorials (one for music, two for remedial reading). It's no wonder that we don't always hear the music in Wayne's "There once was a dog." But if we're going to help children listen to the language of literature and esteem it, we need to create the mental space, the sense of generosity and appreciation, that allows us to see and respond to even a single wonderful line.

Let us pause for a moment to reemphasize that we've concentrated on responding to wonderful language rather than repairing awkward language. Writers learn that language can make an impact on others by seeing and feeling that happen. William Stafford says,

> In the classroom, any time anyone says anything or jots down anything, some of what is said or written is luckier than the rest—and poetry is language with a little luck in it.

Those lucky places—everyone stumbles upon them; they are homogenized into our lives. And in class I try to recognize what comes at me, not to commend or admire, and not even—usually not even—to mention it, but simply to feel it myself. The signals I give off when someone says or writes something that lucks into poetry will come naturally—in my eyes, in the way I lean forward, maybe even in my sudden look of envy.

It is that immediate response to language that counts. (1986, 97–98)

It's easier to notice what youngsters do well if we give ourselves some space to breathe within the writing workshop. If we have some silent writing time each day, it may help us listen well and respond to the language of our children's stories. Then, too, we may want to bring home the notebooks and folders of a few students each evening so that we can read them before the fire.

But it is even more important that children like Wayne have respectful, quiet spaces in which they can listen to and revel in their language. The really important reading that needs to happen is Wayne's rereading his own text. If Wayne had heard and celebrated the music of "There once was a dog," he might have gone back to his story and found ways to keep the song in it going longer. Listening to language has everything to do with generating language. We listen for the phrase, the line, the pages that work, and then we build on that. As Annie Dillard notes in *The Writing Life*,

> It is handed to you, but only if you look for it. You search, you break your heart, your back, your brain, and then—and only then—it is handed to you. . . .
>
> One line of a poem, the poet said—only one line, but thank God for that one line—drops from the ceiling. Thornton Wilder cited this unnamed writer of sonnets: one line of a sonnet falls from the ceiling, and you tap in the others around it with a jeweler's hammer. (1989, 75–76)

Once those of us who teach writing have felt the thrill of saying something just right, once we've found our words leading us to altogether new meanings, then we can invite the young writers around us into that process. We can help youngsters reread their notebooks and drafts, looking for places that were fun to write, for lines that deserve to be read beautifully, for sections that somehow matter in ways the writers themselves may not be able to articulate. When we have experienced the generative process of following our own words deeper and deeper to meaning we didn't know was there, then we can help youngsters to value "good language." But more important, we can also help them listen for places where language can lead to meaning.

Because Judy Davis follows her own language to meaning, she asked Kenny McCloud to reread his notebook looking for words that somehow matter, for language that is exactly true and bristles with possibility. Kenny marked the second half of this entry:

> All days I take the train to school. This morning I was going to school and I fell asleep. When I woke up, I got off the train to go to school. But the strangest thing. I wasn't on 68th Street. I knew I was lost and I was frightened and I felt like I wasn't ever going to see my mother ever again. I felt like I was on another planet. And if I made the least mistake I would disappear.

Kenny's lines are not examples of polished language, but they are exactly what writers look for in their texts. They are a doorway into crucial insights and images. When Kenny writes, "If I made the least mistake I would disappear," the words stand out because they are more real than the smooth, prepackaged words we use in everyday life. Kenny may (or may not) choose to stay a while with these lines, saying more and seeing where it leads. But if he does write more, he will probably write with words that belong to his fear, and they will contain a life of thought and feeling. In this way, Kenny will discover for himself the generative power of language. He will learn to listen not only for good language but for language that can lead to meaning.

— 19 —

Nurturing Writing, Nurturing Teaching

The advice about writing I cherish most has also been advice about living. After my colleague, Susan Pliner, read an early draft of this book, she challenged me to write in a way that was more true and significant: "In your rush to get it all down, Lucy, you sometimes jump too quickly from one good idea to the next as if you were greedy to tell it all—now. It's about patience," she said, and I knew she was talking not only about patience at the desk but also about patience with life itself. She tried to explain, "If you can slow your eye down, your heart down, your mind down, you'll give yourself the opportunity to see all that's there."

In her book, *For the Good of the Earth and Sun*, Georgia Heard tells about a time when she brought her poem to the renowned poet Stanley Kunitz. Georgia watched the wise face of her mentor as he read. She picked up a smooth round stone to hold for good luck. Finally, Kunitz looked up. "You've gone through a revolution, Georgia. This poem is rooted in the flesh and blood of your experience." Georgia let the stone drop. "You used to write poems removed from your experience and your feelings; now they're all one." At the end of the visit, Kunitz said one final thing to Georgia, and it is something that also needs to be said here, at the close of this book. "You must first create the kind of person who will write the kind of poems you want to write," Kunitz said, and then he added, "I'm still working on it at eighty-two."

We nurture our writing by nurturing our souls. Katherine Paterson says:

Writing is something like a seed that grows in the dark . . . or a grain of sand that keeps rubbing at your vitals until you find you are building a coating around it. The growth of a book takes time. . . . I talk, I look, I listen, I hate, I fear, I love, I weep, and somehow all of my life gets wrapped around the grain. (1981, 26)

Our writing grows from repeated encounters with the blank page, but it also grows from our living—from falling in love and sitting with a sketch pad at the foot of a mountain, from walking through city streets and watching the face of a child as she reads. Our poems and stories and speeches and letters grow from our rough drafts and revisions, but they gather energy and substance from the whole of our lives.

In my writing, people have helped me by urging me to linger longer with my feelings and observations, to trust my voice, and to have the courage to fail. But in my teaching, people have tried to help me by suggesting that I rearrange students' desks into a circle, give more frequent assignments, and separate cumulative writing folders from daily ones. This advice on teaching may or may not be wise, but where is the recognition that how I teach comes from all that I am? Teaching well, like writing well, is about lingering longer to see and feel and experience things I might otherwise pass by; it's about being willing to risk failure and trusting my own voice. Like writing, teaching grows out of our passions, our sense of self, our faith in other people, our hope for the world. The way I teach has everything to do with finding a world in the backyard, feeding pigeons on the rooftop, and cherishing a fleet of orange slices on the window sill. I nurture my teaching by nurturing my soul.

We nurture our teaching by watching a cicada bug shed its skin and by curling up in a window seat with a novel and our notebooks, letting the sound of the screen door invoke a world of memories. All of us have these moments, but we don't always draw on them when we teach.

And no wonder. In education courses, we are more apt to hear about "anticipatory frames" and "time-on-task" than about the importance of sitting with a novel and a notebook. When someone observes our teaching, they are more apt to talk about the clarity of our homework assignments than to say, "You used to teach in a way that was removed from your experience and your feelings; now they're one."

There's a great deal of talk these days about teacher burnout and low morale. Publishers and curriculum designers respond by offering prepackaged curricular units and teacher-proof lessons. But what publishers don't realize is that we're not tired of teaching. What we're tired of is the clutter that gets in the way of teaching. We're tired of the tests that turn days, weeks, and months into a wasteland, of being told we can't use the duplicating machine to make copies of our record keeping because it's reserved for important things, of the new mandates that say we're supposed to teach "thinking skills" for twenty minutes a day, as if we haven't always taught thinking. We're tired of the way all this curriculum clutter drains us of our energy and distracts us from our dreams.

When I began teaching I stuck a sign on my refrigerator door that said, "Teaching is a form of loving." Two months later I had added another; this one said, "I'm on my second cup of coffee and I still can't face the day." Those two statements say a lot about this profession. We teachers are an idealistic bunch who struggle to hold onto our dreams. A colleague of mine quit teaching and now works behind the cosmetics counter at Macy's. "When I was teaching I let myself go," she told me. "I didn't fix my hair or care about my clothes or about myself. Now I've got my self-respect back."

In Pat Conroy's novel *The Prince of Tides* (1986), the hero—a teacher—puts into words what many of us feel:

> It had been a winter of deadening seriousness, when all the bright dreams and illusions of my early twenties had withered and died. I did not yet have the internal resources to dream new dreams. I was far too busy mourning the death of the old ones and wondering how I was to survive without them.

In school parking lots, I've seen the bumper sticker "Give up. It hurts less." But of course that's not true. It's hollowness that hurts. For a great many teachers, the teaching of writing and reading has become important because in this field, in this community of educators, in this reform movement, we are finding the interior resources to dream new dreams.

When any one classroom teacher dreams new dreams, it can widen the horizon for all of us. A single wonderful classroom or school can make an amazing difference. By now, hundreds and thousands of people have heard of the little clapboard schoolhouse in Atkinson, New Hampshire. They have heard, too, of the eighth-grade readers and writers in Boothbay, Maine, of the literate communities in Nova Scotia and Arizona, in Denver and Detroit, in New York City and New Zealand. We pass these stories among ourselves, and they change our sense of what's possible. And we shouldn't be surprised that we cherish and remember them more than all the theories and textbooks in the world. This is, after all, the power of literature: In the story of one person learning to write and to read, we see what is possible for all students. In the story of one wonderful classroom, we see the potential for all classrooms.

If we as teachers are going to nurture our souls, we need each other. We need to exchange classes for a day, to share subscriptions to *Language Arts* and *The New Advocate*, to join together in courses of study on poetry and on conferring, to be roommates at a summer institute, to coauthor letters protesting the district's policies on evaluation, to confer with each other about our poems and speeches, to stand together watching a cicada bug shed its skin. Rufus Jones, the great American Quaker, has said, "I pin my hopes on the small circles and quiet processes in which genuine and reforming change takes place." More and more, we are discovering the wisdom of his words.

Recent reforms in Yugoslavia, Poland, Czechoslovakia, and the Soviet Union have happened not by decree from above but because individuals came together, one person with another. So, too, reforms in education are happening as one teacher and another and another come together. If someone were to put pins on a map of the world to mark those places in which teachers are gathering to read, write, and study together and were to ask, "Why here?" we would find that behind each study group there is a single educator . . . joining together with another educator.

A year ago, Donald Graves spoke to a group of whole-language educators. "Our systems of evaluation and streaming have put child against child," he said. "We need to rediscover the spirit of an old-fashioned barn raising, where all hands, young and old, are joined together." All too often school systems have put not only child against child, but also teacher against teacher. All too often those of us who bring aquariums and boxes of books from home smuggle them into the school building through a side door.

Recently I was talking with a friend about the woman who teaches across the hall from her. "She's marvelous with science, isn't she?" I said. "'Yes," my friend answered and then lowered her voice. "But people say she's *ambitious.*" She wanted me to say, "Oh, horrors!" Instead I said, "I hope so." I hope she's ambitious enough to teach according to her beliefs, to know that her teaching can make a difference. I hope we're all ambitious, and ambitious not only for ourselves but for our profession. We need to be.

Teachers are coming together. We're coming together across districts, across grade levels and disciplines, even within our own staffrooms, and we're coming together in the spirit of an old-fashioned barn raising. It's not a barn we're building but a better world for ourselves and our children.

We're coming together partly to celebrate, and when we do, when we step back and look at what's happening to the culture of our classrooms, we see youngsters sitting, arms linked, sharing a story together. We see youngsters beating out on the floor the rhythm of a jazz chant, "I love green, I love black, I love blue and yellow." We see a youngster tape-recording and critiquing early versions of a speech he will deliver to his church congregation. Next to this richly significant work, how trivial the "drill and skill" exercises seem, and the reinforcement dittos, the phonics flashcards, games, records, total drill programs, and software in which, if you push the right button, the creature blows bubbles and perks up its ears. They're glitzy, they're lightweight. Youngsters wander through them just as they wander through the shopping malls. "Dittos? They're okay, they're easy," the youngsters say. "Learning kits? Who cares? You just fill in the circles."

But the stuff of our lives is not glitzy or lightweight. Living our lives wisely and well has little to do with pushing the right buttons or filling in the right circles. The stuff of our lives is, as Richard Wilbur says, a "great cargo," and some of it is heavy. Teachers and children need to bring the great cargoes of our lives to school, because it is by reading and writing and storytelling and musing and painting and sharing that we human beings find meaning.

When children bring the work of their lives to school, they will invest themselves heart and soul. In the course of this book we have seen it happen. Miranda poured herself into the challenge of turning her broccoli story into something lovely and true. Palak danced with excitement over the possibility of turning notebook entries about a turtle and about sleeping on the sofa into a scary adventure story like those he enjoys reading. And because Jakeeya knew that she needed to understand her mother's life in order to create her own, because she knew that writing about her mother as a runaway was important not only for her as a writer but also for her as a person, she was willing to risk bringing the true Ja-keeya into the classroom. It took courage for her to bring the self that feels hurt, that finds solace in reading and writing, to school. It took courage, and it required a friend. "How do you end a really important story like this one?" Ja-keeya asked Anabelle.

"You think from the heart, not from the mind."

When we see Palak, Miranda, Ja-keeya, and the other youngsters working with heart and soul, we know that we as teachers also want to work hard on endeavors of scope and significance. Like Palak, we dance with excitement when we have the opportunity to create something important. Like Miranda, we work tirelessly on goals that are our own. Like Ja-keeya, we need to bring our real selves to school. We need a friend to say, "Teach from the heart." We need to nurture our teaching—to read, think, talk, look, listen, hate, fear, love, weep—to let our entire lives enrich our teaching.

Teaching grows from the whole of our lives. And that's big. It's bigger than a school's yearly goal or a district's five-year plan. It's bigger than any of us or any of our theories. It's big enough to live for.

Works Cited

Agar, Michael H. 1980. *The Professional Stranger: An Informal Introduction to Ethnography*. New York: Academic Press.

Aliki. 1979. *The Two of Them*. New York: Greenwillow Books.

Angelou, Maya. 1969. *I Know Why the Caged Bird Sings*. New York: Bantam.

Atwell, Nancie. 1987. *In the Middle: Writing, Reading, and Learning with Adolescents*. Portsmouth, NH: Boynton/Cook.

Auster, Paul. 1982. *The Invention of Solitude*. New York: Avon Books.

Avi. 1987. Speech. National Council Teachers of English conference. Boston, MA. November.

Baker, Russell. 1982. *Growing Up*. New York: New American Library.

Bang, Molly. 1985. *The Paper Crane*. New York: Greenwillow Books.

Barth, Roland S. 1984. "Sandboxes and Honeybees." *Education Week* (9 May): 24.

Baylor, Byrd. 1983. *The Best Town in the World*. New York: Charles Scribner's Sons.

———. 1986. *I'm In Charge of Celebrations*. New York: Charles Scribner's Sons.

Bemelmans, Ludwig. 1977. *Madeline*. New York: Penguin Books.

Bennet, Jill. 1986. *The Teeny-Tiny Woman*. New York: Putnam.

Birkerts, Sven. 1989. *An Artificial Wilderness: Essays on Twentieth Century Literature*. Boston: Godine.

Bissex, Glenda. 1980. *GNYS AT WRK: A Child Learns to Write and Read*. Cambridge, MA: Harvard University Press.

———. 1986. "What Is a Teacher-Researcher?" *Language Arts* (September).

Blume, Judy. 1984. *The Pain and the Great One*. Scarsdale, NY: Bradbury Press.

Booth, David. 1989. Keynote address. Child-Centered Experience-Based Learning Conference. Winnipeg, Manitoba. February.

Brown, Margaret Wise. 1947. *Goodnight Moon*. New York: Harper.

————. 1972. *The Runaway Bunny*. New York: Harper.

Browne, Anthony. 1985. *Gorilla*. New York: Alfred A. Knopf.

————. 1985. *Willy the Wimp*. New York: Alfred A. Knopf.

Bunting, Eve. 1989. *The Wednesday Surprise*. New York: Ticknor and Fields.

————. 1990. *The Wall*. New York: Clarion Books.

Burningham, John. 1985. *Granpa*. New York: Crown.

Burton, Virginia Lee. 1942. *The Little House*. Boston: Houghton Mifflin Company.

Calkins, Lucy McCormick. 1983. *Lessons from a Child: On the Teaching and Learning of Writing*. Portsmouth, NH: Heinemann.

————. 1986. *The Art of Teaching Writing*. Portsmouth, NH: Heinemann.

Calkins, Lucy McCormick, and Shelley Harwayne. 1987. *The Writing Workshop: A World of Difference*. Portsmouth, NH: Heinemann.

Carle, Eric. 1981. *The Very Hungry Caterpillar*. New York: Putnam.

Carrick, Carol. 1974. *Lost in the Storm*. Boston: Houghton Mifflin Company.

Carter, Forrest. 1986. *The Education of Little Tree*. Albuquerque, NM: University of New Mexico Press.

Cisneros, Sandra. 1986. *The House on Mango Street*. Houston, TX: Arte Publico.

Clark, Roy Peter. 1987. *Free to Write: A Journalist Teaches Young Writers*. Portsmouth, NH: Heinemann.

Cleary, Beverly. 1988. *A Girl From Yamhill*. New York: Morrow.

Coerr, Eleanor B. 1977. *Sadako and the Thousand Paper Cranes*. New York: Putnam.

Conroy, Pat. 1986. *The Prince of Tides*. Boston: Houghton Mifflin Company.

Cooney, Barbara. 1982. *Miss Rumphius*. New York: Penguin Books.

————. 1988. *Island Boy*. New York: Penguin Books.

Csikszentmihalyi, Mihaly, and Reed Larson. 1984. *Being Adolescent: Conflict and Growth in the Teenage Years*. New York: Basic Books.

Cullum, Albert. 1971. *The Geranium on the Window Sill Just Died, But Teacher You Went Right On*. New York: Harlen Quist.

Dahl, Roald. 1988a. *Boy: Tales of Childhood*. New York: Penguin Books.

————. 1988b. *Charlie and the Chocolate Factory*. New York: Penguin Books.

de Brunhoff, Jean. 1937. *The Story of Babar*. New York: Random House.

de Kruif, Paul. 1966. *The Microbe Hunters*. New York: Harcourt Brace Jovanovich.

Didion, Joan. 1980. "Why I Write." In *The Writer on Her Work*. Janet Sternburg, ed. New York: W. W. Norton and Company.

Dillard, Annie. 1987. "To Fashion a Text." In *Inventing the Truth: The Art and Craft of Memoir*. William Zinsser, ed. Boston: Houghton Mifflin Company.

————. 1989a. *The Writing Life*. New York: Harper & Row.

————. 1989b. "'A Girl and Her Books." *American Educator*. (Fall): 40–46.

Doney, Meryl. 1983. *When I Was Little*. New York: Harper.

Dorris, Michael. 1987. *A Yellow Raft in Blue Water*. New York: Henry Holt and Company.

Dr. Seuss. 1940. *Horton Hatches the Egg*. New York: Random House.

———. 1984. *The Butter Battle Book*. New York: Random House.

Dragonwagon, Crescent. 1987. *Diana, Maybe*. New York: Macmillan.

Ehrlich, Gretel. 1985. *The Solace of Open Spaces*. New York: Penguin Books.

Elbow, Peter. 1981. *Writing with Power: Techniques for Mastering the Writing Process*. New York: Oxford University Press

Emberley, Barbara. 1967. *Drummer Hoff*. Englewood Cliffs, NJ: Prentice-Hall.

Esbensen, Barbara J. 1986. *Words with Wrinkled Knees*. New York: Harper.

Farber, Norma. 1979. *How Does It Feel to Be Old*. New York: E. P. Dutton.

Fiday, Beverly, and David Fiday. 1990. *Time to Go*. New York: Harcourt Brace Jovanovich.

Field, Rachel. 1983. "If Once You Have Slept on an Island." In *Random House Book of Poetry for Children*. Jack Prelutsky, ed. New York: Random House.

Fletcher, Ralph. 1991. *Walking Trees: Teaching Teachers in the New York City Schools*. Portsmouth, NH: Heinemann.

Flournoy, Valerie. 1985. *The Patchwork Quilt*. New York: Dial Books.

Fox, Mem. 1985. *Wilfrid Gordon McDonald Partridge*. Brooklyn, NY: Kane/ Miller Book Publishers.

———. 1988a. *Goodnight, Sleep Tight*. Hutchinson, Australia: Century Hutchinson.

———. 1988b. Speech. Teachers College Writing Project Summer Institute. New York, NY. July.

———. 1989a. *Koala Lou*. New York: Harcourt Brace Jovanovich.

———. 1989b. *Night Noises*. New York: Harcourt Brace Jovanovich.

Fox, Paula. 1984. *The One-Eyed Cat*. Scarsdale, NY: Bradbury Press.

Frank, Anne. 1958. *Anne Frank: The Diary of a Young Girl*. New York: Modern Library.

Fritz, Jean. 1982. *Homesick: My Own Story*. New York: G. P. Putnam's Sons.

Gass, William. 1979. *The World Within the Word*. Boston: Godine.

Giacobbe, Mary Ellen. 1989. "Beyond Big Books." Whole Language BOCES Conference. Rochester, NY. October.

Godwin, Gail. 1980. "Becoming a Writer." In *The Writer on Her Work*. Janet Sternburg, ed. New York: W. W. Norton and Company.

Goodfield, June. 1981. *An Imagined World: A Story of Scientific Discovery*. New York: Harper & Row.

Goodlad, John. 1984. *A Place Called School: Prospects for the Future*. New York: McGraw-Hill Book Company.

Gornick, Vivian. 1983. *Women in Science: Portraits from a World in Transition*. New York: Simon and Schuster.

———. 1987. *Fierce Attachments: A Memoir*. New York: Farrar, Straus & Giroux.

Graves, Donald H. 1983. *Writing: Teachers and Children at Work*. Portsmouth, NH: Heinemann.

———. 1988. Speech. Whole Language Conference. Rochester, NY. October.

———. 1989. Speech. Whole Language Conference. Rochester, NY. October.

———. 1990. *Discover Your Own Literacy*. Portsmouth, NH: Heinemann.

Greenfield, Eloise. 1988. *Grandpa's Face*. New York: Philomel.

Greenfield, Eloise, and Lessie Jones Little. 1979. *Childtimes: A Three-Generation Memoir*. New York: Thomas Y. Crowell.

Gregory, Dick, and Robert Lipsyte. 1964. *Nigger*. New York: E. P. Dutton.

Griest, Virginia. 1989. *In Between*. New York: Dutton.

Hall, Donald. 1979. *Ox-cart Man*. New York: Viking.

Heard, Georgia. 1989. *For the Good of the Earth and Sun: Teaching Poetry*. Portsmouth, NH: Heinemann.

Hendershot, Judith. 1987. *In Coal Country*. New York: Alfred A. Knopf.

Himler, Ronald. 1987. *Nettie's Trip South*. New York: Macmillan.

Hoberman, Mary Ann. 1978. *A House Is a House for Me*. New York: Penguin Books.

Howe, James. 1987. "'Reflections." *The Writing Project Quarterly Newsletter* 1: 3 (Spring): 12.

Howe, James, and Deborah Howe. 1980. *Bunnicula: A Rabbit-Tale of Mystery*. New York: Avon.

Huck, Charlotte. 1989. *Princess Furball*. New York: Greenwillow Books.

Hunter, Mollie. 1972. *A Sound of Chariots*. New York: Harper.

Hurston, Zora Neal. 1984. *Dust Tracks on a Road: An Autobiography*. Champaign, IL: University of Illinois Press.

Inner London Education Authority. 1988. *The Primary Language Record: Handbook for Teachers*. London: Centre for Language in Primary Education. (Distributed in the U.S. by Heinemann, Portsmouth, NH.)

Jackson, Jacqueline. 1974. *Turn Not Pale, Beloved Snail*. Boston: Little, Brown and Co.

Jaffe, Dan. 1964. "The Forecast." *Prairie Schooner* 39: 1 (Spring): 48.

John-Steiner, Vera. 1985. *Notebooks of the Mind*. Albuquerque, NM: University of New Mexico Press.

Johnston, Tony. 1985. *The Quilt Story*. New York: Putnam.

———. 1988. *Yonder*. New York: Dial Books.

Khalsa, Dayal Kaur. 1986. *Tales of a Gambling Grandma*. New York: Clarkson N. Potter.

Kincaid, Jamaica. 1986. *Annie John*. New York: New American Library.

King, Martin Luther, Jr. 1963. "I Have a Dream." Speech delivered at March on Washington. Washington, DC. 28 August.

Kingston, Maxine Hong. 1975. *The Woman Warrior: Memoirs of a Girlhood Among Ghosts.* New York: Random House.

Klein, Robin. 1987. *Penny Pollard's Diary.* New York: Oxford University Press.

Kozol, Jonathan. 1988. *Rachel and Her Children: Homeless Families in America.* New York: Fawcett.

Krauss, Ruth. 1945. *The Carrot Seed.* New York: Harper.

————. 1949. *The Happy Day.* New York: Harper.

Kuskin, Karla. 1987. *Jerusalem, Shining Still.* New York: Harper & Row.

Lasky, Kathryn. 1979. *My Island Grandma.* New York: F. Warne.

————. 1983. *Sugaring Time.* New York: Macmillan.

————. 1985a. *The Puppeteer.* New York: Macmillan.

————. 1985b. "Reflecting on Nonfiction." *The Horn Book Magazine* (September/October): 527–32.

————. 1988. *Sea Swan.* New York: Macmillan.

Leaf, Munro. 1936. *The Story of Ferdinand.* New York: Penguin Books.

L'Engle, Madeleine. 1977. *A Circle of Quiet.* Book 1 of *A Crosswicks Journal.* New York: Harper.

Lindbergh, Anne Morrow. 1965. *A Gift from the Sea.* New York: Random House.

Little, Jean. 1986. *Hey World, Here I Am!* New York: Harper & Row.

————. 1987. *Little by Little: A Writer's Education.* New York: Viking.

Lord, Bette B. 1984. *In the Year of the Boar and Jackie Robinson.* New York: Harper.

Lortie, Dan. 1977. *Schoolteacher: A Sociological Study.* Chicago: University of Chicago Press.

Lowry, Lois. 1980. *Autumn Street.* Boston: Houghton Mifflin Company.

McCloskey, Robert. 1940. *Lentel.* New York: Penguin.

————. 1941. *Make Way for Ducklings.* New York: Viking.

————. 1957. *Time of Wonder.* New York: Viking.

MacLachlan, Patricia. 1980. *Through Grandpa's Eyes.* New York: Harper.

————. 1983. *Seven Kisses in a Row.* New York: Harper.

————. 1985. *Sarah, Plain and Tall.* New York: Harper.

MacNeil, Robert. 1989. *Wordstruck.* New York: Viking.

McNulty, Faith. 1986. *Peeping in the Shell: A Whooping Crane Is Hatched.* New York: Harper.

Macrorie, Kenneth. 1985. *Telling Writing.* 4th ed. Portsmouth, NH: Boynton/Cook.

Margolis, Richard. 1984. *Secrets of a Small Brother.* New York: Macmillan.

Martin, Bill, Jr., and John Archambault. 1985. *The Ghost-Eye Tree.* New York: Holt, Rinehart & Winston.

————. 1986. *Barn Dance!* New York: Holt, Rinehart & Winston.

————. 1987. *Knots on a Counting Rope.* New York: Henry Holt and Company.

Maruki, Toshi. 1980. *Hiroshima No Pika*. New York: Lothrop, Lee and Shepard.

Masefield, John. 1912. "Sea-Fever." In *Poems*. New York: Macmillan.

Mathabane, Mark. 1989. *Kaffir Boy*. New York: New American Library.

Meltzer, Milton. 1976. "Where Do All the Prizes Go?" *The Horn Book Magazine* (February): 17–23.

Merriam, Eve. 1962. "A Lazy Thought." In *JAMBOREE: Rhymes for All Times*. New York: Dell.

Morrison, Toni. 1987a. *Beloved*. New York: Alfred A. Knopf.

———. 1987b. "The Site of Memory." In *Inventing the Truth: The Art and Craft of Memoir*. William Zinsser, ed. Boston: Houghton Mifflin Company.

Munsch, Robert. 1982. *Love You Forever: For Their Child Forever*. Buffalo, NY: Firefly Books.

———. 1985. *Thomas' Snowsuit*. Buffalo, NY: Firefly Books.

Murphy, Audie. 1983. *To Hell and Back*. New York: Bantam.

Murray, Donald M. 1968. *A Writer Teaches Writing: A Practical Method of Teaching Composition*. Boston: Houghton Mifflin Company.

———. 1982. "Teaching the Other Self: The Writer's First Reader." In *Learning by Teaching: Selected Articles on Writing and Teaching*. Portsmouth, NH: Boynton/Cook.

———. 1985. Speech. National Council of Teachers of English conference. Philadelphia, PA. November.

———. 1986. "One Writer's Secrets." *College Composition and Communication* 37: 2 (May): 146–53.

———. 1989. *Expecting the Unexpected: Teaching Myself—and Others—to Read and Write*. Portsmouth, NH: Boynton/Cook.

Nelson, Vaunda M. 1988. *Always Gramma*. New York: Putnam.

Parini, Jas. 1989. "The More They Write, The More They Write." *The New York Times* (30 July).

Patent, Dorothy Hinshaw. 1984. *Where the Bald Eagles Gather*. Boston: Houghton Mifflin Company.

Paterson, Katherine. 1977. *Bridge to Terabithia*. New York: Harper.

———. 1981. *Gates of Excellence: On Reading and Writing Books for Children*. New York: Elsevier/Nelson Books.

———. 1988. *Park's Quest*. New York: Lodestar Books.

Peet, Bill. 1989. *Bill Peet: An Autobiography*. Boston: Houghton Mifflin Company.

Polacco, Patricia. 1988. *The Keeping Quilt*. New York: Simon and Schuster.

Pomerantz, Charlotte. 1989. *The Chalk Doll*. New York: Harper.

Putka, Gary. 1988. "Tense Tots." *Wall Street Journal* (6 July).

Quinlen, Anna. 1988. *Living Out Loud*. New York: Random House.

Ratushinskaya, Irina. 1988. *Grey is the Color of Hope*. Trans. Alyona Kojevnikov. New York: Alfred A. Knopf.

Rishile Poets. 1988. "Bring the Cattle Home." In *My Drum: South African Poetry for Young People*. Barbara Meyerowitz et al., eds. Parklands, South Africa: Hippogriff Press.

Rist, Ray. 1973. "The Urban School: A Factory for Failure." In *Risk Makers, Risk Takers, Risk Breakers*. Jo Beth Allen and Jana M. Mason, eds. Cambridge, MA: MIT Press.

Rivas, Barbara Marin. "The Sound of Freedom." South African National Congress Brochure.

Rochman, Hazel. 1988a. "Reading Lifelines." *School Library Journal* (October): 39–41.

———, ed. 1988b. *Somehow Tenderness Survives: Stories of Southern Africa*. New York: Harper & Row.

Rodriguez, Richard. 1982. *Hunger of Memory: The Education of Richard Rodriguez*. New York: Bantam Books.

Roe, Ann. 1952. *The Making of a Scientist*. New York: Dodd Mead.

Rogers, Carl R. 1961. *On Becoming a Person: A Therapist's View of Psychotherapy*. Boston: Houghton Mifflin Company.

Rostkowski, Margaret I. 1988. *After the Dancing Days*. New York: Harper.

Rylant, Cynthia. 1982. *When I Was Young In the Mountains*. New York: Dutton.

———. 1983. *Miss Maggie*. New York: Dutton.

———. 1984a. *Every Living Thing*. Scarsdale, NY: Bradbury Press.

———. 1984b. *This Year's Garden*. Scarsdale, NY: Bradbury Press.

———. 1984c. *Waiting to Waltz: A Childhood*. Scarsdale, NY: Bradbury Press.

———. 1985. *The Relatives Came*. Scarsdale, NY: Bradbury Press.

———. 1987. *Children of Christmas: Stories for the Season*. New York: Orchard Books.

———. 1989. *But I'll Be Back Again: An Album*. New York: Orchard Books.

"Sampan." 1963. In *A Wealth of Poetry: Selected for the Young at Heart*. Winifred Hindley, ed. Cambridge, MA: Basil Blackwell.

Sarason, Seymour. 1972. *The Creation of Settings and the Future Societies*. San Francisco, CA: Josey-Bass.

Scieszka, Jon. 1989. *The True Story of the Three Little Pigs* (by A. Wolf). New York: Viking.

Seixas, Judith S. 1989. *Living with a Parent Who Takes Drugs*. New York: Greenwillow Books.

Sendak, Maurice. 1963. *Where the Wild Things Are*. New York: Harper.

Shecter, Ben. 1989. *Grandma Remembers*. New York: Harper & Row.

Shulevitz, Uri. 1978. *The Treasure*. New York: Farrar, Straus & Giroux.

———. 1985. *Writing with Pictures: How to Write and Illustrate Children's Books*. New York: Watson-Guptill.

Shyer, Marlene F. 1985. *Here I Am, an Only Child*. New York: Macmillan.

Silvey, Anita. 1985. "An Interview with Robert Cormier: Part II." *Horn Book Magazine* (May/June).

———. 1987. "An Interview with Cynthia Rylant. *The Horn Book Magazine* (November/December).

———. 1988. Speech. International Reading Association. New Orleans. May.

Simpson, Louis. 1988. "Poetry and Word Processing: One or the Other, But Not Both." *New York Times Book Review* (3 January): 12.

Sloane, William. 1983. *The Craft of Writing.* New York: W. W. Norton and Company.

Slobodkina, Esphyr. 1947. *Caps for Sale.* New York: Harper.

Smith, Doris B. 1973. *A Taste of Blackberries.* New York: Harper.

Smith, Frank. 1986. *Insult to Intelligence.* Portsmouth, NH: Heinemann.

Smucker, Anna E. 1989. *No Star Nights.* New York: Alfred A. Knopf.

Sobol, Tom. 1987. Inaugural Address, Commissioner of Education for New York State. Albany, NY. 21 October.

Spradley, James P. 1979. *The Ethnographic Interview.* New York: Holt, Rinehart and Winston.

Stafford, William. 1982. "A Way of Writing." In *Claims for Poetry.* Donald Hall, ed. Ann Arbor, MI: University of Michigan Press.

———. 1986. *You Must Revise Your Life.* Ann Arbor, MI: University of Michigan Press.

Stegner, Wallace. 1987. *Crossing to Safety.* New York: Random House.

Steiner, George. 1967. *Language and Silence: Essays on Language, Literature, and the Inhuman.* New York: Atheneum.

Stevenson, James. 1986. *When I Was Nine.* New York: Greenwillow Books.

Taylor, Mildred D. 1976. *Roll of Thunder, Hear My Cry.* New York: Dial Books.

Terhune, Albert P. 1981. *Lad: A Dog.* Cutchogue, NY: Buccaneer Books.

Thornton, Lawrence. 1987. *Imagining Argentina.* New York: Bantam Books.

Tsuchiya, Yukio. 1988. *Faithful Elephants.* Boston: Houghton Mifflin Company.

Tyler, Anne. 1980. "Still Just Writing." In *The Writer on Her Work.* Janet Sternburg, ed. New York: W. W. Norton and Company.

Updike, John. 1989. *Self-Consciousness: Memoirs.* New York: Alfred A. Knopf.

Wells, Gordon. 1986. *The Meaning Makers: Children Learning Language and Using Language to Learn.* Portsmouth, NH: Heinemann.

Wells, Rosemary. 1989. *Max's Chocolate Chicken.* New York: Dial Books.

Welty, Eudora. 1983. *One Writer's Beginnings.* New York: Warner Books.

White, E. B. 1952 *Charlotte's Web.* New York: Harper.

Wiesel, Elie. 1960. *Night.* New York: Bantam.

———. 1986. "Why I Write: Making No Become Yes." *The New York Times Book Review* (14 April).

Wilbur, Richard. 1971. "The Writer." In *The Mind-Reader: New Poems.* New York: Harcourt Brace Jovanovich.

Wilder, Laura Ingalls. 1953. *Little House on the Prairie.* New York: Harper.

Williams, Vera B. 1982. *A Chair for My Mother.* New York: Greenwillow Books.

Wolff, Tobias. 1989. *This Boy's Life: A Memoir*. New York: Atlantic Monthly.

Wood, Audrey. 1984. *The Napping House*. New York: Harcourt Brace Jovanovich.

Woods, Claire. 1988. "Places for Evolving Autobiography." In *The Word for Teaching is Learning*. Martin Lightfoot and Nancy Martin, eds. Portsmouth, NH: Heinemann.

Wyss, J. D. 1981. *Swiss Family Robinson*. New York: Putnam.

Yashima, Taro. 1977. *Crow Boy*. New York: Puffin Books.

Yolen, Jane. 1973. *Writing Books for Children*. Boston: The Writer.

———. 1987. *Owl Moon*. New York: Philomel Books.

Zinsser, William. 1987. *Inventing the Truth: The Art and Craft of Memoir*. Boston: Houghton Mifflin Company.

———. 1988. *On Writing Well: An Informal Guide to Writing Nonfiction*. 3rd ed. New York: Harper & Row.

Zolotow, Charlotte. 1984. *I Know a Lady*. New York: Greenwillow Books.

———. 1987. *I Like to Be Little*. New York: Harper.